THE CLUE BIBLE

THE CLUE BIBLE

The Fully Authorised History of *I'm Sorry I Haven't a Clue*
From Footlights to Mornington Crescent

Jem Roberts

preface
publishing

Published by Preface 2009

10 9 8 7 6 5 4 3 2 1

Copyright © Jem Roberts, 2009

First published in Great Britain in 2009 by Preface Publishing
1 Queen Anne's Gate
London SW1H 9BT

An imprint of The Random House Group Limited

www.rbooks.co.uk
www.prefacepublishing.co.uk

Addresses for companies within The Random House Group Limited
can be found at www.randomhouse.co.uk

The Random House Group Limited Reg. No. 954009

A CIP catalogue record for this book is available from the British Library

ISBN 978 1 84809 130 6

The Random House Group Limited supports The Forest Stewardship Council (FSC),
the leading international forest certification organisation. All our titles that are
printed on Greenpeace approved FSC certified paper carry the FSC logo.
Our paper procurement policy can be found at www.rbooks.co.uk/environment

Mixed Sources
Product group from well-managed
forests and other controlled sources
www.fsc.org   Cert no. TT-COC-2139
© 1996 Forest Stewardship Council
FSC

Typeset in Goudy by Palimpsest Book Production Limited,
Grangemouth, Stirlingshire
Printed and bound in Great Britain by Clays Ltd, St Ives plc

For:

Peter

Willie

Linda

Geoffrey

David

and Humph

Contents

ACKNOWLEDGEMENTS

'Ooh, What A Give Away!'

This book wasn't supposed to be like this. In the wake of the mirth-shattering loss of Humph, anyone spotting this Bible on the bookshelves would be forgiven for sniffing the aroma of 'cash-in', but it's been a long time since this project began, as a light-hearted celebration of the nation's favourite ongoing comedy phenomenon. And now here we are.

Like so many comedy stories, it all begins with Peter Cook. Rediscovering his genius as an adult, it became a source of great pleasure for me to get a regular gig writing about his work for the Official Peter Cook Appreciation Society fagazine, *Publish & Bedazzled*. When that folded in favour of *Kettering: The Magazine of Elderly British Comedy*, I was given carte blanche to write about any old show that took my fancy – and there was only one (or rather two) I could possibly envisage investigating, my favourite radio creation since discovering the tapes at the age of twelve – *I'm Sorry I'll Read That Again* and, of course, *Clue*. So initial thanks must go to Peter Gordon and the whole *Kettering* mob for providing the first impetus; plus Joe Champniss for his original illustrations. However, in terms of importance and support, I must primarily thank the Teams themselves. When *Clue* came to Bristol in 2006, the joyous occasion inspired me to write first about the Antidote to Panel Games, and so began a long period of shivering around stage doors, daring to approach Graeme, Tim, Barry, Colin, Jon, Samantha and Humph. Of course, they were, and have remained, wonderful patrons, amiably handling endless missives, with Jon kindly liaising with Iain and being on hand for advice at all turns.

For the original two articles, I managed to get hold of Graeme and Tim via email only at first, but Barry – being e-sceptic – gave me plenty of phone time. Similarly, it was a joy to have a long chat with Sir David Hatch about the old days, and between them all, I put together pieces which elicited surprisingly glowing feedback from all quarters. A random call from Barry was a nice added extra, saying how much he enjoyed my *Clue* article, and it was with that chat that the idea of extending the *Kettering* pieces to a full-blown book first took root. Keeping to a strict wordcount had been so difficult, and the injustice of the way that Radio Prune had become nothing but a footnote in the Monty Python story was reason enough to celebrate it, loud and clear. To that end, I contacted Sir David and was delighted to receive my very own 'Hatchlet' in reply – 'Dear Jem, Thanks for a sight of the article – I enjoyed it. I'm happy to waffle about the old days anytime, you only have to ask. *I'll Read That Again* book sounds very possible . . . A lot lot more about me next time and I'll enjoy it even more!' The pleasure of receiving this message was still keenly felt and the opening words of this book remained to be written when word came through that he had died.

Agonising reappraisal number one. Could the book go on? I'd had a long chat with Hatch for the article, but we had a lot to cover in the planned chats later in the year. Ultimately his loss made the need to preach about the importance of *ISIRTA* all the more crucial, so the book would now be a tribute to the greatest champion of BBC Radio there had ever been. And so work progressed . . . Humphrey Barclay gave many hours of memories, and some of the greatest images contained herein. Jo Kendall explained to me over a few phone calls that her past was a closed book, that she was happy to chat, but not to be quoted. Her friend, Barclay's ex-secretary Liz Lord, was more comfortable with nostalgia however, and the interviews continued – including the real coup, a whole hour with Stephen Fry, set up by his kind sister and PA, Jo Crocker. Thanks to her, the fact that a man as busy as Fry had taken part gave this book the real stamp of authority.

Not that even Fry's support gave me much hope of getting sight of the lesser-spotted Bill Oddie, and anyone who heard that I planned to interview him gazed at me with astonishment and not a little pity, knowing that he views comedy anoraks with disdain. Ultimately, after a false start and a little pleading via the wonderful Laura Beaumont, I was invited to Oddie Towers for the afternoon where he made tea and happily humoured me until it was pitch black outside, an honour and a pleasure I will always remember. Further chats with Simon Brett, John Lloyd and the late great Geoffrey Perkins were further honours; Toby Rushton offered his aid, and representing the *Clue* guests (despite all of them being preternaturally busy), Tony Hawks, Jeremy Hardy and Rob Brydon kindly found the time, and Neil Innes and Phill Jupitus were close calls. All of the main *Clue* gang were constant sources of support of course, both in sharing memories and inviting me behind the scenes of the Hammersmith show – but having Humph on board was the dream. A friendly chat at the stage door didn't seem to pique the great man's interest, surrounded as he was with adoring fans, but at the very least, his blessing was crucial.

And so the phone call that came one afternoon while busy at the office was quite a shock. Humph was full of apologies, working through his backlog – what was this book all about then? There was some quiet rumination on the end of the line as I ran through the pitch once again, but when the 'Bible' concept was explained, Humph's giggle became contagious. Of course he'd be delighted to be interviewed, and indeed he'd happily sit down when he could and write the foreword. My colleagues had no idea why I was jumping up and down at my desk, but I didn't care – the last part of the puzzle was in place!

Agonising reappraisal number two should need no explanation. Besides our chats, my proper interview with the Chairman had not taken place, to my eternal regret – but such concerns meant nothing compared to the pain of his loss, and the question mark now hanging over my favourite comedy show. Having finalised the book's publication with Trevor Dolby, the official *Clue* publisher, there was no question of giving up now, but the book would have to be a double tribute. Or was it triple? Or quadruple? Any which way, I realised, this Bible had to be finished before its curse struck again.

Its completion, of course, is due in many small ways to a whole host of other helpers and well-wishers, all due respect. My original agent, Peter Buckman, provided initial support which led to Trevor's involvement, also thanks to Graeme's kind intervention. The Giddies were a great source of comfort and goodwill, with Peej Harding, Carrie Yarrow and Jess Pickles especially offering practical help, in that order. I'm especially indebted to them for allowing me access to their fresh Q&A material. Alison Bean of The Goodies fan club provided the right amount of honest feedback untainted by familiarity, suggesting I was on the right path; *ISIRTA* fans Colin Day, Bruce Goatly, Gary C, John Lucas and Giles Wood kindly shared their memories; early encouragement came from Michael Stevens at BBC Audiobooks; the patron saint of comedy historians, Roger Wilmut, gave me sound advice, and then there was famous archivist Andrew Pixley. Our initial fears that we had over-lapping projects soon gave way to comradely support that, along with his partner Julie, also got us closer to the Holy Grail of a complete *Clue* episode guide. Well, we tried. Other archive help was offered by the brilliant Walter Dunlop (who first sent me the treasury of *I'm Sorry* that kick-started the whole project), plus Jonathan Tennet, Andy Walmsley, Ian Gutteridge, Tony Eddie and others – there's still some way to go, but if anyone has any clues to the missing shows, please visit www.missingepisodes.com and join the hunt.

Otherwise, it would be churlish not to thank my family, my employers and colleagues at Future Publishing, Jeff Walden at the BBC Written Archives, all the unnamed PAs and agents who helped me out, Lisa Manekofsky and everyone who helped provide images, the knowledgeable Louis Barfe, Neil Kennedy for collaring Armando Iannucci, and indeed all sparring partners on the website Cookdandbombd, who helped shape my approach to nattering about comedy. Oh, and John Davidson. (Who?)

But final thanks must go to Trevor Dolby, Nicola Taplin, Katherine Fry and the wonderful team at Preface, who had the impossible task of cutting this Bible dramatically down to size, in order for it to stand any chance of fitting on the bookshelves. If this Bible misses any of your favourite gags, games or references, they were probably there originally, but would have required two volumes to get to print – it's down to the team's good taste and judgement that it's in your hands at all. But, like I say, this book wasn't supposed to be like this.

Jem Roberts
April 2009

FOREWORDS

'So, Teams, in the smallest number of words, can you try and sum up a 400-page history of fifty years of radio comedy? Graeme, you can start ...'

It's an alarming experience to find yourself featured heavily in a history book. Even more so to find you're in a Bible. However, personal feelings aside, I have to admit that, as Bibles go, I reckon this is among the top two.

Jem Roberts has gone to extraordinary lengths to track down and interview everyone who has taken part in the *I'm Sorry* shows, and apparently most of the people who have listened to them as well.

The result is a book jam-packed full of facts, anecdotes, quotes and quips illustrating the history of *I'm Sorry I Haven't A Clue* and its antecedents from its Genesis right through to its Apocrypha.

I can't wait to read it.

Graeme Garden

Thirty-seven years having to endure Tim Brooke-Taylor's cunning duplicity, Graeme Garden's Machiavellian machinations, the 'charming' Collin Sell's odious sycophancy and don't get me started on Samantha – we all know how she got the job. You think it's been easy?

Or, to put it another way, thirty-seven years of fun and laughter with old friends, now warmed by the after-glow of Humph. Lucky or what?

Barry Cryer
The Priory, Milton Keynes

This is what I was going to write. That's right, 'this'. But I'd got it wrong. I was actually asked, 'Would I write one of the forewords' not 'one of the four words'. So I'll now go for all four words: 'This book is great.'

Jem Roberts has gone to great lengths to make this an accurate bible. But it's not just accurate, it's also fun as well. I hope you agree.

Tim Brooke-Taylor

PROLOGUE

Last Night a Jazzman Saved My Life . . .

Monday nights can be a bastard. Reintroduced to the world of drudgery with the whole week spread out before you, you wouldn't think that laughter would be one of the prominent features of a Monday evening. But this is the story of that rarest of rare breeds – a comedy show that somehow manages to deliver the required effect, time after time, with a regularity entirely unchallenged by any other long-running show in the world. The ultimate aural antidepressant. The Antidote to Panel Games.

Collapsing exhausted into your meagre accommodation after the first day of a stressful week, soaked from the rain, sour whispers of bills to be paid and debts to be dealt with playing at the back of your mind, the four days until the next weekend seeming like an untraversable desert of obligation and denial, you don't need to be certified bipolar to feel that there's nothing to be done to redress the balance of light and shade required to live to a ripe old age . . . And then, 6.30 p.m., you turn on Radio 4. And you realise that all you needed was the sound of an octogenarian trumpet player reciting a crêpe-paper-thin suggestion that the Light Entertainer Lionel Blair is a sex maniac, and for half an hour there's nothing left to do but give yourself up to the complete amnesia of gut-aching hysteria. You're not alone – millions of others around the British Isles are laughing with you, whether they're at the dinner table, out on the streets, or listening in the car, swerving dangerously as the tears cloud their view of the road ahead. And by the time the jazz man has bid his farewell and the seven o'clock news and *The Archers* has rolled around, you realise that, while such widespread giggly abandon is still possible, things can't be all bad.

With the loss of Humphrey Lyttelton, many lovers of *I'm Sorry I Haven't a Clue* would demand that the book was closed on the show and all its traditions and running gags, after thirty-six years. But what version of *I'm Sorry* did these abolitionists want to preserve? The current model, which probably went back no further than the mid-to-late nineties? The Naismith years, starting from 1991? Everything post-Mornington Crescent, which first appeared in 1978, or the whole show stretching back to 1972? Or did they have the depth of knowledge or long-term memory to recall the Radio Prune days which first gave birth to *Clue*? Was it the whole *I'm Sorry* saga stretching back to 1963 on which they wanted to finally call time?

To the Teams' chagrin, there has been a lot of speculation as to the future of *I'm Sorry I Haven't a Clue* since the end of the triumphant fiftieth series. But you can't pass judgement on the future of the show unless you know where its roots lie and what exactly the high points of this uniquely long-running tradition may be, throughout the last five decades. This Bible is here to try and offer some kind of explanation as to where the astounding phenomenon of *I'm Sorry I Haven't a Clue* comes from, what makes it tick, and where it may go from here.

And, having set out our stall, our search for the Genesis of *Clue* takes us to another stall, the Footlights stall at the 1960 Freshers' Fair at Cambridge University, where a personable young student called David Frost is awaiting a new influx of talent with a large cheesy smile on his face . . .

THE PRUNE TESTAMENT

1

Running Away with the Circus

When it comes to beginnings, there are only two kinds of comedy story that are worth telling: the traditional hard-luck tale of overcoming difficulties to achieve fame (little Richard Pryor playing in brothels, poor wee Dudley Moore all alone in his hospital bed); and the less endearing, extraordinarily easy ride – such as Fry and Laurie and their *Cellar Tapes* friends stepping out of Cambridge to be decanted into the flash car of a cigar-chomping agent, determined to make (most of) them big. The story of the *I'm Sorry I'll Read That Again* alumni belongs firmly to the latter camp.

True, the backgrounds of each individual in the group don't conform to the usual prejudices against Oxbridge comedians, being, if not exactly grammar-school types, then certainly from solid, parochial middle-middle-class backgrounds. But it would be fair to say that, from the first time that the cast we are celebrating moved their belongings into their Cambridge digs and breathed in the last gasps of Peter Cook exhalation that famously lingered in the air, their route to comedy stardom was not a difficult or especially demanding one.

This is not merely a moan, however, but potentially the very root of the free-wheeling, anything-goes atmosphere for which their radio masterpiece is remembered.

Freshers and Footlights

Not that getting their first foothold in Cambridge comedy proved a walkover for the 1960 freshers. The success of Jonathan Miller and Peter Cook made one grand difference to many of this generation of Cambridge undergraduates; they, like Cook and co. before them, had grown up with the dizzying pleasures of *The Goon Show*, but the wild success of *Beyond the Fringe*, just at the time that they were coming to the end of their school careers and facing their futures, gave a very different reason for wanting to get into one of the world's greatest universities. Promising lawyers and doctors had obviously seen

Cambridge as the ultimate establishment at which to train for centuries, but Graham Chapman must surely have been one of the first students to freely admit that the real allure of Cambridge lay not in the chance to graduate from one of the greatest ancient academies in the world, but in joining the Footlights.

The Cambridge Footlights was founded in 1883 – or at least that was the first time that the name had been used for the practice of undergraduates, largely from Trinity College, performing amateur entertainments for the local populace. In the intervening eighty-odd years, it had inspired its fair share of careers – the comic actor Jack Hulbert was perhaps the first pre-war 'name' to emerge from the Footlights, achieving movie fame alongside his wife Cicely Courtneidge. The list of graduates for the next few decades includes the Australian dancer (and *Chitty Chitty Bang Bang*'s Child Catcher) Robert Helpmann and the significantly moustachioed comic legend Jimmy Edwards, alongside Richard Murdoch and Cecil Beaton. Next came the mid-fifties generation which featured Miller, Michael Frayn, Leslie Bricusse and Joe Melia, followed in 1958 by Cook's coterie, comprising John Bird, John Wood (or Fortune, as he became in time), and non-member-because-she-was-a-girl Eleanor Bron, bringing the fifties to a close with the highest standard of revue the club had ever known.

The epicentre of Footlights activity was always the final revue in May Week, which was often hurriedly put together when members should really have been concentrating on their exams. Since Jonathan Miller's time at Cambridge these celebrated shows had begun to be more widely circulated than a short run at Cambridge or London, and were usually broadcast on radio and even television. Chapman always claimed it was a 1958 TV broadcast that caught his eye back at the family home in Melton Mowbray – and it obviously inspired that alumni's immediate successors, in the year that included David Frost, and a young classics student called Humphrey Barclay.

Humphrey Barclay
Born: 24 March 1941, Dorking
Educated: The Old Malthouse, Swanage; Harrow Public School
Humphrey Barclay's only contender for poshest person in this book may well be the other Humphrey, Lyttelton. 'The Barclays arrived with William the Conqueror in that crowded ferry boat,' he confirms, 'and over the ensuing 950 years founded Barclays Bank, Barclays Beers and Humphrey Barclay Productions. We helped abolish the slave trade and reform prisons, and at one time owned one twenty-fourth of New Jersey. We also include a cannibal among our forebears, but that's another story.'

Being of such distinguished stock, descended from the Scottish lairds of Mather and Urie, wee Humphrey's entry into Harrow was no shock, and neither was his rise to becoming Head Boy. However, an early passion for comedy suggested a very unusual career path for the young Barclay, and he names influences such as *The Goons*, Deryck Guyler in *Just Fancy*, Noël Coward, 'Albert and the Lion', Nat Jackley, Laurel & Hardy and 'my uncle Podge' as early comic heroes, as well as his cousin Julian Slade.

Few producers have affected British Comedy quite like Humphrey Barclay, whose work at the BBC and in independent television has influenced millions, although he lists the Maureen Lipman sitcom *Agony*, *A Fine Romance* and *Desmond's* as among his most prized productions. Now mostly retired, he lives 'in London, contentment, and solitude.'

Humphrey Barclay has no OBE but he is, however, an adopted member of the Royal Family – of the African village of Tafo. He explains, 'In 2000, at the funeral in Ghana of my friend the actor Gyearbuor Asante, the Chief of his ancestral town asked me to take on his (unfulfilled) role of development chief. So I now run a charity to enable progress in the small impoverished community of Kwahu-Tafo – friendsoftafo.org.'

Another Footlights graduate made good, Julian Slade, the creator of the hit musical of the fifties, *Salad Days*, was Barclay's real inspiration for joining Footlights. He was already headed for Cambridge, but as he recalls: 'I wouldn't have thought of going anywhere near comedy were it not for the fact that my two cousins, Julian and Adrian Slade, had been members of the Footlights. We all got on very well together, and they used to perform a lot of comedy songs for us at home around the piano, and I do remember probably Adrian saying, "Of course when you get to Cambridge you'll get into the Footlights". And that surprised me, because I had no idea that I'd get involved with anything so grand . . .' Barclay rather thought, like Cook before him, that a job in the Foreign Office would be his final destination, but the flytrap nature of the Footlights would put paid to that.

From this distance, it's quite confusing to try to chart the comings and goings of so many future stars of British comedy at Cambridge University nearly half a century ago – generally speaking, of course, they all studied for three years and ordinarily each year group would be easily separable. But the Footlights demolished these distinctions, which is why as a fresher David Frost could gawp at his hero Peter Cook, that urbane near-graduate, all he liked. Subsequently, Frost would be almost ready to leave university himself when he would see the new gang we are celebrating enter the Footlights clubroom, and they in turn would work alongside later undergraduates such as Eric Idle.

It's no surprise that a continuous relay of inspiration and comic taste is apparent through these years.

But perhaps it wasn't quite the allure of stardom that fuelled the popularity of Footlights. According to Barclay, 'We were very lucky to have this place called the Footlights Clubroom, in an area called Petty Cury . . . it was just a long room, with a stage at one end and a bar at the other; you could go there for a beer and a bun at lunchtime, and hang around there for the afternoon because a sketch needed to be written for such-and-such a smoker, which was a better idea than going away and doing some work, or going for a row on the river or whatever. So we used to hang around together, but – and it's not false modesty – they were the ones reinventing comedy, and I was the affable one hanging around, really.'

These Falcon Yard premises were brand new to the club in 1960, and continued to be the site for this mingling of undergraduates – whether it was to further the artistry of British Comedy or to avoid proper study or even to get a drink after-hours – until its demolition in 1972.

I Thought I Saw It Move

Of course, in later years joining the Footlights was almost invariably seen as a career move – the first time for privileged undergraduate buttocks to settle on the greasy pole that led to a nice job at the BBC. But for those funny freshers whose parents bid them goodbye at the gates to their college in 1960, this was an exciting new move. Perhaps even then the desire to step into Cook's shoes could suggest ambition, but if so, it was an ambition *to be funny*, and *to be with funny people*. What lay beyond that was impossible to tell, but in the meantime, getting into Footlights was all that mattered.

Timothy Julian Brooke-Taylor
Born: 17 July 1940, Buxton
Educated: Winchester College, Hampshire
Tim would be the first to tell you that he isn't anything like as posh as his name suggests, although his family background is not undistinguished, at least in sport – his mother was an international lacrosse player, and his grandfather played football for England in the 1890s. Sport would continue to be a passion for Tim, as a devoted golfer and honorary vice president of the Derby County team. The baby of the family, with several years separating him from his elder brother and sister, Tim was still expected to eventually follow his father and brother into the family firm of solicitors.

But Tim was inspired to follow another path from a very early age, entranced by Norman Evans' Dame on a visit to panto in Manchester, and eagerly soaking up all the radio comedy he could, from *Much Binding in the Marsh* to *Take It*

From Here. At just five, he was expelled from his all-girls school (no, honestly) for teasing Brownies, but this setback didn't prevent him from graduating to Winchester at thirteen, only a year after the death of his father. It was here that his own comic propensities began to be aired, when an intended magic act went hideously wrong, but gained barrels of laughs as a result. Despite this early promise, theatricality was not encouraged at Winchester, and it was only in a panic when being grilled by the Derbyshire Education Board about his reasons for going up to Cambridge that he mentioned the Footlights. Luckily, they still gave him a much-needed grant, allowing young Tim to enrol at Pembroke, like his brother before him, and begin his route towards a career in law.

Outside of *Clue* and *The Goodies*, Tim Brooke-Taylor has continued to be a much-loved presenter and comic and character actor on stage and screen, popping up in *Heartbeat, TLC, One Foot In The Grave, Marple* and more. Married to Christine for over forty years with two grown-up sons, Ben and Edward, Tim has not retired to Berkshire, where he co-owns the village pub. And he has no OBE.

In fact, it clearly mattered a hell of a lot – Tim Brooke-Taylor admits that he never slept a wink in the lead-up to his audition for fear of not being able to follow his brother's footsteps into the club's exclusive premises. 'I went to Cambridge to study law,' he recalls, 'because that's what my family all do, and I could earn a crust … In my case, it was the Education Committee of Derbyshire, God bless them, who gave me the grant, and they asked this question, "What are you going to do when you're not working?" Now I'd prepared a pretty good answer of how hard I was going to work, but I hadn't prepared what I was going to do when I *wasn't* working. So I blurted out "The Footlights!" because my brother had been there.'

Come the time of the freshers' arrival, besides Brooke-Taylor showing an interest in joining up, if you had happened to be loitering around the door of the Guildhall on the day of the University Society's Fair in October 1960, you may have been knocked down by the extraordinary figure of the 21-year-old John Cleese, literally pelting up the street in embarrassed consternation, having admitted to the Footlights secretary (one David Frost) that he could neither sing nor dance. When asked what he *could* do, the lofty youngster murmured 'I try to make people laugh,' and fled. He needn't have feared, judging from Chapman's recollection of the day, on approaching the beaming Secretary at the Footlights stall. 'Frost told me that I couldn't join. I had to be invited to audition. I asked what was the point of having a stall then. He said, "None whatsoever."'

Despite the whisper of change in British society that the early stirrings of the satire boom suggested, Footlights was still a very staid establishment at the time, just as comic revue hadn't *quite* evolved from the genteel smokers performed from the very start of the club's existence. The ability – and will – to sing and dance were still seen as a crucial part of being a member (Cook had famously been in possession of bucketloads of the will, it was the ability that foxed him), and women would not be fully welcomed into Footlights until Eric Idle's time as president in 1964, for all that artists such as Margolyes and Bron have been retrospectively included in the club's success story.

Brooke-Taylor passed the song-and-dance test, but for those less keen on fitting in with the Footlights' cheesy dogma, like Cleese and Chapman, more stealth was required to join the team. Each member of Footlights generally spent two years with the club – first as nervous new boys and then, inevitably, committee members. To gain entrance, this new generation in 1960 had to impress the Frost committee. Cleese knew someone called Alan Hutchison who knew someone called something else, who got him in (his audition piece being imaginary hamster-trampling), but Chapman had to be slightly more wily, staging an independent smoker in his own college, inviting the committee, and plying them with claret. Once both students gained entry, Chapman recalled, 'It became a mission of John Cleese and myself to oust all singing and dancing, which we largely achieved.'

Fundamentally of course, Footlights was only a hobby, and of no greater importance at this stage than the members' other pursuits, such as Cleese's playing football for his college or Humphrey Barclay's cartooning. None of these young people had any great career plan – and it's worth noting that they were especially young for undergraduates, most of them going up to Cambridge fresh out of school now that national service had been made obsolete.

Two of these youngsters – the freakishly tall, bearded elder Cleese, fresh from two years of teaching, and his slighter, blonder, less bearded fellow law student Brooke-Taylor – instantly clicked as comedy fans and indeed comedians, which Brooke-Taylor puts down in many ways to their chosen subject. 'John Cleese I met, funnily enough, through law. We got to know each other partly through the Footlights, but we'd go to law lectures together, and giggle away at the back. John wasn't anything to do with the Pembroke smoking concerts, but he was around at the time. Outside the college I got on with him and Graham Chapman, we were very good friends at that stage.'

Sitting in lectures listening to endless hours of not only pompous rhetoric but tales of hideous misfortune, which translated into hilarity for them (following the law of comedy being pain plus time), gave Tim and John's comedy a certain sick edge even at this early stage. It's easy to imagine the young students reading a legal textbook full of the harshest misfortunes and disasters – road accidents, GBH, manslaughter – and laughing fit to burst.

John Marwood Cleese
Born: 27 October 1939, Weston-super-Mare
Educated: St Peter's Preparatory School, Weston-super-Mare; Clifton College, Bristol

By rights, the name would be Jack Cheese, were it not for his father Reginald's fears of being teased in the trenches when he enrolled to fight in 1915. Facing German machine guns was one thing, but putting up with cheese jokes was obviously beyond the pail. When John was born in the Somerset seaside town of Weston in 1939, his parents Reginald and Muriel were both in their forties, which must have contributed to a notably cosseted childhood. Despite a built-in reserve that wasn't alleviated by his physical appearance, becoming a six-footer by the age of twelve, Cleese was a popular figure at St Peter's. It wasn't until he attended Clifton College in Bristol that his passion for sport was joined by a similar fascination for comedy – notably George Burns & Gracie Allen, and Jimmy Jewel & Ben Warris, who inspired Cleese to write pages of comic dialogue in their style one day when he was too ill to get stuck into any sport. Eventually he developed a habit of collecting jokes, notably from *The Goon Show*, in the same way that other boys collected stamps, or scabs. Cleese's stature had led him to develop a keen sense of humour, being an easy target for low-level bullying, but any inklings of comic genius in his early life were faint. He sneers at the memory of an early turn as Malvolio, but has always proudly recalled his participation in school concerts, one of which boasted a Cleese send-up of one of the masters so biting that another teacher literally fell off his chair laughing.

John did well academically at Clifton, and was offered a place at Cambridge to study law in 1958. However, the end of national service meant that there were simply too many undergraduates for the university to cope with, so he spent two years teaching at his beloved old prep school, gaining an intimate knowledge of the eccentricities of the public school system, as well as, it's fair to presume, a certain patrician tone, both of which would see him in good stead in his eventual career.

Cleese's career has not been uncheckered by any means, but his successes have been of such unparalleled quality and importance – between his Python work on TV, stage and in film, as well as co-creating *Fawlty Towers* with then wife (then not wife) Connie Booth, bagging awards alongside Charles Crichton with *A Fish Called Wanda* and setting up Video Arts – that his place as one of the greatest icons of twentieth-century comedy is inarguable, and history will probably place him on a par with Cook, Milligan, Hancock and Chaplin. In later years he rediscovered his comic voice thanks to his online community at thejohncleese.com.

Cleese has been married three times to date, to three different Americans, and has two daughters, Cynthia and Camilla. He declined the offer of a CBE and a peerage, and has no OBE.

So in time Brooke-Taylor, Cleese and Chapman joined the club, but none of them managed to pass the audition to be one of the team for the 1961 revue. Within their own college smokers, at Pembroke College and elsewhere (Cleese was actually at Downing College but as his fellow law-student friend Brooke-Taylor was a Pembroke man, Cleese had his meals there and generally hung around, being as good as accepted as one of the locals), all of them were beginning to flex their laughter-generating muscles, but the only new blood to scrape into David Frost's final revue, *I Thought I Saw It Move*, was Barclay. He had joined the amateur dramatic society at Cambridge, at first with a view to being a designer, but after auditioning by mistake, ended up 'usually playing sanctimonious vicars'. He continues, 'Because I had fallen into doing comedy parts in plays, they noticed me, whereas they hadn't noticed the lurking Cleese and Chapmans of this world. So, quite bizarrely, they were passed over and I was asked by David Frost to audition.'

I Thought I Saw It Move has gone down in history as Cook-lite, with Frost channelling his hero in a Mr Boylett/E. L. Wisty-style monologue and only minor parts for Barclay. But one item written by Cleese and his pal Hutchison (about a family dog whose rescue from a disused mine had so far claimed the life of three members of its family), did get into the show. As performed by Barclay as a sober newsreader, it is a tantalising seed of what became the central tradition of *ISIRTA* – the silliest and sickest jokes, delivered in news form. Barclay had the staid BBC pronunciation to a T, and it proved a standout item in the revue.

Barclay insists the level of Cook-aping in the rest of the show and elsewhere was perfectly natural: 'I think anybody in any generation is prey to imitating their comedy heroes, and it's certainly true that voices that Peter invented became what you did if you were trying to be funny . . . just as, in a previous generation, we did *The Goons* . . .' And indeed, as subsequent comedians have unwittingly aped the fatuous cadence of Alan Partridge's voice or produced a zany portmanteau which could have been coined by Chris Morris. But there's no denying the density of debt owed to Cook's spirit for that 1961 revue. 'Peter's style and comedy was all-pervasive because he was a towering genius, and we were still in his shadow. We just about emerged from his shadow with *Cambridge Circus*.'

In between Footlights revues and the occasional bout of studying, the 'smoker' evenings at individual colleges during Michaelmas and Lent terms kept performers' skills sharp. It was a great testing ground for material, as the rowdy audiences were often voluble in their abuse if it didn't come up to scratch, making them more akin to a comedy club than a theatre. The Pembroke Smokers were especially infamous thanks to old boy Peter Cook, who would breeze in through his old college on occasion to take to the stage and wipe out all comers with a near-private performance of his incessant wit, as Tim recalls: 'When I got there, he'd just left the term before (Timing, it's all timing!) and *Beyond the Fringe* came through Cambridge when I was there. It's still the funniest thing I've ever seen – hit my head on the seat in front, I mean it was so funny.' These smokers were inevitably even more cliquey events than Footlights shows and there was a great tradition for drag, owing to women only being allowed for certain 'Ladies' Nights', and a general air of inescapable privilege and pomposity that made one undergraduate's blood boil, both then and now.

'We used to do smoking concerts which were appallingly sexist . . . That annoyed me very much. It was only men – and they had a sort of "Ladies' Night" like the bloody Masons . . .'

William Edgar Oddie
Born: 7 July 1941, Rochdale
Educated: King Edward's School, Birmingham
Bill was actually the third or fourth child to be born to Lilian and Harry Oddie, but the first to survive, and it's likely that the post-natal depression suffered by his mother before and after he came along contributed to her being taken away to a mental institution when he was only very young, leaving the young lad to be brought up by his mild-mannered father and imperious grandmother, in the leafy suburbs of Birmingham. It was here that Bill's passion for sport was joined by his greatest hobby of all, ornithology, after an accidental suck on a bad pheasant's egg caused him to vomit wildly over his impressive collection of birds' eggs, ending that unfortunate hobby once and for all, but igniting his passion for caring for birds, rather than robbing them.

Harry worked hard to send his boy to the best schools, and by the time Bill was in long trousers two more passions had joined his little list – an adoration of comedy from *Educating Archie* to the Crazy Gang and, of course, a burgeoning fascination with music. Making up new lyrics to rugby songs at school soon gave way to penning the entire score for King Edward's School's 1959 revue, a tradition Bill took over from classmate Nat Joseph, who would go on to be the head of Transatlantic Records. Between sporting pursuits and his skiffle band, Bill had no distinct career ambitions when he got his place at Cambridge University, but he wasn't going to be short of activities to keep him busy while he decided.

Of course, when The Goodies went their separate ways, Bill's experience as a TV presenter was eventually allied with his passion for birds, wildlife and conservation to great acclaim, making him the nation's favourite cuddly Natural History presenter, with each instalment of *Springwatch*, or its seasonal equivalent, uniting the country in the pursuit of naughty badgers. Despite his cheery persona, he has also been open about his past struggles with a bipolar disorder, and attempts to avoid a relapse. Perhaps his greatest source of protection from this happening is the love of his family, with two daughters from his first marriage to Jean Hart – Bonnie, a choreographer, and actress and director Kate Hardie – and rock star Rosie, from his second marriage, to Laura Beaumont. He also has three grandchildren, and counting.

Bill Oddie has an OBE for services to Wildlife Conservation.

. . . The views of a then twenty-year-old English student called Bill Oddie. Although he continues, 'It wasn't just Pembroke, the whole bloody place was sexist. I wasn't *that* angry about it, but I did think it was a bit much. I mean, I was in no position to be representing the girls or anything like that, except I thought there should be more of them.'

By far the Footlights star with the humblest heritage, Oddie must have cut an extraordinary figure among his peer group. In many ways the polar opposite of his tall, buttoned-up well-to-do law-student friends, the diminutive Oddie made little attempt, Dudley Moore style, to cover up his parochial accent, maintaining a Brummie/Northern burr of his own. He was studying English at Pembroke, but despite his equal talents for music, art and performing, he had no knowledge of Footlights when he first arrived, and certainly never applied to the university with joining the club in mind. But his passion for rock 'n' roll (which had joined his lifelong devotion to ornithology as a significant preoccupation) gave him that one quality which eluded so many others in that environment – cool. Even at this early stage, the chiselled diminutive Mickey Rooney-ish firebrand was something to behold. As Humphrey Barclay recalls from when he first set eyes on Oddie at a Pembroke smoker, Oddie was 'an absolute knock-out. He was a ballsy, bouncy modern performer . . . just fantastic.'

'Bill was in the same college,' recalls Tim, 'so I met him first. It was a sort of charity day, and we were both doing bits and pieces – I was still fairly scared of performing at that stage – but we got on very quickly, and worked in the smokers together. Peter Cook had just left, and we inherited these brilliant revues, so people were going to come to it. And that's the best thing that ever happened, as far as I was concerned – here was a college that had what were bizarrely called smoking concerts, all that meant was a sketch show, in a cellar, with people buying drinks, which is possibly the best way to do comedy. And to work with great people like Bill, and there was a great guy in our first year called Geoffrey Paxton, who really passed on the Peter Cook enthusiasm and brilliance.' But although Oddie's music started to find its way into the main revues, he himself would have to stick to Pembroke Smokers until his final year. He agrees with Tim about the sheer fortuitousness of landing in Pembroke though. 'The Pembroke Smoker was already accepted as being a cut above the others . . . And that, to me, has been the good fortune I've had, and frankly I think, most of my contemporaries too – there was a context for us to fall into and be encouraged by, in a very supportive group . . . If you had an idea, you could do it right then, and nobody was going to boo you off or anything, it wasn't like paying your dues at the open-mic night. You were up next if you were in the audience, so you encouraged them, and they encouraged you. And I'm absolutely certain that that's why people took risks on the type of comedy that they did, because nobody was going to judge them, really.'

Cleese, Brooke-Taylor, Chapman and Oddie were a pretty intimidating quartet of young comics by this time, as well as being good friends. Despite being the looniest of the lot, Graham's rugby-playing machismo made him seem perhaps the most affably normal, whereas the unfathomably tall John was a bizarre sight alongside the tiny but hip Bill, with cock-of-the-walk-to-be Tim completing the set. Cleese recalls today: 'Tim was an almost perfect example of a fairly confident public-school chap. And he was funny, fairly conventional in his thinking, and very easy company. Bill was more eccentric, he didn't give a damn about his dress, which always endeared him to me . . . he and a comb or brush were virtual strangers. He was the only one of us who was really talented, musically.' And as for John himself? 'I think I automatically fell into playing sort of bland middle-class people, you know what I mean, the professionals – the accountants and the lawyers and the architects . . . I think I fell into that because of the public-school background.'

Double Take

With *I Thought I Saw It Move* over, the Footlights committee found that a minor crisis was looming, as Barclay attests. 'They realised in that year, '60–61, that everybody who was anybody in Footlights would be leaving, and they decided that they must – whether they liked it or not – get some new blood in . . . It was David who put me forward, so I owe him a great deal.' With Frost's generation entering the wide world, a brand-new committee had to be formed, and quick. Therefore, the new boys who had really only just begun to find their way around the university suddenly found themselves virtually in charge of the club that they had worked so hard to join in the first place. Barclay took Frost's place as secretary, Brooke-Taylor was junior treasurer, and Cleese became, rather dully, the registrar. It was all part of the process of becoming the big boys, and in the meantime it was back to the smokers, in preparation for the main show for 1962 – the Trevor Nunn-directed offering *Double Take*, with Tim, Graham and John alongside (among others) Miriam Margolyes, *National Lampoon* and *Spitting Image* co-founder Tony Hendra and reluctant performer Humphrey Barclay.

The show was a poor relation to Nunn's other project of that year, *Much Ado About Nothing*. The only way he could afford the play's elaborate wrought-iron set was to use a significant proportion of the revue's budget – which lent a rather random air to the proceedings as the sketches played out against a backdrop of what looked like garden furniture. But there were many important firsts in *Double Take*, which are belied by its cast only recalling embarrassing elements such as a laugh-free musical number featuring them all in animal skins singing 'We are a most important caveman . . .'

Not only would *Double Take* be the very first Footlights revue to play at the ever growing Edinburgh Fringe Festival (which was the brainwave of cast member and then president Robert Atkins, and is now a tradition it would be unthinkable to abandon) but there was also a distinct air of Music Hall nostalgia to the show, again thanks to Atkins and the new boy Brooke-Taylor. With the changes in Footlights personnel, there was an inevitable evolution of style from revue to revue, and between Bill's rocking Adam Faith parody (as performed by Atkins), Humphrey's BBC deadpanning, and the extremes of logical and illogical humour creeping in from Cleese and Chapman, *Double Take* became in many ways the penultimate precursor to *I'm Sorry I'll Read That Again*.

This Edinburgh debut for the Footlights was a formative time for all the cast, but John Cleese learned his greatest lesson in show business, thanks to an unexpected side venture. One entrepreneur had found a small venue not far from the *Double Take* theatre where he decided to set up a nightclub – and with the Cambridge lot having plenty of time to fill before their late-night Curtain Up, Cleese, Chapman and their colleague Alan George were invited to provide twenty minutes of 'light humorous entertainment' at instalments throughout the evening, for a little cash in hand. They pieced together a cabaret act, and were all poised to strut their stuff on the first night when they noticed that not only did their audience consist of just one poor unsuspecting young couple, but also that the female of the two had been so overcome with the embarrassment of the situation that she was sobbing, as her beau comforted her and glared at the trio accusingly. The show stumbled through to its conclusion until the young lovers could finally flee, but it gave Cleese a lifelong superstition, that it is genuinely bad luck for a show's cast to outnumber the audience. It's a fate which befalls enough poor performers at the Fringe even today – but at least John, Graham and Alan had the success of the main show to fall back on.

The show did well for everyone at that year's festival, but with the younger performers only just beginning to get into their stride, the correct recipe wasn't quite there for a hit of *Beyond the Fringe* proportions, or anything like it.

Humphrey Barclay ponders the right recipe. 'I think really the three influences that came in were Bill's music . . . a wit came with John that perhaps hadn't been there before, and then the Music Hall fondness which came with Tim and Robert . . . those were the new elements, and by the time we'd got to *Cambridge Circus*, of course, John had come into his forte, Bill was very strong, and the Music Hall influence had kind of evolved from soft tribute to parody . . . there's a kind of evolution between the shows, I would say, culminating in the very strong gathering which I was lucky enough to be in charge of in my third year.'

But, like many a good student before him, despite many plaudits for his efforts, Barclay never saw himself as a performer and decided to hang up his performing shoes for good as he entered his third and most important year of study. He recalls making a grand gesture of giving away his theatrical make-up. Entering the clubroom, where all the gang were hiding from their homework, he solemnly announced his retirement. 'I wasn't a great performer – I got the straight parts, the poker-faced, posh stuff . . . so I announced that I would not be putting myself up to be in the 1963 revue. Nobody murmured a single word of protest.'

The Fab . . . Seven?

In retracing the *ISIRTA* team's journey from cliquey undergraduates to hot young bucks (plus one doe) of the airwaves, it's irresistible to note parallels with another band of young people who also rose to fame in the early sixties, known as 'The Beatles'. Considering that this comedy movement was taking place at precisely the same time as a similarly culture-changing musical movement, many of the parallels are striking – a gang of kids freed from the oppression of national service who began to hone their craft in their own ad hoc way at home before really putting their talents to the test abroad, who then went on to cause a sensation with their live shows, to the point that the audience's domination began to have a detrimental effect on both their performance, and their will to continue as a group.

Brooke-Taylor (no small Fabs fan himself) agrees that there are parallels.

'I always said how lucky we were to be around at that time, '62–63 specifically; when suddenly we were allowed to do lots of things we weren't before.
Everything was looked at in a new way – it wasn't the dreary fifties, you were
actually allowed to wear coloured clothes and listen to music that was different,
and that was exactly the same with comedy as with music. My theory was
that England was actually entering a pretty good state, and education was so
much better so you didn't have to play down to the audience, you actually
could do what you thought was funny and hoped everyone would go along
with it, whereas before – I loved mother-in-law jokes, don't get me wrong –
but they always implied that the audience didn't know anything at all, which
in the sixties they did! So you could take big leaps . . . Certainly, in *ISIRTA*,
you could go into new areas, and presume people knew history and things
like that . . .'

So this was The Young Generation, doing for comedy what The Beatles
and their lesser contemporaries were doing for music. And, to those comedy
fans for whom a classic show can inspire all the awe and wonder of a classic
album or rock gig, it's the wild genesis of *ISIRTA* that captures the same magic
as The Beatles playing at the Cavern – which doesn't just mean the Footlights
revue or even the Pembroke smokers, but the less rigidly structured gigging
around Cambridge and elsewhere. These extra-curricular shows were mainly
perpetrated by the Cambridge University Light Entertainment Society
(CULES), but every comic was open to trying out material if it would earn
them a bob or two. Back in the days of male-dominated claret-chugging and
obligatory E. L. Wisty voices, it seems that only the medical contingent of the
Cambridge in-crowd took their studies at all seriously, the emphasis rather
being on making each other laugh, and bolstering grants with cabaret performances in Cambridge, London and anywhere else that fancied a slice of the
kind of wit that those frightfully clever 'Fringe' boys were taking from the West
End to Broadway. One of the 1961 freshers, Graeme Garden, recalls: 'One of
the advantages of being in the Footlights, as opposed to one of the other clubs
like CULES, was that the Footlights had the cachet and got booked for May
Balls to do cabarets, and slightly more upmarket gigs. So you'd get a bit of
cash in hand for going along and doing a few sketches to a load of extremely
wealthy students in fancy dresses sitting on the floor at your feet.'

The catch was, of course, that the cloying, Cook-worshipping tenure of
David Frost's presidency of the Footlights had necessitated a subsequent surge
away from satire – this was a whole new generation of ambitious wags and,
for them, silliness was the way forward. Robert Atkins' tenure as president
had seen a whiff of vaudeville creeping in, but now the influence became
more apparent. 'The movement, if it was called anything, was "Back to Music
Hall",' admits Garden. 'That was the subtext – or, in fact, I think it was a

strapline on some of the advertising they did. Satire had really sort of hit the big time with *That Was The Week That Was* (*TW3*), which was going on at about the same time, and people thought, well, we like doing things that are just funny, and we weren't necessarily going to follow the political satire route, which was where it was heading. You know, *TW3* was the first time they'd actually portrayed prime ministers on screen and things like that. The group that was a year ahead of me were very much all about Back to Basics, and funny baggy trousers.'

It's generally accepted that the central instigator of this Music Hall direction, after Robert Atkins' graduation, was Tim Brooke-Taylor who, due to his generally small credit in every *Goodies* titles sequence and lack of involvement in later *ISIRTA* scripts, is often overlooked as an originator of material. His friend Graeme Garden agrees. 'Tim probably knew more about Music Hall than anybody did, and also he had a passion for Buster Keaton and silent comedy as well, and introduced some of that. And certainly he played a lot of the Music Hall comedian roles that turned up in sketches.'

Tim himself puts it down to his childhood love of comedy. 'The only things we had, certainly on radio, were Variety shows – probably when I was very young, seven or eight, I remember being allowed to stay up to listen to things on a Saturday night and you'd get the comics of the time (it was only later that we got more sophisticated, sort of *Round the Horne* and *Much Binding in the Marsh*) and that was where one discovered comedy. I loved it, I had a real adoration for comedians and comedy. I used to go to pantomimes – Norman Evans was the first dame I saw, really part of the tradition, and it was brilliantly funny. And because of my early years I suppose I had this affection for the people who made me laugh. The fact that the sixties had moved into something more sophisticated didn't mean that I didn't revere the people that had gone before. Bill Oddie was pretty into Music Hall as well, to be honest, but I do remember at school in my particular little group we used to do a revue thing, and I remember doing a Music Hall comedian piece. And we were parodying them, but showing affection at the same time. So I was trying to have it both ways I think, sending up what they were doing in Variety, but at the same time thinking "Actually, mate, you're wonderful". That's what Morecambe & Wise were basically, Variety, and I enjoyed everything they ever did.'

Oddie continues the theme, 'We admired the Satire Boom, particularly *Beyond the Fringe* enormously . . . What we meant by "Back to Music Hall" was a recognition that there was some very clever, rather grown-up comedy going on, and we were going to take it back to silliness, really.' Such cheeky, old-fashioned humour and cries of 'I Say, I Say, I Say!' were the last comedic devices that were expected in the wake of *Beyond the Fringe*. But whether the posh punters at each privileged party expected satire or silliness, the random gigging around Cambridge was obviously a popular pastime, with different groups pinching material left, right and centre to pad out an evening's entertainment and make a few quid – and, of course, it was great practice for the main event, a training ground for that year's Footlights revue, destined (by now inevitably) for Edinburgh and from there – who knew?

When the time came for the 1963 revue to be put together, it was Brooke-Taylor's job, having inherited the position of president, to get the ball rolling. Naturally, all the old gang were incredibly busy, and John Cleese had even made the decision to skip that year's show, and concentrate on his work. He put this down partly to falling in love – after which, nothing seemed to matter quite so much, as of course it never does when your heart is broken for the first time. He was also sidetracked, inevitably, by playing football. If a long run of bad weather hadn't fouled up his university football career, that may have been the end of Cleese the performer, which is a terrifying thought.

Having publicly taken his last bow, club secretary Humphrey Barclay was also planning on concentrating on his studies when Brooke-Taylor turned to him to head up the 1963 revue. 'It took me totally by surprise, because I hadn't directed anything at all at Cambridge, but I had worked very closely with Trevor Nunn, who directed *Double Take*. We just got on, and did a lot of the donkey work. You can collect all the smoker sketches that you want, but sooner or later someone has to choose a number to close the first half with, and that kind of thing . . . Trevor and I spent several nights staying up very late in his room at Downing hammering out pathetic lyrics that would *just* be good enough to make some sort of number, which we then forced everybody to do. When he did the same thing for *Cats*, he became a multi-millionaire . . .' The fact was that, having been involved in two shows already, and been a perfect sounding board for all the new sketches and jokes thrown up by the smokers, Barclay was a safe pair of hands. Although he doubts his name was on the top of the list, he 'couldn't say no', even though he didn't have the slightest idea what to do.

Obviously, the first part of the process was to form a team. There were three shoo-ins for the show, of course – Brooke-Taylor, Oddie and Cleese – around whom a team would be built. With Graham Chapman already having left for Bart's hospital to continue his medical training, the core group was then supplemented by Pembroke man Chris Stuart-Clark, who had written material for *Double Take*, and Tony Buffery, who had been in it. But there were still two ingredients missing.

'One of the people who wasn't particularly obvious was David,' admits Barclay, recalling the time when David Hatch was sent for to audition – even though he was actually teaching in Oxford as part of his fourth-year training at the time. 'I have this image of him in a sheepskin coat . . . not a shaggy Afghan thing, more a sort of Home Counties thing . . . and he just had a particular brand of poker-faced, bossy comedy that was very funny, and we needed that. Unfortunately one of the notices for our revue *A Clump of Plinths* said that "Hatch was too often an imitation Barclay . . ." He was a bit nettled by that! But he did tend to play the sort of roles that I had played.'

David Edwin Hatch
Born: 7 May 1939, Surrey
Educated: St John's School, Leatherhead
The youngest of four boys born to a Yorkshire vicar, little David Hatch was turned on to the comedy world via many of the same wireless comedies as his contemporaries at Footlights – *The Goons* and *Much Binding in the Marsh* being prevalent among his favourites. Despite the comedy bug biting him, his rural education saw him tracing the same path as his father, right up to 1959, when he landed a place studying theology at Cambridge, like one of his brothers before him. Deciding while at the university that a secular life may have been more to his tastes (and besides, he couldn't do the Hebrew), he switched to history, and remained at Queen's College to accept his MA and a teaching diploma, before the Footlights revue caught him in its net.

Graduating from *ISIRTA* to managing director of Network Radio, David finally left broadcasting in 1995. Among many public services, he became chair of the National Consumer Council and a justice of the peace, receiving a CBE and a knighthood for his work in the criminal justice system. His marriage to Ann Martin lasted from 1964 until her death in 1997, and together they had two sons and one daughter. Having been introduced by his great friend Terry Wogan and his wife Helen, David eventually tied the knot with Mary Clancy in 1999. Sadly, David Hatch died of cancer at his home in Chalfont St Giles in June 2007.

Hatch would go on to be deservedly lionised for many reasons, but the one main talent he had which has never truly been appreciated is his ability as a comic performer – which was the first thing that struck a comic performer as legendary as Cleese himself. 'I vaguely remember a Footlights concert in which I saw him perform for the first time. And I was very struck that he had some quality that no one else seemed to have, and there was a very strange sketch which started with him, with a very deep voice that he could call up, just saying "Amuse me!" to someone who then sang a song. And at the end, one had totally forgotten the beginning of the sketch, and the guy finished the song, and then David just said, "You amused me."'

After Hatch's entrance came the traditional 'We'd better have a girl in the cast, hadn't we?' moment. Dragging up had thankfully become less prevalent since the early days of Footlights – although Tim Brooke-Taylor's name often gets bandied around when the subject of cross-dressing in college smokers is brought up, and indeed his terrifying feminine side would eventually become a large, wobbly part of *ISIRTA*'s success. But, as the Pythons attest, sometimes, just sometimes, screeching in a badly fitting wig won't do and a real woman (with naughty bits and everything) is the only option.

It would be a severe waste of trees to argue against the suggestion that this group were fundamentally sexist at this point in time. Not, it has to be said, misogynist or chauvinist through any genuine sense of superiority, but the continuing ban on females in Footlights rather seems to be based on a slight fear of the unknown, with a single-sex public-school background generating a prejudice against a certain kind of theatrical female. Tim Brooke-Taylor, whose ultimate responsibility it was to decide how the Footlights functioned, insists to this day that it was more a detestation for 'luvviness' and a desire to keep the club entirely silly that led to the unreconstructed rejection of actresses as official members. 'Bollocks!' says Bill Oddie. 'I remember feeling quite narked for people who clearly were very talented, like Miriam Margolyes, and maybe Germaine Greer after her . . . there was that basic, untrue cliché that women can't be funny. I remember hearing people say it. And I think I heard people I know say it. And I think I heard people who are in this book say it . . .'

While it's impossible for any real comedy fan not to sympathise with the apparent desire in this Footlights generation to avoid pretension and promote daftness, it was not before time that Eric Idle's stint as president in 1964 cleared the way for Footlights to stop being what Barclay terms 'a dreadfully male enclave', and become a unisex establishment – although whether that was down to Idle's own instigation or the involvement of that year's revue star Germaine Greer is moot.

Any which way, in 1963 the comedienne to follow in the footsteps of Bron and Margolyes was not especially concerned with changing club policy – she wasn't even at Cambridge University at the time. However, while teaching at a Cambridge girls' school, she was gaining great notices as an actress in both straight and comedy theatre, and was well known to the Footlights mob. During his experimental dating days, Graham Chapman had even taken this actress out on a date, but his lack of interest must have been blatant. When he approached her for another night out, she replied: 'Should I bring a book with me this time?'

This quick-witted actress, Jo Kendall, had graduated and was teaching in the area when she auditioned for Humphrey Barclay. Her stage performances had already earned her the title of 'Cambridge Queen of Comedy', and whether the first four letters of her name were a coincidence or not, she had funny bones.

However, like her male colleagues, she didn't necessarily have rhythm. 'I'm absolutely famous for not remembering the lyrics to any popular song. And with no notice, I had to sing "My Funny Valentine", which I did, and that was it really . . . la-la-ing where appropriate.' But Barclay had no qualms. 'I don't think there was a great deal of controversy, she seemed to be the obvious candidate, she'd been acting around in Cambridge . . . less obviously comedic, but a witty and clever performer. There was no competition, we all very gladly and warmly welcomed her into the cast.'

And many years of uncomplaining, undervalued vocal gymnastics and surviving the jovial brickbats of this dreadfully male enclave would follow for her. She would be at a disadvantage, being the only one of the gang not to come from the Footlights, and to be serious about acting. But Jo Kendall would certainly be able to fight her own battles.

Josephine Kendall
Born: Leicester
Not everybody relishes the idea of being biographised, and Jo Kendall has always striven to keep her professional and private lives far apart, which this book will respect to the letter. Suffice to say that after a long and successful acting career – largely in the theatre, but also taking in notable roles in the movies *Scum* and *Howards End,* and TV shows *Grange Hill* and *Emmerdale Farm*, as well as radio stardom in *The Burkiss Way* and a role in the first ever episode of *The Hitchhiker's Guide to the Galaxy* – Kendall happily retired to her cottage in the Bury St Edmunds countryside in 2007. She remains a trailblazer for female comedians everywhere, although she has no OBE.

With the team confirmed, the theatre booked for May Week, the band (led by Hugh MacDonald and including a short funny fellow from the year below called Jonathan Lynn) all ready to fill in with the requisite soft jazz, and even the printers ready to churn out the professional programmes, the team had to take the next step, and consider what exactly they were going to *do*.

The Circus Comes To Town
The revue would ultimately be The Best of the Pembroke Smokers, which was inevitable given that the club was now run by the stars of those revues – the unmistakable Cleese/Brooke-Taylor moniker A *Clump of Plinths* shows who was in charge. Neither of the two law students could remember which of them had thought of 'clump' and which 'plinth', but it did the job. Or at

least it did the job far better, it was decided, than the original moniker *You Can't Call A Show 'Cornflakes'*. Some level of relevance in the title was suggested by the stark set design, which consisted of a clump of planks and boxes and shapes which would be rearranged to form different scenes. But even that's pushing it a little far – the name was glorious silliness for its own sake.

Despite a latter-day scepticism as to how directly the show was a reaction to the Satire Boom (Barclay recalls the gang discussing Frost's success with *That Was The Week That Was* with bemusement in the clubroom, failing to see how it differed from what they'd always done at Footlights), the finished revue *A Clump of Plinths* did indeed prove to be an unmistakable move away from the satirical fare that the audience must have expected. Sketches included a mechanical hospital visitor later to resurface in *At Last the 1948 Show* and a Shakespearean Music Hall cross-talk act, 'Swap a Jest', with Brooke-Taylor and Stuart-Clark delivering 'My wife, my wife'-style gags in an approximation of iambic pentameter. And of course there were a few Oddie musical numbers, including the 'London Bus' spiritual show-stopper, an oft-repeated routine involving the whole cast as commuters (surely the inspiration for the embarrassing Footlights skit that opens the *Cellar Tapes* alumni movie *Peter's Friends*).

The closest we have to a record of the original show is the truncated album and the BBC broadcast from the end of 1963, post-London opening and *Cambridge Circus* name change. Although perhaps not as short on memorable hilarity as the oddly gloomy offering from Graeme Garden's generation the following year, *Stuff What Dreams Are Made Of*, it's hard for the latter-day comedy fan to enthuse about a large percentage of *A Clump of Plinths*, at least judging from the BBC broadcast. 'The first show we ever did was the radio version of our stage show,' recalled David Hatch, 'that was the first time we'd ever done a broadcast. And that was very exciting, but also quite easy, because of course we knew the parts well since we'd done it all onstage . . . we knew where the laughs were. From then on it became, not more difficult, but we realised that radio is radio and there were a lot of sight gags, so we had to have different sorts of material. In "Judge Not", there was so much visual stuff in that it couldn't work on the radio, it's an absolutely visual sketch.' And yet the only item that stands out in the recorded version of the show, thanks to a measure of concentrated silliness, is that precise sketch, as written by Cleese, putting the knowledge gleaned while gaining his degree to good use.

'Judge Not' was always the critics' choice at the time – it gave the cast plenty of opportunities for tomfoolery, and even wound up as part of a megamix of legal skits in the first Amnesty comedy show *A Poke in the Eye (With A Sharp Stick)* over a decade later. It's a tangled web of legal piss-taking, presenting the case of Mr Sidney Bottle versus Arnold Fitch, and all the odd asides that entails:

JC: M'Lud, in this case m'learned friend Mr Maltravers appears for the defence and I appear for the money. The case would appear to be a simple one, M'Lud – the prosecution will endeavour to prove that the snivelling, depraved, cowardly wretch whom you see cowering before you returned home on the night of the fourteenth of July in a particularly vicious and unpleasant frame of mind; had words with his wife and then deliberately assaulted his pet ostrich by throwing a watering can at it.

DH: A what?

JC: A watering can, M'Lud – a large cylindrical tin-plated vessel with a perforated pouring piece, much used by the lower classes for the purpose of artificially moistening the surface soil.

DH: Thank you, Mr Bartlett, your knowledge is inexhaustible.

JC: You are very gracious M'Lud. Now, if I may continue, the ostrich, taking fright . . .

DH: The what?

JC: Ostrich, M'Lud. Ostrich, a large hairy flightless bird resident in Africa, remarkable for its speed in running and much prized for its feathers.

DH: Ah, a kind of kookaburra.

JC: No, M'Lud.

Between the antics of the first witness, Music Hall performer Sidney Molar, and a doddering old usher (both played by Brooke-Taylor), plus the insane sight of the dwarf Bottle trying to be seen in the witness box, the endless cries of 'Call Arnold Fitch' that continue throughout the sketch, and Cleese's manic cross-examination, 'Judge Not' descends into complete chaos for an old-fashioned 'rave-up' ending, leaving Hatch's judge to fling over a 'Gone To Lunch' sign, heralding the end of the whole show. But between Cleese's opening remarks and this catastrophic finale, any amount of extemporized silliness could be crowbarred in, making the sketch run for eons and leaving the audience exhausted with laughter. It was a lot easier for Hatch right up there in the Judge's seat though, as he remembered: 'It was a lovely part, because I could watch John go manic every night, and I could watch Tim be a Music Hall comedian, and I could watch Bill Oddie be a dwarf, and I was right at the back of the set, so I could watch it all. I only had about six lines, and I always had them written down because I could never remember the damn things, even after 300 performances . . .'

Another item that made it into the radio broadcast was an Oddie/Cleese take on Somerset Maugham, featuring a couple in the Malayan jungle played by Cleese and Kendall, whose simmering emotions could find no outlet in their strangulated, prim dialogue. Considering the eventual popularity of John and Mary (for it was they), this template for future greatness still holds up brilliantly today. Barclay remembers John and Jo struggling to get the tone right, but giving them the inspiration to summon up the brand of genteel repression shown by Noël Coward and Gertrude Lawrence in *Private Lives* set exactly the right tone.

> JK: So it's all over between us?
> JC: Yes.
> JK: Oh, John. It was all so lovely in Kuala Lumpur in the spring. Do you remember how we used to wade together through the mangrove swamps? And how we used to watch the baby bandicoots frolick-ing in the N'Gumba trees? . . . Did you put the leopard out?
> JC: Yes.
> JK: Oh, what a blind, blind fool I've been!
> JC: I love you! Damn you, I love you!

However, one item that hasn't aged quite as well also contained the root of *ISIRTA*'s most blatant star. The show's Oscar Wilde parody is flimsy as can be on paper, being mainly knocked-up Wildeisms that don't really go any-where. But Brooke-Taylor's Lady Carstairs (a subtly accurate send-up of Dame Edith Evans as Lady Bracknell that was the highlight of the sketch even then) would eventually evolve and mutate into one big, blousy beast of a comedy character, cheered on high not only as Lady Constance, the patron saint of *ISIRTA* but even to this day, whenever Tim rattles his vocal cords in a particular way. Although, ironically, Tim recalls, 'The PR person asked me who would I like to come to the first night, and I said Edith Evans, Lady Bracknell in the original film (we were doing a take-off of *The Importance of Being Earnest*). She came, and I think she was the only person in the theatre who didn't know who I was impersonating! She was very elderly, going, "Ooooh, what's he doing?"'

Although it's undeniably a reserved and dusty forerunner to the shows we are celebrating, *A Clump of Plinths* still has bite, and despite harking back to Music Hall throughout, it is not with pure affection. A short monologue by Bill Oddie sums up the approach:

> BO: I suppose I've been doorman at this theatre for fifty years now. I've seen all the stars of the old-time Music Hall, I have. You want to know about them, you just come to me. I'll tell you about 'em. Cause I've seen 'em. Eddie Kind, George Robey, Marie Lloyd, Harry Lauder . . . they were *rotten*.

No matter what verdict the modern ear reaches on A *Clump of Plinths*, its young stars proved popular enough at the time to inspire impresario Michael White to shift the show over to the New Arts Theatre in London in the summer of '63. The original Cambridge show had already played successfully for one week at the Robin Hood Theatre in Averham and one in York before White (who would, among many other successes, go on to launch *The Rocky Horror Show*) brought the comedy to the capital, with the all-new production opening on 10 July.

I'm Sorry I Must Go

This short run at the New Arts Theatre on Great Newport Street was a real watershed for the show. First of all, it was decided that the whimsical name that had made undergraduates chortle in Cambridge wouldn't appeal to a general West End audience, and so *Cambridge Circus* became the heading which quickly summed up the entertainment on offer. However, the new 'safe' name would ultimately lead to more confusion than A *Clump of Plinths*, not least due to the theatre being some distance from Cambridge Circus itself.

The second change was the loss of Tony Buffery, a popular and wonderfully silly physical performer whom Eric Idle describes as the looniest man in the bunch. He was so loony that, despite remaining attached to comedy, he ultimately spent his life working with gorillas, and became a world-class experimental psychologist. No doubt due to his sometime writing partner's involvement, Buffery's place was swiftly taken by Graham Chapman, who despite qualifying as a doctor, had been earning beer money by gigging around the capital with Tony Hendra.

Combined with its shift to the Lyric Theatre on 16 August, the show ran for well over a hundred performances and had evolved considerably from its rough-and-ready prototype by the time the radio version was recorded in the winter.

It had also cleared their student debts, and now being established in London, all the cast were considering their futures – although none of them (except perhaps Jo and Bill) had seriously considered performing for a career. He and Brooke-Taylor had already abandoned their planned law careers, but Cleese was dissuaded from trying to make a living as a performer at this point by the only moderately appreciative reviews, which singled out Tim and especially Bill for greatness. But there were other jobs in entertainment to be had, as he says: 'I was at Freshfields, solicitors to the Bank of England and I was going to get twelve pounds a week. And writing for Dick Emery and Deryck Guyler I got thirty quid a week, so I was happy and I didn't have to wear a suit.'

There is a cliché about Cambridge graduates during the Cold War period that at some point they would get a tap on the shoulder which would mean either recruitment into the KGB or the BBC. So many years past glasnost, it seems fair to assume that it was only the latter organisation that made offers to the *Cambridge Circus* cast. Humphrey Barclay had no hesitation and the temporarily disillusioned John Cleese had already won his parents' approval to say no to a very nice law firm and join the Corporation. Brooke-Taylor joined ATV as a researcher, while David Hatch became another graduate to be headhunted by the BBC, declining a teaching position in Basingstoke on finding himself at the beginning of an extraordinary career in broadcasting. This was all down to an experienced and pleasantly eccentric BBC man called Peter Titheradge – his official title was Script Editor for the Light Entertainment Department, but this also involved the duty of talent scouting. His eye had already caught these three fresh-faced undergraduates back in Cambridge, but their first test would be the *Cambridge Circus* broadcast.

The intervention of Titheradge was in many ways the real spark that led to *I'm Sorry I'll Read That Again* becoming a reality, and he would go on to become a legend within *ISIRTA* thanks to the gratitude of his recruits. In the twenty-first century, the BBC is more likely to set an online competition to attract ambitious would-be mirth-makers, but back in the sixties somebody from Broadcasting House would actually have to go out and find talent – as Barclay confirms, having had to face the challenge himself in later years. This first run-in with the BBC is still fresh in his memory: 'It was after a performance of *A Clump of Plinths*, we were supping something liquid in the bar at Footlights . . . Tim came over and said he wanted me to come and meet somebody, and I looked over and saw him talking to this rather dry-looking little man and I thought, "Ohhh God, it's probably his tutor or something, I don't think I'm going to go and talk to him . . ." However, thank goodness I did!'

For his very first try-out as a radio producer, Barclay was partnered with experienced comedy producer Edward Taylor, another Cambridge graduate, who also created *The Men from the Ministry*. He penned a special opening for the audio-only version of the show, with two City swells discussing an evening out, taking in a show starring 'a new lot, stars in the making, with new ideas and initiative!' But they finally decide to pop along to catch the strippers at the Windmill instead.

The end of the show was also adapted so Hatch's judge in 'Judge Not' could read the end credits and complain:

DH: When I think that this wireless time might have been used for a programme on ballet, or mime, or nude tableau, the mind boggles. Boggle boggle boggle . . .

The Judge pronounces sentence on everybody involved, but especially damns the producers Barclay and Taylor, who were 'to be taken away and spat upon in the manner to which you have become accustomed'. Right from the off, the shows take comfort from extreme self-abuse, and get the boot in on themselves before anybody else can get the chance. This is in many ways a comedy staple, but no comedy would ever be as proudly voluble about its shortcomings as *ISIRTA* . . .

Although he was still with the team for the shows at the Lyric, the last London curtain would be the final showbiz gesture from Chris Stuart-Clarke, who took the decision to grow up at the end of '63 and enter into teaching, ultimately finishing up as head of first year at Eton and governor of several schools. His parts were at first taken on by Barclay, but ultimately his full-time replacement became Jonathan Lynn.

And a replacement was needed, as White had booked the show in for a tour. A foreign tour! These young hotshots were really going places, and they prepared themselves to face the bright lights of . . . New Zealand in the winter. Not, perhaps, the glamorous next step for *Cambridge Circus* that the cast might have hoped for. But, just as The Beatles had to decamp to Hamburg to perfect their act, nothing would bring this group together and turn them into a seasoned comedy team like that tour down under in 1964.

Before the team could leave for the other side of the world, however, word came from the BBC that they first had to see to the little matter of three further BBC recordings for the Light Programme, tentatively entitled *I'm Sorry I'll Read That Again*.

2

Mrs Muir and I. T. Briddock

Between success in the West End and being snapped up by the BBC, 1963 was the ultimate breakthrough year for those freshers of 1960. In fact, more than any other actual Footlights show, the way A *Clump of Plinths* went on to change and grow and gain plaudits around the world would put pressure on all the revues that followed them – as well as giving rise to the idea that a place in the Footlights revue was the fast track to media stardom. But one detail of the *Cambridge Circus* phenomenon has often been overlooked. With the show doing so nicely in London, who took the show up to Edinburgh that August? It might seem odd today, in a comedy environment in which each comic's material is entirely theirs to perform, but just as *Beyond the Fringe* was taken out on the road by several stand-in casts throughout the years, *Cambridge Circus* was also seen as bankable material, no matter who performed it.

With the London run well under way, it fell to Barclay to ensure that the Edinburgh tradition started by Robert Atkins didn't founder, especially in the eightieth anniversary year for Footlights. And so for one final time he prepared to tread the boards himself, with a carefully constructed team of stand-ins. The younger members keen to do their best to recreate the silliness they'd seen performed by Cleese and company included future knight of the National Theatre Richard Eyre, actor David Gooderson (who would go on to play Dalek creator Davros in *Doctor Who*) and Eric Idle, who had only been in the Footlights since March, and had to be called back from a German holiday via telegram, on the recommendation of fellow Pembroke players Oddie and Brooke-Taylor. The Footlights machine clicked smoothly into action, and everything was sorted for a new permutation of A *Clump of Plinths*, to be called *Footlights '63*.

Graeme and The Young Generation
The only problem was, with the programmes all printed, Richard Eyre dropped out and a last-minute replacement had to be found. Luckily, there was a

second-year medical student at Emmanuel College, a future Footlights president who had failed the audition for the revue first time round, but was still keen to join in, no matter how intimidated he felt by his future cohorts. 'I'd seen the revue in my first year when I went up there, and I thought, "These are very funny, very good people, I can't do that" – I'd been in one school play!' Still, Graeme Garden rallied round, and soon wangled his way into the club with an inspired series of quick charcoal sketches taking the piss out of students, as part of an act which somehow eventually evolved into a famed piece of puppetry involving a frenetic furry vampire bat. 'I had to push to get in, and I was terrified of the president, who was, um . . . Tim. But then I did the *Cambridge Circus* show . . . they were still in London when Edinburgh came up, so the second team went up and did it . . . We shared material, generally speaking, with approval and consent. It was all very amateur at that stage, it was a hobby. None of us were really doing it professionally. I don't think any of us would have actually gone into show business as an individual – none of us had the ambition or the courage to have followed that. But because we were part of a group, doing each other's material and working in various combinations, we had a sort of herd instinct which guided us.' The regard that the senior year had for young Graeme was exemplified by the cliquey handing over of the Footlights presidency, from the graduating Brooke-Taylor to Garden (and then from Graeme to Eric Idle). The medical student clearly had something special, and Tim had hopes that they might work together one day . . .

This generation-spanning group mindset, allied to a reckless notion of not being part of a slick showbiz tradition, is a major part of *ISIRTA*'s anarchic style. Although they were on opposite sides of the globe by the time he became Footlights president, the material shared between the *Cambridge Circus* cast and Graeme, the radio-loving medical student, would soon bring them together, into one legendary team.

David Graeme Garden
Born: 18 February 1943, Aberdeen
Educated: Repton School, Derbyshire
The first child born to Dr Robert and his nurse wife Janet – he has a younger sister, Elizabeth – Graeme's Highland infancy and background ('My maternal ancestors were the McHardys, legendary giants who won all the Braemar Games in the nineteenth century . . . One McHardy was known as 'The Infant', as he only grew to be six feet tall.') was soon forgotten after a period of thorough anglicising both at home, when the Gardens moved to Preston, and at the ancient Repton School in Tim's home county of Derbyshire. A precociously creative little boy, Graeme's passion for cartoons and art soon

became allied to a talent to amuse – especially physically, with an early aptitude for knockabout comedy often employed to entertain the folks at home. Despite his artistic bent, it was in the sciences that young Garden excelled at school, receiving the top marks in chemistry, physics and biology that would get him a place at Emmanuel College, Cambridge, studying natural sciences with every intention of following his father into medicine. Soon, however, entry into the Cambridge University Light Entertainment Society began to turn his head.

Outside of his radio work and *The Goodies*, Graeme has also presented numerous TV shows on history and medicine, written and directed films for Video Arts, made appearances in shows like *Heartbeat, Murder Most Horrid, Yes, Minister, Bromwell High* and, of course, *Holby City* and he continues to write and perform for stage, screen and radio. He has two children, Sally and John, from his first marriage to Liz Grice, and was remarried in 1981 to Emma – they have one son, Tom. He proudly boasts, 'John is having a great time in the music world. Youngest son Tom is a concept artist – catch his work at tomgarden.co.uk – and my daughter Sally is the academic, an assistant head teacher, married and mum to our granddaughter.' Graeme still has no OBE.

The original London run of *Cambridge Circus* closed on 9 November. It had garnered its fair share of plaudits, even if the one critical reaction which most people remember is that of Bernard Levin in the *Daily Mail*: 'Have they got a new Jonathan Miller among them? I may as well get the answer over right away. No.' (However, when you consider that the reaction to Miller's own Footlights show from one critic was 'Jonathan Miller wants to be a chemist and not a theatrical cult. I back his judgement', you'll see that foresight was perennially absent from Footlights reviews in those days.) The success of the show was in part thanks to the fact that it had replaced the long run of *Beyond the Fringe* – it filled the hole left by Cook, Moore, Miller and Bennett admirably. Also like *Beyond the Fringe*, the show was commercially released on an LP produced by George Martin, he having a bit of spare time after completing the recording of *With The Beatles*.

Aside from the December radio broadcast, the gang had time to catch their breath and Cleese, Hatch and Barclay could explore the possibilities of their new BBC posts. In an address to the National Radio Conference in Sydney in 2007, Cleese waxed lyrical about his initial proper job: 'I started in radio in 1963, and that is so long ago, I don't know if you can believe this, it was as though television was just moving in. People still listened on a Sunday lunchtime to the big radio comedy shows, but it was beginning to be displaced, and what was fascinating was the attitude of people in radio, because they'd been king for years, you know?' But these poor deluded stalwarts kept the young boys busy. Barclay had a fiddle with *Twenty Questions*, while Cleese remembers: 'The first thing I was ever asked to do ... there was a Christmas show called *Yule Be Surprised*, with Terry Scott and Brian Rix and for my first professional job, I was asked to take some of the jokes out of it. And then I worked for Dick Emery, and Deryck Guyler, and I've got to say, I loved it.'

It seemed to make sense, with a reasonable wireless hit behind them and this new blood eager to have something to do at Broadcasting House, to attempt a short series of new sketch shows starring the same cast as the earlier theatrical adaptation, and with producer Barclay again backed up by the more experienced input of Ted Taylor. This time, at last, the show featured brand-new material written specifically for the wireless.

A Sober Genesis

A lot of comedy shows – perhaps the majority – take a while to get going, debuting meekly and cautiously to a wary public (the painfully shy audience reaction to the very first edition of *Monty Python's Flying Circus* being a case in point). But comparing this trio of try-out *ISIRTAs* to the eventual bedlam that the recordings generated make it clear that no other programme has ever reached the same extreme of evolution. Looked at as a whole over its ten-year run, *ISIRTA* is a dynamo, starting up with a genteel chuckle and bowing out with a thunderous explosion of unfettered hilarity. The staid air of the initial show is almost uncomfortable to listen to now – as the first of the three has been available on BBC Audio Collection for years, you can hear for yourself. Many jokes are greeted with silence, and, crucially, Oddie's musical numbers have yet to attain the seamless silliness that would become one of the show's main strengths. Even the gentle jazz theme music (though pleasant enough) is a weak prototype for the raucous 'Angus Prune Tune'. Music Hall abandon takes second place to sophisticated urbanity.

The nondescript introduction to the shows is a giveaway. It was flatly described as 'An extravaganza specially written for the wireless by several persons, featuring a number of performers'. Not quite the 'radio custard pie' that it was to become. But then Broadcasting House was clearly no place for levity. Cleese described it as 'a very quiet world, rather like a public-school common room. There's not a great deal of pressure, not very much rivalry. Nobody is ever really dismissed unless they set the building on fire ...' These three shows reflected a twisted version of the respectable atmosphere of BBC Radio with the brand-new title. 'I'm sorry, I'll read that again ...' was the default apology of stumbling BBC newsreaders at the time (which apparently regularly reduced Cleese and Brooke-Taylor to hysterics), yet in isolation it was as meaningless as anything else they could come up with, and therefore appropriate. In fact, at this early stage, much more effort was made to tie the title into the show – each of the three programmes begins with Hatch, as ever, playing the sober newsreader making a slip-up:

> DH: And now here is an announcement of special interest to everyone. It is reported in this week's *Church Gazette* that the Bishop of Dorking revealed no traces of nerves when he undressed the Mothers' Union. I'm sorry, I'll read that again . . .

. . . Cue the gentle jazz. This attempt to make sense out of the show's name didn't last long, but the unnecessarily apologetic prefix 'I'm Sorry' has remained one of the few real mainstays of radio history, and its lasting popularity is a testament to the *Cambridge Circus* team's absolute ambivalence when it comes to names – it's the quality of the half-hour following the title that counts. This problem with names (or, at least, desire to be as random as possible) is underlined by David Hatch, recalling the roster of New Zealand shows that were just around the corner, including not only *The Peter Titheradge Show*, but also *The Cardinal Richelieu Show* (the ubiquitous cardinal had even received a credit in the *Cambridge Circus* programme), *The Mrs Muir Show* . . . 'And one was named after this man (because we had to find titles and we couldn't think of the last one, so John picked up the New Zealand telephone directory, which was not a big directory . . .) called I. T. Briddock. And so we called it *The I. T. Briddock Show*, and we left the next day. And I think we've always wondered what happened to I. T. Briddock, and what people said to him – "Why did they name it after you, Ian?' Or whatever his name was . . . He'd done nothing wrong, his name had just been picked out of a book."

On the other hand, Humphrey Barclay quite rightly identifies the very root of the title *I'm Sorry I'll Read That Again* – 'I think one of the things that John at any rate (and therefore the rest of us) enjoyed was the undermining of authority . . . and so to pick up on the very proper and bottled-up correction, which I suppose we must have heard for real, seems to be just the right tone for the show . . . It was a very good title, and one that we were never sorry about.'

He's right, naturally – from the disdain for OBEs to Cleese's habit of putting silly words to Souza marches to the way that a heavyweight piece of music like Beethoven's Fifth could be summoned up at the optimum daftest moment, cutting through pomposity was *ISIRTA's raison d'être*. The first three notes of Ludwig Van's masterpiece is a particular motif of the early shows. 'The most solemn, pompous bit of music – after all, it must have been in our subconscious somewhere that it had been used as a signal during the war – and it just struck us as endlessly funny,' continues Barclay. 'The whole thing of *I'm Sorry I'll Read That Again* is banana skins under authority.'

Pomposity was similarly pricked in the all-important send-ups of TV shows such as Jonathan Miller's *Monitor*, which gave way to the 'Intelligent Pop Song' by Oddie, again demonstrating this meeting of educated minds with low culture.

> *You would overwhelm, I know,*
> *A Titian or a Renoir or a Picasso,*
> *Every night you seem to me,*
> *Like Aphrodite in a nightie.*
> *I've never had this thrill before,*
> *Except from the statues of Henry Moore,*
> *It's wonderful what those curves will do,*
> *And that's how I feel about you . . .*

Other targets in these pilots include the secret service (with a manic recruitment sketch starring Cleese at his most eccentric which would be repeated in *At Last The 1948 Show*), bank managers and, again thanks to Cleese, public school. A headmaster monologue with more than a shade of the school sequence in *Monty Python's Meaning of Life* provides one of the high points in the third episode broadcast, bristling with a genuine darkness which would raise eyebrows in some quarters even if it were broadcast fresh today.

JC: Major Philips won't be taking carpentry this term. He's in the nuthouse. Two world wars and he never turned a hair, six weeks here and he's running round the field stark naked at the home match. I'm all for a little gentle fun between masters and boys, but *crucifixion*?

There's a harshness there that was rare in radio comedy at the time, and this all-but forgotten strain of black humour would proliferate in *ISIRTA* through to the end – it's amazing what you can get away with when there's a jolly chestnut just around the corner. Cleese's early days on *ISIRTA* were clearly massively influential when it came to the development of his own style of comedy. 'I always liked humour with a bit of an edge to it. And what I discovered was, so did the audience. People have often said, "Well, there's quite an edge in your humour, or a sort of anger underneath it," and the reason is, because people laugh at it. If they hadn't laughed at it, I wouldn't have gone in that direction. But I think it was W. C. Fields who once said, "To make somebody laugh, all you need to do is to dress an actor up as a very old woman and have her dodder along the street and then fall down a coal-hole; but, to make a professional comedian laugh it really has to be an old woman." . . . I like those kind of edgy, sharp jokes. And the producers were always saying to me, "Oh, I don't think we should say that!" And I said, "Let's just say it, it's only radio, and if it doesn't get a laugh, cut it out." And it always got a laugh, so I thought, "well, that's nice".'

These pilot programmes also contained a pleasing piss-take of quiz shows that the team loved so much they took it both to television and, eventually, the stage, when Cleese ordered a middle-aged reprise for the Amnesty show *The Secret Policeman's Other Ball*. The 'Top of the Form' sketch is testament to the fact that there's an *I'm Sorry* legacy of ridiculing quizzes stretching from *I'm Sorry I Haven't a Clue* right back to the very first pilot of *ISIRTA*.

JK: And at the halfway stage, the score is: the boys of King Arthur's Grammar School Newquay, one and a half, the girls of Pudsbury High School Brantwich, nought.

FX: Quick blast of false applause

DH: And now, round seven. Tell the difference. Peter, what is the difference between an elephant and an armchair?

BO: Er, well, um, an elephant is one of those orange boxes you lock books up in and put in the greenhouse, and an armchair is a . . . it's a long plastic pole! A long plastic pole you hang out the window to keep the birds away.

DH: . . . No. I can only give you a half for that, Peter, but I can offer it to you, Elizabeth.

JK: I don't know! Boo-hoo-hoo!

DH: Well tried anyway, Elizabeth . . .

Most of the true highlights of these three pilots, recorded in March and broadcast on the Home Service in April 1964, are the sketches that have clearly been written specifically for radio. In another media spoof, this time a send-up of *Sports Report*, Cleese and Brooke-Taylor examine the prowess of Herbert Crimble, the North-East London area wine-tasting champion.

JC: See what you make of this one, Herbie.

TBT: (*sips professionally.*) Oh it's enchanting – a little playful perhaps, but not extravagant. No. It has a certain – I don't know what – a certain *je ne sais quoi*. No, unless I'm very much mistaken, it's a claret.

JC: You are very much mistaken.

TBT: Oh of course not, silly me, it's not nearly sinful enough for a claret, it is in fact a . . . a Burgundy? . . . No, of course not. It's a pint of bitter, isn't it? . . . Half a bitter? Bitter lemon. Little bitter lemon? Lemon tea? *Lemon squash? Milk? Water? Coffee?*

JC: No, Herbie, I'm sorry, it is in fact a plate of steak and chips.

Already it was clear that the gang were beginning to seize the opportunities for radio to take the audience by surprise, and going beyond the recycling of old cabaret sketches to find their own comic voice for the wireless.

No doubt this experimentation with the medium could have continued right away if their promoter Michael White hadn't organised the New Zealand tour. Only a few weeks after the April broadcast of the first *I'm Sorry I'll Read That Agains*, the full theatrical cast were on a plane bound for the other side of the world. They had no real responsibilities in life, no big plans – John Cleese didn't even have anywhere to live, crashing at Chapman's quarters as he started his career as a writer at the BBC, then later kipping on the floor of Tim Brooke-Taylor's digs at Manchester Square.

Graham Chapman almost skipped the formative experience of touring with *Cambridge Circus*, being immersed in his studies at Bart's, but a royal visit to the hospital gave him the perfect excuse for defying his parents' wish for their singularly unusual child to keep his nose to the grindstone and carve himself a sensible career. As secretary of the student's union, he was invited to take tea with none other than HRH The Queen Mother when she opened a new biochemistry building. This future icon of anarchic comedy sat politely with the old dear, and explained his quandary, having to take time off his studies for theatrical shenanigans in New Zealand. She replied, 'Oh it is such a beautiful place, you *must* go.' And so, Chapman recalled, 'I used that as a kind of Royal Command to my parents, so I was able to go with their blessing. I'd have gone anyway, but that made them feel very much better about the whole deal.'

The Zulus Attack!

So with very little ado (except maybe for the occasion when Cleese took a shower as the plane landed in Karachi, lost his watch and held up the next stage of the journey for an hour as everybody looked for it – much to Graham Chapman's pleasure as it allowed him to get acquainted with a particularly buff Commonwealth sailor), the team eventually reached Christchurch for their six-week tour.

New Zealand in the early sixties was clearly not the *Lord of the Rings*-fuelled tourist hotspot that it is now, and Cleese recalls it as 'a strange time-warp place that felt like England, 1923, South Coast. It had that feeling about it.' Brooke-Taylor goes further: 'New Zealand I think is a great country now, but it was dead then. The pubs would shut at six. Vic Oliver, who was a great comedian, went out to Christchurch and they said "What do you think of Christchurch?" And he said, "It's beautifully laid out. How long has it been dead?"'

There they stood in the lounge of their Wellington boarding house, this awkward bunch of English kids weighed down with luggage, faced with their landlady, Mrs Muir, a bizarre biddy who could have stepped right out of any *Python* pepperpot sketch. The Michael Caine movie *Zulu* had just opened in town, and it must have made quite an impression on the hostess, as she greeted her guests' mumbled greetings with 'Oh, hello – are you the Zulus?' They explained with regret that this was not the case, but she pressed the matter: 'I've got a brother in Africa, do you know him?' Especially in their exhausted state, it's no wonder that her witterings made such an impression on the cast that they named one of their shows for New Zealand radio after her.

Either White had set them up in the worst digs available, or New Zealand was a stranger to customer service forty years ago, as every place the crew stayed during their time in the country has become confused into one nightmarish saga of discomfort, with more than a shade of *Fawlty Towers* about the whole affair. The crippling cold was not alleviated by the lack of heating. Chapman's bed sheets were thick with mildew, while Jo Kendall's complaint about the heating was met with the retort: 'If you're cold, dear, run up and down the corridor.' An early echo of *ISIRTA*'s prune motif is also recalled. At breakfast, in 'a damp room the size of a moist barn', they were told to keep strictly to the tables that corresponded to their room numbers – which meant that they were forced to sit far apart from each other. They were offered a choice of 'fruit or prunes' – the 'fruit' in question being prunes. Similarly, the option of 'cremona or porridge' was somewhat spoiled by the cereal alternative being . . . porridge. When the tea was served, a cup was set down before Tim, who was asked 'Do you take sugar?' 'No,' he replied. 'Well, don't stir it,' snapped back the waitress, and waddled away. On one infamous occasion Chapman asked for a three-egg omelette, and after a few quizzical looks, he was served an omelette with three fried eggs perched on top – a sight so disgusting, he recalled, that 'even people three tables away threw up'.

He called across the room to his friends, 'Don't worry, if it doesn't improve, we'll find somewhere else!' But they didn't.

Worst of all – certainly to a budding alcoholic like Chapman – getting a drink in a country with such stringent licensing laws was a massive challenge. He followed a certain lead with Tim Brooke-Taylor one night to find a low-rent speakeasy where a glass of lager was available to those who knew the right code, as long as they brought along a Coke or orange juice to display if or when the cops turned up. Cleese remembers visiting a draughty restaurant with Jonathan Lynn, in which the house red was served finely chilled. Lynn remarked that at least it was at room temperature.

At first, this unpleasantness was not lessened for the gang by the Kiwis' reception to their comedy. Apparently some of the more ancient contingent in the early audiences asked the management to turn the sound up, thinking they were at the cinema. But as time went on, audiences and reviews picked up – plus there was the learning curve of the four shows thrown together for New Zealand radio. As Hatch recalled: 'We just went into the NZBC studios and we recorded every sketch we'd ever done anywhere – everything any of us could remember, we just recorded and recorded and recorded . . . We have no idea how they turned out, whether they put laughter tracks on . . . we've no idea.' It was certainly a carefree approach to broadcasting – and not only that, there was even a New Zealand TV broadcast. Chapman remembered Barclay fuming at the poor lighting set up by the TV company, getting so worked up about the murkiness that he seemed to be heading for a full-on fit . . . until he realised he still had his dark glasses on.

The live show itself continued to evolve as the cast grew tired of the same old skits. One new addition showed the extent of the sharing of material that went on in the Oxbridge world, as it wasn't even written by a Cambridge man – but it did gain the most outstanding reception. The piece, from that year's Oxford revue, was a mock lecture on the art of slapstick, featuring three men and a lot of custard pies, and was billed as 'Humour Without Tears', by Terry Jones, aged twenty-two and a half. It would go on to prove perhaps one of the all-time great comedy sketches, performed most memorably by Jones, Chapman, Michael Palin and Terry Gilliam in *Monty Python Live at the Hollywood Bowl*.

Still, even with a lauded classic such as that in the show, the *Cambridge Circus* team couldn't pretend that their six-week excursion had been a ripping success – and what would happen now that it was time to return home? There had been subtle mutterings of an American tour – the legendary king of US entertainment Ed Sullivan had seen the show in London and instantly snapped up the American rights, but nothing seemed to have come from that yet.

It was Humphrey Barclay who received the telegram they'd been waiting for. Sullivan had sold the rights to another famed mogul called Sol Hurok. Staging operas and Russian ballets was more his line, but here was the confirmation that the Plymouth Theatre, New York, had been booked for a run of *Cambridge Circus* starting that October. BBC contracts were once again obligingly frozen by the Corporation, accommodation was booked and the bandwagon kept on rolling.

Of course, they all had some time off back in Blighty before the big opening, so it was time to get back on the plane for another gruellingly long flight. Tim Brooke-Taylor and Graham Chapman thought they'd alleviate the pressure by going for a massage in Hong Kong when they stopped there en route, staying for a few days in opulence provided by the mother of one of Chapman's medical friends. But whatever 'added extras' these inexperienced graduates were expecting from their exotic masseuses, they left the parlour disappointed and frustrated. Chapman candidly admitted 'I wanked three times within an hour of the plane leaving Hong Kong'. But luckily, unlike Cleese's missing watch, this didn't impede the plane's journey to its destination.

The Last Show for 50 Miles
With the chill of autumn dabbing away a sticky city summer in New York, 1964, a bright new hoarding was raised onto the Plymouth Theatre, 236 West 45th Street. Down on the sidewalk, gazing up in disbelief at how far the Footlights revue of 1963 had come, was the slight figure of Humphrey Barclay, aged 'twenty-two going on three'. Somebody had to go on ahead to see that Sol Hurok's new signing was on track for Broadway success and, of course, the responsibility was all Humphrey's, taking care of the sensible stuff, just as he had since Brooke-Taylor first picked him to nanny the *Clump of Plinths* cast.

'I remember standing on 45th Street, trying to make myself realise how bizarre and extraordinary it was. Because to a certain extent, as any theatrical person will tell you, when you're touring it's another theatre, another opening, another show. And we had to think "Yes, but – this is Broadway! It's BROADWAY!"'

Although this was four years before Mel Brooks' masterpiece *The Producers* was released, it's irresistible to visualise these days in the Big Apple as taking place in that exact world – from the charming, immaculately bejewelled and coiffeured stage manager to our heroes' ultimate dejection when they were to come up against the money men who ran the show.

It was an overwhelming responsibility for a young graduate to stage a Broadway show without any preliminary touring or testing, and the reaction when the backers saw what they'd actually bought would have floored a less gifted comedy promoter. The cast arrived in New York one by one. Bill Oddie brought along his girlfriend, the talented jazz musician Jean Hart, who was to understudy Jo Kendall – in fact, she herself had already performed at The Establishment and was a charismatic and gifted singer, despite Cook's alleged nickname for her being 'The Singing Housewife'. With the team number now swelled to nine (not including Hugh Macdonald and the band), everyone settled into their hotel (which was naturally mildew-free and offered a far better range of fruit than just prunes), and all the Plymouth theatre staff were friendly and helpful. They were there to assist these alien Oxbridge types to do their thing in any way they could, and all was going according to plan.

There had been preliminary worries about the name of the show – even in New Zealand, there was an element of the audience who bought tickets expecting troupes of elephants, lion-tamers and clowns complete with buckets of confetti. The US backers wanted to avoid any such confusion from the off. So Barclay suggested a splendid replacement title, 'The Last Show for 50 Miles', and was met with vacant stares. '. . . But it isn't!' seemed to be the reaction, and in the frustration the original name stayed. It's a tiresome cliché, and indeed a lie in this day and age to say that Americans don't understand irony, but back in the early sixties . . . it was still, by and large, a foreign language to many on the left-hand side of the Atlantic.

But the wrangling over the name of the show was just a warning shot, a preliminary bit of silliness before the New York promoters unleashed the big guns. Finally, with everything set up and the cast back on the ball and ready to go, the full revue was staged for the sole benefit of the backers. It's diffi-cult to resist picturing these money men sat out in the nearly empty theatre, chewing cigars and possibly even stroking pampered cats as the Bright Young Things strode confidently through the show that they had performed hundreds of times before. At the end of the show, the exhausted cast took their bows to silence and wended their way offstage and out of the theatre, leaving Barclay to deal with any notes that the small, important audience might have.

'I climbed down from the stage – I think the cast had gone off to the hotel – and I was left to hear the reaction of the backers, and it was *terrible*. Here was a show which we had polished through London, and a gruelling tour of gruelling New Zealand and we knew this was a fantastic show – we could prove it!' But the backers were distinctly lacking in enthusiasm:

'Hmm . . . Yes, I see what you've got there.'

'Yes, what do you think?'

'Tell me, the number you use to close the first half, have you got anything else you could use there?'

'Er, no, that's our first-half close, we don't have anything else.'

'Well, the opener will have to go, and the first-half closer, that's no good, and you can't open the second half with that number, nobody will under-stand it . . .'

This was the all-time hit Oscar Wilde parody, Tim Brooke-Taylor's squawking finest hour. Barclay was, to put it very mildly, crestfallen. 'The whole show was just being demolished, and I was gulping and swallowing . . . and eventually I had to go to the cast and say "Um . . ."' They had three days to opening night.

It would be glorious to suggest that the whole team glanced at each other with stiff upper lips and gleams of challenge in their eyes, all ready to take on the Americans and slay them with extemporised wit. But Barclay remembers that it wasn't like that at all. 'I don't think anybody said "Right, let's go and write something new!" What they said was "*Fuck*, what can we remember?"' Once again, it was time to desperately rifle through memory banks for show-stoppers from Pembroke smokers – or even to cut their losses and go home, which was seriously considered for a beat or two. But British pluck won out, and the process of rebuilding *Cambridge Circus* began. Brooke-Taylor admits 'it was pretty frightening. Suddenly you can't use half of your material, or whatever the percentage is . . . With all due respect to Humphrey Barclay, he was brilliant as a producer, but he really did crumple. And it was one of those things, David Hatch and I rallied the troops, and then Humphrey took over again, but it was a very tricky moment. Probably a very good thing, actually, that we were shaken up like that just in time. It was very exciting in many trouser-staining ways.' This was a baptism of fire not just for the young cast, but for Barclay and his ability to effectively string together disparate material from a pool of trusted writers, and can be seen as a high-octane run-through for the creation of each one of *ISIRTA*'s 104 episodes.

With the heat very much on, never had the Cambridge tradition of borrowing and buying other people's material been so beneficial – transatlantic calls were placed, brains were racked for half-forgotten skits, and a musical item by Eric Idle with John Cameron, 'I Want to Hold Your Handel', was quickly pasted in. Having been in the most recent Footlights show with his contemporary Idle, it was Jonathan Lynn who suggested the Fab Four spoof, a crafty cross-breed of Handel's *Messiah* and The Beatles' number one hit. It was clever, and topical, and, of course, guaranteed to please a US audience caught up in the fresh bloom of Beatlemania. They had no time to learn the piece properly, so Tim Brooke-Taylor had the brainwave of performing the song as choirboys, allowing them to have the lyrics in prayer books in front of them. As a finishing touch, somebody was sent out to scour the shops of Broadway for a selection of Beatle wigs, which were not too difficult to locate in New York in 1964.

Graham Chapman's physical prowess was also helping to pad out the rejuvenated line-up, it was at this point that he began to develop his impressive self-wrestling skit, which would eventually become a highlight of Python stage shows, most notably the 'Colin Bomber Harris' match in *Hollywood Bowl*, which Colin inevitably won on points.

Incredibly, after a tortuous session of sitting around in their hotel rooms plundering and begging and memorising, a new *Cambridge Circus* was ready to go just in time. Actually, much of the original remained intact but at last they had a show that the American backers could consider worth their while – or, frankly, could lump it.

Back To Square East
We can presume that backstage toilet cubicles were permanently engaged then, as the clock ticked down to curtain up on the evening of Tuesday 6 October. The opening night for the Broadway run of *Cambridge Circus* was,

by all reports, a riot. Being used to staging quality high-brow entertainment, Hurok had not troubled his wallet with arranging much in the way of advertising or advance media coverage, and of course there hadn't been any pre-show touring in the States. But it was a packed house, peopled with not only Manhattan sophisticates wondering what came next after *Beyond the Fringe*, but also, crucially, Tim Brooke-Taylor's auntie and mother, who kindly patted the great promoter's hand and said, 'Don't worry, I'm sure it will be all right, Mr Hurok, because Tim's quite worried, and when he's worried he's always done well – it was just the same with his exams at school.'

Mrs Brooke-Taylor obviously knew what she was talking about, as the first night seemed to go off without a hitch – the new show was clearly a crowd-pleaser. But next came the *really* unpleasant part – when the after-show party merged into the impatient wait for the early-morning papers, and the critics' response.

The verdict was thoroughly positive, across the board – with only one exception. But only the *New York Times* had the clout to drive readers towards the box office, and nothing less than a 'Rush rush rush!' review would guarantee a success for any show. Sadly, the *Times* sent along a journalist called Tauberman, who was ordinarily their sports correspondent. His reaction to this thoroughly un-American brand of entertainment was, if not scathing, then certainly the antithesis of 'Rush rush rush!' He ultimately signed the death warrant for the show.

Between Hurok's disinclination to push the show via the usual channels, and the *New York Times*' shrug-worthy review, the gang knew that their Broadway hopes were ultimately dashed. The show ran for another twenty-three performances, and ended with a roar of approval on 24 October – just in time for a gushing extended full-colour article to be printed in the *New York Herald Tribune*, by the respected critic Walter Kerr. Singling out Jones' slapstick sketch for especial praise, Kerr ultimately compared the stars of the show favourably with Chaplin, assuring the reader that it was the greatest show that he'd seen in years, and he 'couldn't be more admiring'.

But the damage had been done, and the doors of the Plymouth Theatre were shut to Barclay and co. On the last night, it seems, every member of the troupe shed at least a tear or two as the sad irony of their New York failure, coupled with the bad timing of Kerr's effusive praise, cut them to the quick. Barclay recalls they 'were very soppy that night'. The bad timing of Kerr's sparkling celebration of the troupe made the show's treatment feel all the more unjust.

The irresistible parallels with *The Producers* make the question hard to avoid – was the whole thing some kind of bizarre tax dodge, out of the performers' hands? While recognising the inevitability of the rumour,

Humphrey Barclay reasons: 'Who can say? I don't know. I *think* it was a genuine attempt to put on the show, but "let's not spend much money, it's a bit of a gamble, could these kids pull it off? Ah, they haven't quite – okay, let's cut our losses . . ."'

Whether our heroes were victims of the real life Bialystock & Bloom or not, there were one or two consolations – in November they were invited to perform a shortened version of the show in Connecticut for a concert entitled *In Pursuit of Excellence – an afternoon for the John F. Kennedy Library*, and soon after they continued their pattern of shadowing The Beatles' progress by getting a couple of sketches broadcast coast to coast in an edition of *The Ed Sullivan Show*, on the same bill as Joan Sutherland and The Animals. Oddie took advantage of his passing resemblance to singer Eric Burdon by appearing at windows briefly, to the screaming delight of the teenyboppers down in the street below: 'I remember thinking, "Oh, this is pretty good, I could get used to this."' Perhaps Sullivan, the King of US Entertainment, could have done a better job if he'd retained the rights to *Cambridge Circus*, but his invitation to feature excerpts from the show on his programme suggests he never forgot the quality of what he'd seen in the West End.

In fact, these diversions aside, the *Cambridge Circus* show itself didn't die with the ejection from the Plymouth Theatre. As Cleese takes up the tale, 'Then a couple of guys from a place on Washington Square called Square East asked us if we wanted to come and do the show in this supper club. I loved it there because you could be rather lazy really. There were only about two hundred people in the audience and it was a nice room so you didn't have to knock yourself out getting your voice to the back of these big theatres; you could play at a much more naturalistic level, which suited me better.'

In moving to Square East, the team were actually filling the vacuum left behind by the Second City comedy troupe from Chicago, who had in turn flown over to London for a stint at Peter Cook's Establishment Club. After the pressures of touring and taking a chance on Broadway, this low-key locale in Greenwich Village seemed to suit many of the group far better – not just because it made Cleese's shouting more effective, but because it was a return to the kind of cabarets in which they'd started their careers back in Cambridge, except this time they had the excitement of being in the greatest city in America.

The End of the American Dream
With the New York iteration of the Establishment Club still entertaining punters over on the other side of town (although the London original was already beginning to founder by 1964), it was brave of the Square East entrepreneurs to offer the *Cambridge Circus* team a home. The papers had already

begun to bemoan the British invasion – they'd had *Beyond the Fringe*, The Beatles, The Stones, and a successful run of *Oh What a Lovely War* – and perhaps the shine was beginning to fade somewhat. Nevertheless, the off-Broadway deal seemed to pay off, and in this time the show evolved further, with the team confident enough to write new material on the fly and turn Square East into something more akin to a modern comedy club than a shrunken version of a theatrical show. Having performed the main show so many times, this was the real joy of the New York run, in Bill Oddie's opinion. 'One of the delights of Square East for us was that after the show, we started doing a bit extra. We had a brilliant trio, a really famous jazz pianist called Ray Bryant . . . Originally we had a white band, provided by the Musicians' Union of New York. And they really weren't getting it, and I actually said to the manager, "Can we do anything better than this?" and he said, "Leave it to me. All we have to do is prove that the white guys ain't no good, and then we'll sort it." So he was able to square it with the union, saying, "These guys can't cut it, I'll get my boys" And I knew all three of the band – there was Ray Bryant, his brother Tommy Bryant on bass, and this guy called Walter Perkins, who was a drummer who I knew from lots of records, because I was a jazz fan. And I said – "Fuck!" They were brilliant – not only fantastic musicians, they so enjoyed it, and Tim's often told stories of hearing them propping up the bar talking to all these contemporary jazz people, saying, "That's right, man, we're doing this real hip jazz revue with these English guys . . ." "Er, it's not a *jazz* revue!" But it was brilliant, and we wangled them into the show a bit and that sort of thing. So in this after-show show, we said to the audience, "look, that's the end of the main show, if you want to stick around and drink, that's fine, and we're gonna try out some new material . . ." Jean often sang with the band, and it was great.'

But it wasn't great for everyone, and the first of the gang to bow out of the miniaturised New York run was Barclay. There simply wasn't as much for a producer/director to do in a cosy venue like Square East, and he was beginning to feel like a spare wheel. Also, he recalls, 'Elements of oddity had come in which were against my instincts. In our big famous sketch, "Judge Not", John Cleese came on stage wearing Jean Hart's white fur coat. Now, he was supposed to be the prosecuting counsel! And I'm sufficiently orthodox in a theatrical way, to say "But that's not helping the comedy of the sketch!" Whereas he was now into a Pythonesque world of "Fuck logic!" . . . so it had started to not be my child any more.' So just before Christmas 1964 Humphrey amicably took his leave and set sail for Blighty – his job at the BBC had only been kept open until the festive period, after all, so it was time for him to finally leave the theatre behind and embark on his successful broadcasting career. 'There was no huff or anything like that, it was just ... My Work Here Is Done.'

Jo Kendall was the next to join him. The management at Square East had announced that one girl was all they could afford, and so despite being the original comedienne of the bunch, Kendall found herself caught up in an unpleasant impasse over who was to perform the female roles in the show (and besides, these public-school boys couldn't be expected to write parts for *two* women!). Kendall had enjoyed her time in the Big Apple but eventually, she felt the tug of home too, and left Jean Hart to finally step into the unrewarding female role full-time. Sadly, Hart would apparently be quoted later on as saying that she was the only woman ever to be in *Cambridge Circus* – a ludicrous assertion that would take a warning from lawyers to put right. For the meantime though, she and Oddie were the ruling king and queen of this little world of New York comedy – and of course he had time to take a look at the local birdlife as well.

John Cleese, meanwhile, was lapping up the opportunities shown him by the country that would eventually become his adopted home. He took the time to pretend to fall in love with a Barbie doll in a photostory for *Help!* magazine – thanks to the artist responsible, an enthusiastic long-haired Minnesotan named Terry Gilliam. Equally momentously, he met and genuinely fell in love with a beautiful young waitress who would go on to co-write the most acclaimed sitcom in British history, Connie Booth. It was unquestionably the most productive and exciting time in his life since he first arrived at Cambridge, and Cleese was grasping every opportunity with both hands. One night a dazzling grin from the Square East audience turned out to be the property of UK rockabilly cheese-merchant Tommy Steele, who invited Cleese to audition for a role in the touring version of *Half a Sixpence*. Despite being the kind of boy who was given special dispensation at school never to attempt to make a musical noise, this he did, joining the company after a short period of fooling around with the Establishment company.

The reason Cleese was free to take these chances was that, inevitably, *Cambridge Circus*' time at Square East had wound down by the beginning of 1965. Hatch had packed up and gone home, Jonathan Lynn had followed suit, and Oddie and Hart had moved on as part of the touring live version of *That Was The Week That Was*, along with Brooke-Taylor. The name of this tour could have been questioned under the Trades Descriptions Act on several counts – firstly, it was mainly just the bulk of the *Cambridge Circus* show with Frost's name attached, and secondly the only performer from the TV version of *TW3* in attendance was the burly, moon-faced *Private Eye* co-founder Willie Rushton. Or at least, as Oddie recalls, he was the only *TW3* original there for most of the time. 'David was doing it both in America and Britain – he used to commute, backwards and forwards, across the bleeding Atlantic. But the show was advertised everywhere as *David Frost's That Was The Week That Was*, and his name was in fucking great letters on the posters – which would have been fine if he was actually in it, but he wasn't. He would do a choice gig, you know – there was one on the edge of New York, so he fancied that. There were places where we nearly got lynched!' Not that his few appearances were a boon for everyone either. 'What I got particularly pissed off about was that David would turn up and take all Willie's best material . . . Willie rather meekly sort of said, "Oh, I don't mind, that's fine . . ." And David would take all the juicy bits that Willie had been doing. And I thought, "You bugger . . ."' During a week's holiday mid-tour, while Bill and Jean were off enjoying Florida the way couples do, carefree bachelors Tim and Willie were left to entertain themselves, popping down to Mexico for a few days' undocumented debauchery.

When the *TW3* tour returned to New York, Bill and Tim also took the opportunity to drop in on a friend, unannounced. 'We came back into New York and heard that John was in *Half a Sixpence*, and we went, "I'm sorry I don't *believe* this – he's in *what*? In a MUSICAL? He's camping around in a *musical*?" And so we actually hired a box, which was right over the stage. And John came prancing out, you know – I know he had to do some silly villagers' dance, or the jolly cockney routine, I don't think he had anything to say at all, and he certainly couldn't sing, so why he did it I do not know. And he was flouncing around with a hanky, and then looked up and saw us – "Oh my *God!*" And we were all sitting there, waving, "Hi, John!" It was bizarre.'

Despite the sundry activities of the show's stars, the original *Cambridge Circus* was still clearly capable of doing a good enough trade for a replacement cast to be sought, and Tim had stayed behind briefly to oversee the auditions – and then, to see the makeshift Cleese and co. very quickly fail to capture the magic of *Cambridge Circus*, thanks to the new director's insistence that the poor replacements aped the old cast's performances exactly, down to every tic and pause. Brooke-Taylor recalls that the effect was nothing short of disturbing, like watching a group of animated wax dummies. 'It was extraordinary really, because they were all very good. And then I came back to see them, and it was actually embarrassing, because they were all good comedians, but they hadn't allowed themselves to be themselves, they were actually just doing impersonations of us! It just wasn't right at all, they were even trying English accents, and I thought, the whole point of the thing was being silly, not to try to copy somebody being silly. It lost all its invention, really.' And so, after the best part of two years, *Cambridge Circus*, the show formerly known as *A Clump of Plinths*, finally reached the end of its record-breaking run.

However, back in the sedate corridors of Broadcasting House, Humphrey Barclay had been busy in his campaign to try and pick up where he left off on perfecting a radio home for the Cambridge alumni – to return to *I'm Sorry I'll Read That Again*. At least he already had the name this time – now he just needed some writers, a format . . . and, of course, for his friends to complete their American adventures and return home.

3

A Number of Performers

Surprisingly, the idea was never specifically for Barclay to continue the prototype series the old gang had created at the start of the previous year, but simply to make a brand-new comedy show, the best way he knew how. Still very much a 'baby producer', Barclay worked on several shows, including *The Navy Lark* and what he terms a 'terrible pilot' called *Soup of the Evening*, which convinced him to remain an editor of material rather than an originator. But the BBC remembered the *Cambridge Circus* try-outs, and were keen for him to try to put together something in that vein. He remembers with some discomfort that his new show was going to be called *Get Off My Foot*.

No matter how this planned show would have panned out, the use of Barclay's contacts would have inevitably made it a very similar horse to *I'm Sorry I'll Read That Again* – except, without the concerted spoofing of the establishment that that title suggested, and which was one of the particular strengths of Cleese and co. Barclay would have had a clean sheet to create a new sketch show for the post-Satire Boom comedy landscape. The question was, what did radio comedy need in Britain in 1965? And what did it already have?

Beyond Beyond Our Ken
Without question the number-one show of the time was *Beyond Our Ken*, created by Eric Merriman as a vehicle for the comedy businessman and star of hit RAF sitcom *Much Binding in the Marsh*, Kenneth Horne. Merriman's show had been running successfully since 1958, its popularity due in no small way to the legendary microphone prowess and irrepressible ego of the great Kenneth Williams. Based around a succession of outlandish characters, *Beyond Our Ken* featured Horne as the avuncular central figure, describing his week and bumping into regular freaks and comic turns played by the cast. It had evolved considerably over its seven series, bursting with suggestive silliness and spoofs of celebrities, but at just the time that Barclay was freshly arranging

the pencils on his desk, readjusting to his new career, Merriman had an almighty bust-up with BBC executives that caused the cancellation of the hugely popular series. However, what this really amounted to was the cancellation of Merriman's contract, and a name change for the show. A few doors up from where Barclay sat planning *Get Off My Foot* in his office at Aeolian House, the BBC's Light Entertainment department, writing partners Barry Took and Marty Feldman were putting the starting touches to *Round the Horne*, wresting the baton from Merriman's grip and running with the same old format, but with the added madness that came particularly from Feldman's mind.

Marty Feldman may not have belonged to the same educated Cambridge clique as John Cleese, but his own devotion to *The Goon Show* gave him an almost eerily similar comic voice – as is clear from the similarity of the names of the *Round the Horne* character Dame Celia Molestrangler and John Cleese's alter ego Wing Commander Muriel Volestrangler, a name that would crop up in some form on *ISIRTA* on more than one occasion. Feldman and Took's running of the new Horne show would create an undisputed classic of radio comedy, bursting with suggestive lines and free-flowing nonsense and extended parodies and . . . lots of other things that *ISIRTA* would also boast. It's no surprise that Feldman and Brooke-Taylor became friends so quickly, working and writing together for years. As he recalls: 'Some of the time I was writing with Marty Feldman for part of a week and then he would go off to write *Round the Horne* with Barry Took whereas I went off to write bits for *ISIRTA*.' Tim and Marty became so linked that they performed a sketch together for the Royal Variety Performance in 1970.

What would the college boy Barclay's show need if it was to take on a titan like Horne's programme? Ultimately, the answer has to be: youth. For all that Took & Feldman's scripts can still surprise the ear with unexpected levels of ingenuity, and a brand of filth that can cause amused intakes of breath even in the twenty-first century, *Round the Horne* was still very much an old guard radio show, with comedy-free musical interludes and a much-loved presenter who had been a family favourite since the war – even the theme music had a cosy, military air to it. Despite plenty of pop culture references and all but openly gay characters Julian & Sandy on board, *Round the Horne* was anything but 'with it' (whatever 'it' was). Even while enjoying the witty and surreal jokes performed with gusto by Williams, Hugh Paddick, Betty Marsden and co., there's always the threat of the Fraser Hayes Four waiting around the corner, ready to launch into a rockabilly version of 'Michael Row the Boat Ashore'. Nothing dates a classic radio show like an incongruous musical interlude.

David Hatch was aware that the love for Kenneth Horne's comedy would

make it hard to make an impact, but denies that the *ISIRTA* team felt especially in competition with them. 'We did what seemed to suit us, and the fact
that our show had a not dissimilar structure, in that Ken Horne was the sort
of ringmaster, and in *I'm Sorry* I suppose I played that sort of straight role,
doing the announcements and getting people on and off . . . But I don't think
we were either aping them or conscious that we shared territory – we thought
ourselves very different. They were a lot older, they had Kenny and Hugh
Paddick doing Jules & Sand and all that stuff, and our stuff was completely
different from that. So although people tend to think that we sort of sprang
out of *Round the Horne*, I don't think we did. We sprang out of the stage show,
which sprang out of the Footlights. We had no allegiances to what was going
on in radio at all – except perhaps for the comedy that we liked, like *The
Goon Show*.'

Barclay knew that his shows had always had that extra zing of coming from
the Voice of Youth. So the cry went out for material, both from his old friends
(wherever they were) and jobbing writers like John Esmonde and Bob Larbey,
a duo who began writing together at school but, despite being half a generation older than Barclay, were still very much just getting established as comedy
writers – in 1965 they were many years away from carving their own niche
with shows such as *Please Sir*, *The Good Life* and (from Larbey at least) *As
Time Goes By*. Learning his lesson from *Soup of the Evening*, Barclay concentrated on putting the shows together using random material provided by his
reliable teams of gag merchants, but he knew that the most important thing
a successful radio show needs is a strong regular team of performers. With his
old friends still entertaining diners over in New York, how would he cope?

Is There a Doctor in the Team?

Luckily, something rather like fate seemed to be on hand to save the rookie
producer from a gruelling series of auditions and trial-and-error casting sessions.
'As the year went on, people started to come back from America, so I *began*
to just get the feeling after all, that, "hello, I've got *I'm Sorry* again, why don't
we actually call it that?"' Just in the three half-hours so far created, a definite voice and style of show had begun to develop. And after all, something
like *ISIRTA* was exactly what the BBC had requested – so the arrival of Jo,
and David, and then Tim and Bill back on home turf must have been a relief.

But establishing a permanent radio home for the team was not a completely
friction-free task. Fresh back in the country from his lionisation in the States,
Bill Oddie knew that the one thing this new show needed to stand out from
the dusty competition was . . . him. Oddie's rock 'n' roll sensibilities were to
be this show's secret weapon, so it's little wonder that some form of power
struggle was on the cards from the off. Barclay was of course overjoyed that

Bill was back in town and ready to forge on with *I'm Sorry I'll Read That Again*, but he does recall one tempestuous altercation over the telephone during this time, as they debated the problems of securing a solid team for ISIRTA. 'I do remember shouting at him in slight desperation and panic, "Bill, someone's got to get this together, and I'm the one in that position!" "Yes!" he said, *"and don't forget who put you there!"'* – and slammed down the phone. Although why Bill Oddie was so keen to remind anyone about the debt owed to Peter Titheradge is anyone's guess.

Oddie says that it seemed inevitable that the BBC would demand a series of *ISIRTA*, but at the same time it took years for it to sink in that a comedy career was the way forward for the whole team – Bill had a teaching job lined up, and had also signed up to be a resident naturalist on a Russian expedition, but between *ISIRTA* and work on *The Frost Report*, these were postponed indefinitely. However, even with the key ingredient of Oddie's music being added to the other cast members' strengths, Barclay knew his team wasn't complete. Crucially, John Cleese was still keen on exploring the possibilities of life in the United States, but Barclay made the decision at this point that the missing link was not Cleese's writing partner Graham Chapman, who was not considered as part of the team.

In some interviews Chapman did describe himself as having been 'sacked', but nevertheless he threw himself back into his medical training on return to Blighty, qualifying as a fully-fledged stethoscope-swinger. The truth is that Barclay, keen to create a team with the utmost versatility required to create any scene the script required, had a different medical student in mind to complete the line-up. Fresh from starring in that year's Footlights revue, *Stuff What Dreams are Made of*, newly-ex President of Footlights Graeme Garden was still in training when the call came: 'In a sense, I entered the team because Graham Chapman was going further with his medical career than I did, he actually did his pre-registration work as a doctor, which I didn't do – I just qualified and when I passed the exams I stopped. But I was still a medical student when I was doing the first *ISIRTA* shows.'

Garden's presence in the first series did make a mountain of difference to the show – it's only mild praise to say that his vocal dexterity provided the perfect mortar that held the more experienced team members together. Barclay already knew Garden had what was needed, having seen and heard his potential up in Edinburgh – plus, of course, he could *write*. Reams of jokes dirty and clean, clever and stupid, Garden was good for them. Nevertheless, his huge role in scripting *ISIRTA* was not important at first. 'I was terribly sure that we should have Graeme in the cast, because of his vocal abilities, his wit, and his ability to impersonate,' Barclay insists. 'I just was totally sure. I don't think that I discussed it with anybody.' Besides being as simplistic as suggesting that maybe two Grahams in the cast was too much (no matter how it was spelled), Barclay has no definitive answer as to why Chapman was never considered for the final team. 'Perhaps, from *Cambridge Circus*, I thought of him more as a visual comedian, and therefore Graeme had the edge over him, for radio.'

The importance of impressions and spot-on spoofs of existing radio and TV shows is just one of the cornerstones of *ISIRTA* which tends to get over-looked in the pun-centric appraisals of the show. Just as Hatch was the key to believably lampooning BBC News, Garden and Kendall's powers of mimicry would be put to use time and again when there was a show to be spoofed. Jo Kendall's ability to take off popular performers, for instance, amazes her ex-boss Barclay to this day, when recalling one occasion rehearsing a show. 'I think the script said "A Wendy Craig character" or something, and Jo said two syllables, and I suddenly thought *"That's* impressionism." When you know instantly who she was doing – I was totally struck. She was kind of unsung and taken for granted, and that was all very unfair.' From lisping children to matronly grannies with a wide array of husky sexpots in between (the audio equivalent of a Carol Cleveland bimbo), Kendall could do them all, making her and Garden an audio cast of varieties between them.

If Eamonn Andrews was required for a merciless *This Is Your Life* lampoon, or a crotchety Walter Gabriel for a fun poke at *The Archers*, Garden could do it. But by far his most loudly cheered impression was always Eddie Waring, the gabbling rugby commentator who was almost as funny in real life as he was in any spoof. 'I think a lot of the voices were off the peg – a "here's one I can do!" sort of voice,' Graeme admits, 'The reason we sent him up was that it's a terribly funny voice – you don't need to know who he is. The first time you see Eddie Waring, you think, "What is that man talking about?" It's wonderful!' *Monty Python's Flying Circus* also featured a bravado Waring impression from Garden's flatmate for much of the early sixties, Eric Idle. But Garden recalls that there was no competition – Waring himself insisted that Graeme's impression was the best. 'I didn't go to the recordings of the first lot. But I remember hearing them when I went home – for a holiday or something – and I enjoyed hearing it on the radio, I remember thinking, "Oh, that sounds fun to do." I was delighted when Humphrey Barclay came through and said, "Would you like to join the team and do some writing?"'

So that was How the Gang Got Together. And it's worth a brief pause here to reflect what a momentous event this was, when Barclay's cast first signed on the dotted line back in the spring of 1965. Of course, from one point of view, the trio known as the Goodies were working together for the first time. But, more importantly for our story, a friendship and professional partnership was cemented that would go on to provide radio laughs for nearly half a century – Tim Brooke-Taylor and Graeme Garden were both part of the *I'm Sorry* team at last. And they're still there to this day.

Rhubarb Tart and Beethoven's Fifth

It was May 1965 and the Cambridge Queen of Comedy, three Goodies and a Radio 2 Controller-to-be stood together for the first time with just a script and a microphone separating them from the first proper *I'm Sorry* audience. Outside the Playhouse Theatre, that home of radio legends where the Goons had recorded their own brand of anarchy years earlier, the monochrome streets of London were creeping into bright Technicolor, and Carnaby Street shop-keepers were only just beginning to get an inkling that sales were up. But for comedy fans in the know, something equally exciting was happening onstage every Sunday evening. The mix of old-time Music Hall with fresh new comedy was the perfect comedy answer to a culture that was on the brink of flitting around in archaic military garb, listening to rock 'n' roll as well as trippy music inspired by old 78s. The sixties were an eclectic web of innovation and nostalgia, and *ISIRTA* would be the show to fully reflect this mix.

The first episode wasn't a 100 per cent success with the *Listener* at first, which opined on 25 October 1965: 'On Mondays now, the Light Programme offers "I'm sorry I'll read that again", which they say is a new kind of laughing – so perhaps one shouldn't expect either a good, old-fashioned belly laugh or the delight of those short cuts through time, space and appearances that were normality for the Goons. On a first hearing this new show's chief characteristic is abundant energy . . . Certainly all the noise and activity is exhilarating, but you need more than that to get away with jokes about manic Wing Commanders and mothers-in-law (even if the last-named is an inanimate bundle to be stuck in the luggage compartment of a bus) . . . However, it's early days and for all my strictures, I look forward to the next battering.' The forgotten reviewer was wise to hedge his (or her) bets, as the show was just beginning a very long process of evolution that would turn it into the loudest success on the wireless.

Gone were the awkward attempts to incorporate the title into the intro of every show, but each programme was still introduced by a play on the original deliberately bland summary – such as: 'This is *I'm Sorry I'll Read That Again*, approximately 1800 seconds of japes, pranks and idiosyncrasies, written by a number of ideos, and featuring several syncracies.' It's fascinating to hear the team starting to find their feet, honestly admitting that the show offers nothing but 'a laughable mixture of impractical jokes' and 'hilarious hoojamuflicks'. Where today the majority of radio sketch shows are tested and templated to within an inch of their lives before the first free-ticket holder files into the theatre, everyone involved in *ISIRTA* was simply feeling their way. 'I don't remember saying to any of the writers, "That's a bit too like ..."' recalls Barclay, denying any inspiration from Horne or anyone like him. 'We were aware that we were a rabble – and we knew we weren't the most original thing. There was just a kind of youthful anarchism which appealed to the audience. And to be honest, we were making a lot of it up as we went along.' Hatch agrees that it was a far cry from today's producer-led shows. 'Nobody was ever told, you know, "Go away and write about a woodpecker." Nobody was told to do anything, they just handed in their stuff. Comedy shouldn't be done by focus group – nobody would tell the Pythons what to write, they just wrote what they liked.'

Without the Prune framework, these early shows perhaps have a slightly more scattergun approach than those from later on in the run, but the way that Barclay arranged each programme – always with spoof credits and titles, not allowing a single minute to move away from the full-on silliness – indicated some inspired ideas, some of which would be picked up by future comics. The first episode, for instance, closes with the cast sitting around as critics, pulling apart the preceding half-hour, in the exact way that Stephen Fry and Hugh Laurie's superlative BBC2 sketch show *A Bit of Fry & Laurie* would kick off their first series.

From start to finish, *ISIRTA* is replete with viciously self-flagellating gags that rip apart individual sketches or performances. Any latter-day producer would advise against pre-empting criticism in this way, but Fry admits that it's a natural source of material. 'To my knowledge I never heard that episode, but I think Hugh and I shared with John in particular the slight paranoid sense that whenever we did anything, we could almost fill in all the negative reviews we could hear in our heads as we were doing it. And therefore there's this huge desire to get your retaliation in first, as the phrase has it. I mean, I do it to myself all the time, so when I'm in a film or something I'm actually muttering the *Time Out* review in my head while I'm waiting for the lighting to be done ...' A long *ISIRTA* sketch featuring a very silly foreign-language course could also have subconsciously inspired Fry, who would develop the idea in his own classic radio show *Saturday Night Fry*, with his 'Learn to speak Strom' sketches.

There's a plethora of left-field items throughout the first series, with the show's loose format allowing each item to hit the ground running with no strained introduction, and proving that the team knew how to make the most of being in sound only. There's an estate agent who shows customers around habitable animals ('There's some very nice bed-sitting-rabbits, or you could be very cosy in a kangaroo if you don't mind sharing.'), a public-school pickpocket who steals his victim's clothes as he speaks to them, an interview with an invading alien, and all manner of random skits.

Nevertheless, the team knew that as well as random sketches, running gags were crucial to building an audience. So there are many themes present and correct in the first series, some of which would stand the test of time, such as numerous references to Beethoven's Fifth Symphony, guest appearances from the Tillingbourne Madrigal Society (who debut in show two with their trilling take on The Animals' 'House of the Rising Sun'), the regular play on the word 'spot', which inspires an instant response from young Brooke-Taylor every time it's mentioned ('And now we come to the high spot of the programme' – 'WOOF!') and rhubarb tart. Don't forget the rhubarb tart.

To make the best rhubarb tart, you take a light shortcrust pastry and lay it in a dish, before stewing five finely diced sticks of rhubarb in a quarter-pound of jam sugar. Then you add a little lemon peel and pour it into the tart casing before baking it for half an hour at gas mark 4. Leave to cool, and you have a fine, tasty rhubarb tart. However, why this should be in the least bit amusing is, in itself, impossible to say. Bill Oddie believes that it was a Cleese preoccupation that took hold despite nobody finding it very funny at first – but it didn't matter, repetition was the key to making commonplace phrases hilarious, as the *ISIRTA* team would shamelessly admit on air in the years to come. Soon the dish would be name checked at any and every opportunity.

That is *So* Old!

The first mention of the baked delicacy was in a stream of nonsense during a horse-racing sketch, but it started to resemble a motif in episode 5, when it was used as the password to the den of an evil Fagin-type figure in the middle of the early extended sketch 'Martin Copperwick' – 'I was born in the little town of Chunky Plantagenet in the county of Lincolnshire. This came as a great surprise to my parents, who were living in Wigan at the time . . .' – an inspired Dickens pastiche that shows that yet another *ISIRTA* hallmark was present right from the start. These genre spoofs weren't yet performed under the name of Prune Playhouse, or Prune Play of the Week, being intro-duced as 'The *I'm Sorry* Sagas'. But much of the shows in season one were to be taken up with elongated lampoons of famous stories, starting with the Sherlock Holmes-inspired 'The Case of the Workington Shillelagh', and it's here we find the germ of the reliance on chestnuts and groanworthy gags that would ultimately become *ISIRTA*'s albatross. They even do the 'Call me a hansom cab', 'You're a hansom–' 'Watch it!' gag, with Hatch's Dr Watson character unabashedly crowing 'That joke is *so old*!' throughout. Puns, smut and silliness with a shamelessly corny panto flavour . . . it's astonishing how soon the cast found their voice.

The rest of the series would feature similar pun-packed pastiches, including the US Civil War tale 'The Battle of Whispering Mouse', Chandleresque narrative 'The O'Rafferty Case', featuring Garden as Private Dick Mike Spanner and, best of all, in show eight, 'Doctor Why and the Thing'. This last is an especial triumph, and the popularity of Russell T. Davies' *Doctor Who* relaunch makes it a cert for commercial release if the BBC have any sense.

Already the tradition of having Tim play the central character is in place, as he goes on to narrate the tale as Peter Potts, the hero of the terrible tale of The Thing: 'It seems as if it happened just yesterday. In fact it began this morning.' Potts goes to visit Garden's Doctor Why – a Hartnell-era clucking old loony professor who shows him his new time machine, and urges him to travel forward to the year 3000 AD:

TBT: But gosh, I mean, I haven't brought a toothbrush!

GG: Then you'll just have to leave your teeth behind!

TBT: No, but who will look after my poor bed-ridden grey-headed old . . . budgie?

GG: Oh very well . . . What do you care? Why should anyone care? They laughed at Galileo, they laughed at Newton, they laughed at Einstein – WHY WON'T THEY LAUGH AT ME???

TBT: It's partly the lines, but mostly the delivery, actually.

Most Unimportant Cavemen

Some attempts at running jokes and characters were to fall by the wayside, however. One interesting forgotten double act that popped up occasionally was Cosmo & Thingy – a kind of prehistoric Pete & Dud played by Garden and Oddie, the latter a gullible squeaky sidekick with more than a hint of the Dagenham Dud about him. The laconic pair would debate the basics of life, inevitably ending with Cosmo pulling a fast one on Thingy. They were actually the creations of Esmonde & Larbey, who went on to try a whole sitcom with the characters on ITV in 1972.

The influence of Cook & Moore, which is easily picked up in these shows is perhaps especially telling when you realise that the very first broadcast of the double act's series *Not Only But Also* (and therefore the debut of the Pete and Dud characters) had occurred just a few short months before the *ISIRTA* recordings began. It's little wonder that Peter Cook's madness was still rubbing off on his Cambridge successors – John Cleese always considered Cook a guru and a friend, and to this day Tim Brooke-Taylor doesn't lose a beat in proclaiming Cook the God of Comedy. About half of Cleese's range of voices are filched from Cook, with stunningly accurate reproductions of Cook's toffee-nosed 'Domonic' voice rolled out with no apology several times in

ISIRTA – although the major voice which was unavoidable at every turn was E. L. Wisty's nasal suburban monotone. This became 'the voice' for comedic losers, accountants and bores forever more, culminating in the election of a prime minister, John Major, who was mocked for having the exact same voice. The *ISIRTA* team would also be grateful for the E. L. Wisty sketch format which was always a handy template not just for the radio, but in TV shows such as *At Last the 1948 Show*, *It's Marty* and indeed *Monty Python's Flying Circus*. In a nutshell, a straight man tries to mind his own business as a loony sits by him and bamboozles the poor normal with dull flights of fancy – which often turn out to be completely true. Paul Merton was still embracing the format in his own show in 1993.

The main forgotten regular character, however, was Bill Oddie's Filthy Old Tramp. This character provided the main format for Oddie's songs, in the days before the team had the guts to just be themselves. 'I think that might have been slightly inherited from *Cambridge Circus*,' he recalls, 'because there was a sort of a character . . . well, it's wasn't really a character, it was just a costume, sort of an old mac and a flat cap, and I did a couple of songs in the show dressed like that – which were otherwise sophisticated songs, or appeared to be, so the clash appeared to be weird . . . And basically I was there to be kicked around to a certain extent. When you've got big tall people like John Cleese and Graham Chapman, obviously it's the big person/little person routine, like Pete & Dud.'

These amusing dead ends aside, the first full series of *ISIRTA* grew in confidence and anarchy, bowing out on its last broadcast in December, with a full-blown 'History of Radio Light Entertainment', packed with piss-takes of the stalwarts of 'Good Old Steam Radio'.

The shows bristle with vicious attacks on other radio shows, especially the truly dire standard of comedy offered by Jimmy Clitheroe – Cleese's cry of 'It's *I'm Sorry I'll Read That Again*, Mutha, Again!' gives *The Clitheroe Kid* a reference in almost every show. But the 'History of Radio Light Entertainment' special is particularly full of attacks on the Wonder Show's stablemates – there's a governmentally approved version of *The Archers*, filled with unsubtle news items, memories of the time when the BBC broadcast nothing but rolling episodes of *Mrs Dale's Diary* (Kendall's intoning of 'I'm worried about Jim . . .' was an instantly recognisable reference at the time), plus a grab bag of quicker spoofs, of commercial radio and of course old-time Music Hall. Perhaps the reason why this last episode so boldly shows the way forward for the show is because it was written solely by Bill Oddie, Tim Brooke-Taylor and Graeme Garden. It even pilots a feature which would sustain right up until today, when Garden introduces the first ever Dirty Songbook – Expurgated Version. As a crotchety old censor, he announces a burlesque song by Oddie packed with buzzes in the optimum places – 'In this way, a song that sounds slightly suggestive can quite simply be made to sound absolutely filthy.' Despite becoming a *Clue* stalwart, Oddie claims the revelation of the joke as his own: 'There was no way of escaping the fact that we were having to produce a lot of material. And so we were looking for a format which you could repeat, and the gift one was the Dirty Songbooks – Julie Andrews and Rolf Harris. I thought, "Oh God, we can do this for just about anything!"'

In this first run, there's one last debut of a creation that would go on to epitomise the whole show. 'The Battle of Whispering Mouse' had already featured a character called Backwoodsman Prune (a colleague of General Custard, naturally), but towards the end of show 9, a comic beat group performing an odd version of 'Come into the Garden, Maud' (the musical version of the Tennyson poem that, again, is still a regular in *I'm Sorry I Haven't a Clue*) is preceded by a number performed by Angus Prune and Rosie Bedsocks. At last, the future proprietor of the whole show had put in an appearance – the road to Radio Prune was open.

But Angus Prune wasn't the only person who would make a difference to *ISIRTA*. The first complete series of recordings was in the can by August '65 (it's usually listed as the second series, following the original trilogy of try-outs, and there's some confusion when it comes to the numbering of *ISIRTA* series but the BBC releases stick to the idea that the pilots were a series in themselves), yet by the time the show finished broadcasting to the nation in December, Barclay already had a third run of *ISIRTA* pencilled in, ready to begin recording the following February. It had gone down well with critics, the *Guardian* labelling the show 'witty, exuberant and very free-ranging – no dominating father figure, no set convention . . . just all the boys together, writing and acting and apparently – also genuinely, one imagines – enjoying themselves energetically'.

It definitely qualified as 'a flying start', but things could only be improved by a new arrival. Done with touring the States, writing (very temporarily) for *Newsweek* and generally experimenting with life, young John Cleese was back in the UK, and ready for some fun. Like so much in sixties comedy, the thanks for this go to David Frost, who lured him back home for *The Frost Report*.

Something Completely Different
The first episode of the second full series (now shifted over from the Home Service to Radio 2 forerunner the Light Programme) immediately trumpeted the fundamental strength of the show – the personalities of the troupe. Regular self-reference and even self-mythologising is the secret of getting an audience to warm to a cast, often (crucially) to the extent of accepting corny material, when it's performed with panache by familiar faces – or, indeed, voices. Getting

the audience to love the performer on a personal level is worth a thousand top-grade gags, which is, for instance, partly why the *Carry Ons* remained so massively popular throughout the sixties and seventies, and why French & Saunders regularly have taken pride of place on Christmas evening TV, performing flimsy movie pastiches that ultimately allow them to be their own familiar selves.

The *ISIRTA* cast had begun to appear in episodes as themselves even in the first series, arguing about credits and whatnot, but it's not until series 3 that their individual personas are spelled out for the listener. With Hatch's place as 'Announcer' under debate, the team trade off their roles:

TBT: This is the first programme . . .
DH: Just a minute, what do you think you're doing?
TBT: I'm doing the announcement.
DH: I see.
TBT: You can do the dirty old man bits.
DH: No I can't do those. I'll do the songs.
TBT: No no no, Bill Oddie does the songs.
DH: No, he's doing the woman's parts. What about Jo Kendall?
TBT: She's doing the dirty old man bits . . .

Until finally the dispute is settled by the debut announcement:

JC: My name is John Cleese and I am the star of the show.

This boast is rubbished of course, and the tall newbie gets the job of announcing every show, in an increasingly silly voice, for evermore – just as he would on *Monty Python's Flying Circus*. Although the *Cambridge Circus* reviews had singled out Oddie and Brooke-Taylor for praise, there had never been any doubt within the team that Cleese was a truly ominous talent. Therefore, even though he was at this point far from being a household name (*The Frost Report* wouldn't make his elongated frame a regular sight on TV screens until 1966), he still had a towering presence in the radio show from the start, which would become both a boon and a burden as his radio persona very quickly mutated into the snarling, radio-mocking anarchist John 'Otto' Cleese. 'Otto' had always been his favoured middle moniker, perhaps stemming from embarrassment at his real middle name of Marwood – but even his despairing mother was never able to establish a real motive for the Germanic replacement. Nonetheless, the name Otto would continue to be a Cleese favourite right up until Kevin Kline played the villain of that name in *A Fish Called Wanda*.

ISIRTA would give Cleese his freest comedic arena, not just allowing him his own pet name, but also space to moan about the standard of the scripts, both on- and off-air. In his keynote speech to the National Radio Conference of Australia, Cleese insisted: 'Radio has always been my favourite medium. This is not just something that comes on as you get old . . . You're just there with the microphone, you know, it's all about the CONTENT! Isn't that wonderful?' However, as with *Python*, Cleese could not be constrained, and it's a testament to the rest of the cast that later Cleeseless shows are not poorer for his absence. There was always a place in the show for John, it just happened that as he grew more successful, his presence would depend more on his whim than anything else. 'The only problem with radio,' he admits, 'was the money. When I started on *ISIRTA* I got £22 an episode, and after we'd done over a hundred, we managed to get it up to £32 an episode. So I realised that as I needed this stuff called food, I thought I would head for the lush pastures of BBC Television . . .' Generally, the lure of lucrative TV versus fun but inexpensive radio created a tension that would ultimately spell the end of *I'm Sorry I'll Read That Again*, and the birth of *I'm Sorry I Haven't a Clue*.

Importantly, though, no matter how keen every member of the *ISIRTA* team was to hurl abuse unabashedly at every other member while in front of a microphone, from 'Boring Old' Hatch to famously feminine Brooke-Taylor (not to mention the extremely ungentlemanly conduct towards Kendall, who remains perhaps the most undervalued female comedy performer of the last century), each part of the gang was welcome to participate, if they could – as Hatch said, 'We knew radio didn't pay an awful lot, but it was very nice to get the money that we *did* get. And if someone did say "Well, I've got a television show to do that's paying me money, I won't be there for this series", you said "Fine" . . . It wasn't a loyalty contest. It was basically survival, and you'd go with the guy paying the bigger cheques.' This must ultimately come down to the impetus behind the group being friendship before show business. For now, Barclay had his revamped complete Wonder Team of old friends, the audience loved them, and it was all hands to the pump to keep this fresh new comic scene going, using the Cambridge network not just for the cast, but also for the scripts.

4

Specially Written for the Wireless

No other sketch show in any media has ever offered quite the level of random unpredictability of *ISIRTA* in the main body of each programme. Especially before the later series gelled around the concept of the show being broadcast from the fictional station, Radio Prune (a framework which many shows would be grateful for, from *Radio Active* to *On The Hour*), laying a bet on which genre of comedy each following sketch would fit into would be an idiotic waste of money – a Music Hall pastiche? a confusingly surreal piece of crosstalk, incorporating rhubarb tarts and furry friends of choice? an audience-baiting arrangement of puns and chestnuts, or a positively filthy rock song? To any truly green audience member of today, attuned to expecting the same roll-call of comic characters predictably lining up to do their schtick, such unstructured variety would surely be a real shock – and yet *ISIRTA* offered so much breadth that they even had room for precisely the same kind of recognisable returning popular characters, eliciting gigantic roars of welcome, in among the array of oddments. The obvious mingles with the startling in every show.

In this century, it's definitely this unpredictability and variety that most marks *ISIRTA* out from any other radio institution. And the reason for this inspirational dexterity and knock-'em-for-sixteen randomness? Presented with the two suggestions, that either each half-hour script was assembled with an ambitious intention of catching the listener off guard with a carefully crafted structure of deliberately disparate comedy sketches and songs designed to build an overall picture of all-encompassing variety and high-class anarchy, or that the team were generally glad to paste together any scrap of new material they could lay their hands on to fill the requisite thirteen-odd half-hours, hoping that their undoubted talents and likeable personalities would allow them to wing it in front of a sympathetic audience . . . few of the *ISIRTA* team deny that the second option would be closer to the facts.

'I think it was a grateful acceptance of all the material that was available,'

Hatch confessed, 'I don't think any conscious decision was made that "we're now going to make the biggest casserole there's ever been". It was a bit like when I started *Week Ending*, I just got a load of writers and said "write", and they all wrote! With *I'm Sorry*, Humphrey had thirteen half-hours to find the material for. So we all wrote – Tim wrote some stuff, I wrote some stuff . . . Bill and Graeme wrote most of it by a mile, there were freelancers who wrote stuff, and everyone has different styles, different things that made them laugh, so it had the eclectic mix – at one time bawdy, the next quite sharp, and then puns . . . it was whatever Humphrey could get his hands on, and edit down into something that made a good half-hour. So I don't think it was deliberate in any way, it was simply "you take what you can get."'

But when the people giving you what you could get included John Cleese, Graham Chapman, Eric Idle, Johnny Mortimer & Brian Cooke, Clive James, Peter and David Lund, Bernard King, Peter Hutchins, Alan Hutchison, David McKenna, Simon Brett, John Esmonde & Bob Larbey *and* Tim Brooke-Taylor, Bill Oddie and Graeme Garden, it's no wonder that the sound of barrel-scraping is so rare in *ISIRTA's* 104 episodes – and when that desperate scraping sound is heard, it's usually deliberate. Perhaps when you've set yourself up as a vaudevillian free-wheeling comedy gang, you have the licence to ignore the bottom of the barrel and go straight through, thriving on the buzz of the audience and the thrill of messing about in front of a microphone.

With each series averaging at around thirteen episodes, it's no surprise that compiling the scripts used up all the organisational and critical flair that Barclay and the cast had shown on Broadway. Garden was as hands-on as anyone in the team right from the start, and remembers: 'There was certainly grateful acceptance for somebody who'd send in a funny sketch – be it a science-fiction parody or a Music Hall song or whatever it might be, and if it worked, we would do it. When we were doing our own things, we'd think the best way to go for that target is in one of Bill's songs or have an episode, a big parody of a Shakespeare play or whatever it is, to end with . . . we had some characters that did reappear, but what we didn't have was, every week, the Rambling Sid Rumpo slot or the Julian & Sandy slot, we didn't have that structure, which the Kenneth Horne shows did . . . I think that's probably why I prefer the *Mitchell & Webb* approach to the *Little Britain* approach. Mitchell & Webb's show tends to be a bit more varied – "what comes next?"'

With both Idle and of course Cleese working on the show, it's no surprise to find ideas that would be explored by the Pythons later on littered throughout *ISIRTA*. Eric was pursuing an acting career, having graduated from Cambridge, and yet, thanks to Barclay's encouragement, he spent most of his time in the wings or dressing room scribbling down comedy sketches, while questioning his thespian powers in shows like *Oh What A Lovely War* and a farce called *One for the Pot* – missing a crucial cue in the latter thanks to being immersed in an extended sketch for *ISIRTA*. The actor giving him his cue even had to track him down to his dressing room, where he sat writing nonsense about rhubarb tarts. After that experience, Idle knew that comedy writing was to be his forte, and *ISIRTA* was a major part of his income in these early years. Brooke-Taylor remembers, 'Eric idle and I used to write for the show together at one stage. He had grown up with us at Cambridge, he worked with Bill Oddie and myself in our college revue, so he knew exactly what was required.' Oddie also recalls giving Idle his first break. 'Originally poor Eric had to sing my songs in Edinburgh, so I like to think I inspired him, because he was determined that he could do better than me. He's very sweet, we went to the first night of *Spamalot*, and he actually thanked the Goodies, as it were. He got us to stand up and said, "I wouldn't be doing this if it wasn't for these three." Tim and I had auditioned Eric for the Pembroke Smoker or something.'

With so much sharing of material it's almost fruitless to try and untie exactly who wrote what, but it's tempting to see the seeds of *Python* more strongly in *ISIRTA* sketches such as the investigation into gangs of old ladies that terrorise innocent youths (or a salty crew of chartered accountants who sing shanties about their book-balancing exploits, or a vet who insists that a poorly dog is actually a budgie, or Idle-esque lines such as 'The situation at noon today was 12.00 precisely, and has been getting steadily later throughout the day'), than in perhaps any other *Monty Python* forebear. Cleese even drew on an early sketch starring Brooke-Taylor as one of his 'Butterling'-style pathetic employees (in this case an ineffectual zookeeper) when he came to write his *A Fish Called Wanda* follow-up *Fierce Creatures*: 'This was the second largest zoo in the whole of Europe. We had over 6000 animals. All we have left is a rhinoceros, two hyenas and a ferret with a wooden leg.'

Another arguably Pythonesque element that would play a huge part in series 7 was the regular debate between a rabble of ridiculous aged blustering fogies, soon to be known as The Buffies, who were fixated on the behaviour of long-haired youngsters. No matter what the theme of each *I'm Sorry* investigation was that week, from Housing to Love to London, they would bark to each other about the good old days:

TBT: I had all my hair blown off in the war. Look, I've got a wooden wig.

DH: Oh yes. I thought it was odd, you combing your hair with a chisel.

JC: When I was in France, I lost three legs. And a gramophone!

DH: I had my gramophone blown off.

BO: I had my hat blown off.

GG: I had EVERYTHING blown off! I'm completely wooden, you know ...

TBT: You tell that to these modern youngsters, they'd laugh in your face.

JC: Long-haired hippies ...

TBT: AND ANOTHER THING! These miniskirts ...

GG: What about 'em?

TBT: I mean, you look all right but I just haven't got the legs ...

It doesn't take a Professor of Comedy Sketches to see the similarity with the Cleese/Brooke-Taylor/Chapman/Feldman classic from *At Last the 1948 Show*, 'The Four Yorkshiremen' sketch, since tenuously added to the *Python* canon.

Add to this *Python*-flavoured brew the burgeoning talents of Johnny Mortimer & Brian Cooke – whose way with youthful dialogue (honed in *ISIRTA*'s young lover sketches, which featured Brooke-Taylor and Kendall as a passionate couple without a clue what to do with each other) would come in handy as the creators of genre-defining flatmate comedy *Man About the House*, and spin-offs *Robin's Nest* and *George & Mildred*, not to mention the US version *Three's Company* – and of course Esmonde & Larbey, and you've got an eclectic mix of the best of 1960s and 70s comedy writing.

The comic world of *The Goodies*, however, was increasingly the strongest element in the shows, in sketches such as an early run for the celebrated 'Kitten Kong' episode in which a gigantic budgie terrorises its owner, or the regular occasions on which the ever-patriotic Brooke-Taylor would make an impassioned speech to the strains of 'Land of Hope and Glory', but perhaps most notably in the Garden/Oddie-led extended sketches which began to be a fixture of every half-hour.

Love, Marriage and Babies

It's incredible how the third series of *ISIRTA* gradually introduced every major tradition of the show during its thirteen episodes. Firstly, David Hatch introduced a trio of characters who would always elicit a cheer whenever they were wheeled out: Hugh, Cyril and Rupert (or Johnny as he was first known), the three-month-old babies forever sat outside the supermarket in their prams, complaining about the baby's lot. The idea of voicing the thoughts of tots may seem commonplace now, but it was a stroke of genius from Hatch – and all thanks to his new-found role as a father. 'I was the first member of the cast to get married and have children. The baby sketches were quite successful.'

JC: What's that stain on your bib?

DH: Fish and macaroni . . . I spit it out every time, but she will go on giving it to me. I tell you, she's no idea . . . Hey, here comes Cyril and his ghastly mother. Come on, scream everyone.

ALL: WAH!

TBT: Well, what's new with you, Hugh?

DH: Oh, I saw my father the other day. Funny looking bloke. He kept throwing me up in the air and laughing. Strange sense of humour, right after fish and macaroni . . .

'Quite successful' is clearly false modesty from Hatch, but one of the reasons why Hugh, Cyril and co. were always welcome in any episode was simply because, as Garden has suggested, they were regular characters, without being a predictable part of every show. Whenever any of the team became a proud parent, it was only a matter of time before watching their bouncing progeny's behaviour would inspire a new Babies sketch.

A couple of episodes after the Babies' debut, another irregular sketch format returned, which would provide some of the best dialogue throughout *ISIRTA*. Gone were Tim and Jo's confused young lovers, and back in the team came John & Mary, the Maugham-influenced romantically repressed couple from *Cambridge Circus*:

JC: Ah, how I love to be alone in the country.

JK: John?

JC: Yes?

JK: I'm with you.

JC: How I love to be alone in the country.

JK: But John – you brought me with you!

JC: I didn't. You hid in the back.

JK: But you must have noticed.

JC: Not at all – it's a very large tandem . . .

JK: Oh, John – why don't you admit it? You don't love me any more.

JC: All right, I admit it.

JK: John – once we had something that was pure, and wonderful, and – and good . . . what's happened to it?

JC: You spent it all.

JK: That's all that matters to you, isn't it? Money. I despise you, I hate you. I don't know how I've been able to stand it. I suppose it's because I love you. I do love you, John. I love you more than I can say. I need you, John, I . . . I . . . Please, John, don't look at pictures of nude women while I'm talking to you!

With a hefty dose of kitchen-sink drama thrown into the brew, plus a no-holds-barred attitude to both surrealism and sickness, the John & Mary duo must be the single most dysfunctional couple in comedy history, giving Cleese masses of inspiration for both his works on psychiatry and the relationship between Basil and Sybil Fawlty. Their situations often changed, but John & Mary remained the same buttoned-up painfully unaffectionate couple throughout the whole of *ISIRTA*'s run:

JK: Oh John – talk to me!

JC: I'm sorry, I've got things on my mind. I'm tired . . . God knows I haven't had much sleep, skinning that bison last night . . . I'm going to sleep.

JK: John, talk to me – say something to me. Say you hate me, say I'm ugly . . .

JC: Which?

JK: Say I'm ugly.

JC: You're ugly.

JK: You're only saying that – you don't really mean it! You don't care, you never think about me – up and down all night, warming the milk, mashing the rusks, all the crying and the bedwetting . . .

JC: Yes I know . . .

JK: I wouldn't mind if we had a baby.

JC: I'm sorry, but I prefer bisons – good night.

Despite their quarrels, their family troubles, having numerous children, bisons, and a dead mother-in-law to support, they always somehow stayed together – perhaps they're still together to this day. What is certain is that the John & Mary sketches contain the very best quality dialogue in the series, with an old-fashioned Groucho Marx-style quickness and zaniness to the gags which belies the show's reputation for being mainly composed of chestnuts, cheers and groans.

Did Somebody Call?

By far the greatest source of much-loved insanity, however, was to come from the yet-to-be-named Prune Playhouse section of every show, which in the second series contained plays on Robin Hood, 'Dr Heckle & Mr Jibe', Agatha Christie, and in the second show, there was 'Moll Flounders', which would thrust two comic icons into the limelight at once.

The buxom young heroine (played of course by Kendall) visits the home of her betrothed, Sir Roger De Coverlet (Cleese). When she arrives, the door is answered by Oddie in the guise of a humble, dishevelled, wrinkled retainer, name of Grimbling:

BO: Your mother wishes to see you in the Green Room.
JC: Get on with it.
BO: I'm afraid she's not very well today, she's been seeing spots before her eyes.
JC: Dear me, has she seen the doctor?
BO: No sir, just spots.
JC: That's a very old joke.
BO: I'm a VERY old butler, sir.

Just popping in for that one joke, Grimbling has a long way to go to be the fully-rounded, down-trodden, sweet-natured dirty old man who we remember – and who Bill Oddie used to get hounded to transmogrify into any time a fan stopped him on the street. It was in some ways an evolution of the sad little tramp 'character', but Oddie admits today that, like so much else in the show, 'It wasn't a burden – if you find a voice which can get a round of applause without doing anything, then consider yourself lucky . . . Same with Tim, he *relished* it, absolutely.'

Brooke-Taylor's familiar character would become central, although far more dramatic character development was required for Roger's mother – 'A tall, regal, gracious bit o'crackling. She was sitting too close to the fire . . .' – to become the true star of *ISIRTA*. Having said that, Brooke-Taylor's Lady Constance De Coverlet, emerging from his turn as Lady Carstairs in the Oscar Wilde sketch, certainly has one thing right from the start – she's an insatiable sexpot. In her very first scene, she warbles, 'It is time for my tea and muffins. Tell Grimbling to bring the tea, and tell Muffins I want him . . .' and (those who want to avoid spoilers look away from the book now), she returns at the end of the show to steal away Moll's love, the Highwayman Dick Turpentine. Admittedly in this sketch Lady Constance is a logical character, but as the crowd's taste for Brooke-Taylor's lusty old lush grew, the incongruous ways that Her Ladyship would be inserted into every escapade would be half the fun of the character. This is not to mention her amazing ability to grow and shrink as the plot required, from a diminutive roly-poly sexaholic to a saucy titan capable of being mistaken for an iceberg. Or a planet. Or the demon Hecate. Or Frankenstein's Monster. Or even a steam train.

'It was one of those characters where, if you've got a voice, you use it,' shrugs Brooke-Taylor. 'I think Graeme wrote some of the serials, which I think are the highlights of the series, where it just grew. I don't think I claim much credit for it, but I *loved* Lady Constance – I think she was very useful to the writers, to be perfectly honest.'

With her invisible bulk and warbling yelps of greeting – somewhere between a duchess and a chicken – Lady Constance was of course pure radio. Nobody would want even to try and fully visualise such a blood-chillingly egregious frilly monster of a woman. But, with the sex drive of Mae West in a boys' locker room and a physical presence that makes grown men run for the hills covering their unmentionables, Lady Constance De Coverlet rapidly became a smash with the crowd, and an episode couldn't go by without her. No matter where the plot meandered, everybody knew that sooner or later a dreadful phrase like 'What's that? In the distance! A great, fat blubbery, monstrous, misshapen creature . . .' would herald the First Lady of Filth onto the stage. In later series, the band would always strike up a brash rendition of 'Happy Days Are Here Again' every time she steamed into the show, with a cheeky Brooke-Taylor wink at the audience and a plot-advancing dirty insinuation towards that week's male heroes:

TBT: Oh, adrift in the pitiless ocean on a tiny raft, miles from land, alone, just me and two men, ooohhh . . . TERRIFIC!
JK: What about me?
TBT: Certainly not, you're far too butch . . . Wait, I have an idea! I'll take all my clothes off.
DH: Yes.
TBT: Then I'll nail them up to the mast.
DH: Yes, and then?
TBT: That's rather up to you . . .

A colossus in every way, Lady Constance became the very hub of *ISIRTA*, the Fairy Prunemother, the true mascot of the show – whether the cast (Brooke-Taylor aside) liked it or not. Once the crowds got a taste for her, there was no getting rid of this good-time gal, any more than it was possible for any male character to escape her gasping sexual attention.

The unholy trinity of *ISIRTA* heroes played by Tim, Bill and Graeme was completed with the *Tom Brown's Schooldays* spoof towards the end of this run, which introduced the eponymous Tim Brown's teacher, the antique rambler whose every line would become the exact definition of the word doddering, Mr Arnold P. Totteridge. Totteridge's dithering is a verbal display that's impossible to capture on the page, but Graeme Garden's marathon amnesiac monologues would grow ever more extended as the character fermented, allowing the team to fill whole precious minutes of airtime with circuitous meandering, often involving the repetition of the phrase 'Good evening' several times, many repeated mutterings of 'How d'you do, d'you do, do you do, do you?' and always leading to the polite, apologetic '. . . I'm, er, I'm not boring you, am I?' 'He wasn't based on anybody or any particular affliction,' says Graeme. 'There was just a strange wiring he had in his brain,

I think. His logic streams were somewhat mangled. The audience seemed to like it . . .'

Enter the Prune

Angus Prune and Rosie Bedsocks had entered the arena way back in the first series in name only, but Angus didn't really start to develop into the ephemeral ringmaster of the show that he would ultimately become until the gang were a couple of dozen episodes up. In fact, for his first epic outing, 'Beezer Soccer Yarn, The Angus Prune Story', he would turn out to be some kind of Georgie Best figure, years before Best himself would become an iconic footie hero. But all this football business was forgotten by series 4, in which Hatch and Kendall portrayed Prune and Bedsocks as the archetypal boss and secretary struggling to keep their love affair secret from the wife – a situation made especially tricky by the fact that Rosie *is* the wife. But then continuity wasn't important – Angus Prune was a funny name, to be used whenever possible. The team eventually decided that Angus Prune was 'the average *ISIRTA* listener' – a sort of composite schmuck that personified the entire noisy Audience.

Prune wouldn't become the real mascot for the show until a particularly boring day in the *ISIRTA* office, when it was decided that something was missing from the theme tune. Elizabeth Lord (or Lizzie Evans as she was then known) had elected to join the Light Entertainment Department of the BBC as a personal secretary just before Barclay arrived, and she would go on to be an indispensable aide to both him and his successors on *ISIRTA*, involved in every stage of each show's production. One evening in 1965 she was taking a bath and mulling over that week's show when she realised there was something missing – a sing-a-long theme. The original instrumental theme tune had for a time been accompanied by a frankly disturbing way of actually laughing the tune (usually by Garden), but what the already-titled 'Angus Prune Tune' needed was words – and so she pitched her idea to Barclay, who recalls: 'I and my secretary Liz Evans wrote the words in the office one day. Just for fun, we had nothing better to do. I can see myself now sitting at my desk in Aeolian Hall and hammering out the lyrics, and Liz, who was sitting opposite, behind her big typewriter, joined in . . . We were always desperate for ways to open and close the show and my instinct was not to waste a second of airtime, so I think I basically wrote those Humphrey Barclay jokes at the end of the show simply because, rather like the *Today* programme, we wanted to use every last second.' An admirable ambition of course, but with a tightly packed knockabout show like *ISIRTA*, you need a big finale to bookend the dense silliness. From the middle of season three onwards, you knew that the end was nigh when John Otto Cleese squeaked his farewell and Oddie, as Prune, piped up with the truly inane boasts:

My name is Angus Prune, and I always listen to I'm Sorry I'll Read That
    Again (YOU DON'T!)

My name is Angus Prune, and I never miss I'm Sorry I'll Read That Again
    (GET AWAY!)

I sit in my bath and I have a good laugh, 'cause the sig tune is named after
    me! (CHANGE THE NAME!)

My name is Angus Prune, and this is my tune, it goes –

I – S – I – R – T – A, I'm Sorry, I'll Read That Again!

And that was all for that week, folks.

In Tune with Prune
Until the death of Kenneth Horne cut the show off at four series in 1968,
Round the Horne was certainly the King of Radio Comedy in its time, popular
with all the family (well, all the ones who hadn't become addicted to television). The long-haired Oxbridge types over on the Light Programme doffed
their caps to Feldman & Took's creation, however, safe in the knowledge that
their programme was more than a sketch show.

Given the familiar nature of the basic format, *ISIRTA* had one crucial
element that set it apart from its competitors and predecessors, far more
tangible than the intellectually silly nature of the humour and the youth
of its stars – *I'm Sorry I'll Read That Again* had RHYTHM. David Hatch
insists that the show always had an unmistakable sound all its own – 'If
you passed a shop doorway and heard it going, you knew it was *I'm Sorry*
because that was the feel of it, it had its own noise.' This essential ingredient came courtesy of Dave Lee and his 'Boys'. 'Dave Lee was the musical
director on *That Was The Week That Was*,' remembers Oddie, 'that's when
I first met him . . . and he'd been in charge of some very complicated
musical things, because *TW3* was very innovative. So when *ISIRTA* came
up, it was just a question of asking him whether he'd do it. And he got
the band together – there was a pool of I guess what you'd call session
musicians, and a lot of them were seriously good. Sometimes I'd be trying
to get a Spike Jones-type sound out of them, the next it would be a rock
'n' roll number, or a country number, we just covered everything.' With
Lee on piano backed up by trumpet, trombone, clarinet, drums, bass and
guitar, the Boys didn't just play the theme tune and back up Bill – they
knitted the entire show together, punctuating the jokes and bridging the
wildly differing sketches. They even got their own intro in one early episode,
for a Tubby The Tuba-style 'Introduction to the Orchestra' sketch. Hatch
went through the whole ensemble, each playing a sarcastic riff when
announced:

DH: Of course, quite a few people work in a band like this. And quite a few don't. So let's just run over some of the musicians. Now here's Brian, he's on bass ... Here's Donald, he's on drums ... Here's Derek, he's on clarinet ... and here's Kenneth ... he's on gin and tonic, there's Cedric playing the guitar ... Brian playing the trombone ... and David ... playing the fool. Well, there they are, the musicians and their instruments. For best results, keep them well oiled.

Most sketch and Variety shows had a resident band to provide stings, links and the like, but naturally, as *ISIRTA* developed, the playing got tighter, the atmosphere got more anarchic, and the band's madcap way of lurching from spot-on pastiche to squealing din-making made the Boys one of the most important 'characters' in the whole set-up – and their hearty leading of the laughter and cheers didn't do any harm either.

Devotees of classic pre-*ISIRTA* shows such as *The Goon Show* and *Beyond Our Ken* can argue quite correctly that the humour of those programmes was often as anarchic and unpredictable as any modern comedy, but when it came to music, the laughter nearly always stopped. Thankfully, since the days when Ronnie Corbett would disappoint millions, halting the laughs by introducing Barbara Dickson halfway through an episode of *The Two Ronnies*, the practice of inserting humour-free musical numbers in the middle of comedy shows now seems almost unthinkable. It's not that the music of Ray Ellington and the like are unentertaining – far from it – but there's a discomfiting insinuation that comedy alone is not enough, so an old-fashioned torch song or a crazy jazz number is needed to offer a full half-hour's entertainment.

With William Edgar Oddie on board, that whole tradition was due to be blown away.

He's Just My Bill
By Oddie's own admission, this was more to do with enthusiasm than musical ability – from one of his earliest *ISIRTA* numbers, 'Ain't Got Rhythm', right down to his appearance on 2007's musical celeb show *Play It Again*, Oddie has been up front about his own lack of technical musical ability: 'My instrument was a very ancient Grundig reel-to-reel tape recorder, at which I was very expert, recording tunes and tapping the table to give a drum rhythm.' But with musical director Leon Cohen around to take Oddie's ideas and turn them into tuneful reality thanks to Dave Lee and a full band, there was nothing that was off-limits for *ISIRTA*, musically speaking. 'Leon was the copyist basically, I wouldn't say "arranger" as such – although he probably did. And I used to go up to Dave's house – fortunately he lived about a

hundred yards away from me, maybe that's why we chose him – and Leon
would be there as well. And because I didn't write music, I would take the
tape along, and then sing the song to them, and tap out a rhythm, and he'd
offer me chords. And I'd say, "have you got something better than that? Something a bit funkier?" I couldn't play anything, and that's still the case. But I
did write songs, and I was very much into pop music . . . It would be silly to
deny, I've obviously got a musical streak in me from somewhere. I can sing
reasonably well, I do my own tunes, I can recognise chords when they're *wrong*
. . . So I had to work with them, and Dave would ask what style the song
was, and I'd say, "Look, OK, this is the melody," and I'd put it on the tape
recorder if necessary. And the lyrics, you know, the two came together. And
once we'd got it down, Leon would go away and write the charts. Dave had
a long and successful career, and I did hear from him not that long ago –
when I got the OBE he sent me a splendidly sarcastic letter, as well he might.
Fully deserved . . .'

Tim Brooke-Taylor happily states the obvious. 'Bill's music was a *huge* part
of it. The problem with him is that he's too good a musician, so that once
he's writing really good melody-filled songs, he moves onto something slightly
more modern, and you go, "Ooh, let's have more of those tuneful songs, Bill!"
It did help that we could have the musical bit, but it was never straight.'
Dudley Moore had, of course, been the saviour of *Beyond the Fringe*'s need for
musical interludes, and his cultured pastiches were also a great escape from
the traditional revue torch song. But mixing genuinely contemporary pop
music with genuinely funny jokes was Bill Oddie's triumph. 'I don't think it
was conscious,' he admits, 'but as it was, I found myself the only person doing
comedy music. Because, for some odd reason, music in revues was either the
sort of Flanders & Swann/Weston Brothers type thing, which I also wrote a
parody of – you know, the two guys at the piano . . . slightly topical, always
the same form . . . three rhymes and a pay-off, like a limerick form, almost.
They were either that, or serious songs, which was even worse. The standard
cliché was you'd have all this clever-clever comedy and then you'd get a
nostalgia song, with a couple of guys in boaters singing about great days on
the Cam (but not funnily!), or you'd get the song sung by the girl . . . I
remember going to see the Footlights revue in the first year, and I think this
is what was happening in London as well, it was probably copied off that,
and you'd have all these silly sketches, and then the girl (probably under
protest, the guys trying to keep them in their place or something) would be
there in a black dress with a bit of a slit up the side of it, leaning on a pillar
with a Scotch in her hand, and singing some bitter-sweet song about how
lonely it was and being world-weary, you know? And it was dead straight!
How the hell it got into revue I'll never know, but that was the tradition and

it went on for ages . . . And I said, "Why are they doing this?" It didn't make any sense. So I had an open field.'

Making the songs genuinely cool was also crucial. 'I think the secret of the success was that the sort of Cambridge students who didn't really want to admit to liking pop music could like it, because it was funny now. I often thought, "You're responding just as much to the fact that this is a rock 'n' roll song as to the actual lyrics.' It made it OK to like pop music, if it was actually rather clever and sending it up. Which of course wasn't the case at all, I just enjoyed singing that way!'

As can be seen from his 1967 album *Distinctly Oddie*, with its mix of balladeering, cockney knees-ups and rock 'n'roll, Bill Oddie was the perfect example of a rock star trapped in a comic's body. If he did tend to be the most irascible member of the team, then perhaps there's good reason – not only was he the most feted star of *Cambridge Circus*, from the least privileged background, he also probably worked the hardest out of any cast member on *ISIRTA*, not just performing and singing, but writing the scripts, overseeing the creation of the music and even many of the sound effects. He could also boast one of the greatest rock screams of any sixties performer.

Despite his lack of technical expertise, Oddie was hardly a complete musical novice. He released his first singles at almost the same time as he started work on *ISIRTA*, with the non-humorous juvenile delinquent rocker 'Nothing Better to Do' backed with 'Traffic Island' (complete with accompaniment from the first Mrs Oddie, Jean Hart), going out on George Martin's Parlophone label in 1964 – the same label as leading jazzman Humphrey Lyttelton. 'George Martin did comedy – he did the Peter Sellers records,' says Bill, and 'he'd done the *Cambridge Circus* live thing, and my agent at that time was to do with the music business, so it was a perfectly standard thing to do, it wasn't like being given a major producer . . . "Nothing Better to Do" was one of two records that I've had banned by the BBC. Basically satirical – this was my *TW3* training – it was about mods and rockers beating the shit out of each other in Brighton at the time. It's quite embarrassing to listen to now, because it wasn't funny. And that got banned by the BBC with the splendid reasoning that "it might incite people to violence". They could imagine mods and rockers marching into war singing that song. If only!'

Polydor released Oddie's first full album in 1967, complete with groovy bright red artwork and photos of the clean-cut wee moptop playing the saxophone. *Distinctly Oddie* is undoubtedly an *I'm Sorry* product, boasting tracks like 'The Rhubarb Tart Blues' and a pop version of Beethoven's Fifth, as well as *ISIRTA* songs such as 'The Ferrets of Old England' and the Police Constable Herbert Platt ballad 'The Lawman' – but none of the songs were released as singles. Bill was still attempting solo success right up to 1969, with a little number called 'Jimmy Young', but chart success wouldn't come along until the Goodies pulled on dungarees and began whooping like funky gibbons. A post-1966 World Cup victory song recording the heroic exploits of footballer Nobby Styles was all set for blanket promotion, when Styles' lawyers foolishly pulled the plug. 'I also did a couple of demos for George Martin, fairly funky songs, and the band included, would you believe, Rick Wakeman on piano, John Paul Jones on bass, and Mitch Mitchell on drums. If you want name-dropping, you can't do better than that – eventual Yes, Led Zeppelin and Hendrix, produced by George Martin of The Beatles.'

Again like The Beatles, one of Bill Oddie's greatest virtues was versatility, with a breadth of style that told of a deep love for everything from psychedelic rock to bluegrass to Noël Coward. This was the sixties after all, when The Bonzo Dog Doo-Dah Band (and, to a far lesser extent, The Temperance Seven) were reminding their hip contemporaries of the ripping joys of jazz – and they shared a major influence with Oddie, in Spike Jones. Garden admits, 'Some of the songs are direct homages. Not parodies, we weren't sending up Spike Jones, we were learning from the master.'

Jones, who died in 1965 at the silly age of fifty-four, is probably the closest thing to a single godfather of *ISIRTA*'s sound that anyone can pinpoint. His way of cutting through the po-faced ballads and pulp pop of the thirties and forties, adding rude sound effects and silly voices to the point of audio pandemonium, is an exact precursor of the show's attitude to sacred cows, and the team and sound effects people often killed themselves trying to perform Jones-style numbers live for *ISIRTA*. It's the vaudevillian Spike Jones element – the crazy percussion and use of random whoops, whistles, honks and hoots – that really defined the *ISIRTA* sound, when it began to creep in from halfway through series 2.

Dave Lee's interpretation of this cartoony comic jazz, performed by full band, is the true punctuation of *ISIRTA*'s humour. It added to the anarchic atmosphere, with the hip rock pastiches providing the groovy youth polish – Oddie's version of 'On Ilkley Moor Bar T'at' in the style of Joe Cocker, was after all released on John Peel's record label Dandelion in 1970, which is as high a commendation of both musicality and cool as anyone can claim. Peel heard Bill's rendition while listening to *ISIRTA* one night, and decided it was just the thing to drum up some publicity for his label, so he even went so far as to hire most of Cocker's original line-up from 'With A Little Help From My Friends', the Grease Band, to back Bill up on the number. (John Lennon loved the track when he heard it too, even if he did attribute it to John Cleese.) The flipside of the single showed another interest of Oddie's – taking the piss out of The Beatles' later perceived pretensions, with 'Harry Krishna', a George Harrison-baiting squib featuring the mantra 'Harry Secombe,

Secombe Secombe . . .' which made the whole record a kind of double spoof of what was happening in sixties pop. In fact, there was hardly a single twist or innovation in the world of pop music throughout that seminal decade that didn't catch Oddie's ear and result in a note-perfect pastiche: Motown, folk, Merseybeat, soul, Beach Boys, virtuoso rock . . . *ISIRTA* featured them all, filtered through Oddie, Cohen and Lee's Prune machine.

'On Ilkley Moor . . .' was the culmination of Oddie's sideline in silly covers of other people's songs that in many ways presaged 'One Song to the Tune of Another'. Perhaps the most famous instance of this is Oddie's Louis Armstrong impression, peaking with the fully extended rendition of 'What a Wonderful World', in which the singer's trademark gravelly sound is finally perfected to crystal-clear tones by his being rushed to hospital mid-song to have his tonsils out. Fittingly, Oddie had laryngitis when he came up with the idea.

Despite (or perhaps because of) Oddie's impressive input into every show, his musical interludes were perennially presented as an embarrassment to everyone. As an extension of the brow-beaten pathetic characters he tended to play in sketches, eventually it would be Oddie as himself who would line up for abuse from everyone before launching into bigger numbers such as the epic 'Magical Mystery Bore' Beatles pastiche, the jubilant 'Julie Andrews' or prototypes of Goodies numbers like 'I'm Taking my Oyster for Walkies' and the wild country hoedown 'Stuff That Gibbon', which would never recapture the excitement of the live version when re-recorded for vinyl. As the sixties gave way to the seventies, Oddie moved into funkier territory, with the hip session musicians edging closer to the Goodies sound – especially in a raunchy ode to bestiality based on the Troggs' 'Wild Thing' ('*Hey Wild Thing, look I'm on the hunt / I love your legs both back and front . . .*') and the 'Theme From *Shaft*' spoof, with wailing electric guitar paying tribute to Andy Pandy.

Throughout the Prune years, Oddie wrote well over a hundred original songs, so it's little wonder that he soon began to incorporate crazy cover versions. The team even went so far as to invite listeners to come up with their own song titles to inspire Bill, but the resultant number, 'Mao Tse-Tung was a Scotsman' proved to be so confusingly meaningless as to put them off that idea for good. Still, it's an awesome achievement and Roger Wilmut, in his masterly work *From Fringe to Flying Circus*, put his finger on the genius of Oddie's music exactly when he noted that the trick was to write songs that were great to listen to in their own right – toe-tapping tunes, memorable melodies and lyrics that were interesting or amusing even if their references were well past their sell-by date – which is why the 'Andy Pandy' song's stablemate, a Simon & Garfunkel-style ode to Kenneth Wolstenholme, is still an enjoyable song years after the great sports commentator himself has passed on, and his celebrity has passed out of general public knowledge.

The Hills Are Alive . . .

Oddie was certainly not the only musically oriented member of the team though – they had all passed the Footlights auditions, after all. And when a more communal song was suggested, it usually came in the form of a recital by the Tillingbourne Folk and Madrigal Society, of the Tillingbourne Valley. This was often an excuse for a more highbrow or traditional form of close-harmony silliness, but they could also rock out when required. The sixties folk boom had been in the firing line from the start of *ISIRTA*, with Bill, Graeme and Jo delivering a storming medley of folk hits in the first series, such as Bob Dylan's take on 'The Eton Boating Song'. But the Society's greatest achievement was released on the first *ISIRTA* cassette compilation, the stirring anthem 'There Was a Ship That Put to Sea' – a song that 'falls into the vocal tradition of sung music, and contains features that undeniably suggest': *There was a ship that put to sea, all in the month of May / With a Fa-La-La-La* . . . The joke is of course that the complicated, lengthy, seemingly endless harmonious repetition leads to the blunt pay-off '. . . *sank!*', but for the joke to work, the choral work had to be magnificent. Oddie, Cohen and Lee must have worked hard to make the cast sound so perfectly in tune. Yet, that's certainly not how Jo Kendall recalls the experience today, remembering only the briefest of once-overs leading to the terrifying feat of delivering a humorously complex choral work in front of a live audience, practically on the hoof. Bill and the Boys took time to run through the numbers, but if it involved other members of the cast, they were generally flying by the seat of their pants.

Every member of the cast was called on to sing a number or two, and even the eardrum-smasher of Clifton College, John Cleese, voluntarily sang – although he admits today that 'I used to say to my children that if they didn't behave I would sing to them'. The exaggeratedly painful voice of Cleese was often the one chosen to deliver the random but insistent musical references in sketches, most often an uncalled-for rendition of an excerpt from *The Student Prince*: 'Overhead the moon is beaming – beam, beam beam . . .' But otherwise, after the titanic success of its cinema release in 1965, *The Sound of Music* inspired the most ridicule.

The sickly Nazi musical's main function was to be referenced by Cleese in the most staggeringly tenuous puns – often a play on 'The hills are alive . . .', but also regular perverse attempts were made to crowbar in the stirring 'Climb Every Mountain', such as Cleese's complex monologue about giant rodent teeth in the *Daktari* spoof 'Dentisti', in which the audience are taken to the brink of rebellion by an exhaustingly ponderous set-up just so Cleese could break into a tuneless sampling of . . . wait for it . . . '*Prime ivory mouse-tusks* . . .'

But Otto also has a small but terrifying roster of songs to his credit, some of which crossed over into the *Python* legend, with his perversely precise biographical song 'Oliver Cromwell' turning up on the album *Monty Python Sings*. This was set to the tune of Chopin's Polonaise in A-Flat Major. Being endlessly less musical than Bill, John's songs infamously pilfer from the classics, with American march composer John Philip Sousa (writer, of course, of the *Monty Python* theme 'Liberty Bell') providing a very rough melody (inspired by 'The Washington Post') for 'The Rhubarb Tart Song'. The Cleese masterpiece, however, takes its tune from the Ivor Novello ballad 'Rose of England', its stirring, sentimental melody the perfect setting for the timeless 'Ferret Song'. The call-and response nature of the rodent/nostril-themed classic makes it an epochal moment of *ISIRTA*, with a reprisal in one of the rare 'Best of' medleys featured in the show – as well as TV exposure as the denouement of *At Last The 1948 Show* and an entry in the *Monty Python* songbook. 'The Ferret Song' is irrepressible . . . except within the Monty Python team. Cleese reportedly begged his colleagues to let him work the number into the *Python* stage shows, but it was always strenuously vetoed by everyone else.

These classic musical moments were only possible due to the one thing that is almost beyond imagination for any latter-day show of its kind – a full band, onstage. Today's shows are lucky to run to a trio of session players and a synthesiser, but nothing can compare to the sheer oomph of a full band – in fact, if pushed, Graeme Garden insists that it's the one thing he misses most about the *ISIRTA* days: 'We'd have a live band on stage who'd be playing links, and jumping in with snatches of music and stings and things, and it was terrific. It's what we love about *Hamish and Dougal* having a live band, it's just fun . . . I loved the lift of it, and the music that they would bash in behind you and suddenly that whole sketch would come to life, or the audience would cheer, and at the end of a sketch there'd be a huge fanfare and a sting from the band, that was wonderful.'

'How De Do Dere, Honey?'

Another element of the writing and performing of *ISIRTA* which ties in with the old-fashioned comic-strip stylings of The Bonzo Dog Doo-Dah Band is the frankly unpleasant question of racism – not to mention sexism and homophobia – which crops up from time to time in the shows.

Were the *ISIRTA* team racist? No, of course not, any more than The Bonzos were batting for the National Front when Viv Stanshall sang '*Through the twilight I can hear the humming of a melancholy coon* . . .' in the song 'Tubas in the Moonlight'. To call the sixties 'a more innocent time' with reference to the depiction of certain minorities would be a cliché, but it is hard for many nowadays to think back to a time when a jam company having a golliwog for a corporate mascot wasn't considered remotely questionable, or for one of the best friends of Bonzo Dog icon and *Beano* legend Lord Snooty to be a crudely drawn rubber-lipped Negro. 'Where am dat warty-melon'-style voices were par for the course, and for the *ISIRTA* generation, the unacceptable crudeness of the references were already part of the joke. So *ISIRTA* does undeniably wring laughs from such woeful stereotypes, but on balance, given the unreconstructed times in which the show was recorded, *ISIRTA* was generally forward-looking in its denunciation of racism.

This was after all long before the BBC cancelled *The Black & White Minstrel Show* in 1978, and yet Radio Prune made it clear at the time just how unacceptable the show was. One spoof of the show kicked off with a typical rendition of 'Camptown Races' delivered with Jolsonesque verve, only to be disrupted by Cleese's intervention: 'Stop it at once, this is most offensive. We at the BBC have finally and definitely made up our minds . . . for the time being anyway. This "Black & White" nonsense is offensive, and has to stop. So wipe that silly black stuff off your faces, and do the show some other way.' This intervention is admirable, of course, except for the fact that the team's solution is at first to attempt an offensive oriental version called 'The Yellow & White Minstrel Show', and finally a poofy replacement called 'The Pink & White Minstrel Show', where they sing the real 'Camptown Races'.

The fact is, if you set out with an 'anything for a laugh' philosophy, and add to that a desire to be as consciously offensive as possible, as *ISIRTA* often had . . .

GG: Each week, after the show, we receive many thousands of letters . . . of complaint. And our switchboards are jammed with abusive phone calls. So to avoid the congestion we're going to tell you now who we'll be offending in this week's show, so you can start writing straight away. And those of you who want to make abusive phone calls, please make them at ten-second intervals in alphabetical order. If you all call at once it's very difficult for us to ignore them.

JK: So here is this week's list of people we'll be offending.

DH: All vicars, colonels, prime ministers, Tony Blackburn, gibbon fanciers and Julie Felix, housewives, radio listeners, Tony Blackburn again, and John Davidson–

EVERYONE: *Who?*

BO: –the Musicians' Union, all Director Generals of the
                 BBC, and at least one contemporary English MP for
                 Wolverhampton with a small moustache and the initials
                 E. P.

GG: Also, small people will be slightly sneered at.

TBT: Well, I'm sorry we couldn't include everyone in that list,
                 but if you do specially feel that you ought to be offended,
                 please write and tell us, enclosing a stamped addressed
                 OBE.

. . . then, yes, minorities of all sorts are going to come in for a childish ribbing,
if it gets a laugh. Oddie believes that ultimately any perceived 'ism' in the
show is a 'funny-voice-ism': 'They were caricature-isms, I mean, let's face it,
we're talking about an era where you still had golliwogs advertising marmalade.
You don't for one second think that it's actually anti-black people.' Besides,
even when caught in a cycle of offensiveness, the underlying anti-racist sentiment in the show is usually part and parcel of the joke, as in the numerous
digs at the execrable policies of Enoch Powell, only touched on above.

Race-related silly voices were a regular occurrence, based on the understanding that this younger generation knew full well that they were beyond
the pail. Musical director Leon Cohen's Jewishness was ramped up with every
cartoonish 'All right, already', and the shameless spirit of Peter Sellers'
'Goodness Gracious Me' Indian voice was summoned up regularly: 'and unless
you can be persuading people that you're Johnny Speight, they'll think you're
in very bad taste.'

It would seem a taboo to mention the occasional lapse of political correctness in the show, were it not for the fact that the few genuinely uncomfortable
episodes, racially speaking, have all been made commercially available. There's
a *Brer Rabbit* Prune Play bursting with wince-inducing *Song of the South*
voices on *ISIRTA* Volume 4, and the *Canterbury Tales* play included on
Volume 3 is also pretty unpleasant listening, featuring as it does a clumsy
attempt to get laughs out of Asian immigration throughout the sixties – everybody in the British Isles becomes afflicted with a plague called the 'Brown
Collywobbles'.

There was one major regular running gag of Bill Oddie's which assuredly
comes under the heading of 'Best Before Political Correctness', when his
terrible patois-inspired line 'How de do dere, honey?' is thrown in unnecessarily, and all too often. 'When I did "How de do dere honey" for anything
that was black, I was doing the joke black stereotype as done by minstrels
and people like that, who were white,' insists Oddie. 'It was an easy laugh,
but it wasn't racist. It was just a cheap reaction – you might as well say we

were dowagerist.' Even in the show, though, at times this 'funny black man' turn genuinely seems to irritate Cleese especially, as in this extract from the gambling scene in the flapper-era gangster spoof, 'Bunny and Claude'. The lines following Bill's gag come across as genuinely off-script.

> JK: Come on, W.C., play a spade.
> BO: How de do dere, honey? (*Audience groan.*)
> JC: Oh God, I thought we'd got rid of him.
> BO: Well, it's been a long time, I haven't done him for–
> DH: Now, Claude, you play a queen.
> TBT: . . . What d'you think I've been doing?

Two for the price of one, there! And the subject of Tim's infamous penchant (or, to be fair, inescapable reputation) for playing women and camper-than-camp men, as instanced by his lisping Claude above, brings us to the next sour subject . . . Were the *ISIRTA* team homophobic? Again, no – for the time, the writers and performers were notably enlightened and even sympathetic to the newly legalised lifestyle choice, as could only be expected from the gang that once included Graham Chapman, who had proudly thrown his own coming-out party in the summer of 1967. Admittedly, Chapman's writing partner Cleese had a hard time coming to terms with his friend's revelation at first, but it's crucial to remember that these comedians were young, white middle-class lads from a buttoned-up world living through a period of massive social change. Until the legalisation of homosexuality it had been one of many 'perversions' ripe for mickey-taking, or, more often, simply an unspoken taboo.

So, although there was certainly no genuinely anti-gay feeling in the *ISIRTA* camp, comedy queens abound in *ISIRTA*, because they made the crowd roar with laughter. Brooke-Taylor and Cleese especially had a distinctive line in catty queens likely to spitefully insist 'If you touch my earrings I'll wince!' at the drop of a feather boa.

In the twenty-first century, of course, twenty years on from the supremacy of right-on alternative humour throughout the eighties, comedy racial stereotypes and outrageous queenery are now quite all right for mainstream BBC1 humour once again. *Little Britain* showing a white man pretending to be an oriental transsexual called Ting Tong Macadangdang is fine today, somehow. The homophobic or racist undertones and indeed overtones in shows such as *Bo Selecta* or *Extras*, or in the stand-up of Ricky Gervais or Jimmy Carr, are deemed cosily ironic, whereas many may think that a show recorded by twenty-something Cambridge graduates in the sixties could only be unreconstructed bigotry and therefore as offensively outdated as Alf Garnett cuddling a golliwog.

The truth is that each generation of dodgy jokes is as offensive and indeed as knowing as the other; it's whether the material's funny enough to be worth risking any offence that should matter.

However, Tim now admits, 'The one thing I do regret is the large number of gay jokes. At the time it was liberal to be able to do "poofter" jokes at last – *Round the Horne* did them brilliantly. But it went on too long and I remember thinking, "if I do this in a 'whoops' voice it will get a laugh." I'm happy to say I gave that route up eventually. Fast-forward many years until I played a part in the new *Crossroads*, where I was the gay partner of the chef. I played him as seriously and non-camp as I could and at the time said this is one way of apologising and doing something positive. My character, mind you, was dead in a week.'

Lovely Girls

But were the *ISIRTA* team sexist? In many ways, yes – especially when later series really let rip in order to offend, such as the first female newsreader on Radio Prune being incapable of delivering bulletins without them turning into never-ending streams of gossip.

But then it's hard to think of any comedy of the period – Oxbridge or otherwise – which wasn't ultimately chauvinistic in its depiction of women. Admittedly the proliferation of dolly birds, feather-brained housewives, hideous nags and the like in sixties comedy reflected the unreconstructed times – Germaine Greer's *The Female Eunuch* was not published until 1970, and it's possible that the hidebound attitudes of her male colleagues in the Footlights and the Pembroke Players may have played a part in her study of gender politics.

Because, as Carol Cleveland has opined on many a *Monty Python* talking heads show, this generation of comics were public-school boys who had barely grown up since entering showbusiness. The repeated protestations from the Pythons that they could only write parts for busty young maidens or hideous old crones applies in many ways to *ISIRTA* as well. 'They were all very nice, very well-brought-up upper-class boys,' remembers Liz Lord, 'well, apart from Bill, but the people in those days did have good manners and they were all Cambridge-educated. But I think they automatically assumed that they were in charge. Well, they *were* as far as I was concerned, I was just Humphrey's secretary – considered a very glamorous job in those days.' (No doubt the allusion there was to Bill not being upper class only.) Have sympathy for poor Jo Kendall, then, fighting to survive among this gaggle of patrician post-grads; playing lisping girlies, heavy-breathing good-time girls and miserable matrons.

The undeniable erosion of broad public popularity for radio comedy has meant that most people's idea of young female comediennes in the 1960s probably stretches as far as professional dolly birds Carol Cleveland and Barbara Windsor, or at the most perhaps Establishment performer Eleanor Bron or then sitcom star Sheila Hancock. But in many ways Jo Kendall, the Cambridge Queen of Comedy, outdid them all. As part of a popular sketch troupe, appearing in character as herself every week throughout the decade, Kendall was part of a comedy team, not just an actress. She had had to stand up for herself to protect her part from Jean Hart, and contend with the brickbats that came from keeping up with the rest of the boys. It's one thing for a gang of lads to throw around personal abuse, but it is a small early blow for women's lib for Kendall to have accepted and dished out as much dirt as the rest:

JC: You stay here and I'll go off with Timothy.
JK: Why?
JC: Well then you can have a love scene with Bill Oddie.
JK: Oh, boring.
BO: What's the matter with that then?
JK: Well I'm all for little surprises, but not that little.

And yet (and the reason why Kendall deserves to be remembered head and shoulders above many sixties female comedy icons) she did eventually get to contribute her own material for the show as well – which would be unthinkable from Cleveland or the Lovely Aimi Macdonald. Writing the funnies was man's turf.

Luckily, as well as the continued support of producer Barclay, and Hatch and Titheradge, Jo did have another girl in the gang to turn to. 'I think Jo found a very good ally in me,' says Lord. Barclay's assistant was the first woman to write material for *ISIRTA* and this acted as a catalyst for Kendall. She just had funny bones, so why shouldn't she get a bit of cash for pitching in with a sketch or two? 'Maybe she noticed that actually as I seemed to be writing scripts for things, then for God's sake, at least she could. I was only the humble typewritist, you know?' Jo, on the other hand, was an actress – certainly the only serious actor in the team at this stage. Even today, she believes that real acting ability was in short supply in *ISIRTA*, and although she hails Tim as 'one of the greatest wits in the world', she doesn't rate his straight thespian skills – the only member of the Wonder Team she has ever rated as an actual actor is Graeme. Bill agrees. 'She *was* an actress, whereas the other people in the show – we didn't want to be actors! Certainly in my case, I didn't want to be. I don't think there was much sexist humour in the show, unless by implication – there's one girl, and she appears not to be getting as many laughs.' But after so many years in the team, Kendall *could* have a go at writing jokes, serious actress or not. Even in conversation today, Kendall is in fact the most jokey of the *ISIRTA* alumni, still picking up on puns and finding double entendres irresistible – it's little wonder that she ended up with a credit or two.

Admittedly, the percentage of *ISIRTA*'s fifty-plus hours of material which was written by Kendall or Lord is very small. But the entire output of sixties Oxbridge comedy is so overwhelmingly male-dominated, this still marks them out as inspiring. So yes, right from the first days *I'm Sorry* was sexist, fundamentally a Boy's Own Club, yet with her input into the show, and her output of thousands of characters and impressions over the years, Jo Kendall certainly held her own. Which undeniably suggests.

5

Introducing Dermot Staveacre the Singing Baboon!

So we have our Magnificent Six and a Half standing, script in hand, behind the array of microphones but in front of the rowdy band, who are stretched across the stage, with Dave Lee on the piano. There's just one ingredient to add, and it's probably the most important one: Meet the Audience.

In radio comedy, it may seem a little cute to single out the audience as a central component of the proceedings, but *I'm Sorry I'll Read That Again*'s Audience very quickly became a lot more than a bunch of spectators, which is why actually getting to be there for one of the recordings was such a hot ticket. With such an explosion of youthful entertainment in the sixties, where else could you find the comedy equivalent of a rock concert? The Establishment Club had fizzled out, and TV recordings were hardly the place for reckless abandon. Getting a pass to see these Cambridge types at the Playhouse was like being asked to join a gang and invited to an exclusive party all at once – and it's an experience which has continued right through to the present day, at the recordings for *Clue*.

Every One a Maserati!
It may also seem rather facetious to say that jokes were important to *ISIRTA*. But the show's specific obsession with jokes ties in with the importance of the Audience – because there's no denying that a significant proportion of the jokes in *ISIRTA* were deliberately, cringingly *bad*. As we've already seen, every half-hour was an unpredictable grab bag of surreal humour, satire, wit, impressions, rock music and character comedy. And yet the one thing that unthinking commentators choose to remember about *I'm Sorry I'll Read That Again* is that it was full of painful old puns. The reason that this unfair reputation sticks is probably because the advent of every creaking old joke was the time for the avid Audience to join in and *groan* their disapproval – not to mention booing and barracking in extreme cases. And it's when the Audience are joining in that the show takes off.

With the possible exception of Fozzie Bear and his hopeless chestnuts, the concept of gleefully groaning at jokes that you know are unfunny is a peculiarly British institution. At the risk of getting unnecessarily academic, Dr Richard Wiseman, a professor in public understanding of psychology at the University of Hertfordshire, has a theory as to why we take pleasure from crap jokes. 'Clearly it's nothing to do with the laughter. I suspect what's happening is that you have a shared experience . . . somebody tells a joke, and the nature of the psychology of humour, is that any joke will make some people laugh but not others – which isn't a shared, bonding experience. But if you tell a *bad* joke, everyone groans, we're all in it together. And it also takes the pressure off the joke-teller. If you've got a good joke and tell it badly, everyone says "Oh, you just messed that up", and you feel bad . . . If you've got a bad joke in your hand, you can't tell it badly, it's a bad joke! If no-one laughs, you blame the piece of paper, not yourself.'

That rather sums up the use of puns in *ISIRTA*. There's an abundance of them because it allows for a high, quick-fire joke rate, because it encourages everyone to join in . . . and because it absolves the cast of real blame for the script's failings (Oh, what a giveaway!). Which is quite a safety net for any writer/producer having to piece together thirteen half-hours.

Each week's journey through the World of Prune would be gloriously, gratuitously littered with rapid puns allowing the cast to interject with terrible asides, the quicker the better (and the quickest were the worst). There were fish puns ('Fish and Quips'), cookery puns ('Pots and Puns'), planetary puns and many, many gibbon puns. In the early days the cast would even desperately force in completely random punning references to 'Ring a ring o'roses' (anything that sounded like a sneeze would elicit a unanimous 'All fall down!') or 'Hands, Knees and Boomps-a-daisy' to provoke a response from the crowd – any meaningless crowbarred-in song title always went down well.

If Hatch's narration left even the vaguest room for wordplay, the cast would be in there. It didn't matter if they couldn't find an accompanying voice – after all, what does the sun, or a rock, or a leaf sound like? Never mind – one could just perform it 'in my leaf voice!'

But soon even the cast, especially Otto, would openly show their displeasure at the cheesy lines, and Cleese's delivery of them gets more flatly dismissive with every episode.

DH: On this particular day, a crowd had gathered listening to an old sailor, who was busy smashing up shellfish.

GG: Oh, a prawnbroker! (*Audience groan.*)

DH: All right, all right, all right. Just for once I thought we could do a sea story without the fish jokes, but I was wrong. If you want to do the fish jokes, all right, do the fish jokes, I don't care. Let's get 'em all out of the way before we start then. Come on.

JC: Good evening. Here are the fish jokes. Come back to my plaice and we'll have a whale of a time. Then you put your skates on and I'll wear my new shoes with Dover soles with the electric eels to give you a nasty shark on porpoise. Then we'll go for a long hake on the road to Manta-rays singing the tuna of 'Salmon Chanted Evening', 'Oyster The Mainsail' and 'Clam Every Mountain'. Finally, we'll visit the home of whales, kippers and whelks made out of the hide of eels . . . (*Audience sound unsettled.*) *Whale-Kipper-Whelk Home in the Eel's Hide* . . . (*Audience shout 'rubbish', 'off!' etc.*) And you can have that in whiting. And that concludes the fish jokes for today. Thank cod!

On another occasion, 'The *ISIRTA* team scored 22 fish jokes in 45.3 seconds, a new European world record. They will now collect their prize of three squid each.'

The *ISIRTA* team really cared about jokes, old and new, and were keen for the show to act as a safe haven for gags which may have seen better days, but deserved a fitting retirement. One of their ultimate tests came in an episode in which they faced certain death at the hands of Pirate Cleese:

TBT: . . . No, I am not Fred Shadow. Nor are these the wicked accountants you may have taken them for . . . I am Tim Brooke-Taylor and these are the cast of *I'm Sorry I'll Read That Again*.

JC: In that case, KILL THEM ALL!

TBT: Very well. Kill us, we won't be here for much longer anyway. (*Everyone weeps*)

GRAMS: Mournful music.

TBT: But please grant us one last favour. Spare our poor grey-headed jokes. They served us well as they did generations before us. Don't let them die. PLEASE DON'T LET THEM DIE! PLEEEASE . . . Was I all right? . . .

JC: . . . Well, Audience, it's up to you now. We've saved these good old jokes, so when we're gone, keep using them and if you bump into them let us know how they're getting on. And perhaps you'd like to write for details of our 'Adopt An Old Joke' scheme . . .

On the other hand, a notably Cleese-styled sketch revealed the darker side of jokes, with a hard-hitting documentary on the shady world of joke-swapping.

This bleak exposé closely follows the same lines as *Monty Python*'s sketch 'The Mouse Problem', but with Tim as a recovering joke addict.

TBT: As the evening wore on I sensed that something was up and I didn't think it was something an ordinary fella like me should get involved in. So I turned to Blanche, the bloke I was with . . . and I said, 'Let's get out of here.'

JC: But something made you stay on.

TBT: But something made me stay on. Well, the rest is easy to guess – since then joke-swapping has become part of my life.

JC: But where does this traffic in jokes go on?

TBT: In pubs mainly, a pusher will come up to you and say something like, 'I've got a good one here for you.' And of course, you know what he means . . .

In *ISIRTA*, jokes were not a laughing matter. They were a serious business, worthy of official announcements and warnings – on one occasion allowing Hatch to slip in an unusually cheeky dig at the competition: 'And now the *I'm Sorry I'll Read That Again* Spot the Joke competition number two . . . If you do spot any jokes, write them down on a postcard, and send them to *Round the Horne*. They want them back.' One episode in series 8 even began to sink under the weight of puns during the Prune Play '20,000 Leaks Under The Sea', and the cast had to man the life jokes just to stay afloat (and keep the Audience at bay).

The problem with puns, of course, is that they are seen as cheap. Children read joke books, while adult humour is supposed to be subtle, witty, dry. The sad thing is that *ISIRTA* had all that sophistication in abundance, but the Audience made the most noise when a pun was belted out, and that memory seems to have overshadowed the show's other strengths. Still, this weight of schoolboy howlers, lollipop-stick puns and groan-inducing grey-haired old woofers is undeniably the real fuel of *ISIRTA*, binding the Audience together into a barracking rabble of apparent comedy experts. On more than one occasion were these hundreds of punters heard to cry sarcastically 'Ha bloody ha!' in unison. And yet – listen to any episode you want – they're all audibly having the time of their lives. Giggling, roaring, moaning, groaning, hooting, cheering, booing, hissing – even telling their own jokes in unison – the *ISIRTA* Audience is louder and more present in every episode than any other radio comedy audience. And, as they join in with the traditional ritual of cheers and groans, every last one of them knows they're part of an exclusive club.

It's undeniably a cop-out, but the effect that *ISIRTA* had on the Audience at the Playhouse Theatre four decades ago can only be explained away with the trite adage 'You had to be there'. The fact that this raucous atmosphere became a holy grail to television producers (who would fail quite dismally in attempts to recreate the effect) proves that there was just something about the laid-back atmosphere generated at *that* time, and in *that* place, by *those* people. There's no replicating the chemistry that made it happen.

It's Sunday Evening . . .

But the laid-back atmosphere took a lot of work to generate. 'I had a pretty easy ride,' Barclay says, 'apart from the sheer slog of getting it done – I used to feel totally sick every Sunday. I could never eat all day, I was just a bundle of nerves . . .' Brooke-Taylor also remembers those 'days of rest' as hectic: 'The day never seemed long enough. Most of the effort went into the songs and fitting in the sound effects. We also tried to cut it down to length and some of this meant rewriting on the spot. The Sherlock Holmes pub was originally a retreat but, eventually, it seemed to contain most of the Audience . . .'

A typical Sunday recording would begin with everyone travelling from their homes dotted around the capital – Garden from the flat he shared with Eric Idle, Oddie from his leafy corner of Hampstead, Lizzie Evans (as was) and Jo Kendall from their flat in Earls Court, and so on – arriving at the theatre for 10.30 a.m., and getting their first of many caffeine fixes from the kindly woman who manned a tiny kiosk on the top floor. Only then would the group begin to go through that week's script.

Graeme Garden recalls: 'In the early days we used to meet during the week for a read-through of an evening, and then rehearse it on a Sunday, we'd all get together. We stopped doing that after a while, partly I think because the read-through tended to be when we would try stuff out and so we'd be selecting material, and if something didn't work then we'd have to look for another sketch to replace it with.' Lizzie Lord also recalls the Sunday morning meetings: 'We'd go through the script and be completely ruthless . . . nobody had seen the script until then, which I had laboriously typed and then run off on an old Roneo machine . . . Whole pages would be discarded. Whole new pages would be written. I remember Graeme saying once as we threw page twenty-one away "I think we could say page twenty-one has been tightened!" I recall a great amount of laughter – there were also arguments, but usually it was very funny. These were the days before computers, and I didn't even have a typewriter at the theatre so all script changes were made by hand by the cast on their own scripts. I had to keep track of it all and make sure everyone had all the changes.' Garden continues, 'Once Bill and I started writing the whole thing, we used to just get together on a Sunday, and do little bits of trims and rewrites in the afternoon, and then record the show in the evening. At the Playhouse Theatre in Charing Cross, once owned by Jeffrey Archer . . .

A superb, beautiful theatre, the one with the famous carvings of half-naked ladies on the side of the stage.' It is indeed a fine building, still standing, despite the dangerous period of dilapidation that followed its twenty-five years of use by the BBC, from *The Goon Show* right up to 1975. 'The recordings were terrific fun – we used to go to Lyons Corner House for steak afterwards, and it was a jolly day.'

Lord agrees: 'It was the best day of the week, Sunday ... After more or less agreeing the script, which would take all morning, we would take a break for lunch, which was always whatever the lady in the kiosk had on offer – nothing more glamorous than a few ham sandwiches and the odd bun ... Some of us would sometimes go out for a walk for ten minutes or so to get some fresh air, along the river. One day I walked along there and sat on a bench and chatted with John. He asked me what was going on in my life, and I told him my boyfriend wanted me to go round the world with him. I said I wanted to, but was worried about leaving the Beeb. John said I must be mad and that I should follow my heart – so I have John Cleese to thank for the fact that I've been married now for nearly forty years!'

As the cast ran through bits and pieces for the show, Evans and Barclay or Hatch would repair to the recording studio at the back of the theatre, where the studio managers would be, and run through the technical side of things, especially the sound effects both from library stock and recorded on the hoof, usually mastered by BBC audio buff Andy Cartledge. Many sketches and songs required a huge line-up of whistles and duck-calls and gongs and spot-effect props, most of them performed live by Oddie and others. Bill delighted in giving Cleese the job of providing some complicated musical sound effect, reducing the musically dyslexic star to a pool of nerves. By the time the props were dished out, Dave Lee, Leon Cohen and the Boys of all shapes and sizes had arrived and Bill would have a run-through of the songs and musical links. If necessary, rewrites of the sketches would also still be going on, very often by Cleese. He wasn't going to perform any material that he felt would make him look *too* ridiculous, if he could help it.

The final part of preparation was the full run-through with music and sound effects (played in on gramophone) at 5 p.m. This was the last chance to tighten up the show and throw out any gags which would fail to get even a convincing groan – after which, Lord remembers, 'everybody would go to the Sherlock Holmes pub for a half of bitter before the recording (which now I suppose nobody would dare do), while the Audience which had been queuing patiently outside filed in and took their seats – and then they'd do the show. It was very new, very young, and it was like a follow-on from *The Goon Show*, but sort of going in hand with the young revolution. In the sixties, every-thing was about being very young ...' In fact, great swathes of the Audience were under twenty, with blocks of tickets going to schools and a youth-led fan club. The chief Angus Prune Appreciation Society became so numerous that Humphrey Barclay wrote to BBC Enterprises begging them to help out with all the requests for signed photographs, badges, and printed lyrics for Bill's songs – not to mention the fan-made cuddly ferrets which were fast becoming a collector's item – but nothing came of his enquiry. Still, the fanbase was enthusiastic, and organized – and of course, they knew the score when it came to joining in with every show.

As well as Eric Idle and Terry Jones becoming fixtures in the crowd, the front row was often commandeered by Graham Chapman and his medical pals. He may have been dropped from the team, but Chapman's loyalty to his writing partner Cleese made the Sunday recording sessions a regular date, with his gang of boozy doctors-to-be. Clearly, if you're looking to create a boisterous, lively atmosphere, a mix of teenagers and drunk medical students is a great place to start.

Put On the Red Light

The show itself would kick off when Humphrey Barclay took to the stage to warm up the eager punters, crack a few jokes and explain the dos and don'ts of radio recordings. Or rather, the show would really begin when the cast appeared behind the dapper producer and began to take the piss. This tradition was the perfect weekly introduction to the show's philosophy of not standing for authority figures of any kind – Barclay may have been in many ways a long-standing servant of his wayward fellow graduates, but on the day he was The Man, and ripe for shaking. On the gang would troop, fresh from the pub – Oddie in garish flower-child get-up, Garden looking all of twelve in dark-rimmed specs and brilliantined quiff, Hatch naturally beautifully turned out in smart attire, Brooke-Taylor similarly dandy in sports jacket and tie, petite Kendall sporting hip Dylan cap and 'the latest fancy trends' and unquestionably not least, the stage-dominating figure of John Otto Cleese, the loudest mocker of them all.

'We were a good team, but all very different,' says Tim. 'Jo was different for fairly obvious reasons. A talented, attractive girl – though we were all attractive on radio. We did tend to play extensions of ourselves. John did not suffer fools. David as producer was by definition "Boring Old Hatch" – though of course he wasn't. Bill was a highly talented time bomb waiting to go off – fortunately the explosions were usually during his excellent songs. Graeme was the best at voices, impressions and writing . . . Though I was best at everything really.'

Having been unceremoniously booted offstage by the script-clutching rabble, Barclay would retreat to the recording booth, where Lizzie Evans was poised with her stopwatch, waiting for the official take to begin. Each show would always kick off with an almost arbitrary intro, with no fanfare, designed to catch the average Light Programme listener off guard. Perhaps an episode of *The Archers* would start, only for the characters to tune into *ISIRTA*, or there would be an experiment in stereo, or the latest from the Dwarf Olympics, or a special location report from John Cleese's bathtub (specifically, from somewhere on his right knee), anything to mess about with the format and shout from the hills that what would follow is not just another cosy comedy programme. Upon which, nothing could gee the crowd of excited spectators up more than the Angus Prune Tune. ('In accordance with tradition, whenever this piece of music is played, the audience rise, and leave the room.')

Graeme Garden had to be absent for a stretch, as he continued his medical training right up until 1967 – very often his submissions for each show would arrive on the back of envelopes sent up from wherever he was poking his stethoscope at the time. On one occasion in series 5, Kendall was also absent, and Jean Hart understudied just as she had done in New York – even going so far as to play Jo's part in a John & Mary sketch – albeit an odd 'prequel', in which John proposes.

Fluctuating casts aside, these early shows were bursting with jokes old and new, especially the in-jokes which the Audience were primed to cheer to the intricate rafters of the Playhouse every time. The planting of the seeds which eventually bloomed into these running gags was unspoken, with the repetition of references ever so subtly building up into wonderfully cheap laughs. For anyone unfamiliar with the shows, the Pavlovian response to random mentions of Dermot Staveacre or 'Hands, Knees and Boomps-a-daisy' must be confusing. Barclay insists that the eager Audience were never specifically led. 'We never held up signs or anything like that. We would just try to create an atmosphere – I would go on and do the warm-up, and encourage the cast to come on behind me and send me up. So that instantly established a kind of anarchy. Sometimes it would be written in a sketch that we wanted the Audience to shout out something, but we never whooped it up with signals for applause and all that kind of thing . . . and in those days when we were editing a show, we didn't sweeten it, or add any laughter. It was kind of unstoppable, we're all jolly glad to say.'

The experience of those Sundays down at the Playhouse is one that everybody there will take with them to their place of rest. David Hatch said that 'it wasn't just doing a show and wanting it to be good, it was seeing people and having a good chat with them, and seeing how people were getting on, getting married, having kids, and it's that sort of camaraderie that of course you miss. So if I miss anything it's the fact that we don't meet up occasionally on a Sunday and see how life is getting on.'

Audio pandemonium in the can, the cast and crew would head back to the Sherlock Holmes – or perhaps pop off for supper at Lyons Corner House – before wending their ways back home to the wives, or boyfriends, or kittens, with another half-hour of crowd-pleasing filth under their belts. Not the most relaxing way to spend a Sunday, and not especially lucrative either – but there's not a member of the team that doesn't remember the times fondly.

The Search for the Green Eye
The familiarity of so many of the show's traditions was especially aided by the two running serials which cropped up in *ISIRTA*'s lifetime. For the fourth series, kicking off at the end of 1966, Graeme Garden was unavoidably detained in a hospital in Plymouth, studying midwifery, but the shows were held together despite the loss of his vocal powers by the introduction of a regular story, 'The Curse of the Flying Wombat'. It was basically a way to hook the listener in with increasingly silly cliffhanger endings, and each instalment of the serial filled the Prune Play slot at the end of the programme. This aimless, facetious play on *Treasure Island* had a wavering plot that only a madman would try to summarise, but nevertheless . . .

The tale unfolds in London, 1850 (ten to seven). Like in so many of the previous Prune tales, the hero is the wet Everyman Timothy Brown-Windsor, who is press-ganged by a dodgy salt name of Old Hatch, onto the good ship *Flying Wombat*. There he meets Jimlad, who turns out to be 'a feminine female woman of the opposite', called Fiona Rabbit-Vacuum; not to mention the insane tyrannical Cap'n Otto Cleese, 'a tall barrel-chested, gimlet-eyed, beetle-browed, cheese & onion-flavoured man'. Their mission is to find the precious Green Eye of the Little Yellow Dog – a task instantly hampered by the discovery of a bomb on board, and before long the mighty ship starts sinking. Rather than plug the hole with a rhubarb tart, the problem is solved by the cry of 'Full steam upwards!' The villains of the piece, Oddie's Irish Casey O'Sullivan and his sidekick Masher Wilkins (Cleese with a pre-Gumby idiot voice to which he became so attached that Masher soon became another semi-regular character, bawling, yelling and threatening the hero whenever the plot required it), are introduced just prior to the much anticipated arrival of Grimbling (by carrier pigeon) and, of course, Brown-Windsor's auntie Lady Constance, who boards the *Flying Wombat* in Aberdeen. From then on, and throughout the story, much fun is made of Tim Brooke-Taylor's near-schizophrenic need to double up, and talk to himself in character ('In the theatre they call this versatility, in radio we call it economy'). The problem is redoubled when Lady Constance's sister Hurricane Flossie (also played by Tim) joins the crew and poor Tim tries to retain his sanity playing all three parts at once – although Kendall also becomes the star of several schizophrenic monologues, having to play all the female roles that aren't wobbly old sex maniacs. With all this confusion, it's no wonder that everybody forgets the plot.

But there's no need for spoiler warnings when it comes to the conclusion of 'The Curse of the Flying Wombat' – scribblers Oddie and Garden had strung the meandering escapade out to the end of the series' thirteen episodes, and that was the main point. Captain Cleese grabs the Green Eye and claims that he's Lady Constance, everybody else claims to be everybody else, and the story dissolves into catastrophe one more time . . .

'They Don't Make Children Like They Used To!'
. . . Only to bleed right into that year's Christmas special, 'Jack and the Beanstalk', which only kicks off because the Green Eye turns out to be still attached to the Little Yellow Dog, who then reveals himself to be the Director General of the BBC, played here by Cleese (although Garden would just as readily step into the role of Corporation bully later on, when Cleese was absent).

This breed of fascistic BBC Management chappie would be a prime motivator throughout the rest of *ISIRTA*'s run – a perfect threatening old fool, personifying the Corporation management types who would turn to Barclay and co. whenever the show raised any heckles within the Reithian halls, and intone, as Bill recalls, 'There once was a programme called *The Goon Show* and they don't work for us any more, so don't get uppity with us!' Cleese's DG was, again, the authority figure, ripe for raspberries and boos from the Audience. There was also a marked similarity to Graham Chapman's Colonel character in *Monty Python*, stepping in when the Prune gang were being too silly, and ordering them to shape up and offer some decent entertainment. But on this occasion, he steps in to launch the first ever *ISIRTA* panto.

The raucous pantomime every Christmas made perfect use of the show's traditions – often they weren't even tagged onto a run, but were a special end-of-year reunion months after that year's series, making those recordings even merrier and boozier than normal. The team are keen to point out that panto specials were commonplace back then, but no show suited the corniness and sauciness of pantomime better than *ISIRTA*. From 'Dick Whittington and his Wonderful Hat' to 'A Christmas Carrot', each Yuletide special still stands up today as a perfect encapsulation of the jovial, lackadaisical revelry of the recording nights, positively unprofessional in their let-it-all-hang-out exuberance. But they obviously weren't *real* pantos, being big sprawling spoofs of the whole pantomime tradition. And they weren't kid's stuff.

When the show was halfway through its lifespan (and at roughly the same time that a 'Best of' album was released by EMI, allowing the youthful Prune fanatic to relisten to shows for the first time ever), the Powers That

Were decided to grant it the distinction of an earlier broadcast than its regular 10 p.m. slot, with a repeat at the usual time. Hitherto it had always gone out at the later hour, with a more low-key Saturday lunchtime repeat. Barclay trumpeted the move to 5 p.m. in the *Radio Times* in April 1967:

Two phone calls and a postcard flooded in from all over the country when *ISIRTA* left the air in January, and within a week the letters had reached the astonishing and fish-paste total of five. We realised that there was nothing ferret but to bring back the Wonder Show as soon as possible ... 'Are there any changes?' the fans will want to know. ('*Aren't* there any changes?' plead the others.) Well, it's at a New Time on a New Day, and if all goes as planned, around the fourth programme there should be a New Joke. Otherwise what the *Daily Sketch* calls 'Radio's funniest show' will continue to bring joy to the masses in its own inimitable down your way ...

Naturally, publicity for the show was Barclay's job – as a cartoonist and artist (like so many others featured in this book), he always took great care in designing every bit of Prune bumph, working on designs for the EMI album and accompanying press articles with brilliant caricatures of the team that emphasised their glaring physical differences. He also masterminded many inspired photo sessions – the team with Barclay himself messing around with custard pies, Oddie sitting on Cleese's knee like a slightly more lifelike Archie Andrews, Kendall mocking the boys as they are all hung up on a row of coat-hooks, and of course the whole gang posing with specially made woolly ferrets.

But in authorising an earlier repeat, the schedulers seemed to be making the same mistaken assumption that would end up being made about *The Goodies* – that because the show was youthful, and fun, and appealed to younger listeners, that it could double as a 'kids' show'. The complexity and filthiness of the jokes seemed to pass BBC Management by, but no matter how clearly childish laughter is heard in the Audience, *ISIRTA* was not made for kids. Oddie is adamant that 'I personally *hate* panto, and probably half the fun I had in writing them is how much I hate them. I don't mind the stupid routines, as long as they are then recognised as stupid routines and sent up, you know. But the actual lack of care that goes into your average commercial pantomime is evil, I think. When people bemoan the death of pantomime, I'd dance on its grave any day.' Oddie's distaste is especially obvious in 'Jack and the Beanstalk' (Beanstalk played by Otto Cleese), in which the perverse crowd of ragamuffins insist on constantly booing poor Widow Liketo-bebesidetheseaside (played by Lady Constance/Brooke-Taylor), and cheering Hatch's villainous landlord. This is despite Cleese's threats that unless the 'boys and girls' do as they're told and refrain from rustling sweet papers, they will be shot. But the rebellious crowd's refusal to play ball continues:

JC: They don't make children like they used to!
BO: How are they doing it then?

One of the pitfalls of attracting a younger listenership was the attention from the BBC censors, who would obviously be casting a careful eye on any show airing on the Light Programme at teatime. As Roger Wilmut observes in *From Fringe to Flying Circus*, the trick was to place something broadly bawdy, and inevitably destined to fall beneath the censor's blue pencil, right next to a far more subtle, but ultimately far more risqué gag. Thus it was that the *ISIRTA* team managed to get a character called Martha Farquar onto the airwaves just as the nation's families settled down to their tea. But Oddie doesn't recall any notable struggles: 'Radio comedy has almost *always* been filthy – I mean, *Round the Horne* was non-stop, and ours was pretty bad sometimes . . . But by and large we didn't have a fantastic amount of trouble with censorship, and it got easier as the years went by. I think we were very well protected by our producers.'

Barclay himself says he had a pretty easy ride. Despite the early hour of broadcast, they had 'a freedom that we all relished, and eventually the lack of that I suppose got on top of one or two of us in the television world . . . We were never censored – I think one of the most borderline speeches was in the Robin Hood sketch, where Friar Tuck was dismissed with "And now Friar, Tuck – off!"'

David Hatch always treasured the laughably draconian Green Variety Producer Policy Guide with which all BBC producers were issued in the early days. This very silly document precluded mentions of 'suggestive references to honeymoon couples, chambermaids, fig-leaves, prostitution, ladies underwear (e.g. "Winter draws on . . ."), animal habits (e.g. rabbits), lodgers, commercial travellers . . . Pre-natal influences (e.g. "his mother was frightened by a donkey . . .").' These rules were of course made to be broken, and Tim Brooke-Taylor believes that the need to be suitable for a teatime audience was actually helpful, making everyone work harder to get the dirtiest jokes past the Powers That Be: 'That's why it got naughtier and naughtier. It got to the stage where Peter Titheradge cut something out, and I asked him why – he'd got into such a neurotic state, he said "Because the Audience laughed!" Because he didn't understand the line himself, he assumed it must be absolutely filthy.' The filthy-minded Boys that backed up Dave Lee were also a great barometer of a joke's suitability – if they laughed more than anyone else at a joke, there was probably a second meaning so dirty that it would have to be cut.

But it wasn't just filth that caught the attention of the BBC bods. In 1967 Bill Oddie was arrested for assaulting a policeman and a gag about the extra strain his antics put on the Metropolitan Police had to be taken out, as the matter still hadn't been settled in court by the time the episode was broadcast. Graeme attended Bill's eventual trial, and recalled that 'when the six-foot copper claimed Bill had kicked him in the chest a titter ran round the courtroom'.

With so much airtime and such an enthusiastic young, impressionable fan base, the show had never been more popular. 'Radio Rosemary' in the *Telegraph* wrote, on 23 July 1967, 'It is a worthy echo of *The Goons*, voices and all, and keeps a sharp eye on the quirks of other entertainers . . . Producer Humphrey Barclay should be given a free hand to flood the oily holiday beaches with his own brand of sound.' A sixth series was a cert. With a twice-weekly outing at new times, a successful new LP of highlights available in the shops, and a raucous crew of Prune groupies both in the Playhouse and in front of wire-lesses around the country, *I'm Sorry I'll Read That Again* was riding high throughout 1967. But then came a double change.

Oh, What a Giveaway!

First of all, and perhaps most historically, BBC Radio underwent the greatest alteration since its inception. In October 1967 the Home Service, the Light Programme and the Third Network were split into Radios 1, 2, 3 and 4, and the Prune team were quietly shifted over to Radio 2. There was no way they were going to let this pass unmentioned when they returned for the sixth series in the summer of '68. Once they'd wrung all the laughs out of bewailing the loss of the Light Programme, the team realised that the distinct person-alities of the new stations would give them brand-new jokes and clear targets, especially Jimmy Young and a whole host of 'cool' new DJs (or old codgers posing as new DJs – with the 46-year-old Young getting the worst of the abuse), many of whom, such as Emperor Roscoe, used to broadcast across both stations simultaneously in those early days:

DH: It's the David Hatch Show! Yes, it's Dave the rave on the medium wave – with another happy go-go ringing-dinging, bunky-futting, fronty-bucking, grunty-funking, funting-bunting . . . (That was close!) funky-butting funtime of fun and frolics on Radio Hatch!

EVERYONE: GET ON WITH IT!

The 'Groovy Hatch' phenomenon would become a regular joke, with each opening episode of the series featuring a narrative tale of the gang getting back together, as told by 'Dave's Diary'. This was the perfect way for the gang to remind everyone of their individual personalities from the off, so the in-jokes could hit the ground running – references to Jo Kendall's horse fixation and female impersonator Tim Brooke-Taylor's conspicuous status as the last unmarried man in the team being just some of the unsubtle slights.

However, the second big difference in the sixth series was a far more momentous watershed for the show. Humphrey Barclay had gone. As he remembers today, this was in no small way due to the young crowd that *ISIRTA* had been attracting: 'It was very interesting watching the evolution of this being late-night sophisticated comedy . . . to it being moved to midday, because clearly there was a young audience for it . . . and of course that's what led to my getting a television job in the end.' Yes, ironically for the man who had written into the credits many pokes at the lucrative world of 'sight radio', such as 'the script was by Tim Brooke-Taylor, David Hatch, Alan Hutchison, Eric Idle and Bill Oddie; and not John Cleese, who has sold all his to television . . .' Barclay was the first to be permanently lured away to TV – and not just any old TV, but collecting the commercial sovereign.

'I was extremely happy at the BBC,' he insists, 'I had decided in my mind that I had been a very lucky man, being carried by this host of amazingly funny and creative people, and this wouldn't last, the tide would go out one day, and they would all go off and do other things and I would be left beached, with no confidence in my ability to create anything else . . . When I went into the BBC people had kind of patted me on the head, and said "Ooh, future Director General", so I thought maybe that's the answer, that one day there would be a more protected role in management. Curiously, of course, that's what happened to David . . . So I applied for a traineeship to BBC Television Light Entertainment and got it, and was about to go and do it, when I got this letter from Jeremy Isaacs at Rediffusion [a company whose contract was already dying, it had seven months to go] and blow me, they wanted me to go to television and invent a children's show which had the same appeal as *I'm Sorry* . . .' The company already had the title – *Do Not Adjust Your Set* – but Barclay would honour their brief for a funny, raucous kids' show by hiring the best of the talent he had nurtured, who had not yet had a fair crack of the whip – *ISIRTA* stalwart Eric Idle would be defaulting on his decision to stay behind the pen and step in front of the cameras, along with his fellow regular Playhouse attendee Terry Jones, and Jones' writing partner Michael Palin. Joining them would be the gifted young comic actor David Jason, comedienne Denise Coffey and (providing the same kind of musical oomph that came from Bill, Dave Lee and the Boys) legendary art school misfits The Bonzo Dog Doo-Dah Band. And it would be a smash. But first he had to break it to the Beeb.

'Of course, it was incredibly difficult to go back to the BBC, and say I'd had an offer. The first person I had to go and speak to of course was Peter Titheradge, because I owed everything to him . . . and he instantly said, "You must go, dear boy, you must go." I then had to go and see the Head of Light Entertainment Tom Sloane . . . He said, "If you stay with the BBC, and come to television we'd give you the best training in the world, and then it's possible that at the end of that time you might be eligible to be considered for a post which might conceivably lead to being the assistant to . . ."' It didn't take long for Barclay to see that immediate creative control of his own show outclassed this offer several times over, and so off he went.

Many producers are easily forgotten, but Barclay's participation in each of his shows was always a conspicuous stamp of quality and his name became well known, not least due to the way that 'the blame' for each episode of *I'm Sorry I'll Read That Again* was always loudly laid at his door in the closing credits to each show – on one occasion he had to close the show on his own when John Otto Cleese ordered the whole cast to walk out with him, in disgust at the Audience's behaviour. Over the next forty years, Barclay would produce countless great half-hours, often with heavy Cambridge links, including the *Doctor* series, *End of Part One*, *Up the Garden Path*, *Surgical Spirit*, Simon Nye's ITV Christmas pantos of the nineties, and Simon Pegg and Jessica Stephenson's slacker comedy *Spaced*. But these successes as the Great Producer would never match up to the experience he had learning his trade alongside his contemporaries on *I'm Sorry I'll Read That Again*. From answering Brooke-Taylor's call for an organiser in the Footlights clubroom, to New Zealand and Broadway, to the BBC and years of carefully building the perfect audio home for his protégés, selecting the best sketches and funniest sound effects, *I'm Sorry . . .* was undeniably Barclay's baby.

And yet, with each of the team now enjoying their own success outside of the world of Prune, the loss of the originator was not exactly the apocalypse it might have been. There was no stopping Radio Prune now. And so, when Barclay gathered his old friends together to tell them the bad news at the end of 1967, he recalls with a laugh that the bombshell was met with 'roars of apathy'. Just as when he broke the news of his retirement from revue performance back in the Footlights clubroom, or when he bowed out of the New York run of *Cambridge Circus*, Barclay left quietly, and amiably, with best wishes from everyone, and the show went on.

6

Full-Frontal Radio

The tensions between radio and television within the BBC had been marked since the rise of TV's popularity in the 1950s. When the *ISIRTA* team first began broadcasting, the wireless bosses may have still looked down their noses at their brasher sister, but by just 1958, the number of houses in the UK with TV sets already outnumbered those with only radio. Transferring radio stardom to TV stardom had been a goal for many performers since before *Hancock*'s successful move to the visual medium, so it's no surprise that the Prune performers had all dipped their toe in TV comedy long before Barclay made his decisive move.

Tim Brooke-Taylor was the first to make his mark on the small, grey flickering screen, becoming well known for all the wrong reasons when he took over from Peter Cook's E. L. Wisty slot on ATV's *On The Braden Beat*, not long after his return to Blighty after the New York run of *Cambridge Circus*. He experienced a similar problem to Warren Mitchell while playing Alf Garnett in *Till Death Us Do Part*, coming on every week as a bowler-hatted City gent who believes himself to be the soul of liberality, but displays the most appallingly snobbish prejudices against all walks of life. 'It was certainly terrifying following Peter Cook – I still think he's the funniest person I've ever met, so to follow someone like that is not easy. It was a different character, and it was extraordinary doing him . . . but when you realise some people are starting to take this person seriously, you know it's time to stop. I actually heard people in the pub agreeing with my character, it was just awful. I'd say things that were trying to be right, like "They work like slaves, blacks – extremely hard", you know, but that's how people would talk in those days.' Tim found that censorship of TV comedy was much harsher than anything he'd come up against before. 'When I was doing that, Kenneth Tynan was saying "fuck" for the first time, and I was being censored for material on Princess Margaret, because she was misbehaving, and I'd say things like 'She must remember she's British – at least on her mother's side'. They actually censored that and downgraded the sound, almost to the minute that Tynan was saying "fuck"!' Bill Oddie fared slightly better, chipping in with a few songs on the show, plus walk-on parts in *TW3*, before getting the job of performing topical numbers on Ned Sherrin's 1965 follow-up show, *BBC 3*.

A Frosty Reception

It was Cleese, however, who made the first real splash on the box, as part of the team on David Frost's massively popular *Frost Report*, performing sketches live alongside Ronnies Barker and Corbett, and self-confessedly coming close to fouling himself with sheer terror at the experience. Of course, there's hardly an icon of sixties or seventies comedy that wasn't thankful for *The Frost Report* – the show's hunger for material meant that writers from stalwart Denis Norden to relatively green scribes like the young Barry Cryer all earned daily bread from turning in jokes.

David Frost's titanic influence was felt on the careers of almost every performer featured in this book, from his promotion of Cleese to the inclusion of Willie Rushton in the *TW3* team. But it's no wonder that his enormous success (allied to his legendary reputation for 'borrowing' from his hero Peter Cook) set him up as a popular hate figure among the *ISIRTA* team. The older and wiser comics would now no doubt insist that 'hate' is putting it far too strongly, but there are few figures dealt with in such a bitchy manner in *ISIRTA* than the jet-setting Son of a Preacher Man – he was after all ubiquitous, and so the slightest squeaky 'Thank you, thank you' from Cleese would get a roar of recognition from the Audience. Even in the very first show, 'David Frost and himself' are listed among the roll-call of famous love stories; but Frost was most comprehensively targeted in a sketch similar to a sequence later on in *Monty Python* (starring Eric Idle in 'Timmy Williams' Coffee Time!'), directly showing the falseness behind the trailblazer's cheesy persona, in 'The Kevin Mousetrap Show':

GG: Ladies and gentlemen, it's the Kevin Mousetrap Show!

<u>GRAMS:</u> <u>Cheesy TV Theme.</u>

GG: Yes, Kevin Mousetrap, what's he doing tonight? Who's he talking to? Where is he? What's he up to? Here am I waiting at home, his supper will be stone cold, gallivanting off, never so much as a by-your-leave, I don't know . . .

DH: And here he is, Kevin Mousetrap! (*Audience applaud.*)

JC: Thank you, thank you, very much, well, we've got a wonderful marvellous super terrific show for you tonight and you'll be meeting some wonderful marvellous super terrific people, so straight away here's the first wonderful marvellous super terrific

guest star celebrity personality of the show – ME! . . . This
brings us to our next guest – philosopher, wit, traveller, and
appalling old bore, Arnold P. Totteridge.

GG: Ah, good evening. (*Audience roar!*) How d'you do, d'you do
d'you do . . . do you?

Over forty years on, Garden obviously underplays the distaste shown for the
man who would go on to become the great knight of TV political interviews:
'In those days there wasn't a route from university to show business like there
is now, it was kind of opened up by *Beyond the Fringe*, and then David Frost
took it by the horns and really went for it career-wise – and was a bit resented
for it at the time, although over the years I think he's done people's careers
much more good than harm.'

Besides, it wasn't just Frost – TV was sent up at every opportunity in
ISIRTA, from Hughie Greene's transatlantic drivelling in *Opportunity Knocks*
to the random cries of 'Open the box!' and 'Take the money!' alluding to
Take Your Pick. The team also weren't averse to blatantly pointing out just
how badly paid radio work was in comparison to TV writing and performing,
in one episode begging a half-crown from their Fairy Prunemother to make
an entire series. There's even a reference to the growing attitude towards radio
as a secondary medium in one of the early episodes, dealing with listener's
letters:

DH: 'Dear sir. I only ever listen to good old steam radio, because I
can't afford a television. I think it's deplorable that because of
this I am denied the pleasure of the visual arts. I feel I am being
rigorously victimised. Radio must have more visual appeal, otherwise I shan't watch it. So there. P.S. There must be thousands
like me.'

TBT: I very much doubt it . . .

Certainly, to survive in London (let alone convince their parents that they
weren't squandering their highfalutin degrees), the *ISIRTA* team knew
they had to find some form of lucrative work outside of the World of Prune.
The late sixties was infamously a time for experimentation for young people,
and the Footlights alumni experimented with comedy in a TV format a great
deal before any of them got it right. As Cleese recalls, 'It was a general pool
of people who got together in different manifestations. Sort of like watching
little amoebae under a microscope, all moving around and joining up with each
other. And occasionally people would break into one group or another . . .'

After *The Frost Report*, Frost had packed Cleese and Chapman off to Ibiza to work on the screenplay for his company Paradine Productions' movie vehicle for Peter Cook, the crafty satirical flop *The Rise and Rise of Michael Rimmer*. Tim Brooke-Taylor and *Frost Report* head writer Marty Feldman flew over to the island to meet them for a brief holiday in the sun towards the end of 1966. The four of them gelled so well that when Frost joined the party and invited Cleese and Brooke-Taylor to star in their own ITV sketch show, it was only natural for first Chapman, then (at both John and Tim's insistence) Feldman to come on board. Frost and the channel heads weren't too sure about presenting Feldman's bug-eyed features to the British Public – and he had misgivings of his own, having kept strictly adhered to the typewriter for years, firing out filth for Rambling Sid Rumpo or centrepiece sketches on *The Frost Report*.

But the three Cambridge lads and the startling ex-Music Hall clown scored a small but palpable hit with *At Last the 1948 Show*, which first aired in February 1967, making a clear leap from the days of the satire boom with two series bursting with an anarchy and insanity unlike anything else in TV comedy at the time. Although the show now exists mainly in compilation form filched from Swedish TV and wobbly off-air recordings discovered in somebody's attic on the other side of the Earth, it's perhaps the single strongest representation of *ISIRTA* humour on television that we have.

Certainly a weight of Cleese/Chapman/Brooke-Taylor material from the radio show turns up translated into a three-camera set-up. And often, it still works even with the loss of the imagination required to hear the dialogue and sound effects alone. A sketch in which Chapman plays a politician who literally falls to pieces while being interviewed by Brooke-Taylor was almost word-for-word recycled from *ISIRTA*, in which the parts were played by Hatch and Cleese. The *ISIRTA* version only pre-dates the TV sketch by a few months, and is of course set in a TV studio in the first place, but the original is still probably superior for allowing the listener's imagination to run riot as the politician gradually disassembles – although Chapman's visible dismay at his misfortune when playing the Cleese role for TV does go some way to make up for the sketch's radio roots.

Similarly, one of the first episodes of *At Last the 1948 Show* features the age-old 'Top of the Form' sketch, but more laughter comes from Feldman, Chapman and Brooke-Taylor switching costumes at top speed to play both the boys' and girls' teams than from the script itself. The efforts put in to create great TV from great radio paid off brilliantly (which makes listening to the LP released of *At Last The 1948 Show* highlights an odd experience for any listener familiar with *ISIRTA*).

So much material, going all the way back to *Cambridge Circus*, was repeated in *At Last the 1948 Show* that it's no wonder that most of *ISIRTA*'s Magnificent

Six and a Half show up at some point during the two series that bookended 1967. Bill Oddie put in several appearances, most notably as a distraught patient dealing with Brooke-Taylor's malfunctioning automated hospital visitor in the old *Cambridge Circus* sketch 'Patients, For the Use of', and Jo Kendall's appearances include the only televised version of the original classic John & Mary sketch.

Cleese and Kendall appeared as lovers again in an extended sketch, sending up the danger of live drama in much the same way that Victoria Wood's *Acorn Antiques* sketches would perfect twenty years later. The pair play actors in a Victorian melodrama called 'The Willetts of Littlehampton' contending with an invasion from Tim as a TV executive showing around a gaggle of rich Arabs, and particularly one cheeky specimen played by Feldman, who opts to sit between the romantic leads during their passionate love scene, grinningly lasciviously.

A similar extended sketch gave a bigger part for Oddie, as a tiny sidekick to Cleese's villainous Macdonald, also featuring Brooke-Taylor as an inept James Bond cipher. The melodramatic thriller 'Mice Laugh Softly, Charlotte':

INT. A COUNTRY HOUSE STUDY. NIGHT.
Oddish(Brooke-Taylor) breaks into a study by nightfall, only to be trussed up in a chair by the menacing Kobalski (Oddie), as the lights come up and Macdonald (Cleese) is discovered in an armchair, disguised in dark glasses, with a pistol trained on Oddish. Beside him is a chess table.

JC: Good evening, Mister Oddish. Welcome to Locksby.
TBT: Doctor Atkins! (*Macdonald removes his sunglasses, revealing an eyepatch.*) Professor Nuberg! (*Macdonald shifts the eyepatch to the other eye.*) Fu Tong! (*He removes the eyepatch altogether.*) Macdonald!
JC: The same.
TBT: So it was a trap!
JC: Yes. Checkmate, Mister Oddish, you have made your last move. (*He moves a chesspiece, and then eats it.*)
TBT: I wouldn't be too sure, Macdonald, I still have one or two tricks up my sleeve.
JC: Kobalski! Search his sleeves! Especially – up them!
       Kobalski examines Oddish.
BO: Nothing!
JC: Nothing? I'll teach you to bluff me, Oddish! All right! Kobalski, go to Moresby, fetch the car, and collect the girl. (*Exit Kobalski.*)
TBT: Not – Susan!

JC: Yes, Mister Oddish, your pretty little Miss Hinton.

TBT: You swine!

Macdonald strikes Oddish several times, unconvincingly – the camera angle reveals that no strikes connect. Re-enter Kobalski.

JC: What is it, Kobalski?

BO: I can't drive!

JC: You can't drive? FOOL! DOLT! PIG! (*He hammers Kobalski into the floor*) I'll teach you to drive . . .

BO: Oh, thank you, sir!

As the spoof dissolved into frantic Marx Brothers-style chaos (like so many other sketches in the series), 'Mice Laugh Softly, Charlotte' called for one of many supporting roles to be played by a youthful Buddy Holly lookalike called Barry Cryer, who popped up more than any other bit-part player – even Eric Idle, who had by now recovered his acting chops and was soaking up the TV-making process immediately prior to being given his first proper break by Barclay, in *Do Not Adjust Your Set*.

With its constant stream of spoofs, 'The Story So Far . . .' intros, pompous news items and silly extended sketches, *At Last the 1948 Show* is definitely the most cogent visual accompaniment to *ISIRTA* that we have. The fact that Cleese and Brooke-Taylor were given the rare distinction of being 'Editors' of the show proves that the quartet were given extraordinary freedom. So as *Cambridge Circus* and *ISIRTA* were what they knew best, it's no wonder that the series so closely resembles *ISIRTA*, right up to the epic rendition of 'The Ferret Song' that closes the first series, made even funnier by the spectacle of everyone from the cast lined up in evening dress, solemnly giving the silly ditty their all.

But, bar the odd appearance from Bill and Jo, *At Last the 1948 Show* was only half an *ISIRTA* show. The true raucous spirit that had come to dominate the radio recordings was absent – but plans were afoot to do something about that.

Medicine's Loss . . .

The only really conscious attempt to recreate the mayhem of *I'm Sorry I'll Read That Again* on TV is also the one real reason why showbiz finally managed to lure Doctor Graeme Garden away from a life in medicine. By 1967 he had completed his studies and only required one year of active doctoring as a resident to be fully qualified. However, sharing a flat with the ambitious young Eric Idle could not fail to be a deciding factor in Garden's decision to stick with comedy. It's tempting to see these two young hungry comics, living together in the middle of London in the swinging sixties, as a very hip couple of young bucks, but Garden is keen to disabuse anyone of that impression. 'We used to go out and have meals together and go to the pub, but we used to have separate circles of friends – and also the people we were working with, because Eric was getting in to working with Jones and Palin at the time, so they used to breeze round quite often. It wasn't a particularly wild time, as I recall it. But I was engaged, and about to get married for the first time. And I was leading a particularly boring life at that point, because my fiancée wasn't around . . . I had to leave the swinging for a while. It was on hold.'

Having signed up with Idle's legendary showbiz agent, Tony's brother Roger Hancock, Garden was still split between the stethoscope and the tickling stick when he went in to see the great man, one day slap bang in the Summer of Love. The elder expert in the business of show was trying to impress on Garden the gravity of his decision. 'Now, Graeme, you can't just muck about at it, you've got to decide whether you just want to go on writing as a hobby, or whether you're prepared to go out and get the work, because nobody's going to ring up and ask for you . . .' At that moment, the phone rang, and on the other end was a Cambridge contemporary of Graeme's called Tony Palmer, who was setting up a new TV project. 'Hello. I understand you represent Graeme Garden – would he like to appear in a new comedy show called *Twice a Fortnight*?' As Roger's eyes popped out of his head, the grin on the bespectacled young Garden sitting opposite gave him the only answer he needed. Medicine was deferred until further notice.

'I thought, "Well, I could put the medical job off for six months, till the next round of them comes up, but I'll probably never have another offer of a TV series, and I'd really like to try that and see what it's like." So I put the medical job off, and did the TV series, and one thing led to another . . . I don't know how because it was such a dreadful series.' Unlike *At Last the 1948 Show*, there's so little left of *Twice a Fortnight*, at least visually, that it's hard to refute Garden's summary. 'It was in a way a kind of breakthrough show. Tony Palmer's idea was to get some of the chaos and the wildness of the radio – I don't think he realised that it was quite as carefully planned on the radio as it was, he thought we just went on and made it up as we went along or something.' The title was Eric Idle's idea (as was the inclusion of Garden, no doubt), and the elements that made up the show came from many sources, though *ISIRTA* was definitely the main inspiration.

Although the producer himself has laid the blame for the idea firmly at Oddie's door in the past, history has decided that it was Palmer who wanted to deliver in a TV format the kind of party atmosphere created at the Playhouse Theatre on those Sunday nights. But his methods weren't ideal. 'He gave the audience party-squeakers and glasses of wine as they came in so they'd sound even more like a football crowd than the radio audience,' continues Garden, 'which was disastrous, just asking for trouble. And it was a completely chaotic show – it was my first experience of doing a TV series, so I thought they were all like that. But it was ridiculous.' Oddie remembers the realisation that they were going to go out, live, to a baying mob as rowdy as any Prune Audience. 'When we saw they had squeakers, we were going "oh, fucking hell – they're *armed* now!" It was murder.' The plan to create a comedy supergroup of Oxford and Cambridge stars, which would yield such legendary results as *Monty Python*, simply didn't gel, and the atmosphere in the studio is recalled as fraught to say the least, with Palmer earning a reputation for being an *enfant terrible* (which, as Garden pointed out, translated as 'awful child'), with tantrums a regular danger on-set. Palmer was a distinguished maker of music documentaries, well connected with all the hottest bands, and also produced Jonathan Miller's *Alice in Wonderland* film (in which Eric Idle was an extra), but this one experiment with TV comedy did not play to his strengths.

There were saving graces though – 'There was some good filmed stuff that Mike Palin and Terry Jones put together and wrote, and we went off and filmed together, and that was fun,' says Garden. 'It was during that that we did the send-up of *The Seventh Seal*, which I think they used in one of the *Python* movies. Me as the Knight, and Terry Jones as Death, playing chess on the beach.' This footage ended up being spliced into an early trailer for *Holy Grail*, marking the only appearance from a Goodie in any Python product. Oddie found it impossible to resist getting involved with the filmed inserts, aiming to 'tickle up' Palin and Jones's slow-paced ideas, and gaining crucial film knowledge that would come in handy for *The Goodies* just a few years later.

With this frankly jarring mix of pastoral movie inserts and ramped-up live bedlam, it's no surprise that the audio footage of *Twice a Fortnight* is a confusing relic – old stalwarts from the *Cambridge Circus* days Tony Hendra and Jonathan Lynn, plus Germaine Greer, were on hand to perform in the studio sketches, but between the rowdiness of the crowd and the filmed-as-live pressure the performers were under, few of the studio items hit the mark. 'It's a show I wish there was some footage of, I've never seen any,' admits Oddie today. 'But God almighty, it was a mess. Nevertheless, it had some very interesting precedents in it – I think in a weird way it was a bit ahead of its time. In a funny sort of way it was a bit Vic & Bob, I could see a sort of relationship to that kind of show which is actually a bit of a mess, really, but there's a place for it.'

The Prune flavour of the proceeds is apparent from Oddie's signature tune – another Spike Jones-inspired number kicking off the anarchy every week. Each sketch was also punctuated with vaudevillian stings from the band, identical to those on the radio show. The first episode even ended with part two of a pirate serial (featuring a Grimbling-a-like called Gooseberry), bursting with gags from 'The Curse of the Flying Wombat', many of which elicit groans from the audience. But while the groaning seems affectionate in *ISIRTA*, here it seems damning – even when the cheapness of gags is acknowledged, such as Jonathan Lynn's line "Tis very rough, sir!' to which Captain Garden replies, 'I know, but we still get paid for it . . .'

JL: Look up there in the sky! 'Tis a bird!

TH: 'Tis a plane!

GG: No, 'tis a bird . . .

JL: 'Tis a messenger pigeon!

GG: Aye, and what's that tied to its leg?

JL: A messenger!
We hear a bird shriek and a body fall, and GOOSEBERRY (Oddie) enters.

BO: Oh, blimey. Good morning gentlemen!

GG: Why, 'tis Gooseberry, our faithful messenger boy!

BO: Two days have I been travelling like that!

GG: You poor old soul. Your hair has turned quite white!

BO: Well if you'd been tied under a pigeon for two days, your hair would be white.

JL: That's a very old and rather unpleasant joke.

BO: It was a very old and rather unpleasant pigeon, actually.

'There was a bit of crossover from *ISIRTA*,' Graeme recalls, 'I'm sure we did the odd Doctor sketch or something, but I honestly can't remember what was in it.' In fact, few people bar the most devoted archivists care to remember much about *Twice a Fortnight*. One of the few things that people *do* care to remember about it, however, was the amazing array of rock bands that performed in the studio. The music documentary-maker Palmer managed to get vintage performances out of The Small Faces, Cream, Cat Stevens and The Who, who gave a storming rendition of 'I Can See for Miles' in the very first show. This in itself did not best please Oddie, who, despite being a fan of all the bands on the bill, was looking for a way to present his own music on TV. Not long after the untrumpeted finale of *Twice a Fortnight*, Bill's management would be contacting BBC TV about a new musical vehicle for him, which would never see the light of day.

Twice a Fortnight ran for ten weeks in the autumn of 1967, alongside the second outing for *At Last the 1948 Show*, and wasn't such a hopeless case that a follow-up series wasn't mooted. The late Saturday night slot hadn't helped the viewing figures (Oddie subtitled the show 'Match of the Day Part 2' to try and bump up the ratings), but given time it could well have taken root as the first genuinely cool youth comedy programme on TV, a kind of precursor to *Saturday Live*. The show also takes the honour of planting the passion for visual humour that would set both Palin & Jones and Oddie & Garden in good stead for their individual successes in *Monty Python* and *The Goodies*. But the next TV excursion from the *ISIRTA* camp featured a completely new duo, as Brooke-Taylor and Garden teamed up for *Broaden Your Mind*.

Banana Men

Ironically, *At Last the 1948 Show* proved the most immediate success for the one member of the team who was nearly prevented from taking part. The BBC gave Marty Feldman his own show (in colour!) almost immediately after series two finished, and Tim Brooke-Taylor stepped down to become a supporting player and co-writer of Feldman's frenetic, bizarre programmes. Playing straight men in *Marty* and *It's Marty* at least kept his face on the box (even as second banana) and also provided his first professional link to John Junkin (as third banana). In the next show to emerge from the *ISIRTA* fold, Junkin would be promoted to second banana, as well as conducting the studio warm-ups.

TV bosses were still more than keen to try and find the right visual vehicle for these frightfully funny young Oxbridge comedians, even if a red-hot, stone-cold TV hit was yet to be made by any of them. With so much potential recognised in these fellows, it's little wonder that, while working on *Marty*, Tim was given the go-ahead to put together his own show, inspired by the then current popularity of encyclopedias bought in regular instalments. *Broaden Your Mind: An Encyclopedia of the Air* was entirely Tim's baby, but he decided not to go it alone, roping in Graeme to form a double act. 'I think, partly, I've got to thank Eric Idle for that,' he remembers, 'I knew Graeme of course, from *ISIRTA* and to a certain extent, Cambridge. But I'd been writing some stuff with Eric and meeting up and going to the football with him, and I remember saying, "Gosh, who do you think would be good?" I can't remember if Graeme had just given up medicine, but he was sharing a flat with Eric. And that was the sort of matchmaking, really. Graeme and I have always got on, but we didn't know each other that well then. And of course it was the best decision I've ever made.'

Despite his talents, Tim insists, 'I always lack confidence in writing, and that's why I was much better writing with people. I always find that if you're on your own, you think, "Oh, that's rubbish," and you put it away, but I did enjoy writing with – well, John Cleese, Graham Chapman and Marty Feldman.' With Dr Garden, such an industrious writer (he'd managed to steer 'The Flying Wombat' through weeks of adventures while delivering babies in Plymouth), Tim had really struck platinum. 'He's always been a good writer.

He's probably the most underestimated person I've ever met. I mean, the rest of the world is *beginning* to learn how good he is, but it's extraordinary . . . because he hasn't got that pushy-pushy side to him, they don't realise what an incredibly good performer he is, and a very clever writer. Why is *If I Ruled The World* not still on? It's so much better than all the other rubbish, and he was really good in that. He's not pushy enough, but that's part of his talent. It subtly creeps up on you . . .'

Especially with Garden's convincingly academic tones opening each episode, *Broaden Your Mind* was, in essence, Peter Serafinowicz and Robert Popper's cult hit *Look Around You*, thirty-five years early. Garden and Brooke-Taylor introduced each show in the TV studio in front of a live audience (who were thankfully not inebriated or in possession of toy squeakers), presenting a series of sketches in the studio and on film, and dispensing silly information and competition questions.

So many episodes of *ISIRTA* contained extended sketches taking a cheeky look at aspects of modern life in a documentary style (unemployment, housing, marriage, etc.) that Brooke-Taylor and Garden had a huge amount of scope for making quick-fire TV mockumentaries about serious issues. As the sixth series of *ISIRTA* was practically concurrent with *Broaden Your Mind*, fans of both shows would have had the strange experience of seeing the same comic ideas being broadcast on the wireless and on the television within months of each other. The Old Colonel characters for instance, who always cropped up in the *I'm Sorry* investigations grumbling about that week's topic, were reproduced on the TV by Garden, Brooke-Taylor and supporting actor Roland MacLeod, as 'The Buffies'.

Broaden Your Mind reused a fair bit of *ISIRTA* material, although Garden believes that the recycled sketches proved to be low points in the show, having not been written specifically for the medium. The most popular characters from the first series were certainly the bumbling ancient anti-raconteurs Teddy & Freddy, but even these originated from *ISIRTA*, with David Hatch accompanying Tim, who was known as Timmy. The names may differ between TV and radio, but the characters' role in the show remains the same – to bumble on with something to say about history, or art or science, but then get caught in a never-ending stream of decrepit misunderstanding, effectively splitting Garden's Totteridge character into two in much the same way as the Dagenham philosophers Pete & Dud emerged from a last-minute sharing of an E. L. Wisty monologue (although in *The Complete Goodies*, Robert Ross accurately notes that Teddy & Freddy could also be seen as a less childishly filthy version of Newman & Baddiel's 'History Today' professors featured in *The Mary Whitehouse Experience* twenty-five years later).

Garden and Brooke-Taylor admit that their love of the Teddy & Freddy characters could have led them to continue doing them forever, self-indulgently basking in their lovable ditherings – indeed, the characters still have life in them today, being only slightly dusted down for an encore in the pair's 2005–7 *Goodies* tour. But after the first series of *Broaden Your Mind* went out at the end of 1968, it was decided that lovability was one of the things holding the show back (indeed, viewer feedback from the very first episode reported that the 'two nice young men' who starred, were 'much more warmly regarded than their material'), and so Bill Oddie was brought in full-time at the suggestion of regular contributor Barry Cryer to inject a bit of his own personal nastiness into the proceedings. He'd already been a key part of the first series, finally getting the chance to put some of his favourite *ISIRTA* numbers on the screen – such as performances of songs like 'My Identikit Gal' and the centrepiece of Oddie's concept musical 'The Sound of Monks', the Julie Andrews-flavoured 'Antibellumlaudedaturarmamutarum' – and another link to *ISIRTA*, all of these musical moments were masterminded by the trusty Dave Lee.

But between Oddie's bigger role in the proceedings and Teddy & Freddy being reduced to just one appearance, the second series of *Broaden Your Mind* was quite a different show when it went out in 1969. With the union of Brooke-Taylor, Garden and Oddie, the direction of Jim Franklin, and even details such as Garden's regular use of an enormous computer throughout the series, the foundations of *The Goodies* was set, at roughly the same time that Cleese was preparing to make the phone call to Michael Palin that would provide the spark for his ideal TV vehicle, *Monty Python's Flying Circus*. Cleese had submitted material to *Broaden Your Mind* when it started out (along with Feldman, Took, Chapman, Cryer, Idle, Palin, Jones and *ISIRTA* alumni Chris Stuart-Clark, Simon Brett and David McKellar), but soon *Python* would provide a home for all his sketch material, which he could bring to the screen on his own terms.

So by the end of the decade no one single TV translation of *ISIRTA* had really taken off, and now the lines were beginning to be drawn up between the different factions of the *Cambridge Circus* team.

Humphrey Barclay's move to commercial TV was no great defection, then – they'd all got there before him. And indeed, a few members of the *ISIRTA* team were to be grateful for Barclay's move to TV. After giving the careers of Idle, Palin, Jones, Jason and Terry Gilliam a boost with *Do Not Adjust Your Set* (even writing letters to the US government to help prevent Gilliam from being drafted into the US Army), Barclay was given the task of adapting the *Doctor* books by Richard Gordon into a sitcom format. David Hatch had already scored a hit producing a radio version starring Richard Briers a couple of years previously, but writing the scripts for the TV version would prove a lucrative sideline for Oddie & Dr Garden and Cleese & Dr Chapman, and even provide the initial inspiration for *Fawlty Towers* in a Cleese episode featuring a pompous, rude hotel manager. Garden was still flexing his medical funny bone for Barclay decades later when the latter invited him to write for ITV hospital sitcom, *Surgical Spirit*.

A Two for One Deal

Humphrey Barclay wished the team well, but he does admit to being pleased to note one big difference when *ISIRTA* returned to the air in the spring of '68 – it required two people to do his job. David Hatch of course was an obvious choice to take the reins, having been producing radio shows successfully since the very start of his time at the BBC – nobody knew the ins and outs of putting together *I'm Sorry I'll Read That Again* like he did. The extra money couldn't have hurt either, with a young family to support.

But he did have the problem of not being able to be in two places at once, and so he roped in everybody's friend Peter Titheradge (who wasn't even officially a producer, enjoying the pleasingly vague title of the Organiser of the Light Entertainment Department). 'When it was clear that Humphrey was going, it was felt, because I was already a radio producer, that I would take over, but I couldn't do it all because I was on the stage as well. So I needed somebody to sit in the box, and make sure that everything was working properly. So Peter (who'd never produced a programme in his life, but was a dear friend and a great mentor of us all) said "I'll do it" – and he was quite old at this point, probably fifty-five or something, and we were all in our twenties. So he used to sit in the box, smoking furiously, and at the end I'd ask if it had all gone OK, and he'd say "I wouldn't mind a retake on that or that . . ." and we'd do it.' Lizzie Lord, who stayed behind to assist Hatch and Titheradge, remembers the man fondly: 'I thought he was as old as God, but he was probably forty-five! He was unmarried, a certain type of man, very artistic, very theatrical in his tastes . . . a delightfully charming man. He was very supportive of Jo, I think she was a bit out on a limb . . .'

Titheradge had started out as a writer (besides several other pre-BBC careers, not to mention his adventurous exploits with the British Army in India), but Graham Chapman was to state that 'he'd given up writing because he said, "I'm just not angry any more, at anything," and I think a lot of the thing with writing is you have to be angry about something; you have to inject some kind of message into what you're saying, even though it's not obvious. You're not stuck for a subject if you're angry about something . . . I'm angry about almost everybody.' Nevertheless, Titheradge remained a man of words to the end, with a number of celebrated poems to his name.

Hatch always had great respect for his predecessor, insisting that 'Humphrey was the guy who really put the stage show together, he had picked the cast and chosen the material – with some input from us, but basically he was the producer/director, and he decided what the items would be and in which order they would run. So he was sort of our guru ... a very good editor of material, he knew what would work and what would not. He was respected by us all.' But at the end of the day, the whole ethos of *ISIRTA* had been anarchy, built on a gleeful lack of professionalism. 'We were all guilty of it – Humphrey in particular going. "I don't really know this medium, I'd better play it safe and this is the kind of stuff that seems to go on the radio." So that's what we did. And then later on of course we got rid of those hoops of steel around us and Bill and Graeme let rip, we all realised that anything was possible; as indeed *The Goon Show* had shown before.'

With so many dozens of half-hours under their belt, it's little wonder that the team now had a shorthand, or that Oddie & Garden could take the responsibility of putting together every script on their own – they'd been writing the bulk of the shows, the serials and Prune Plays, for years anyway. As Garden says today, it just made sense. 'It sort of streamlined the process a lot, because we wrote half the show each, they couldn't really reject either of us, because they'd only have half a show that week. So they had to accept what we gave them, and we had to keep our part of the bargain and write something that was pretty good. But we saved all the time of trying to attract people to write, and having to go through the sifting process. It is a nightmare, I know, because I've done shows more recently which have been written by many, many authors, and it's really quite tricky to put them together and get them balanced. Whereas if you're writing it more as a piece between two people, you can get a balance. Bill and I used to talk about ideas together, and then write half each. Which is basically how we used to do *The Goodies*, as well.'

'We divided it up in different ways,' recalls Bill, 'so we'd go away and work separately for a few days, and then come back together and read each other's essay, as it were. Which I always resented for two reasons, first of all, because Graeme was better at performing things just off the top of his head than I was, and even more intimidating was the fact that he typed his scripts out, and I didn't. As I did explain to him, I said, "I wish you'd stop doing that because it makes me feel like I'm making you go and retype something that's finished, because it's all neat, you know?" Whereas if I'd just scribbled a pile of rubbish, he never felt any compunction about criticising mine. And he'd say, "It's all right, I type quickly ..." But he never learned, he always intimidated me by being neater and better.'

Oddie and Garden's move to take control of the *ISIRTA* scripts was a positive decision, Oddie remembers. There were plenty of other talented sketch writers out there, but they decided, '"Why bother? Let's keep this within the group," and also it meant therefore that we could theme the whole programme a bit more too, the reappearance of catchphrases and all that would be built into it, so it was more of a fluid piece that way. Graeme and I, I think very positively, said, "Look, let's face it, really this is our show – we're going to write it." That was an overt statement, almost militant.' The move paid off, when Oddie and Garden won the Writers' Guild of Great Britain Award in 1968.

A Sound Sensation Across the Nation

So, if Barclay was apprehensive (or perhaps even a tiny bit hopeful) that *ISIRTA* would founder without its founder, the vim with which Radio Prune burst into action once ensconced on Radio 2 would leave no room for mistaking that Angus Prune was not only alive and well, he sounded reinvigorated and groovier than ever before.

The whole shake-up of BBC Radio – in fact, wireless broadcasting in general – allowed Bill and Graeme to practically relaunch *ISIRTA*, drawing on the wonders of commercial radio for the establishment of a whole new station. It had been mooted in previous episodes, but not until the seventy-fifth show, in the middle of series 6, would Radio Prune finally get off the ground, and on the air.

> DH: You are now about to witness an historic event . . . we're about to celebrate the opening of a new local radio station. And tonight's local is the Dog & Muffin in Buxton, where the cast of *I'm Sorry I'll Read That Again* are now ready to inaugurate the first broadcast of Radio Prune.
>
> JC: Radio Prune, named after the producer; because, like a prune, he too is small and wrinkled and keeps us going.
>
> TBT: And now the Postmaster General will launch the new station in traditional manner by smashing a bottle of champagne on David Hatch.
>
> FX: Swanee whistle plunge – smash!
>
> DH: Ooooow!
>
> JC: What a terrible thing to do! All that champagne wasted!

The team swore on a copy of the *Radio Times* that the station would contain full-frontal nudes bulletins every hour, and maintain a complete disregard for the BBC Censorship Committee, who were 'just a small cross-section of average retired colonels, puritans, saints, nuns and, of course, loonies' – epitomised, naturally, by 'the Buffies', now the traditional shorthand for the older generation moaning about 'long-haired nancies'.

'Yes, but – this is Broadway!
It's BROADWAY!' Cambridge Circus at
the Plymouth Theatre, New York 1964.

Cleese, Stuart-Clark and Sidney
Molar, the man who knows the truth
about the dwarf and the ice-cream.

'My spouse, my spouse, she's no virginal!
Tim and Chris Stuart-Clark. 'Swap a Jest',
Cambridge Circus 1963.

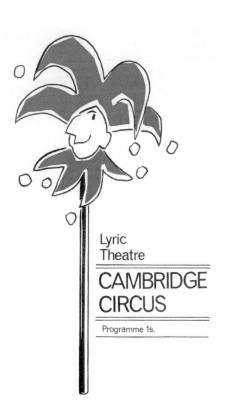

Lyric
Theatre

CAMBRIDGE
CIRCUS

Programme 1s.

This is what 'Hilarious hoojamuflicks' must look like. The Wonder Team mug for the cameras, 1965.

Sexually frustrated young globetrotters. John, Tim, and Graham with orgasmic fans. Hong Kong 1964.

'I'm all for little surprises, but not that little.' The actress and the comic, mid-sixties.

The Fairy Prunemother and the dirty little man, as envisaged by Producer Humphrey Barclay.

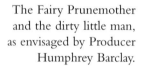

Humphrey Barclay's rough artwork for the first ISIRTA commercial release.

'There was a ship that put to sea, all in the month of May.' A rare shot of the Tillingbourne Madrigal Society in full flow, 1969.

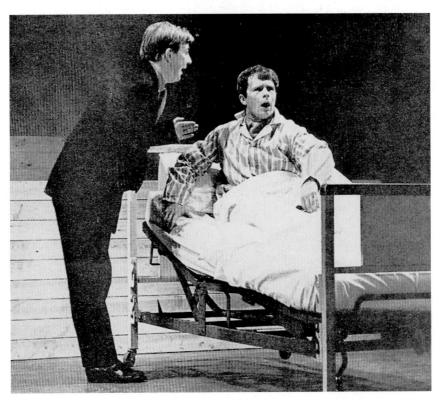

'Patients, For the Use of' – Tim and Bill go through the motions of a skit performed from Cambridge to New York to At Last The 1948 Show.

Barclay bumph for
the *Radio Times*, 1966.

It's I.S.I.R.T.A. again

LIGHT

10.0

EVER since *I'm Sorry, I'll Read That Again*
began in 1964, listeners have complained.
They have complained that it's hard to
visualise the young comedians who make up
the cast, and they have asked us to help.

So, for the new series which begins tonight,
Angus Prune and I got together and prepared this
first ever Do-It-Yourself Visual Aid Kit For I.S.I.R.T.A.
Listeners. Attractive to look at and easy to make, it
is designed to take all the tedium out of 'listening in.'

HUMPHREY BARCLAY

INSTRUCTIONS

1. Carefully cut out
   whole drawing.
2. Carefully stick on to
   some cardboard.
3. Cut out figures and
   'Mike.'
4. Carefully bend back
   bottom flaps.
5. Stand figures round
   'Mike.'
6. Carefully switch on
   'Down Your Way.'

The winners of
the 1968 Writers'
Guild of Great
Britain Award
enjoy their success.

Hot tickets for 'The Match of the Day Part Two' – Twice a Fortnight, 1967

A painfully young Brooke-Taylor locks horns with Sir Announcer David Kipperfeet Hatch, CBE, JP, No OBE.

The Goodies with a large collection of Goodie-lings, in the magical yesteryear known as the 1970s.

By popular acclaim, these later editions tend to be remembered as the pinnacle of *ISIRTA*'s quality, with series 8 being the most pilfered run in the BBC Audio releases. And this is despite the gang's preoccupation with finding a successful TV format during this time. But then, as Cleese admitted only slightly patronisingly, the freedom that radio could provide to just mess about without the worry of grabbing ratings was part of the appeal. 'I used to regard it as wonderful practice. It was like warming up in the nets before you go out to the middle to play cricket. It was great, but you knew that this was not as important as live television, peak hour. But it was tremendously useful and it gave me a chance to play off the audience. If you do a hundred shows, you learn a bit in that time in terms of technique.'

It was the eighth series that boasted programmes to appeal across the board, such as 'Home This Afternoon A Go-Go', and endless commercial breaks for products such as 'Poo-Gone Deodorant Spray', presaging *The Goodies*' fake ad breaks. Even news bulletins sneaked in advertising when Radio Prune went commercial, with Hatch intoning catchy jingles mid-bulletin such as '*What a lovely girl you are, in a panty girdle bra./ Milo-Pew will show you how, why look like a fat old cow?*'

The show also generated brand-new running gags as it went on, with an obsession with gibbons finally coming to the fore. Oddie and Garden's pre-occupation with the primate, which would reach horrific proportions when 'The Funky Gibbon' hit the charts, was as random and facetious as the earlier preoccupation with rhubarb tart. It did, however, help that Graeme could deliver a stirring impression of a whooping tree-swinger. The Tillingbourne Madrigal Society were even brought out of retirement to lead the crowd in a storming rendition of the country song 'Stuff That Gibbon', and the infamous primate would be name checked at every opportunity – 'gibbon half a chance . . .'

Spot the Mistake
This period also finally saw the introduction of the Prune Play of the Week, now fronted by Oddie's Hughie Greene figure (albeit referred to by Kendall as 'Eamonn' or 'Mr Monkhouse'), as he rated each new playwright's sub-mission on the old Boo-o-meter. Most of them of course registered as 'truly offal'.

With the shorthand down pat, Oddie and Garden produced the best of their Prune Plays in this time, including classics like 'The Taming of the Shrew' (with Cleese giving an early, silly performance of Petruchio, which he was to play straight for Jonathan Miller's TV version a decade later), the Bond pastiche 'The 3:17 to Cleethorpes' (starring Hatch as Cliff Hanger-Ending, charged with the task of saving the honours list from falling into the clutches of foreign spies), 'Henry VIII and his Six Wives' (which he married en masse, of course), and a spoof of *Star Trek* which is utterly derailed by Otto's petulance at his lack of a decent role – once his infantile pouting wears down producer Hatch's authority, Cleese takes charge and makes the entire crew of the Enterprise Welsh for no reason whatsoever.

These later Prune Plays also introduced another great tradition of *I'm Sorry* – a joke format which would be an unavoidable part of the franchise for decades to come. It's rare in a sketch when there isn't some form of formal announcement just waiting to be made, at a grand function or society party. And somebody would have the task of announcing the Late Arrivals, such as: 'My lords, ladies and gen'men . . . The Duke and Duchess of Lawdown, and their daughter, Lady Lawdown . . . An easy one to start off with.' Or: 'The well-known newspaper baron, Sir Q. Lation . . . wait a minute, you can't come in, you're not funny enough.'

Part of the reason why these later spoofs are so sure-footed is because of the further tightening up of the show's running gags that was afforded by a second weekly serial, which ran throughout the seventh series – 'Professor Prune and the Electric Time Trousers'. If anything, this extended play on *Doctor Who* is even more summary-proof than 'The Curse of the Flying Wombat', being a random odyssey through time and space in which Garden's aged Professor, his irritatingly cute niece and nephew Basil and Trixie (played by Oddie and Kendall) and his nerdy assistant Percy Plimsoll (Cleese) zoom about in a pair of fantastic trousers, battling a race of robotic Antipodean villains called the Aussies and meeting famous figures from history as they race to retrieve their trousers from Prune's arch-nemesis the evil Fetish (also Garden).

The absence of Tim Brooke-Taylor from the gang of main heroes in this final *ISIRTA* serial was deliberate. After the constant doubling up in 'Flying Wombat', no chances were taken with Tim's roles, so he was crestfallen to be given the role of the Professor's dog Spot – his one line being 'Woof!' The whole enterprise backfired, however – none of the cast having taken into account the sheer adoration that the crowd had for Brooke-Taylor and his stable of silly voices, which meant that from the very first episode, the merest mention of 'Spot' or slightest bark from Tim would elicit a roar from the Audience which sounded quite enough to knock the entire cast back on their heels. It's little wonder that the exasperated writers quickly killed off the popular pooch, but Spot always found a way back into the narrative somehow.

Although the Tim-baiting is obviously affectionate, it's clear by series 7 that both writers and cast felt somewhat trapped by the need to keep on dragging out the same old characters and ideas that the Audience loved – as proved by the similarly dismissive way in which Lady Constance is treated in 'Time Trousers'. The naughty old lush is in hot pursuit of Professor Prune from the first, but the gang speed away before she can squeeze her bloated form into the trousers. If one were feeling pretentious, you could argue that the resultant chase across time and space (in which Lady Constance turns up everywhere, as Queens Elizabeth and Victoria, or as the space nymphette Boobarella) is allegorical of the *ISIRTA* team trying to escape the by now quite onerous demands of the Audience. After years of building up a devoted following, it was quite rewarding at first to be able to generate enormous cheers and applause just by having Tim warble on as Lady Constance (or going 'Woof!'), but there was a point at which the easy way of getting laughs began to pall. Cleese especially was vociferous in his quite genuine contempt for the easily-pleased punters, and can be heard yelling 'Easy! Easy!' whenever a particularly obvious gag causes hilarity.

Was this just in-character Audience-baiting from Otto? Certainly his role as cast bully comes to the fore in these later series – Brooke-Taylor wasn't the only one of the team feeling left out, with Hatch's anxiety over his precarious role as part producer, part boring old Announcer spilling over into apoplectic indignance of an almost Kenneth Williams magnitude, with a little goading from Otto.

> DH: I'm fed up with being a boring old announcer! I never get any
> exciting bits, I only get the dull old factual links! . . . You lot do
> all the kinky parts and blue jokes, I'm not made of stone, you
> know! Mmm, I can put on women's voices and do passionate love
> scenes! I'm as kinky as they come, you know! I can do that and
> a lot more, you know!
> JC: Who's a little fibber?
> DH: . . . I am.

Hatch gets his own back later on in the story when he realises the power of his role as storyteller, and narrates Cleese into sitting on a wasp – and then of course, everybody wants to have a go at being narrator. The final instalment of 'Professor Prune and the Electric Time Trousers' dissolves into a silly series of scenes with each member of the cast knocking each other out so they can take over the reins of narration and give their character the best happy ending. The violent relays of frying-pan batterings as each one of the Wonder Team wrestles control would make Reeves & Mortimer blanch.

No Puns, No Puns, and No Puns
By this stage the gang were (comedically at least) at each other's throats – the days when only Bill came under fire for being small and hairy were long gone. During an instalment of 'Time Trousers', when Professor Prune is being

cross-examined by Fetish in an *Alice in Wonderland*-style courtroom scene, Cleese interjects:

JC: We may as well point out at this stage that Graeme Garden is playing both of these parts. The following passage is not so much an exercise in humour, as in verbal expertise. We do not expect many laughs during it but Mr Garden would appreciate a round of applause when it's all over, as this will persuade listeners at home that it was very difficult to do, which it isn't. Carry on, bighead . . .

. . . Which is all well and good as part of the show, but the fact is that by this point, with *Monty Python* in the offing and a busy work schedule, Cleese felt that he had outgrown *ISIRTA* by quite some way. Now happily settled down with Connie Booth, he did genuinely resent having to leave his marital home and give up the vast majority of his day of rest to deliver what he saw as button-pushing material to a horde of screaming regulars (or 'joke fodder', as Otto dubbed them) who didn't much care about the quality of the comedy, when they were having such a good time. 'Suddenly the Audience changed, it started getting like playing at the cup final. Instead of having a nice Audience that laughed, suddenly there was a football crowd atmosphere . . . Eventually, the Audience became so much an integral part of the programme, and being a bit of a purist, as I certainly was in those days, I got fed up with the fact that so much was based on puns, which I did think was the lowest form of wit . . .' Cleese has gone on record as saying that his one adage throughout his solo career has been 'No puns, no puns, and no puns . . .'

'Well, he broke that rule a few times,' chuckles Barry Cryer, who was another regular Audience member back in the sixties, on hand to witness Cleese's genuine consternation at the atmosphere: 'John hated the mob atmosphere that grew up in the Audience. They started being treated like a rock band when they came on – the roars! – and there'd be people in the circles at the Playhouse in the old days stringing banners across, and John was horrified. The reaction became so over the top – which it deserved, but comedy's about laughter, not about whoops and shouts. Steve Martin was the most brilliant stand-up, but he became completely disenchanted because he played big arenas and they just whooped at him. I have an aversion to whoops.'

The team were finding that the rapport with the Audience they'd carefully built up was now beginning to overpower the entire show. Barclay shudders to recall, 'You want it to begin with, and then the monster takes over . . .' And it wasn't just Cleese who tried to tame the rabid crowd (even going so far as to threaten them with Shakespearean jokes unless they began to show proper appreciation for the *ISIRTA* gags, beyond just roaring and cheering), Hatch, as head prefect, also tried to calm the grinning sea of rapscallions:

DH: Shut up! Quiet! What do you think that sounds like to those at home? They don't know that Tim's camping around with no trousers on! We have lately received a number of complaints that this programme is too noisy, and that our Audience has been laughing too loud and clapping too much! In fact, we do make a fortune by exporting our applause to *The Andy Williams Show*. BUT! We can't help agreeing that our studio Audience is barbaric, rowdy, and totally out of control! You at home, think yourself lucky that you can't *see* them as well! Anyway, we're now going to do the next lot of jokes very very quietly. And you lot will laugh, and you will clap, very very softly – WON'T YOU?

AUDIENCE (*whispers*): Yes . . .

'They were a liability, that lot,' laughs Oddie. 'Some of my favourite moments involved John Cleese haranguing the Audience, and them just screaming with joy thinking it's all part of the show . . . "Are you actually *listening* to this or not?" The Audience became a many-headed monster without any doubt, and took over. Used to scare the life out of me . . .'

The boisterous crowd reaction was never a worry to Garden though. 'I used to enjoy it, it gave you time to think apart from anything else. That's why playing comedy to a half-empty house is so difficult, because the Audience don't laugh long enough for you to catch your breath. John, I think, has always found it difficult – he's never quite found an audience that he really respected. He keeps trying to find an audience of people he admires as much as they admire him. I loved the fact that the Audience were that enthusiastic, like a football crowd cheering the goals. I think on television when we tried to artificially stir the audience up, I didn't like that, because that wasn't real. It was the Audience's idea in *ISIRTA* to groan or cheer.' But even the patron saint of *I'm Sorry* has to admit that the knee-jerk reactions from the fans could work against the comedy. 'It *was* a bit irritating when, if they heard a pun, they would automatically groan and then realise it was quite funny and laugh. And you'd think, "Well, why did you bother to groan in the first place?"' Brooke-Taylor agrees that this was the one irritant from which the whole cast suffered. 'Loud was OK – we love it on *Clue*. The Audience would groan, which in a way meant they were comfortable, but they got into the habit of groaning as a reflex action and then laughing when they'd heard the joke properly. This annoyed us all and made timing almost impossible (fortunately, the *Clue* Audience is not like this). It got to the point where you almost wanted to say, "Calm down, dears – we haven't reached the joke yet!"' Artists finding that the roar of the excited crowd compromised their performances? We're back in Beatles territory . . .

Of course, with everyone being such good friends since late adolescence, genuine bad feeling between the stars tended to be kept to a minimum – even with the gulf between Kendall the actor and Oddie the comic taken into consideration. Barclay remembers, 'If we look back, we never had any rows, through all the shows . . . I mean, touring can be pretty fierce, but no – we never had that "Oh my God, so-and-so's not talking to so-and-so" . . . We used to resent John for other things, like he couldn't be bothered to turn up for rehearsal – he was very intolerant about rehearsal . . . He'd slot in rather late and just read what he was given, or sit in the dressing room and write extra bits into the script which he then wouldn't tell me about, and perform them live at the microphone . . . I can hear now Bill's grumpiness about John sailing in and stealing the show, because Bill had been there all day slogging away with Dave Lee getting the music right, and all the sound effects and so on, which was hard work. And then John just had to come in and read the lines. But nothing ever broke out into difficulty.'

'In some of the later series,' Garden continues, 'John used to have it written into his contract that he didn't have to turn up to rehearsal. It's interesting, having a look at Michael Palin's diaries, to see that they had the same sort of problem with John on *Python*, he rapidly lost interest in the TV series I think . . . But he was just like that, he always had rather grand schedules and timetables and diaries, and he'd put aside a certain time of the year for Rest & Relaxation, and there was no way he was going to work then, and that sort of thing. He always gave the impression of being terribly organised.'

Despite protestations that show business was never really the right career choice for him, Cleese had always been ambitious, and with ambition comes the need to leave behind old associations and move on to the next thing. But there was always a place in *ISIRTA* for the vicious Otto. 'The Audience loved him, and he was terribly funny,' says Garden, 'so as long as he delivered on the day we let him do that . . . Bit annoying that the rest of us had to turn up and rehearse and rewrite the script while he wasn't there, but that's the price you pay – and he's gone on behaving like that, as far as I can see!'

By the eighth series, however, with *Monty Python* starting to get real acclaim and taking up so much of his time, Cleese was absent for several episodes altogether – yet the quality of these shows remains high. As even his old friend Brooke-Taylor says, 'Cleese's absences were a bit of a relief occasionally as he found our Audience very difficult to deal with.' Otto's so-called quitting of the show has always been exaggerated, however – he was very much back in the saddle for the last few shows of the run. This may have been because it was apparent by now that the whole cast had outgrown Radio Prune, and that the 1970 series would be the last one.

It seemed inevitable as the decade drew to a close that Radio Prune's days on the air were numbered, and as the series continued, Garden and Oddie once again used as material the actual problems involved in making the show, airing their dirty laundry in every show and ramping up the air of amateurism week by week – the less they seemed to care about the show, the looser and funnier it became.

Garden and Oddie happily threw away all trace of artifice, even admitting at the top of show eleven that 'if you repeat something often enough, no matter how meaningless it is, people will laugh at it'. But while pointing out the meaninglessness of so many running gags, Graeme and Bill were still introducing more of them as the show went on. The Order of the British Empire was the strongest of the new repeated references by the eighth series. More banana skins under authority, the meaninglessness of ten-a-penny honours was the gang's new war cry, and never was an opportunity missed to bring them up, and put them down, with OBEs flung around like choccy drops. The whole cast even gave themselves OBEs in the end credits – well, all except for Bill Oddie, who somehow didn't qualify.

The in-show depiction of the cast as a gang of naughty schoolchildren faced with the cane-flexing masters from the top of the BBC hierarchy had reached 'Bash Street' proportions. But the series-closing musical extravaganza that was 'The Raymond Nostril Story' (actually a kind of Broadway musical stitched together from some of Bill's greatest hits, not to mention another outing for 'the Rhubarb Tart Song') would seem to have been the last straw. Even Lady Constance, by now Radio Prune's head of programming, could only stand by as Parliament rushed through a bill to close the station down, with immediate effect. After only thirteen weeks, the MCC – the 'Buffies' who colluded with the BBC bosses to sneer at and repress everything Prune stood for – were battering on the door like bailiffs, preparing to cut Radio Prune down in its prime.

So that was that – the game was up. All that remained was for the Director General to hand out the beatings, with all the cast sentenced to obscure jobs on lesser radio programmes, like *Mrs Dale's Diary* or Jimmy Young's show. Their last request, to sing 'The Angus Prune Tune' one final time, is granted, and shakily the team bid the Audience goodbye with a tear in their eye. TV was beckoning, and Radio Prune was no more.

7

I'm Sorry I'll Read That Again . . .
Thrice More

With the final episode recorded in April, the rest of 1970 played out without any stirrings in the *ISIRTA* camp. Series 2 of *Monty Python's Flying Circus* and the first shows from *The Goodies* were created, Hatch had his own radio shows to see to, and Kendall returned to the stage as well as appearing as Anne Stanhope in the Emmy Award-winning BBC series *The Six Wives of Henry VIII*. It looked like the aged Buffies of this world had finally seen off the brash antics of Radio Prune . . .

But there was a tradition to hold up, and after so many years of panto pandemonium every Yuletide at the Playhouse, Hatch wasn't about to let standards slip (or indeed, improve). So, once again, and now for a positively final time, the gang regrouped for their seasonal special just a few days before Christmas Day 1970 – with the show going out on New Year's Eve.

And so, that festive evening, the show opened with the whole band of scamps regrouping to try to sneak Radio Prune back on the airwaves. However, the Blue Meanies of their fictional BBC were waiting in the shadows:

GG: This is the Director General of BBC Radio speaking . . . Now you just can't come sneaking back on my radio station like that. Where have you all been for the past year, come on, where have you been?

EVERYONE: Please sir, please, we've been doing television and things, sir . . .

GG: Television? TELEVISION? . . . What's television?

TBT: Well, sir, it's a sort of radio with pictures, sir.

GG: Rubbish. It'll never catch on.

BO: Please, sir, we've been doing *The Goodies*, sir.

JC: And *Monty Python's Flying Circus*!

JK: And *The Wives of Henry VIII*.

BO: . . . What?

GG: Never heard of them, they sound silly. SILLY! Now come on, confess, you've been earning money, haven't you? . . . Aren't you ashamed of yourselves? Well, don't you come crawling back to me. I've said it before, people who want to earn money have no place on BBC Radio.

Eventually, the DG grants them a respite, as long as they can make everyone laugh within five seconds ('Knickers!' 'No good, it has to be clean.' 'Clean knickers!'), but they are warned not to dare to do their traditional panto, no matter how much they might be tempted to sneak in the usual fare – hence the title of that year's show, 'Doctor Zhivago . . . and his Wonderful Lamp'.

It's little wonder that, once again, the Scroogey topic of money came up in the show. The fact was that everyone in the *ISIRTA* team had begun their careers in broadcasting as callow graduates, but were now, sadly, grown-ups. By now most of the chaps had families to support – even Tim had jumped off the dock, defying his on-air reputation for whoopsiness by marrying his girlfriend Christine in 1968.

When trying to earn a living in comedy, says Brooke-Taylor, 'You try and do it all . . . I know that when John and I were working for the *Frost* programme as editors, we had an office together, and we spent most of the time writing bits for *I'm Sorry I'll Read That Again*, or checking through the script for it. You didn't think this was your life, doing *ISIRTA*, because nobody could just exist on radio. The traditional comedians would be off doing summer seasons and things like that, and radio would just be part of it . . . But you stayed loyal to it, the radio, even though it was ridiculously paid at one stage, because you were working with such great guys, and you were given a platform. But you'd never think that was your real job.'

So with the lure of TV lucre calling them, you couldn't blame Oddie and Garden for throwing in perhaps the most blatant exposure of their formula for Prune pandemonium. After all, this was the end of the road, there was no need to hide the machinery of the show any more.

JK: The team at *I'm Sorry I'll Read That Again* have been at it for seven years now . . . (*Audience cheer.*) And they've been doing the programme for a long time.

JC: Through seven years . . . we have sweated and toiled to write and perform over fifty hours of material, and always we have striven to make it ever fresh, subtle and sophisticated . . . And yet, even now people stop us in the street to say 'When's Spot coming back?' or even, 'Do your Grimbling voice', it makes you sick. You rabble don't care about the clever stuff, all you want is these

	inane catchphrases. Well you want 'em, here they come. The
	whole putrid lot!
TBT:	Thank you, John Cleese. In 1965 we brought you . . .
JC:	Ferrets.
TBT:	In 1966 . . .
BO:	'How de do dere, honey?' . . .
GG:	In 1968!
TBT:	Woof! (*Cries of 'More!'*)
JC:	In 1969!
DH:	Gibbons.
TBT:	In 1970!
JK:	OBEs.
JC:	Right, that's the lot done with. It's like feeding time at the zoo.
GG:	Now, did any of you spot –
TBT:	Woof!
GG:	Shut up! Did any of you notice the deliberate omission?
TBT:	Yes! Yes I did – Tim Brooke-Taylor speaking. Tim Brooke-Taylor,
	I'm the one who does Lady – (*Muffled noises as he's gagged.*)
GG:	That was a clue. She may be on later, if *he* pays up.

But she did turn up of course, for a veritable Dickensian smorgasbord of chestnuts for Auld Lang Syne – Eddie Waring, the Buffies, a Christmas carol dirty songbook (expurgated version), late arrivals at the Russian ball, a rendition of 'Lenin on a Lamp Post', and, finally the entrance of Lady C, the Fairy Prunemother herself. Sadly, the presence of a man dressed as a woman in the show proved to be the final straw and the whole edifice of Radio Prune was trampled by the BBC's Pantomime Extermination Unit. Even the sexual attentions of the titanic saucepot herself couldn't change the DG's mind and save the show from extinction, and, with a quick emotional rendition of 'We'll Meet Again', the last seasonal special was finished, as was *ISIRTA*.

Graeme Garden knew that the show had run its course, and simply took too much time and effort for far too little financial reward. And yet the Audience was still there, tooting their horns and baying for bad gags. One diehard young fan, Colin Day, was lucky enough to be the first member of the crowd to discover that this was Radio Prune's planned swansong, thanks to a chance encounter: 'After the recording was over my friend Mole and I were heading down Northumberland Avenue when we saw John Cleese, Graeme Garden and Tim Brooke-Taylor walking up towards us, so we stopped and asked them about the show and if there was going to be another series. They explained that they were all doing other things and that they didn't have the time to produce another series with all of their other commitments. John Cleese indicated how big a pile of scripts for a series would be, a pile about two feet high. We thanked them for talking to us and walked off thinking we had probably seen the last ever *ISIRTA* . . .' How could any self-respecting comic leave a hungry crowd like that, eager for more? There had to be an answer. Then Graeme Garden had an idea. He took whizz-kid BBC producer David Hatch to the pub, and a plan began to take root . . . A quick-fire alternative to Radio Prune was in the offing.

The Cheeky Boys

As the post-Prune careers of all the gang blossomed, only the fans were left languishing. *Monty Python* and *The Goodies* were in their heyday, Jo Kendall became one of the earliest stars of *Emmerdale Farm*, playing Peggy Silbeck, and David Hatch was continuing a career in BBC Radio Light Entertainment more fruitful and fascinating than perhaps any other in the history of the corporation.

Having already launched, devised, presented or otherwise produced many of the most successful radio comedies of the sixties and early seventies (including his perfect audio adaptations of P. G. Wodehouse's *Jeeves* stories and the *Doctor* radio series), Hatch still had time for more. As well as the panel game thing he was kicking about with Graeme Garden, Hatch was to be the first producer of a brand new sketch show starring Tim Brooke-Taylor, alongside old bananas Barry Cryer and John Junkin. It was to be an absolutely shameless grab bag of ludicrous puns, lunatic quickies and leering innuendo . . . It would be no giveaway to draw parallels with Tim's previous sketch vehicle.

Although it seems almost like Brooke-Taylor's 'solo album' after the break-up of *ISIRTA*, *Hello, Cheeky* came about, ultimately, because of *The Goodies*. 'If there had been more *I'm Sorry I'll Read That Again* I'd have been happy to do those, but . . . when it had been established that Bill and Graeme were basically going to write *The Goodies*, I needed to do something! Although I was involved in the writing for *The Goodies* too, it didn't take up much of my time, so that was me looking for something else to do, basically.'

What Tim found to do was to team up with two colleagues at equally loose ends to create their own free and easy radio show. 'John Junkin I didn't know at all until I did *Marty*, and we worked together for a very long time afterwards . . . I can't remember exactly the first time I met Barry, it must have been probably around the same time as *The Frost Report*. But we always got on, and he and Junkin used to do warm-ups for nearly every comedy show at that time.' Brooke-Taylor and Junkin had already recorded a BBC TV pilot in 1971 for a sort of prototype *Men Behaving Badly* called *The Rough with the Smooth*, about two comedy writers called Tim and John who were constantly chasing 'skirt' . . . But before the BBC could come to a decision about that, along came this radio opportunity. Ultimately, the critical drubbing for similarly lairy Leslie Phillips sitcom vehicle *Casanova '73* would kill off *The Rough with the Smooth* – a seven-part series was broadcast without much publicity, but it was never recommissioned.

With so many Prune fans yearning for more *ISIRTA*, perhaps it's no surprise that what this seasoned trio came up with was a saucy, silly hotchpotch of popular songs, outrageous wordplay, oceans of subtle and not-so-subtle filth, and a special regard for groanworthy gags. They hit the ground running – note the early entry for The Uxbridge English Dictionary:

BC:	And so the Guatemalan midget in the top hat said, 'No, madam, not in these trousers!'
TBT:	That joke was requested by Edith and all the girls at Hannegan's Truss Boutique. So we know what kind of girls *they* are, don't we?
JJ:	Meanwhile, on a cricket ground not a thousand miles from Crewe Junction . . .
GRAMS:	Fanfare.
JJ:	University Of The Air. What is 'syntax'?
TBT:	It's the money Catholics put in the collection after they've been to confession.

As the name suggests, *Hello, Cheeky* was perhaps the ultimate undiluted display of Tim Brooke-Taylor's love of naughty, ribald Music Hall humour. Tim had always most completely personified the Music Hall approach of *ISIRTA* – the grotesque wink, mechanical elbow-nudge and cry of 'Eh? Eh?' which follow any of his cheekier chestnuts is a Brooke-Taylor trademark that no one else can quite pull off. With this new show far more weighted towards him – plus the presence of seasoned Music Hall chairman Cryer – it's no wonder that the name of *Hello, Cheeky* is still legendary in the field of outrageous throw-away punnery and stunning innuendo. The gags may have seen better days, but it pioneered *The Fast Show*'s quick-fire format twenty years early – set-up, gag, and move on. No sketch, skit, song or item is allowed to linger in *Hello, Cheeky*, with more quickies per episode than was thought scientifically possible at the time. Cryer, Junkin and Brooke-Taylor would present the show as themselves, lined up before the microphone just like the old *ISIRTA* days and occasionally hurling abuse at each other, musician Denis King or a special guest (including Frank Bough, who was 'amusingly' accused of transvestism in the show years before the tabloids ended his career). The rapid pace of the show ensured that the audience were certainly kept on their toes, not to mention the sound-effects man. The groans and hoots rise and fall much like in *ISIRTA*, but at twice the pace – and yet somehow *Hello, Cheeky* always manages to seem far from frenetic, mainly down to the sheer carefree, almost careless delivery of the trio, who appear just to be taking the piss and having the time of their life doing so.

'It was one of the few things I've done where all three writers sat in the same room and just worked away,' says Tim. 'It was actually really rather good to sit in a room – one of us, usually me or John, would be at the typewriter – and just jabber away. I'd started working with John doing *The Rough with the Smooth*, where we used to say, "We'll do four pages today and then we'll play Scrabble . . ."'

Like all the best comedy shows, *Hello, Cheeky* allowed its creators just to do what made them laugh. Whether Brooke-Taylor or producer Hatch intended it to be so, it was in many ways a placebo for *ISIRTA* when it was first broadcast in the spring of 1973. However, before the series had even finished its first run, it was becoming clear that perhaps a placebo wasn't going to be needed.

That Old Gang of Mine

Hatch was keen to cater for the fans with some proper scripted *I'm Sorry*, but knew that radio wages were unlikely to lure the stars back onto the airwaves. Jo Kendall was available for more, as indeed was Tim. The tricky thing would be convincing Bill and Graeme to invest the time in writing new scripts – and of course press-ganging Cleese back into action. Despite their preoccupation with *The Goodies*, Bill insists that *ISIRTA* was never far from his and Graeme's thoughts. 'We still loved writing it. I would have been happy writing it for years! It was just all those jokes that never failed to make us laugh.'

But, almost by pure coincidence, it just so happened that everyone in the team became available towards the end of that year. Brooke-Taylor says, 'I don't think it was a surprise – there was quite a demand for it and people wanted to do it – but I do remember feeling "this is one step too far, we've lost the continuity here." You do need everybody working week by week rather than just coming back, and deigning to do it in a way. I remember thinking, "It's a shame if it doesn't go on much longer, but I don't think it will."' Nevertheless, whizz-kid Hatch had managed the impossible, and lined up a brand-new series of *ISIRTA*, albeit for a shorter run of only eight episodes, to go out at the end of 1973.

This was the first series with any real break, after a steady run throughout the sixties – this would be the *ISIRTA* of the seventies. Between pioneering spoofs of radio phone-ins, more savage Radio 1 attacks and references to the Osmonds, Radio Prune was dragged up to date.

JC:	You still have to move with the times, this is 1957!
JK:	No it's not!
JC:	It is in the BBC . . .
DH:	Oh rubbish, we can still live off our loveable old catch-phrases, can't we?
JC:	No, you need new catchphrases, new ideas, new blood, new guts – giblets, dismembered weasels, oh I love it, I love it, it's good to be back . . .
<u>FX:</u>	<u>Door slams.</u>
DH:	He may be a loony, but he has a point. Public tastes have changed, we've got to give them what they want. We've got to have a new catchphrase. I suggest 'Can I do you now, sir?'
BO:	It's been done.
JC:	What about 'And now for something completely . . .'
EVERYONE:	Nooo!
BO:	Don't be ridiculous . . . terrapins! Bound to get a laugh, that. Terrapins.
DH:	Bill, terrapins have never got a laugh, and they never will.
BO:	Oh yes they will! Listen to this – TERRAPINS!
AUDIENCE:	HA BLOODY HA!
BO:	All right! Phase two!
JC:	This is an exercise in Audience brain-washing – 'The Terrapin Song' . . .

One stutteringly catchy Oddie number and the last fresh animal motif is introduced into Prune folklore, alongside gibbons, ferrets and Cleese's 'eke'-ing mice, not to mention our inanimate friends the teapot, the rhubarb tart and, of course, the OBE. But the final series of *ISIRTA* still doesn't quite feel like business as usual – the OBE-baiting anarchy of the old shows is far more visceral. Often Full Frontal Radio verges on the hardcore, with a psychedelic 'Alice in Wonderland' packed with drugs references (and a depiction of Lewis Carroll as an incredibly dirty old man that's even more shocking today than it was at the time), a whole show devoted to pornography, sex and violence (featuring explicit ads for waterbeds, the *Des O'Connor Dirty Songbook*, Bill's perverted song 'The Masochist's Rag' and the clothes-swapping panel game *What's My Kink?*), and the following opening sketch, which proves that Caroline Aherne and Craig Cash were not the first team to create a sitcom called anything like 'The Royal Family':

GRAMS:	'Steptoe & Son' reworking of 'Land Of Hope & Glory'.
BO:	The Royal Family.
DH:	I should like to point out that any similarity between the characters and any actual living or dead royal personages . . . is nothing to do with me.
EVERYONE:	Creep!
DH:	Anyway, Mrs Royal is sitting at home, counting her spare bedrooms and polishing her tiaras, while Mr Royal is out in his gardens, practicing his polo.
FX:	A polo ball is whacked, and smashes a window. A door opens.
JK:	Has one had a good day, dear?
JC:	(*Bawling costermonger voice*) OI! Where's me (*beep*)ing polo ball? If that (*beep*)ing corgi's chewed it again I'll wring its (*beep*)ing neck!
JK:	We do wish that you wouldn't swear so much.
JC:	Don't you talk to me like that, who d'you think you are the – the Queen or somebody?
JK:	We are.
JC:	Yeah, and I'm the (*beep*) King. Where's me dinner?
JK:	It's in the oven.
FX:	Enormous chamber being opened.
JC:	Gordon Bennett, what's this, flamin' roast swan again? Friggin' caviar, lobster bisque? Well you can stuff that lot up yer coronet! What's for pudding? Oh Gor BLIMEY! Can't we 'ave nothin' but zabaglione and crepes suzetteys? I'll show you what you can do with yer zabaglione and crepe suzetteys . . .
FX:	Plates smashing.
JC:	(. . .) And yer lobster bisque and yer lousy swan – RIGHT! I could do with a pint!
FX:	Service bell ringing.
JC:	'Ello? WHERE'S ME CHATEAU NEUF DE PAP? I keep twelve bottles in the fridge regular, where is it?
JK:	You don't understand, dear. Things are much more expensive these days. It's not fifteen pounds a bottle any more, my love. The nation has had to tighten one's belts.
JC:	What, are you tellin' me you don't get enough money, eh? Two million quid a week! Gor blimey! That's more than a coalminer gets in a month!

This stunningly loud, raucous sketch goes on to feature a Goons-obsessed ugly Prince (with Garden running the whole gamut of *Goon Show* voices) and a horse-fixated Princess, and generally manages to pre-empt *Spitting Image* by at least a decade. The old piss-taking of pointless honours like the OBE had mutated into the team (well, bar Hatch, of course) dishing out blatant, hilarious childish volleys at the reigning Windsors themselves.

With this last free-wheeling foray into Full Frontal Radio after years of financially and creatively rewarding but pretty restrictive TV work, Cleese especially is on top form in the final episodes of *ISIRTA*, and only stayed at home enjoying a quiet Sabbath of kitten-maintenance for just the one week. Indeed, Otto didn't just deign to give up his time for his radio pals; by 1973 he had left the *Monty Python's Flying Circus* television programme for good. Always on the lookout for bigger and better things, he felt the TV shows were beginning to repeat themselves and absented himself from the fourth and final series. However, returning to the Prune fold was an unexpected move, and certainly one that flummoxed Michael Palin. In his diary for 1973, Palin records how Cleese's loss of interest in the *Flying Circus* shows was a source of confusion, when they were all riding high – Palin's friend and Hampstead neighbour Oddie insisted that John had decided to come back to *ISIRTA* purely 'because he thinks it will be fun', while conversely Tim asked John at one *ISIRTA* recording if he was still dithering about whether to leave the *Flying Circus* TV series. 'Er . . . not really,' was the reply. This caused consternation and jealousy within the Monty Python camp at the time. There was (indeed, there still is) a clear division between The Goodies and The Pythons now, and some people feel that the former group (especially long-time Cleese and Chapman collaborator Brooke-Taylor), had rather missed the boat by not 'qualifying' for Python status. Cleese's loyalty to his old gang in 1973 flew in the face of this received opinion. The other Pythons simply could not understand how John could walk away from a successful TV series for a radio show fuelled by puns and cheeky Music Hall silliness – but John was just having fun with his old friends. Weeks spent rehearsing and filming *Monty Python's Flying Circus* versus the odd Sunday evening at the Playhouse, doing silly voices with no costume, no make-up, with the chaps he'd been friends with since he was a fresher? No contest. It may not have paid well, but the pleasure Cleese was having spitting out *ISIRTA*'s gags right to the end is apparent in every show – certainly series 9 contains far more blatant corpsing and giggly mistakes than ever before.

'I don't remember *not* corpsing,' laughs Oddie. 'I was the worst, I was very bad at corpsing. But on radio, you can cut it out . . .' The show often collapsed into genuine hysteria, but Hatch always left the funniest errors in the edit. Some, like a slip-up from a pressured Tim Brooke-Taylor getting muddled up while playing Lady Constance, her sister Flossie and Timothy Brown-Windsor all at once even made it to the LP recording, and remains a favourite moment of his: 'I enjoyed the bits where I was doing three characters and failing – on the LP, that was a genuine mistake, when I got the wrong one – one of the best moments, and entirely unintentional . . .'

The players' quickness to gleefully mock anyone's mistakes is another sign of their closeness, after so many years of working together. 'I think we were very lucky as a group, to know each other and get on with each other,' continues Tim. 'I've never been a good one-man performer, I think the best thing you can possibly do in comedy is spark off each other, and that's why I love working in teams.' Perhaps this infectious daftness is the reason that the final run is also the most plundered series for commercial release, with five of the eight shows considered worthy of inclusion on CD, to date.

So maybe Brooke-Taylor was wrong to feel that the team had 'jumped the shark' – seeing as the show had always thrived on its anarchic, laid-back atmosphere, having the team casually dash off one final audio lap of honour suits the comedy perfectly. Perhaps random reunions would be a possibility for exactly this reason, and so the final episode of the series, which aired on 23 December 1973, had no great sense of finality – there's no 'We'll Meet Again', no tearful farewell, and Lady Constance does not explode. Announcer Hatch does, admittedly, become an alcoholic when his schoolmasterly ways provoke the rest of the team into setting up rival station Radio Terrapin (Bill was right – it did catch on), finally causing Radio Prune to close down. All this is soon forgotten though when he rehires them for his own station, Radio Hatch, and they launch into a classic World War II prisoner-of-war send-up, 'Ice Cubes Down My Cleavage, or The Coldtitz Story'.

'The Angus Prune Tune' played, the old friends bade each other a warm farewell that Sunday evening at the Playhouse, and went back to their families, their private lives, and their own comedy careers. Tim, Bill and Graeme would be tied together forever as The Goodies, and Tim and Graeme would ever remain true to wireless broadcasting, but as for the gang as a whole . . . their paths were diverging. From then on, The Audience would have to get by without their healthy regular dose of Prune.

Wonderful Radio Hatch

Announcer Hatch may have been lambasted by his cohorts in every show as a swot and a creep – the Cuthbert Cringeworthy to their Bash Street Kids. But in reality, Hatch was not the type to play it safe when it came to radio comedy. He had already paved the way for *Spitting Image* in a sense by joining up with fresh young radio bod Simon Brett to launch the satirical series *Week Ending,* in 1970. Brett was an Oxford protégé of Humphrey Barclay, just as

Barclay and Hatch had been Peter Titheradge's Cambridge discoveries, and recalls his indoctrination into this great tradition of BBC recruitment: 'I directed a late-night revue on the Fringe at the Edinburgh Festival in 1967, and I'd been in the one the year before in 1966. And then Humphrey Barclay came up, talent-spotting, saw my show, bought me a drink and asked if I would be interested in pursuing that avenue. He introduced me to Peter Titheradge, and then it sort of went quiet . . . and I became a Father Christmas in a department store for about seven weeks. But then fortunately I was offered a year's contract as a trainee radio producer, starting on the first of January 1968, which was a working day in those days.' But, although he doesn't deny that there was a definite Oxbridge monopoly in British comedy, Brett believes there was little choice. 'I think, to put it in context, in those days there really wasn't any comedy "scene". Now you've got stand-ups in every pub, virtually, but then . . . if, in Light Entertainment, you were trying to engage with the younger audience which everyone was convinced was out there, there really was nowhere else to look. There was that great John Peel quote, that when he joined the BBC it was all run by ex-fighter pilots, which wasn't actually a million miles from the truth. When I started I spent a lot of my first couple of years going to retirement parties of really quite elderly people who'd been through the war . . . They needed to get a younger generation in somehow. You couldn't go to comedy clubs because they just didn't exist. So the only places where there was a kind of tradition of revue, where you could find someone who had a comedy instinct, were Oxford and Cambridge, and Bristol as well, to a lesser extent . . . It did seem kind of elitist, but on the other hand there weren't many other places to look.'

One of Brett's first BBC jobs was to pitch in with a few *ISIRTA* pieces: 'I only had two or three sketches on, because I think they were very much their own writers, but I had a few things. There was very definitely a style to what they did, which was sort of very silly, very pun-filled, and slightly child-ish – in the best way.' He was also another familiar face at the Playhouse. 'I attended a few recordings – particularly when my stuff was on, but it was just an amazing sort of cultish atmosphere that I hadn't encountered anywhere before. The queue outside, down the bottom of Northumberland Avenue . . . it was an amazing Audience response. There was a huge gulf between them and the comedy writers like Frank Muir and Denis Norden, who were absolutely wonderful, but were then probably in their fifties, and there was really very little for the young. There was a kind of void that needed filling. Radio 1 had just started in 1967, so musically the young were catered for, and before that with the pirate stations . . . but young people weren't expected to look to comedy, put it that way.'

When Hatch and Brett teamed up on *Week Ending*, they took the original spoof news element of *ISIRTA* to the extreme, replacing the fake newsreader's get-out clause of 'I'm sorry I'll read that again' with 'And now here is *next week's* news . . .' However, the greatest difference between the shows lies in *Week Ending's* lack of an audience, with each episode edited together by the producers with no laughter track, putting topicality and realism before *joie de vivre.* By the time the show limped to its close in 1998 it was generally seen as toothless and clapped-out; but over its thirty-year history, *Week Ending* provided a ferociously fecund breeding ground for generations of comic giants, giving a leg-up to more names than even David Frost could boast. As well as featuring Hatch's close friend David Jason in its early shows, plus *Quote Unquote* deviser Nigel Rees (of whom we shall hear more), not to mention Tracey Ullman, ex-Footlighter Morwenna Banks and stalwart Bill Wallis on performing duty over the years, the show's very charitable open-door policy for writers meant that over the decades precious minutes' worth of writers' fees were accumulated by Andy Hamilton, Guy Jenkin, Jack Docherty, Moray Hunter, Kevin Cecil, Andy Riley, Stewart Lee, Richard Herring, Peter Baynham, the late Debbie Barham and many more.

But it was the role of the producer that was filled by the most eminent roster – and this is where the unavoidable Oxbridge mafia subtext of this period of the *I'm Sorry* story becomes more marked. In later years luminaries like Harry Thompson and Armando Iannucci teethed in the producer's chair, but under Hatch and Brett's supervision, the earliest Oxford and Cambridge graduates to start off their careers making *Week Ending* were Griff Rhys Jones, John Lloyd and Douglas Adams. These last two, along with Hatch and Brett, would go on to be involved with the first likely successor to *ISIRTA* – *The Burkiss Way*, written by two young eager comedy writers who between them had no connection whatsoever to either Oxford or Cambridge – David Renwick and Andrew Marshall.

Indeed, both writers were earning their living writing for BBC Radio right from the age when most of their contemporaries were just setting off for university. Renwick arrived at Aeolian House at the age of only nineteen, on the strength of several random comedy sketches written while working for his local newspaper in Luton. Anyone familiar with Marshall & Renwick's sketch shows will be left in no doubt as to their debt to *Monty Python*, with sketches in shows such as *Alexei Sayle's Stuff* that often seem tantamount to *Python* fan fiction (featuring, say, the Marxist-Leninist star unconvincingly dragged up as a housewife who keeps a bishop as a pet, or Angus Deayton as an ancient Greek foreman who employs Pythagoras as a dung-shoveller). However, arriving at the BBC when the Pythons were only just beginning to hit their stride, Renwick's true inspiration as a comedy writer lay elsewhere.

Just as Cleese, Garden and co. had slavishly tuned into *The Goon Show* in their teens, and gobbled up every last joke for recycling in the playground the following day, David Renwick was a committed fan of *I'm Sorry I'll Read That Again*. Every week he would avidly tune in to Radio Prune, and write down every torturous pun that caught his ear so he and his school friends could relive the latest machinations of Lady Constance and friends at leisure. So the excitement he must have felt when the then head of radio comedy, Ted Taylor, kindly brought him to the attention of producer David Hatch must have been immense. As the star of Radio 2's most raucous hit, Hatch was the hip young face of BBC Management, and Renwick's loony ideas appealed greatly to him.

Put to work in the Oxbridge-heavy environment of *Week Ending*, it's no surprise that Renwick most easily identified with the younger Marshall – as a grammar-school prodigy, he seemed to be the only other regular writer in the team who hadn't been part of Footlights, or the Oxford equivalent. After years of gag construction in the foothills of radio comedy, in 1975 the duo were given their own comedy try-out in the alien atmosphere of Radio 3, abetted by co-writer John Mason and producer Simon Brett. This short spell of pilots took its cue from *Broaden Your Mind*, with a similarly academic theme – in this case, a spoof of Open University programmes entitled *The Half Open University*.

Minus Mason's regular input, this idea transferred to Radio 4 the following year as the first series of *The Burkiss Way*, in which a Professor Emile Burkiss presented his own Dynamic Way of Living – which was only the vaguest excuse for a sketch show in which anything could happen. In fact, perhaps more than any other radio comedy show since the Goons were riding high, *The Burkiss Way* went furthest out of its way to ensure that absolutely anything *did* happen.

Marshall & Renwick were always trying to catch the listener (not to mention the BBC announcer) well and truly off guard. False endings, hoax beginnings, spoofs so real they could confuse a clever person and a sense of loony logic that came from years of Cleese study, ensured that *The Burkiss Way* was one of the most adventurous radio shows of the seventies – every bit as much as *The Hitchhiker's Guide to the Galaxy*, which would itself be a returning source of mockery in the show once regular contributor Douglas 'Mr Different' Adams had scored a hit with it.

In the early days, before Marshall & Renwick took over sole duty of scripting *The Burkiss Way*, the cast line-up was veteran voice Chris Emmett, That Nigel Rees Again, *Play School* legend and Chockaboy Fred Harris, and comedienne Denise Coffey. But when Coffey was unavailable for the second series, Simon Brett knew just the woman for the job – someone who could not only be relied on to provide pitch-perfect mimicry, but who was the original star of

Marshall & Renwick's main radio inspiration – Jo Kendall. 'As I say, there was no comedy tradition,' he recalls, 'so funny women were like gold dust, they always were. Now of course there are many more funny women, but then there were few who could be relied on to do comedy stuff. So Jo, with her *I'm Sorry* credentials, was a natural piece of casting.' Kendall fitted right in with this inspired brew of pastiches and puns, and in fact being the more experienced woman with a team of three actors rather than just one of the gang alongside five rowdy hams rather allowed her to shine in the series. 'It was probably more an acting job than a team job, in a way. The other lot had been together so long, they'd spent time backstage and that kind of thing, whereas with the *Burkiss* team, she probably knew some of them before she joined, but there was less of that shared history.' John Lloyd – perhaps the most influential of all of Hatch's producing protégés – would also work closely with Jo and the team in his time in the producer's chair, and agrees with Brett that Kendall was in many ways ahead of her time as a versatile comedienne, as opposed to a token showgirl. 'That was one of the main things with *Not the Nine O'Clock News*, that we thought, we're not going to do that, we're not going to have the girl who'd be just the bimbo; if she's going to do a bimbo, she's going to be very conscious that she's sending all that up, and she's going to play doctors and barristers . . . Jo Kendall was there ten years before.'

There was no live band for *The Burkiss Way* recordings unlike in the Prune days – the show simply had brief brassy jazz/rock credits slotted in generally wherever it suited the writers' needs. But from 1976 to 1980 *The Burkiss Way* was a radio sensation very nearly as wild as its sixties forebear, even without a live band, and it was also the first show to be directly influenced by *ISIRTA*. The following it attracted was devoted, even though there was only really one returning character – a miserable old git called Eric Pode of Croydon, of whom David Hatch recalled, 'He was greeted on his first speech of each episode with the kind of wild enthusiasm from the audience last seen with Lady Constance . . . The roots for an audience having a particular hero or heroine one can trace back through Jules and Sand in *Round the Horne* to Eccles in *The Goons*.' Besides Eric and his regular interviews with Fred Harris, there were a handful of trademark vocal tics, such as calling people 'Jobes' or 'Smoth', but that was as far as the in-jokes tended to go. Nevertheless, it still felt like a continuation of Radio Prune, filled with many an 'Oh, what a give-away!' when the writers revealed their inspiration too transparently. Comparisons were also inevitable, given the rowdiness of the audience every time a pun overstepped the mark. Eyewitness accounts portray the recordings for *The Burkiss Way* as pandemonium, with the venue often so packed to the rafters that fans took to sitting on the stage at the performers' feet.

As Simon Brett followed his mentor Humphrey Barclay to London Weekend Television, producer extraordinaire John Lloyd took over for the third series, before teaming up with Adams for not only their joint sci-fi comedy series idea, but also a special project for Christmas 1978. But *The Burkiss Way* was so important (or perhaps so fun) that the big boss, 'Hatch of the BBC' himself, took over the producer's role for the fourth series. Perhaps in tribute, the first episode features a sterling Lady Constance impression from Kendall herself, who had heard it often enough at close range. Hatch had just returned to London after a spell as head of BBC Network Radio in Manchester, but now being Head of Radio Light Entertainment, he certainly didn't need to get his hands dirty on the factory floor. *The Burkiss Way* would be the last show he actually produced, so it's clear that he really wanted to keep the show running, and in good quality. Simon Brett believes that the arrangement suited Marshall & Renwick as well. 'David had worked a lot with David Renwick and Andrew Marshall as they were developing new ideas, so I think they trusted him. They certainly liked *ISIRTA*, and they're both extremely verbal writers ... the punning and all that kind of thing obviously were in a direct tradition from *I'm Sorry* ...'

To celebrate this last foray into audio comedy producing, a subtle homage to *ISIRTA* was not enough for Hatch, and Tim Brooke-Taylor himself was invited to make a brief but incredibly noisy guest appearance:

FH: There's only one door left – it's my last chance of escape!

FX: Door opens. Hollow dripping sounds.

FH: At last I've – Oh God, no. No, I ... I feel all hot and feverish! My skin is red and blotchy, what manner of evil horror ...

TBT: (*Lady Constance*) Ooooeeeugggghhhhoeauhhh! (*Audience explode into lengthy ovation*). Oh, thank you! Good to see you! Ooohhh!

FH: Who's that?

TBT: Ooohhh! Eric Pode of Croydon!

FH: Now, come on, stop trying to pretend you're Lady Constance.

TBT: Oh, very well, spoilsport!

It's clear why David Hatch took it upon himself to keep *The Burkiss Way* running right up to 1980, when its writers made the inevitable transference to TV, both through an LWT attempt to televise *The Burkiss Way* (a Kendall-less series of spoof sketches entitled *End of Part One*, produced by Barclay and Brett), and, eventually, apocalyptic sitcom *Whoops Apocalypse*. As a show that united a large and loud audience with its anything-for-a-laugh atmosphere, *The Burkiss Way* gives a tantalising idea of what *ISIRTA* would have been like in the late seventies. Simon Brett thinks this was the case, at least 'in terms of the audience appeal and certainly the audience reactions in the studio, which probably built more after I moved to LWT . . . But the anarchic set-up had been established.' The cultural references had obviously moved on, the air of rebellion may have intensified in the wake of punk (the last ever episode, 'Wave Goodbye to CBEs the Burkiss Way', was drastically edited, taking out six minutes mocking Radio 4's grovelling coverage of the Queen's birthday – when broadcast, the gaps were filled with guitar music), but replace Eric Pode of Croydon with Grimbling, mix in a few funky Oddie tracks, and *The Burkiss Way* is positively *ISIRTA* Mark II.

Panto Season Again
One other Radio 4 presentation in the late seventies roused the sleeping Prune at the station, and if ever there was an Oxbridge (or more specifically, Cambridge) Mafia jamboree, it was *Black Cinderella Two Goes East*. In hindsight it may not seem a logical starting point for the duo behind *The Hitchhiker's Guide to the Galaxy* to advance their joint broadcasting career, but the first thing that John Lloyd and Douglas Adams did on leaving *The Burkiss Way* was to put on a pantomime. With Hatch in charge of Light Entertainment, the old festive excitement of an *ISIRTA* panto piss-take at the Playhouse was going to be recreated, in the winter of 1978. The same year, Hatch also pieced together an album of *ISIRTA* moments from the later series, with a cover featuring a transistor radio dunked in a bowl of prunes and custard – only the second official release, and a vinyl rarity today.

Shockingly, the idea for the show originated from Douglas Adams himself, and was to be his one original project as a radio producer. 'It was his idea to do *Black Cinderella Two Goes East*', confirms John Lloyd, 'but Douglas, as everybody knows, was the most disorganised person. The idea that anyone would make Douglas a producer is completely nuts. So he really struggled, and didn't know what to do, it was his first radio production, apart from the odd edition of *Week Ending*. So I, as Douglas' best friend, in the next office, was called in to help at the very last minute – if not days before the recording, then not much more than that. I came along because at least I knew about, you know, warm-ups and how to do read-throughs and all that. Douglas was fantastically creative, but he frequently couldn't make up his mind and get down to things . . . I was honoured to be asked, we just thought it was so brilliant that all these people had come along, all the *I'm Sorry* people, and other oddballs like John Pardoe, the Liberal MP.'

The fact that Adams instigated this full *ISIRTA* reunion is made all the odder by the fact that he never appeared in a single Footlights show – and the same club had sacked John Lloyd for fear that he would ruin a serious play that they were taking to Edinburgh. 'We both had a slightly strange relationship with Footlights, because they never put Douglas in a revue, they always thought he was too arcane, even though he was a big star in the St John's revue. I literally went up to Cambridge not knowing what the Footlights was, I'd never heard of it – I was that ignorant! And although I loved jokes, it took me quite a long time to get into it, and I never thought of joining Footlights until I was in my last year in '73, because I did college revues, just as Douglas was doing.' Nevertheless, their association with the club put them in Hatch and Brett's sights as talent scouts, and in the end Lloyd's start in broadcasting seemed to echo Hatch's own a decade earlier. 'At that time, Footlights was seen as kind of superannuated and hopeless. There hadn't been a really, really funny revue since *Cambridge Circus*. And ours wasn't considered in any way the most innovative revue, but a return to that old tradition of great jokes, lots of fun and larks and all that kind of thing. The worst thing about it was the title, it was called *Every Packet Carries a Government Health Warning*.' The arrival of this vintage of Footlights on radio, however, did not prove as hardy as *ISIRTA*, with their offering *Oh No It Isn't* only running for six episodes. In the meantime, Lloyd continued to follow in Hatch's footsteps producing *Week Ending, Just a Minute*, several pilots and generally earning himself a reputation as a safe pair of hands, and the perfect co-producer to bring Adams' pantomime into being.

Hatch naturally approved the project with gusto, and Adams and Lloyd fulfilled their remit by zooming up to Cambridge like they were attached to the alma mater by a piece of elastic, recruiting a pair of undergraduates to script the thing, rather than Oddie and Garden or any other established team – or indeed, coming up with the puns themselves. But getting the finished scripts out of the writers Clive Anderson and Rory McGrath was not as easy as they thought. Adams himself had to doggedly shadow the pair to make sure they got the job done, which was ironic given that Adams' later novels required him to be similarly coerced into getting words on the page, if not actually locked in his room with a pad, a pencil and a rudimentary Apple Mac.

Considering the equally head-splitting problems that the producers had getting the cast together, perhaps it's not surprising that *Black Cinderella* was one of Douglas Adams' few producing jobs. Casting the show should have been easy, as the entire company was made up of Footlights graduates – Richard Murdoch's aged tones were perfect for Baron Hardup/Oddbeef, younger members of the troupe were Maggie Henderson and Dr Rob Buckman as Cinderella and Prince Charming, and probably the biggest coup was roping in King of Cambridge Peter Cook as Prince Disgusting. Still coming down from the final *Derek & Clive* outing, Cook plays the role in the spirit of his alterego Clive throughout – leering, gravelly, sick-minded and carefree, barely bothering to curb his language, as if it will spill out into full-on *Get the Horn* profanity at any moment.

With that group bagged, getting Hatch to reunite his old *ISIRTA* pals would be a walkover, surely? Jo Kendall was certainly happy to play not only the Wicked Stepmother but several female roles, and Tim and Graeme were naturals for the Ugly Sisters, of course – Tim would go on to don the dame's insane garb for many a panto season in years to come, still allowing the Lady Constance within him the odd rare chance to air her bloomers. Garden, meanwhile, put on a 'Moaning Minnie' voice based on legendary panto dame Norman Evans. The pair made an unlikely brace of daughters for Kendall and Murdoch:

JK: How pathetic you are. Our marriage is becoming a farce. You never liked me as a person, all you ever wanted was my body. Well you can't have it – I've buried it.

RM: Oh that's awful, and unspeakably hideous! What a ghastly prospect . . .

TBT: (*Lady C*) Ah, you've noticed me at last! Ooeughh! (*Audience cheer*) Oh, thank you, you're older than you look! Ah, Mumsie! (*Kissing noise*) Dadsie! (*Kissing noise*) Cinders! (*Kissing noise*)

BO: Why does he keep kissing his hand like that?

TBT: Any more of your lip and you'll find it difficult to eat!

JK: Where's my other daughter, Gardenia?

GG: Ee, 'ello everybody, 'ere I am. I'm sorry I'm late, but I've been putting my face on and I ran out of clamps. Never mind, I've had an invigorating bath and now I feel like a new man.

TBT: Oh, but Gardenia, you're a girl!

GG: Oh, so it was a loofah then . . .

Bill's role in the panto was more problematic, however, which is why he's officially credited as 'The Pantomime Bill Oddie', and generally grumbles entertainingly about his casting throughout the proceedings, as well as usually taking the place of the much hated Buttons when the need arises. He also gets to sing a bizarre song with Graeme and Tim called 'Sisters . . . and Bill Oddie'.

Getting John Cleese on board was – perhaps inevitably – even more diffi-cult. Unhappy with the BBC's treatment of a programme he'd worked on with producer John Cassels entitled *John Cleese's Sketchbook*, which also featured his wife Connie Booth, he absolutely refused to be in the Footlights reunion panto, or attend a recording. The despairing Adams and Lloyd eventually managed to beat him down on the first point, at least, strong-arming the comic by arranging to set up a tape recorder at his home so he could record his lines as the Fairy Godperson there and then. It was a bizarre ploy to which the *ISIRTA* team never had to resort, and it lent a deathly quality to Cleese's contribution to the panto when his lines were played in, especially with such a rowdy audience in attendance. The joke turned out to be on John by the end of the story anyway, as the rest of the cast legged it for the pub early, leaving his recorded voice all on its own. Bill had used a similar tactic to get John involved in a project when he recorded a Cleese sporting commentary for a pop single called 'Superspike' to raise money for British Olympiads, in 1976. Oddie went on to perform the song on *Top of the Pops*, but Cleese never had to leave his sofa.

Cleese's bodily absence aside, this festive reunion must have been a convivial way to see in 1979, but *Black Cinderella Two Goes East* never really came alive when broadcast and it was to be the last attempt to revive the *ISIRTA* panto tradition, especially with Hatch no longer on the ground floor of radio production. The recording remains a fascinating comedy oddment, though, with so many comic giants involved in one hour of fluff, and there's plenty there to satisfy the *ISIRTA* fan. As well as Tim's Lady Constance turn and the Buffies that rule the tale's Kingdom of Saxmania, there's Oddie's singing, puns in abundance and even a groan-laden 'Arrivals at the Ball' (including not only an excruciating 'Walter Wall-Carpeting' but also 'Mr and Mrs Champions, and their diminutive son Wee Arthur Champions'). But, with TV and indeed movie careers to maintain – plus Hatch's move to Controller of Radio 2 in 1980 – this tenuous *ISIRTA* reunion was a blip, and there were no more attempts to revive Prune on the horizon.

A Kick Up the Eighties

In the 1980s, the wonders of radio sketch comedy were probably best embraced by the team who would go on to create the ridiculously underappreciated Channel 4 sketch show *Absolutely* – experienced BBC writers Jack Docherty and Moray Hunter with their colleagues Pete Baikie and Gordon Kennedy, plus non-Scots contingent Morwenna Banks and John Sparkes. Between *In Other Words the Bodgers* in 1985 and *Bodgers, Banks & Sparkes* the following year, they created ten episodes of brilliantly clever radio comedy, weaving together insane sketches that catch the listener off guard in much the same way that *The Burkiss Way* made good use of the medium.

But an earlier hugely successful radio show which contained contributions from Hunter & Docherty (including one of the best remembered sketches, in which a director tries to convince one of his actors that the best way to play the part is to *be a better actor*) owed a lot more to *ISIRTA*. This was due not least to being based on a fictional 'national local radio station' which gave the team the licence to cram in any sketch they wanted, be it a spoof of an existing programme, a bizarre interview, or a ridiculous news story. *Radio Active* picked up where *The Burkiss Way* left off in 1980, and its similarities to *ISIRTA* didn't stop at the radio station format. The team, which was formed for the Oxford Revue of 1978, contained a young Angus Deayton (dry, saturnine, destined to contend with comparisons to John Cleese throughout his early career), Helen Atkinson-Wood (a talented mimic and the only female in the group), Philip Pope (the king of musical pastiches), Michael Fenton-Stevens (a gifted all-round comedy actor with a particular knack for playing women) and, by the time they reached Radio 4, Geoffrey Perkins (the driving force of the show, and already a radio comedy producer by the time *Radio Active* debuted. He would go on to be the BBC's Head of Comedy and, indeed, producer of *I'm Sorry I Haven't a Clue*). Having scored a hit in Australia with the Hee Bee Gee Bees single 'Meaningless Songs (In Very High Voices)', the team also enjoyed a successful tour of the Antipodes together.

The parallels to the Radio Prune staff are irresistible of course, but the main difference with *Radio Active* was the extent to which the format was rigidly followed. Where Angus Prune was the originator of Radio Prune, Radio Active was owned by the execrable despot Sir Normal Tonsil, but the main presenters – Anna Daptor, Mike Channel, Mike Flex and of course Mike Hunt – helped create a complete cogent fictional radio station, unlike the entirely meandering set-up of Radio Prune, which only came into play for a bit of a laugh. No one was ever seriously expected to ignore the fact that *ISIRTA* was a bunch of kids messing about in front of a live crowd. But *Radio Active* (with its returning advertisements for 'Honest Ron' and whatever housewives June and Mary were flogging each week) managed to maintain the facade of being a national local radio station throughout over fifty episodes in seven series – not to mention the TV spin-off *KYTV* and a reunion special in 2002.

The *Radio Active* reunion special was, of course, not unprecedented. Perhaps the most famous example of a radio show being revived after a long time off-air was the famous *Last Goon Show of All*, which proved a perfect celebration of the wonders of sound broadcasting, in that it was 'like they'd never been away'. Unlike on telly, it doesn't matter how the years have treated the stars of a radio show – as long as they've got a voice, a new edition can be made to sound just like the old days.

This must have occurred to David Hatch when the twenty-fifth anniversary of the first try-out *ISIRTAs* came around in 1988. Apart from a small book of selected scripts (mainly from the later series) put together by Bill and Graeme and released by Javelin Books in 1985, there had been little activity in the *ISIRTA* camp throughout the decade, and Hatch arrived back at the

BBC's Light Entertainment Department to find a world very short on the spirit of Prune.

Having been boss of both Radio 2 and Radio 4, David Hatch was promoted first of all to Director of Programmes, and, in 1987, to Managing Director of BBC Radio, with a seat on the board of management – quite some progress for the vicar's son who almost became a teacher, before opting to be a clown. But the silent critics of what was seen as an Oxbridge old-school-tie network (not to mention the far louder critics, especially in the 1980s) would not have questioned Hatch's rise through the ranks if they ever worked with him. As well as being a funny and agreeable person to work for, he had an ear for sound radio, and comedy in particular, like nobody else in the business – as Phil Spector or George Martin were to popular music, David Hatch was to radio comedy. And he was loyal to BBC Radio, not just as part of the old high-ranking governing body that he used to mock so regularly in *ISIRTA*, but as a truly interested, hands-on creator of quality radio.

That's why, only a year or two after taking the top job in radio, he was once more, and for an absolutely final time, hearing the call. It was time for Kipperfeet 'Boring Old Announcer' Hatch to leap into the saddle once again. To put it in his own words: 'The entire nation trembled as it heard once more that dreadful sound that it hoped never to hear again . . .' No, not the World War II air-raid siren – 'the Angus Prune Tune'.

That's right, it was *I'm Sorry I'll Read That Again* . . . *Again* . . . *Once More! Again*.

8

The Prune Legacy

'I can't remember how the reunion happened,' Tim Brooke-Taylor says, helpfully, 'but I do know I pushed for it – it seemed a fun thing to do.' He was right, of course; huge fun was inevitable when this old gang of Cambridge graduates, now in their late forties, took to the stage of the Playhouse theatre one last time, in late 1989. Hatch detailed radio producer Richard Wilcox to take the reins, but ultimately the anniversary special was his party. Not that it was an easy one to arrange.

The tale of Hatch's mission to reunite the whole *Cambridge Circus* lot to mark the twenty-fifth anniversary of the original *I'm Sorry I'll Read That Again* pilots is remarkably well told within the special itself. For once, herding 'the voices, and what's left of the bodies . . .' of the Magnificent Six and a Half back behind the microphones must have been every bit as ambitious in real life as it was within the World of Prune. As ever, this was mainly due to Cleese, whose success with *A Fish Called Wanda* had just made him the least likely Hollywood sex symbol since Dudley Moore got caught in Bo Derek's hair-beads. Even an old personal friend and high-flying BBC bod like Hatch (referred to within the show as 'Managing Director of Radio, I/C Drama and Variety Shows', or Man-DRICDAVs – Mandy for short) would surely have a job convincing an award-winning movie star to return to the dusty halls of radio, even for one night?

Bill confirms that luring Cleese back was a Herculean feat. 'Graeme and I had been asked to write it, and we were quite happy, we were sure he was going to do it . . . and then we kept getting these messages from John's agent saying, "John's actually having Rest and Recuperation, he's decided he really can't do it at all," and we were really angry about that, because we'd written the bloody thing, you know? And then they came back and said "All right, he'll do it, but he only wants to do a half-hour show." And I remember Graeme and me saying "Don't tell him – tell him it's a half-hour show" – and we did about two hours or something.'

While David was climbing the ziggurat of BBC Management, of course Tim, Bill and Graeme had lived whole lives as *The Goodies*, a sensation on TV and – briefly – in the charts. But their individual solo careers had taken each of the trio in different directions by the late eighties. Post *Hello, Cheeky*, Tim joined the other two in the much maligned *Dandy*-inspired cartoon series *Bananaman* (no three people were better suited to bringing any D. C. Thomson comic to life), but Bill's involvement with children's TV went a lot further than his colleagues', co-creating the stage-school sitcom *From the Top* in 1985. *From the Top* echoes the same love of Music Hall as *ISIRTA*, telling the story of William Worthington, a bank manager who was born to a would-be showbiz starlet round the back of a Variety theatre during the Blitz. With the Music Hall in his blood, he joins a stage school to achieve his ambitions of becoming a star. Both the show and its equally entertaining novelisation were co-written with the second Mrs Oddie, author and former *Sale of the Century* hostess Laura Beaumont – Oddie and Jean Hart having had a parting of the ways in the mid-seventies, and officially divorcing in 1981. Laura had to suffer an excruciatingly uncomfortable honeymoon in New Guinea for Bill's first ever wildlife series, *Oddie in Paradise*. Once he had convinced the BBC Natural History bosses that he wasn't just an ex-comic chancing his arm at ornithology, Oddie's second – or was it third? – career was stretching ahead of him.

During the time that Bill was working on projects for children with his wife and gaining a reputation as the UK's most famous birdwatcher, Garden was putting his training to good use, presenting the BBC medical series *Body Matters*, and Tim was gaining an infamous reputation for starring in the cosiest of mainstream sitcoms, playing Richard O'Sullivan's best mate in the successful ITV show *Me and My Girl*, as well as the eponymous emasculated spouse in middle-middle class comedy *You Must Be the Husband*. This was obviously all grist to the mill for the show, in which Tim has taken up residence in the horrifically twee new town of Milton Sitcom. Hatch knows of only two men that can save him:

DH: Hello, I'm Mandy. You'll probably remember me better as Old Kipperfeet.

BO: Good Lord! It's boring old Hatch!

GG: What can we do for you, Mandy?

DH: . . . I'm looking for a load of pathetic old gags, feeble puns, stupid voices, appalling songs, so naturally I've come to you. You are still writers, aren't you?

BO/GG: Oh yes, I should say so, yes . . .

DH: Are you sure?

GG: Yes! Look, here's something I wrote this morning!
DH: It's a prescription.
GG: . . . It's quite a funny one.
DH: You're obviously not writers, you're a doctor and a birdwatcher.
GG: Oh, give us a break, Mandy! All we have to do is dig up an old *I'm Sorry I'll Read That Again* script . . .
BO: Yes, then cut out all the jokes that are rude or offensive or bad taste or out of date or unfunny . . .
GG: Then stick them all together to make a show!

Jo gets off lightly – having continued with her successful stage career, her thespian powers are only sent up by the suggestion that she changed her name to Meryl Streep to get work. But bringing Cleese back into the fold is a different matter – the 'squillionaire recluse' John Otto Cleese? Even in the Prune fantasy, Bill and Graeme doubt that he'd say yes. The great movie star is discovered in Howard Hughes-style seclusion (bar Oddie as his trusty side-kick Robin), counting his money while 'orbiting the Earth aboard his customised space shuttle, the *Ferret 1*. The ageing crazed eccentric cut a sorry figure, encased in empty Kleenex boxes and latex rubber sheeting, because of his neurotic obsession with not being mistaken for Basil Fawlty. His long grey beard hung down to his knees, looped up behind his back and swirled round the top of his head in a bouffant quiff, held in place with Blu-tack to conceal the ravages of a failed, rather pathetic hair transplant.'

Despite his celebrity, it was no surprise that Cleese finally opted to revel in an evening's nostalgia at the Playhouse in 1989; but within the show's plot, his willingness to rejoin comes with two conditions: 1) that he be allowed to do a silly walk (in contrast to real life of course, in which people asking him to wave his legs around was a painful daily occurrence – Cleese believes that years of reluctant silly walking contributed to his need for a hip replacement in 2001), and 2) that he be allowed to perform 'The Ferret Song' one last time.

BO: Oh no no no, they'll never agree to that, sir!
JC: Well, please ask them, Robin, please . . . Please let me do the silly walk, please! Do you realise what it's been like all these years, not being allowed to do the comedy legs? In *Silverado*, they wouldn't even let me hop! The part of the sheriff was crying out for it, but they wouldn't even let the horse do it! And 'The Ferret Song' was cut too, my God, Robin! Even in my own movie they held me back! You know, it was going to be *A Ferret Called Wanda*, but no! Oh no, Mister Smart-Arse-Kevin-Clock-My-Oscar-Kline-Bastard

said 'let's make it a fish!' A fish! And I protested! (*Audience cheer.*)
Shut up! I protested! But Michael-Two-Face-Kill-My-Dogs-Palin
said "A fish? Brilliant!" Bloody Palin . . . 80 *Days*? More like 80
years. Stick a chip up his nose and he's anybody's. I mean, a fish
can't do a silly walk, can it? Not like a ferret . . .

Bill and Graeme's script is every bit as relevant today as it was in 1989, in
making the theme of the show global warming and ecological disaster – the
hot air being created by Radio 1 DJs and the appalling Radio 2 shows of
Derek 'Do they mean me? They surely do!' Jameson is threatening the ozone
layer, and so Greenpeace advises the BBC to recycle their programmes for
the good of the environment (giving Nature Boy Bill Oddie a perfect excuse
to launch into a joyous pun-laden rendition of his song 'Spring, Spring Spring'
which far outstrips the original). As the DG's gofer, Hatch is ordered to dig
up any old rubbish for recycling, and naturally there's only one show on his
mind.

The central Prune Play of the reunion show is the only recycled part. Tim
Brooke-Taylor admits today, 'In hindsight, I wish we'd had a bit more time
and completely rewritten it, so it was completely original. But it was fun to
do, and good to go down memory lane, although one can't do that too often
. . .' The environmentally friendly spoof chosen was series 9's 'Jack the Ripper'
story, a 'Phantom Raspberry Blower of Old London Town'-style escapade that
may not have been among the greatest Prune Plays ever staged, but gave plenty
of exposure to everyone's talents. Plus it had that world-beating line:

GG: It's up to us, Superintendent!
JC: I suppose so, we should go to Whitechapel this very night, he's
      bound to strike again. Oh, look at that fog, it's a real, a real . . .
GG: Pea-souper?
JC: No thanks, Sergeant, just had one.

Also, it wasn't just a re-recording, but a fully recycled pastiche, with a fair
amount of rejigging from Oddie and Garden. It's interesting to compare the
two versions of 'Jack the Ripper' (and quite easy, given that both versions
were perversely included on the BBC cassettes), and to hear the strikingly
different performances from the team, over fifteen years apart. They ad-lib in
different places, a dodgy 'How de do dere, honey?' voice is thankfully expunged,
and Oddie adds an important caveat to his Hughie Greene impression, for
the late-eighties audience: 'Who is Jack the Ripper, and while you're at it,
who the hell am I?' But perhaps the biggest cut came in the loss of Tim's
gut-achingly funny inept Sherlock Holmes, a highlight of the original.

Their bit for the planet done, Lady Constance and the team round off the reunion special by giving John Otto Cleese such a sustained drubbing that you'd think the whole show was arranged by Cleese's therapist to dampen his award-inflated ego. The vigour with which Cleese enthusiastically puts himself up for abuse shows, once again, the affection he held for these old college pals of his – no one but his contemporaries, who had known him since he was an undergraduate with only an honourable mention in theatre reviews, could get away with such character assassination. His sex-symbol status is ridiculed, his Video Arts company is mocked (rich, considering Graeme had written and directed a fair few of the company's corporate training films), and of course, the silly walk proves to be rotten radio.

JC: Hang on, I get it, you're laughing at me, aren't you?
EVERYONE: Oh, no, no . . .
JC: Why are you being so horrid to me? We all used to be such chums!
DH: WHEN?
JC: You used to encourage my feeble attempts to be funny. Remember, it was you lot who first introduced me to ferrets! I've still got the toothmarks . . . And so have the ferrets. Nothing's changed. We're still the same fun-loving, zany pranksters trying to brighten people's lives with a smile and a merry quip, it's just that I'm paid twenty million times as much as you! That's not my fault, it's just because I'm twenty million times more talented, but that's no reason to be beastly to me . . .

In later life, Cleese has freely rhapsodised about the joys of radio, but at the height of his career, there was a tendency to rubbish his comic roots, Oddie says. 'He did tend to give us the impression that he didn't like the humour, but I think we knew how to slightly annoy him to get the best out of him. It's terrible when you're deified, and it must be hard to handle really. But I remember when we did that reunion thing, he was getting a bit huffy about something and I just sort of grabbed hold of him and said, "John, it's only us, don't worry!"'

Finally, this Cleese-centred last foray into the World of Prune leaves the whole gang (not to mention the Buffies of the BBC Board of Governors, and indeed the whole BBC) up for auction to the highest bidder . . . who of course, turns out to be a squillionaire recluse with a desperate need to perform a song about having a rodent up his nose. At last, Otto, owner of the BBC

(Broadcasting By Cleese), gets to end the entire *I'm Sorry I'll Read That Again* saga with a rousing recitation of 'The Ferret Song'.

You can bet that there were plenty of old hands in the crowd that Sunday night, cheering as the middle-aged Prune alumni delivered the old, old favourites, and every much loved character and gag was welcomed (or groaned at) with heightened volume. Humphrey Barclay (then with LWT) was not in attendance, but his trusty secretary Elizabeth Lord took that sentimental journey – and she wasn't just a guest either. Jo Kendall may have been far from centre stage in the reunion special, but that didn't matter when she'd already joined forces with her friend Liz to write not just a great sketch, but one last eavesdrop into the painful marriage of John and Mary, on their twenty-fifth anniversary:

JK: John, is that you? I'm in the bedroom.

JC: Eleanor darling!

JK: Eleanor? John, it's me . . . your wife! Mary!

JC: Oh, I'm so sorry, darling, I'd forgotten who you were . . .

JK: John, come through to the other room, won't you? I've got a surprise for you.

JC: Not after all these years, you haven't. Why are we in darkness, darling?

JK: I just thought you'd enjoy a romantic candlelit dinner for two.

JC: Oh good, who's coming? Where are you going then?

JK: John. It's for us. You and me. The two of us. It's our 25th.

JC: Ah, no wonder I'm exhausted . . .

JK: . . . I understand you with your little peccadilloes.

JC: Ah, how I love their little snouts and scaly backs.

JK: Those are armadillos!

JC: Well, of course they're armadillos, we bred them, remember?

JK: Yes, John – that was the most painful thing you asked me to do for you.

JC: Still, we laughed, didn't we? Gosh, how we laughed as we plunged them into the boiling fat . . .

JK: John, why do you have to be so cruel?

JC: Oh, I don't have to be, I just enjoy it, it's purely voluntary.

It was final proof of just how well deserved the name 'Cambridge Queen of Comedy' was – the slickness of the gags required for Cleese and Oddie's patter is not easy to replicate, and Jo and Liz captured the tone perfectly. So much for the 'old boy network' – Lord and Kendall were two women with good reason to grin through that last Sunday evening of all.

A Home for Old Jokes

'I don't think any of us came away from the reunion thinking "we must do another series",' says Graeme, 'but it was huge fun to do as a one-off . . . It was very much of its time, and of our time too.' The nostalgic success of the *ISIRTA* reunion inspired a bit of a Prune revival in the early nineties. Repeats popped up on Radio 2 and David Hatch oversaw four commercial releases for the show on BBC Audio cassette between November 1989 and 1997. These provide a perfect introduction to the show for any curious comedy fan born after the programme's demise.

The one note of preparation the rookie listener is given comes in the form of a reworking of the original LP sleevenotes, by Hatch:

> Despite Radio Prune's pioneering work in employing a woman, a small furry idiot and a future Managing Director of BBC Radio, nobody in the entire history of the show was ever awarded the O.B.E., and that is a record of which they can all be proud. This, on the other hand, isn't a record of which anybody can be proud, but then it was made in the old money, by unfortunates. Look after it please.

ISIRTA received plenty of repeats on national radio over the years, on a rather ad hoc basis, until the idea of filling half an hour with anything recorded more than six months ago became something of a taboo on British radio. So it's likely that the comedy fan who came home with one of these BBC double-tapes would know nothing of these famous comics' radio roots.

Radio *Prune*? Who's stuffing a gibbon? What does 'grimbling' mean? Who's John Davidson? Why are those people wildly cheering a man who sounds like a horny chicken? Getting a foothold in this in-joke-riddled world of madcap jazz, marital anguish and small furry creatures is a daunting task to the uninitiated. But, even decades on from their recording, that's how these repeated gags work – they hook you in, you want to know why everyone is enjoying the silliness quite so much. And before long, a new devotee of Radio Prune is created. In the nineties, this was more than likely thanks to Hatch's selection of shows on cassette.

'Anything But Broadcasting!'

At around the time the Managing Director of Radio was overseeing these early releases, however, the BBC was changing beyond all recognition. The Buffies and members of the MCC that once made up the BBC's Board of Governors were all dead and gone – Hatch was now on the board himself, in many ways poacher turned gamekeeper. But the BBC was going to have to evolve a lot further if it was to move towards the new millennium – and ensure the renewal of their charter by the Conservative government.

Despite having the most successful roster of radio shows to his name of any hands-on producer, Hatch's career in Management had not been free from anguish. While running Radio 4, his ambitious attempt to relaunch the morning scheduling into a running programme called *Rollercoaster* met with predictable bile from the station's legion of traditionalist listeners who boiled their eggs to the split-second timing of the station's hallowed schedules. And another headache awaited him when he was entrusted with launching a brand-new station, BBC Radio 5, in 1990. Its mix of sport, education and children's programmes was not embraced by a huge listenership, and when the Gulf War necessitated the introduction of rolling news, Hatch was put under pressure to turn the new station over to News and Current Affairs. One of the strongest voices in favour of this move was the Deputy Director General John Birt, and Hatch's victory in the Gulf War (Radio 4 carried the news service throughout) had, in many people's view, signed his own resignation for when Birt took the top job.

It was actually a shock for many when Birt became the DG, as Hatch had been widely tipped for the role himself. His devotion to quality broadcasting and combination of leadership skills and good humour seemed to set him in good stead, but the BBC as a Corporation was moving in a different direction. Not long after the inevitable happened in 1992, Hatch recalled, 'What happened was that I think it was decided that I should be moved out of radio. I didn't like that very much; I didn't *like* the way it happened. Apparently my successor was appointed six weeks before I was myself told.' However, thanks partly to the intervention of then Heritage Secretary David Mellor, Hatch was not actually kicked out, but made a 'special adviser' to Birt himself, or as Hatch himself had it (and didn't he have it?), he was 'a sort of minister without portfolio': 'I believe passionately in the BBC, and my task . . . with John Birt, has been to try and tell him what the soul of the BBC is about . . .' He had his work cut out putting a friendly face on the Birt regime.

The rise of Birtism at the BBC was probably best summarised in *Alexei Sayle's Stuff*, in which the self-styled 'fat bastard' has to wait for his dinner in the BBC canteen while accountants carry out an audit on his apple turnover. The grey, management-speak-spouting bureaucratic corporate faces taking the reins of broadcasting mirrored John Major's government exactly, but they were anathema to Hatch's passionate, jovial approach to broadcast management. Nevertheless, he was a loyal adviser, publicly defending the DG against accusations of tax irregularities, and keeping him up to date with a flurry of personal notes and pearls of wisdom gleaned from Hatch's four decades in radio production. And he had the satisfaction of at least one more enormous success, having exerted pressure to ensure a return to Radio 2 breakfast time for his friend Terry Wogan – there are many thousands of TOGs out there who owe a lot to Announcer Hatch. In a strange kind of repayment, a while after Hatch's wife Ann passed away in 1997, he was introduced to his second wife, Mary Clancy, by Terry and his wife Helen. Wogan was even best man at their wedding in 1999.

Hatch had always been an attentive boss, in his office at six thirty every morning, regularly popping into studios during broadcasts and geeing up the talent, as well as firing out hundreds of memos or 'Hatchlets' – witty and good-natured notes of encouragement, advice or censure, in the latter case often signed 'Cluck cluck, Mother Hen!' This was not just a professional trait, but extended to anyone who came into Hatch's sphere of influence – his quirky and thoughtful handwritten notes were appreciated by everybody who received them. In a job in which an ambition to transfer from radio to TV broadcasting was the norm, no other producer or manager retained such enthusiasm for and belief in radio as David Hatch. 'I do think that Radio 4 is the soul of the BBC. I remember saying in an interview in Thatcher's time, that if Thatcher . . . were going to destroy the BBC, the last bastion that we should all cluster round is Radio 4. Get rid of BBC1, BBC2, all the other channels, 4 is the soul of the BBC.' 'Radio 4,' he also wrote, in a decidedly Prune-ish vein, 'should be a daily anthem of joy – and anthem is as anthem does.'

Despite his devotion to radio, Hatch knew when he was sidelined, and so he took early retirement from the BBC in 1995. John Birt heralded him as 'an astute, straight-dealing and utterly committed champion of the medium' as he left. Ever the public servant, however, he didn't put his feet up, but signed up for whatever duty a highly experienced elder statesman could fulfil. When he completed the form, in the space where the applicant is allowed to specify their preferred area of public service, Hatch wrote 'Anything but broadcasting!'

He became not only a JP, but chair of the National Consumer Council in 1996, chair of the Parole Board of England and Wales in 2000 . . . and chairman of his own panel game, the radio-themed *Wireless Wise*, in 2003. He couldn't keep away from broadcasting for long.

Post-Prune Programming

There was an undeniable debunking spirit throughout the eighties when it came to Footlights, and the Oxbridge Mafia in general. This would perhaps be best demonstrated by the legendary 'Bambi', from the second series of *The Young Ones* in 1984 (in which the filthy heroes take on the might of 'Footlights College Oxbridge' on *University Challenge*, managing to blow up the toffs before being crushed to death by a giant chocolate eclair), if it wasn't for the fact that Footlighters Stephen Fry, Hugh Laurie and Emma

Thompson merrily joined in these vicious swipes, proving that the savaging was toothless.

In truth, not least thanks to this generation of Footlights graduates, Cambridge and Oxford continued to provide vast amounts of top-quality comedy throughout the eighties and nineties, on radio just as much as TV. As well as Fry's peerless non-live sketch show *Saturday Night Fry* in 1988, Cambridge graduate and CULES member Andy Hamilton hooked up with Comedy Store compere Nick Revell, taking the baton from *Radio Active* for several series of *The Million Pound Radio Show* between 1985 and 1992, with a reunion in 1996. The show was more along the lines of *Round the Horne* than *ISIRTA*, generally building a montage of sketches from the duo's weekly activity.

Many of these radio comedy originals benefited greatly from David Hatch's support, while he was still managing director, for a new weeknight 11 p.m. comedy slot on Radio 4. The spot helped to launch the careers of a whole new generation of comics, from Cambridge and elsewhere. That said, however, another nineties Cambridge sketch show in the traditional revue vein was *And Now in Colour*, written and performed by four Footlights boys, including *Preston Front* scribe Tim Firth and comedian turned barrister William Vandyck – but its two series of sketches and songs, broadcast on Radio 4 at the start of the decade, made no great impression. Two other comedy shows – one purely Cambridge in origin, and the other filled with Oxford and Bristol graduates – were to prove considerably more influential as the decade unfolded.

Rob Newman & David Baddiel, and Steve Punt & Hugh Dennis, though two hugely different kinds of double act, were all at Cambridge in the mid-eighties – all bar Newman were in the Footlights, but they never performed as a team in their college years. Herded together post-graduation by producer Bill Dare (son of *Just a Minute* and *Hitchhiker's* icon Peter Jones), they formed the central team of their own zeitgeist-strangling semi-topical sketch show *The Mary Whitehouse Experience*, piloted in 1989. They may have seemed to be yet another male quartet of Cam-punting graduates, but they introduced a far sharper, harsher brand of comedy than the *And Now in Colour* team, who had actually followed them into the Footlights.

TMWE benefited from stand-up spots from the likes of Mark Thomas and Jo Brand to add credibility to their radio incarnation, and the very fact that they broke through on Radio 1 rather than 2 or 4 shows that they were beginning the process of genuinely achieving that philosopher's stone of all radio producers, so rare since *ISIRTA*'s popularity in the sixties: Making BBC Radio Comedy Cool for a Younger Generation. Within just a few years Newman & Baddiel's national success on TV and with their live tour would help coin the cliché 'comedy is the new rock 'n' roll' and, in turn, inspire the growth of comedy as an enormously powerful industry in its own right, rather than just another branch of Light Entertainment.

Perhaps more influential in terms of comedy form, however, was *On the Hour*, which was launched in 1991 when the Oxford-educated producer of *The Mary Whitehouse Experience*, Armando Iannucci, contacted Bristol graduate and Greater London Radio DJ Chris Morris and suggested that they team up to exploit Morris' inspired spoof radio stylings in a half-hour format. Iannucci himself was no dunce when it came to sound production, and their joint skills (not just with language and absurdity, but with razor and tape) made *On the Hour* a genuine landmark in radio comedy. It took the accurate news spoofing that first characterised *I'm Sorry I'll Read That Again* and pushed it about as far as it can possibly go, updated for the brasher news broadcasting of the nineties. Rather than hilarious *Two Ronnies*-esque howlers like 'Late last night a supermarket in west London was broken into. Seven pounds of cheese and fifty bottles of aftershave were stolen. Police are looking for a very very sexy mouse', *On the Hour*'s news in brief ran more like 'The Bank of England has lost the pound', 'Where now for man raised by puffins?' or 'Following a low reading on the Royalty Meter, Prince Edward is to be executed'. Both Morris and Iannucci were true lovers of radio, and just like *ISIRTA*, barely a scruple of the BBC's wireless broadcasting was left unmocked in *On the Hour*'s twelve episodes.

Most of these shows of course leapt onto television rapidly, with BBC Radio more than ever being expected to know its place, as a kind of wet nurse for the VIP that was BBC TV – in fact, not only the BBC but the independent production companies that practically ran TV comedy in the 1990s, such as Hat Trick or Talkback, both established and run by Oxbridge graduates, who pounced on these radio gems and gave many of the stars namechecked in the last few pages TV careers. The *ISIRTA* team had been among the first post-*Hancock* generation for which the move to TV from radio success was not just possible, but almost expected, and the tradition was going stronger than ever throughout the nineties and indeed in the twenty-first century. The radio series *On the Town with the League of Gentlemen* caused some discontent among radio producers who had a Hatch-like loyalty to the medium, presented as it was to the radio comedy department as almost a fait accompli, to act as a tester for the twistedly theatrical North Country sketch performers' all-but-commissioned TV show. For many new comedy names, the briefest flirt with sound broadcasting was becoming quite enough training ground for the full TV and movie career experience, with very few performers returning to work for radio fees once their DVDs were in the shops.

The proliferation of comedy clubs and general evolution of the comedy industry – be it in clubs, on tour, on radio, TV, cinema, print or online – has obviously provided far greater scope for the radio producer looking to put together a new comedy show than just the Cambridge Footlights, or the Oxford revue. Comedy is such big business that the idea of talent-spotting seems archaic to many modern producers, who just have to set up an online competition and watch the hopeful entries flood in. There is, however, still a huge roster of Oxbridge names that make up the structure of the comedy industry, and although getting into the Footlights is far from being a golden ticket to comedy greatness, some graduates continue to break through.

Stephen Fry recalls being certain that the glory days were already well in the past when he was performing the silliest of sketches in the Footlights clubroom back in the late seventies. The young committee members would trawl through the archives, marvelling at what their great comic forebears had come up with when they were still just larking about at Cambridge. 'I was very aware of *Cambridge Circus* as a student, and there were pictures of them on the wall in the clubroom, all in duffel coats, and that classic sort of sixties student look . . . It was very interesting, that whole sense of a connection, of the continuity of the Footlights all the way through. And of course, you believe when you're there that it's over, you think, "Those were the glory days, and we're just an embarrassment." And one doesn't realise that it's going to go on twenty years after you, there'll be people like Sacha Baron Cohen and Mitchell & Webb to carry on the tradition . . .'

Aren't You a Little Past It?

A great boon to all the radio shows mentioned in this book was the birth of the digital radio station BBC Radio 7, which was officially launched by Paul Merton in 2002. Specialising in repeating comedy broadcasts over three years after their original airing, the station has done wonders for the status of several wrongly forgotten comedy series. It even provided a platform for both Hatch and Oddie to present their own choice of classic radio comedy, with Oddie presenting his own thesis on why radio comedy has greatly improved since the bad old days – 'I'm sixty-four, and tend to have friends of roughly the same age. And one of the things I absolutely hate is when they go on about "Oh, they don't do comedy like they used to . . ." Generally speaking, my response to that is THANK GOD!' – and goes on to prove his point with episodes of *On the Hour* and *On the Town with the League of Gentlemen*. As both these shows were by then too old to be representative of contemporary radio comedy, it wasn't a watertight argument – but he remembers the whole show being recorded against his better judgement, and the old shows he was compelled to include were so piss-poor as to put him off the entire project.

Hatch was more in control with his own stint as a comedy DJ, playing favourites chosen from his own productions, including an episode of *The Burkiss Way*, but eschewing an *ISIRTA* episode because, thanks to digital radio, it got 'plenty of airings anyway'. Although a mighty creation like *I'm Sorry I'll Read that Again* was not exactly forgotten by the comedy-loving public, the regular repeats of Radio Prune silliness on Radio 7 has been a boon for fans of puns, ferrets and rhubarb tart. When the station started there had been no commercial releases since 1997, no sign of the shows finally arriving on CD, and the individual *ISIRTA* team members weren't just far apart working on their own projects, they were all reaching the age when they would have retired – had *Cambridge Circus* not come along to change their lives. Jo Kendall, in fact, has retired to a comfortable cottage in Bury St Edmunds after a long, successful career in the theatre with a modest but colourful roster of TV and movie appearances on her CV. Kendall left radio comedy behind her years ago.

As indeed did Bill Oddie, who is more famous as a TV naturalist and conservationist than he ever was as a comedian, or indeed a musician. Oddie has blown hot and cold on the comedy business in his later years, one minute all but disowning his comic legacy, the next reducing everyone on panel games such as *Eight Out of Ten Cats* and *Never Mind the Buzzcocks* to panicked bemusement with his bizarre moods and eccentricities. Oddie's humour is an inseparable part of his personality, it's there in all his television programmes, but there's little doubt that it's Bill's wildlife shows that have made him that cosiest of things, a national treasure, whether he likes it or not. Indeed, he is an institution. Indeed . . . he has an OBE.

Yes, in 2003 Bill Oddie, the wild rock-singing rebel of Radio Prune, accepted an invitation to Buckingham Palace to receive an OBE for his services to wildlife conservation. *ISIRTA* may have mercilessly mocked honours for years, treating them as royally approved choccy drops . . .

GG: Ah, Hanger-Ending, do come in, take a seat. Have an OBE.
DH: No thanks, sir, I've already got one.
GG: Now, listen, I have a job for you. A very secret mission. I need hardly tell you that this job is absolutely Top Secret.
DH: I see, sir.
GG: Right, that'll be all.
DH: But what do you want me to do?
GG: Ah, well, that's the secret. Now you run along and do the job . . . and I'll tell you what it was when you get back.
DH: No, that's not much better, sir.
GG: No, it isn't, is it? Tell you what, I'll give you three guesses.

DH: You want me to carry a package of secret documents to Cleethorpes, documents which, if they fell into the wrong hands, could topple the government and plunge Europe into war?

GG: Got it in one, good man! Have another OBE.

DH: No thanks, sir, I'm trying to give them up.

. . . but Hatch himself had received the CBE for services to broadcasting way back in 1994, and would actually be knighted for his work with the criminal justice system the year after Oddie's OBE acceptance. As Hatch himself laughed in early 2007, 'When we gave ourselves all those OBEs, who'd have thought we'd finish up with a knight of the realm with a CBE, it was all quite weird really.' It would be ludicrous to accuse Bill Oddie of 'selling out' for accepting some recognition for his devotion to conservation . . . though it has to be said, Bill wasn't too comfortable with the idea of bowing to the royals and the archaic system he'd spent so long sending up. But he shrugs, 'You can say what you like about it, I don't care. If it had been three weeks later I wouldn't have accepted it, once Blair had gone into Iraq . . . I thought about not accepting it – the only reason I did is that I know how those things are awarded, which isn't anything to do with the Queen or the prime minister or anybody else, but they ask peer group people. So I know they would have gone round David Attenborough and a few others, and people put you up, I was probably nominated by someone in the conservation world, the RSPB and the Wildlife Trusts, and I thought, "Well, actually it's a bit of an insult to them," I'd have to ring everybody up and say sorry. So I thought, "Oh fuck it, let's go along with it." And my family obviously wanted to go to the palace and have a bit of a giggle, which we certainly did! The healthy disrespect for the whole thing I thought was quite splendid. It was like a bunch of naughty schoolboys, with the posh lot – Keeper of the Queen's Corgis or something – over there. I've only worn the OBE once, to a fancy dress party, as a bit of bling.'

Oddie would have been forgiven for being a little paranoid as he and his proud family made their way out of the palace with his medal, though, as sooner or later he knew he would be facing a grinning Tim Brooke-Taylor and Graeme Garden, who says, 'I'm still laughing. Not quite so loudly, but still laughing. Ah, the look on his face when we first met him afterwards was priceless . . .' Besides the gong, an equally dramatic about-turn in Oddie policy came from his advertising for the Post Office in 2007, after devoting a whole episode of *ISIRTA* to how rubbish they are: 'Second class is lower class . . .'

With all this irresistible material to work with, how on earth could they possibly avoid just one more special reunion of the old *Cambridge Circus* team for a positively final foray into the World of Prune? Comedy being the commercial titan that it is nowadays, getting Cleese and co. back together would have seemed an incredibly worthwhile project – Cleese had after all managed to synchronise with the surviving Pythons for a thirtieth anniversary special in 1999, and Tim and Graeme (and occasionally Bill, who was mainly present in pre-recorded form) had scored a huge hit touring their stage show *The Goodies Still Rule OK,* in the wake of finally getting the shows released on DVD after years of frustration. The two of them made the UK leg of the tour (which swept triumphantly through Australia with Oddie in 2005) a more personal odyssey through their comedy creations, not just giving Freddy & Teddy their own spot on the show, but performing a heavily stripped-down *ISIRTA* script, allowing Tim to burst into Lady Constance's warble to delighted audiences up and down the country for the first time in generations. In Australia, Bill was on hand with all the sound-effect props just like in the old days, and all three recreated the tried and tested 'Jack the Ripper' Prune Play to great acclaim.

So the death of Graham Chapman in 1989 (and the busy schedule of Bill Oddie) hadn't stood in the way of these comedy reunions. But, asked in 2006 about the likelihood of one more helping of *ISIRTA,* the one man who remains constant through the entire *I'm Sorry* story, Tim Brooke-Taylor, had to admit: 'I'd be very happy to do another one, but I don't think this would happen. Bill and John have moved on. Graeme and I very much enjoyed doing a bit from *ISIRTA* in our *Goodies* stage show . . . Judging by the audience reaction at the Edinburgh Festival and our tours of Australia it's one of the highlights of the show. It's great doing Lady Constance again.' 'Yeah, that was great fun to do, no doubt about it,' agrees Bill. 'There would be no reason not to do something like that . . .'

Thankfully, without any involvement of the producers, writers or performers, *I'm Sorry I'll Read That Again* landed on BBC CD in 2007, ten years after the last commercial release. The TV and radio archivist Andrew Pixley had been badgering his friends at BBC Audiobooks for new *ISIRTA* products for a long time, and finally commissioning editor Michael Stevens oversaw a repackaged box set of all the episodes already released on cassette, only rearranged into chronological order. There was even a brand-new CD, Volume 5, containing especially classic episodes 'Dentisti', 'Bunny and Claude' (featuring Bill's *Magical Mystery Tour* pastiche), the Northern melodrama 'Incompetence', and the incomparable disaster that was 'Star Trek'. The earlier releases had been very sparsely designed, with the usual snaps sourced from the mid-sixties photo sessions of the gang bound together in audio tape and the like, but these new releases were brash, colourful collectibles, with an almost *Carry On* style to the packaging.

Could there really not be just one special one-off episode to coincide with the CD relaunch? The time was ripe – none of the team were getting any younger, and John Cleese was rediscovering his comic voice at his leisure (between filming guest appearances in huge movies), by using his Web portal thejohncleese.com as a medium for some semi-improvised comedy sketches all performed at his American ranch. Taking his stage show *John Cleese – His Life, Times and Current Medical Problems* on tour in New Zealand in 2005 must also have aroused the sleeping Otto in him somewhat – and in 2005 it was already sixteen years since the last reunion, which had been sixteen years on from the end of the show's proper run. If Brooke-Taylor had been up for it, he would easily have brought John into the fold– it was Cleese who dubbed Tim 'The only man who could get Hitler and Churchill to come to tea together'.

When asked in early 2007 about the possibility of some kind of reunion happening, David Hatch was certainly all for it, if just for a chance to meet up with his old pals at the Playhouse and have a laugh. Recalling the 1989 reunion, he said, 'It was great to be back on the stage with everyone. Because we had spent a long time together, with the stage show, and then over the ten-year period of doing *I'm Sorry*, when there were regular bouts of us down at the Playhouse on Sundays – and it wasn't just doing a show and wanting it to be good, it was seeing people and having a good chat with them, and seeing how people were getting on, getting married, having kids – it's that sort of camaraderie that of course you miss.' However, he added, 'I think the people to ask about a reunion are Bill and Graeme, because it'd have to be written by somebody. But I think most of us are still in touch – I had lunch with John about two months ago when he was over here, Graeme and I were emailing each other when I was in South Africa, so there is a circuit of people still in touch with each other.'

But unfortunately, only a few months after these words were spoken, the chances of rounding up the Magnificent Six and a Half for one last geriatric serving of the Wonder Show became nil. David Hatch died of cancer in June 2007.

Hatch of the BBC

Hatch was not the first of the *ISIRTA* architects to shuffle off this mortal coil – Peter Titheradge passed away in March 1989, seven months before Graham Chapman, and his friends and colleagues all paid due respect to the man who had, ultimately, made *everything* possible. It's hard to emphasise sufficiently just how meekly many of the comic icons featured in this book were drifting towards the daily grind of law, medicine, education etc. when they neared graduation – none of these middle-class graduates had showbiz in their blood. John Cleese has always wavered on whether he has showbusiness in his nature, and is convinced that he was set for a quiet life. 'All the people in my year – 1963 – we all had jobs, we were in advertising, or teaching. I was going to be a lawyer, a solicitor . . . and then this show happened out of the blue, which was much better than we expected, because we had some talented people . . . And suddenly there were people there in suits, talking about putting it in the West End, and other people, different people, in different suits, asking us whether we wanted to join the BBC . . . And I thought, "I think writing jokes would be much nicer than sitting in a lawyers' office." Plus I got paid two and half times as much!'

If Titheradge hadn't gone out on his talent-scouting mission and been suitably bowled over by *A Clump of Plinths*, then *Monty Python*, *The Goodies* and, in turn, British Comedy as we know it simply wouldn't exist. Humphrey Barclay paid tribute to the poet, wit, adventurer and producer in his funeral eulogy: 'If someone were to ask what the following have in common: the Managing Director of BBC Network Radio; the author of Thames TV's comedy success; and this year's British Academy Best Film Actor – anyone outside this circle of friends might have difficulty. But for any of *us*, there's an instant answer: Peter. Peter the talent spotter, Peter the mentor, Peter the champion, Peter the wise, Peter the friend . . . to whom David Hatch, Simon Brett and John Cleese, among so many of us, acknowledge our unpayable debt. I spoke to John as we were planning a send-off for Peter before his departure for New Zealand. He was instantly enthusiastic, because, he said: "I love that man." John called me from America as soon as he heard that Peter had died, and he was in tears.'

Peter Titheradge, then, achieved a lot more than he probably realised, even given the full and variety-filled life he led. Although David Hatch is responsible for half of the most successful radio shows of the last forty years, he would not have had the opportunity without Titheradge. The difference with Hatch's death, though, was that this wasn't the loss of one of the originators of *ISIRTA*, it was the loss in many ways of the star – 'Boring Old Announcer' Hatch, the whistle-blowing prefect with a liability to take you unawares with the looniest fit at the drop of a hat.

Only his closest friends had known about David's illness, but even they were taken by surprise by the suddenness of his passing. John Cleese had flown in to visit him just a few days before his death, and 'It was absolutely typical that he couldn't wait to peel back the bedclothes to show me a T-shirt he was wearing which was a London Underground map with the words "I'm Going Underground", which he thought was absolutely hilarious'. The newspaper obituaries were rich with praise for a great defender of British radio, but his real comic powers as a performer and writer were sadly overlooked, several papers mistakenly referring to him as 'a straight man'. One obituary described his *ISIRTA* persona as 'unflappable', which is way off the mark – Announcer Hatch would be sedate and urbane one minute, and whine and scream and yell at the unfairness of his boring persona the next, in a way that would make Kenneth Williams back away cautiously. Hatch's range of voices and personas, from Footlights to the final episode of *ISIRTA*, was never less than impressive, deserving the waves of adoring laughter that they inspired.

Cleese's speech at the memorial service elicited a roar of laughter by beginning with the words 'I always had the feeling that David thought I was a bit of a wanker . . .' but the loss of his great friend inspired a lengthy and sincere tribute. 'I found David totally congenial,' Cleese says, 'I was trying to remember, over forty years or whatever it is you expect to have a few disagreements with friends, but right now I can't recall one with David. I was very reassured that someone as utterly decent as him was in charge.' Humphrey Barclay also has fond memories of his colleague and friend – and not just during the *ISIRTA* years: 'It's been the most happy experience, how we've all gone on, happily together – with two sad losses, Graham, and now David. He had a wonderful relish for life, and for talent. He was intolerant when talent didn't come up to the mark, but nobody was a greater encourager . . . He was totally distinct. A big heart, and a big talent.'

'In itself, it's a wonderful bit of history, really,' Bill Oddie reflects, 'to have someone who *played* the man from the BBC, the little Announcer man who was cross that nobody ever gave him proper parts to play and that, end up as the big boss – Sir David!'

John Lloyd got his first break in comedy broadcasting thanks to Hatch, whose guidance and encouragement to succeed would eventually result in Lloyd's production of shows such as *Not the Nine O'Clock News*, *Spitting Image*, *Blackadder* and *QI*. 'Nobody who met David didn't hugely respect him, and we were very good friends, and stayed good friends. I went to his memorial service and his funeral as well, which was heartbreaking, because he was such a well-loved guy. Both places were absolutely jammed with people. I said to his wife Mary, "David was like a second father to me", because he was such a supportive, energetic guy, and he gave me my life's motivation in a way, because he showed that it was a great thing to be the person behind the scenes. That it wasn't a lesser thing to be the producer, but it was a noble and brave and difficult job, and that somebody has to do it, and you may as well do it well. And that's sort of gone, really, to a large extent. Unless you're a celeb, you don't count these days – they don't give a shit who the producer is, it's, you know, "Can you get Graham Norton?" But what is extraordinary about David is that he lived his life so well. He was a man of the most extraordinary integrity and kindness, and diligence, and he was a genuinely good person. That's a very rare thing, you don't find those people around very much. He was just such a brilliant bringer of vibrant life to everything.'

Those who had hoped for just one more *ISIRTA* reunion special, with every member of the team still around to have some fun, realised the end of that hope was part and parcel of the sadness of Hatch's loss. However . . . the BBC has yet to make any move to give Hatch the tribute he so clearly deserves – and besides, a stage show recreation of *Round the Horne* was a huge hit in 2004, even receiving a broadcast on BBC4 despite the fact that none of the stars or main writers were involved, most of them being long gone. Also, The Bonzo Dog Band staged a triumphant tour down memory lane in the twenty-first century, despite the *enormous* absence of lead singer Viv Stanshall. These mixes of reunion, tribute and good old-fashioned crowd-pleasing can be a joyous and cathartic appendix to any comic or musical legacy.

Tim Brooke-Taylor has already been the subject of a strange Australian stage play (which envisaged an alternate universe in which Oddie became a huge pop star and left him and Graeme to continue without him), and also agrees that some form of tribute is inevitable, but it could never be quite as enjoyable as a full reunion would have been: 'You almost think you can do these shows, because they become sort of tributes, in a way, but it is a shame . . .'

No Need to Apologise . . .

I'm Sorry I'll Read That Again remains the single greatest radio sketch show of all time. How can that statement be justified? All right, so it may never have transferred directly to TV and spawned a million talking dolls or official BBC mugs that shout 'Teapot!' when you put hot water into them, and it may not have the international reputation of *The Goon Show*, but . . . just listen to that football-crowd atmosphere. No other radio sketch show has ever united an audience in such a dogged, joyous fashion, and no other such programme ever will again – it's just impossible. The days when any sketch show on radio could attract a devoted following without transferring to TV, going on tour and making a movie are long gone. Just as no band could ever hope to top The Beatles, because those four young men were around at the right place at the right time, breaking boundaries and being the first to experiment with their chosen art form, the *ISIRTA* team, haphazardly blasting into public consciousness at the same time as the Fab Four, broke the mould. All we can do is listen to them doing it, and wish that we had been around at the time to witness the first yelps of British comedy being kicked up the arse by a younger generation. Everyone knows that the Swinging Sixties had an effect on music, on fashion, on theatre, on television, and so on. But if you want to hear how it affected radio comedy, Radio Prune is the place to be.

Architect of so much of the Prune universe, Bill Oddie, may champion modern radio comedy (albeit under duress), but when he goes on to state 'if I were to say what is so wonderful about radio, I think it is that you can conjure up pictures with sound effects and voices, pictures that couldn't actually exist, you couldn't actually show them. And that is what radio is about, for me; that is the magic of radio. To do something that simply couldn't transfer to the television', then his chosen champions of 'new' radio comedy hardly compare to *ISIRTA*, translating to telly in *The Day Today* and *The League of Gentlemen*. But *I'm Sorry I'll Read That Again* couldn't be captured in a TV format – there's just too much in it. The show's 104 episodes have such a wealth of both variety and mental spectacle that no one TV show could contain it all, and so it begat two – *Monty Python* and *The Goodies*.

Yes, the show's performers occasionally had cause to turn their noses up at the obvious puns and groanworthy gags, but that's what the fans loved. Whether laughing or groaning, those youths you hear in any archive show are having a great time, and Cleese considers such spreading of sweetness and light a crucial part of existence to this day – forty years old or not, the shows still have a great power to provoke laughter. 'I don't think at this moment in history there's all that much optimism and happiness in the world, and I think every time somebody laughs a bit . . . momentarily the world is a wonderful place. I think it's immensely important.' It may be regrettable that the relationship between the catchphrase-hungry Audience and the performers has left *ISIRTA* with its ridiculously simplistic reputation for corniness, when for every lame pun there's a razor-sharp witticism, but those who still tune in to actually listen to a show will rapidly hear the artistry in the scripts' stringing together of laborious wordplay, inventive filth, intellectual references and all the other multitudinous ingredients we've examined. Throughout over fifty hours and ten years, the *ISIRTA* team seemed to touch upon every possible vein of humour, and they've left behind an incredible archive of unsurpassed comic song, dialogue and noise.

But of course . . . there is one other reason that *ISIRTA* must always be applauded and appreciated as a comedy classic above all others – because it never *really* ended in 1973 at all. The *I'm Sorry* philosophy of 'banana skins under authority' and doing or saying anything for a laugh has extended its direct influence well into the new millennium with a spin-off that remains the most popular comedy show on the wireless, right here in the twenty-first century. If *Cambridge Circus* had not mutated into *I'm Sorry I'll Read That Again*, millions of comedy fans would have been robbed of the best laughing experiences of their lives. *ISIRTA* remains part of our culture thanks to its direct descendant and partial namesake: the ultimate aural antidepressant, the Antidote to Panel Games.

And, starter for ten, what is the name of this world-beating long-running legend of radio comedy for which we must all be eternally grateful to Angus Prune and his legion of ferrets, gibbons, terrapins, randy dowagers, dirty old men, 'eke'-ing mice, unhappy couples, sneering babies, OBEs, teapots and rhubarb tarts?

I'm Sorry, I Haven't a Clue.

THE CLUE TESTAMENT

9

Money for Old Rope

The Sherlock Holmes pub, just a quick stumble from the Playhouse Theatre where over a hundred episodes of *I'm Sorry I'll Read That Again* were joyfully played out before a roaring crowd, was naturally the local of choice for the Prune Players for many years. Before and after most shows, Hatch, Garden, Brooke-Taylor, Oddie, Cleese and Kendall would pop in for a swift half and, in Sir David's words, 'see how life is getting on'. However, as Tim once observed, as soon as the Prune-loving fans discovered that this was where their heroes wetted their whistles, it became increasingly difficult to have a quiet drink in there without being asked to sign autographs or do a Lady Constance impression.

Therefore it's not surprising that when 29-year-old co-scriptwriter of *ISIRTA* and the man Barry Cryer describes as 'very much the oracle' of *Clue*, Dr Graeme Garden, decided that he wanted a serious chat with David Hatch, they walked the extra distance to the Guinea pub in Mayfair. Producer Hatch ordered the drinks (on BBC expenses, of course) and they sat outside, to make the most of the late-spring sunshine one afternoon in 1970. The eighth (and, to all intents and purposes, final) series of *I'm Sorry I'll Read That Again* was being broadcast on Radio 2, and the recordings of the last few episodes were still fresh in the memory. Those Sunday-night recordings were a source of pleasure for performers and fans alike, but Graeme knew that the time had come to call it a day.

It was natural that Hatch would be the first person Garden would consult when putting his plan into action – David was the prefect of the band of unruly rebels that made up the *ISIRTA* team, and his BBC bosses had already made it clear that another series of Prune silliness was required. Bill and Graeme, enthused with their brand-new 'anything, anytime' TV project, had already been face to face with the Corporation top brass at a BBC luncheon, and told them straight that there was no way they could afford to invest their time and energy in creating more *ISIRTA* shows, no matter how much they loved working on radio. Like all the other guys on the team, they had not only burgeoning TV careers to take care of, they had families, mortgages and responsibilities that simply weren't there when the exciting offer to work on BBC Radio was first made to them. 'Writing for radio takes as long as writing for television', Garden reasoned, 'and is paid a great deal less. It's also in many ways much harder – every bit of it has to be dialogue, and the jokes have to work in a very restricted way. It's brilliant, great fun to do, but we found it was getting very difficult to earn a living and keep writing radio at the same time.'

Hatch understood Garden's decision to concentrate on more lucrative work – he knew it wasn't easy to make ends meet with a young family, and had plenty of sidelines himself: 'I was also doing a quiz programme called *Quiz International* for the World Service, then I did a programme called *Information Please*, about people seeking all sorts of facts, and I'd research things and do other bits of performing. I was on an interesting contract where I could produce and write and perform, so I was allowed to do what I wanted to do. Which was of course the only way you could make a living in those days, particularly when you're married and having children.' Naturally, whatever the nature of the compromise that Garden had contacted Hatch about, it was bound to be worth a try.

The Parsons Project

Not only was Sir David Hatch one of the Prune players, and the founder of shows like *Week Ending* and the *Jeeves* and *Doctor* radio series, there's also one titan of radio comedy on his CV that we haven't yet examined – *Just a Minute*. The long-running radio panel game owes its success to Hatch, as well as much of its structure and content. The idea of a panel game in which raconteurs are given a subject to talk about for sixty seconds, without hesitation, repetition or deviating from the subject, came of course from the legendary deviser Ian Messiter. He was inspired in turn by his old Latin master, Percival Parry Jones, who would punish boys by making them stand up and talk for a minute without hesitation. The memory of this childhood challenge appealed to Messiter, who remembered the experience one morning on the number 13 bus which took him to his job at the BBC, and he leapt on it as an ideal radio format. He added the extra rules and scoring, and set about trying to turn it into a broadcast-worthy game show to join the existing big hitters like *What's My Line?* on television, or *Round Britain Quiz* on radio (which was first broadcast back in 1947, and is still running today). *Round Britain Quiz*, however (like *Brain of Britain*, which started in 1953), was then a general knowledge quiz for members of the public throughout the regions – but Hatch knew that *Just a Minute* would thrive only on the wit and wisdom of well-known panellists.

Messiter had attempted an earlier show featuring Kenneth Horne called *One Minute Please* which hadn't caught the public's imagination, so when Hatch was brought in on the project at the time of the launch of Radio 4 in 1967, hopes weren't high. However, he took Messiter's idea and gave it just the shape and feel that it needed to thrive. First he hired Jimmy Edwards as the chairman – his cane-flexing *Whacko* persona making him perfect for keeping control of a frenetic and polysyllabic bunch of orators. When Edwards became unavailable, however, Hatch promoted the squeaky-clean, charming actor (and Arthur Haynes' straight man) Nicholas Parsons from the panel. Parsons managed to hold down the job for over forty years, so it wasn't as inane a piece of casting as it at first seemed – who better to control a vain gang of limelight-hogging raconteurs than a polite straight man? Hatch went on to oversee the hiring of the regular line-up of Clement Freud, Derek Nimmo and, in subsequent series, Peter Jones and, the *pièce de résistance*, Kenneth Williams. This equally talented but vastly mismatched collection of extemporisers provided the real chemistry that launched *Just a Minute* on its unstoppable march to greatness – Freud keenly haggling for points and dourly listing objects when it was his turn to speak, Nimmo lyrically bursting into extensive theatrical anecdotes with gusto, Jones – ever the subversive – saying less than anyone else but making his input count with the sharpest, withering one-liners, and finally, that squawking, intellectually unbound citizen of Great Portland Street Williams, shamelessly playing up to the audience with every honeyed speech and self-aggrandising tirade – just as he always had done in *Round the Horne*.

But it wasn't just Hatch's creative input that got *Just a Minute* off to such a great start – it was his determination, and passion for his work. When the first pilot (featuring Freud, Nimmo, Wilma Ewart and Beryl Reid) was put out in December 1967, BBC Management were far from impressed, and informed Hatch that the show was not going to continue. Upon which, Hatch informed them that if *Just a Minute* didn't continue, then neither did he, and tendered his resignation from BBC Radio. The respect which 'Hatch of the BBC' had already garnered so early in his career was so great that his bosses climbed down – and the show has now been running for more than fifty-five series.

Hatch had also had a slightly less stellar success with a programme entitled *The Tennis Elbow Foot Game*, launched the year after *Just a Minute*. Despite the confusing title, this was a pretty straight word-association game in which a Chairman would start a strand with one word and set up a metronome, and the panellists would come up with their own logical associated word within a strict time limit – or were gonged off if they dried up. It was a better title than it was a show, but in spite of the obvious limitations of the format, there were two lengthy series of the game before Hatch called it a day. The game concept would be completely torn apart by Garden in the eventual regular *Clue* round 'Word for Word', in which only words with no connection whatsoever to the last were acceptable, and the opposing team would have to buzz in if any link could be made between consecutive words. (Incidentally, perhaps the riddle of who out of Cleese or Brooke-Taylor favoured 'clump or 'plinth' back in 1962 is answered by the fact that the word 'plinth' remained a regular motif of 'Word for Word' for decades after Cleese's exit, and is still worth listening out for today. Also: 'elephant's foot umbrella stand'.)

The Tennis Elbow Foot Game was far from a flop, and *Just a Minute* was a massive hit. Graeme Garden needed someone who really knew how to launch a show that would succeed, who had a good track record when it came to panel games, and of course, who got the *I'm Sorry* brand of humour. Who else would he suggest a drink to, but Hatch? He remembers pitching the basic concept of *I'm Sorry I Haven't a Clue* to him back in 1970. 'I'd been on a panel game, I think, with Gyles Brandreth, and I thought "This is money for old rope!" You get people who are quite amusing, get them to play a silly game, and just hope that they'll come up with something funny.' Garden had been on many panel shows (as had most of his colleagues), such as *Many a Slip* (basically 'spot the difference' but with comic monologues) and *The Tennis Elbow Foot Game*, but the probable identity of the silly panel game that gave Graeme his idea is *The Clever Stupid Game*, produced by Ted Taylor in 1969. Although he was a regular, alongside Cyril Fletcher and June Whitfield, of this Brandreth-devised panel game, he has no recall of what it entailed, other than being entirely pointless, and not terribly funny. He realised, while sitting there not being terribly funny, that the Prune gang would gel together much better as a quiz team.

The fact that the pilot was almost entitled *Old Rope* betrays the odd truth that this most successful of joy-bringers was first forged in a spirit of 'greed and laziness'. Looking around at the devoted pandemonium of the final days of *ISIRTA*, and looking at the comparable size of the cheque that he and Oddie were receiving for writing *The Goodies* for TV, Garden decided that what was needed was an alternative show that could 'achieve the atmosphere and enjoyment of *ISIRTA* . . . without our having to do the chore of writing a script for it. It was almost as cold-blooded as that.' Besides, it was clear that the success of the individual *ISIRTA* members, Cleese especially, was making it harder to physically get the team together to record tightly scripted shows. Accordingly, Garden and Hatch worked together on the format for a show in which the well-loved regulars could gratify their devotedly raucous Audience with the same gob-smacking puns, insistent innuendo and seemingly haphazard horseplay, except without the script. Naturally, there would be no actual score to keep or game to play. Early episodes would make some incongruous attempts to 'keep track', but – whisper it – the whole show would just be an endless excuse for shameless laughs.

Hatch had a lot of input into the pitch, including the selection of the theme, 'The Schickel Shamble', or Haydn's 'Austrian Hymn' as interpreted by film composer Ron Goodwin – a recording which only seems incongruous now in its original context, the 1969 caper movie *Monte Carlo or Bust* (which incidentally featured a cameo from Willie Rushton). Certainly, the opening notes of 'Deutschland Über Alles' isn't really what you'd associate with a jolly panel game, but its brassy fanfare has been the indispensable opening to every single episode, as stirring an opening jolt as the Marseillaise opening on 'All You Need is Love'. Then the staggering, clown-like trombone tune that follows is a perfect musical primer for the meandering silliness that fills the subsequent half-hour. Hatch played Garden his choice of tune in the office as they continued to plan out the pilot, and asked for his thoughts. 'That's totally inappropriate,' replied Graeme, 'It'll do!'

The Panel Beaters

It seems that pilots for Radio 4 panel games were as numerous and fleeting in the seventies as Beatles reunion rumours, or chart entries from the Wombles. Just a brief look through the BBC contracts for our *ISIRTA* regulars throws up a wave of try-out panel games, whose rules and quirks have long since been forgotten. John Cleese had a go at *Home Late* and *Right or Wrong*, not to mention *There's No Time Like the Present*; Tim Brooke-Taylor could have been heard on *Second Time Around* or *Spoof* if they had managed to catch the audience's imagination; Graeme Garden's presence on the show *Speakeasy* didn't make it a success, and so on. The celebrity panel game was a thriving genre of entertainment, with *Call My Bluff* already a notable TV institution (it also ran on radio, with Cleese an occasional guest). But *Just a Minute* had been the first radio show to really show where a panel game's strength should lie – unlike game shows, which members of the public took very seriously, a celebrity panel game should be entertaining first, with point-scoring a sorry second. It's no surprise that, in his dotage, Nicholas Parsons began to award more points to panellists 'because the audience loved it' than for actually playing by the rules of *Just a Minute*. Hatch and Messiter's success in attracting a radio audience with only the simplest of concepts and the most ragged of rules had clearly opened the floodgates for new panel games staffed with funny chaps but with only a tagged-on game aspect – it's just that so few of them got beyond the pilot stage.

This conveyor belt of parlour games was ripe for mocking, in much the same way that *ISIRTA* had sent up *Top of the Form* and *Ask the Family* years earlier – with a witheringly superior questionmaster and a bunch of clueless contestants trying to solve the riddle of 'What's the weight of thirty-eight Brazilian anacondas?' or what a 'gallysporrancobbler' is – except the new spoof would have fewer boundaries, no schoolgirl wigs and that all-important aspect – no script.

The original intention of ad-libbing an entire half-hour was not quite as earth-shatteringly radical back then as it may seem. The cast of the Establishment – Bron, Bird, Fortune and so on – had been inspired by Chicago's Second City troupe (especially Mike Nichols and Elaine May) to extemporise sketches and material since the start of the sixties, some of it spilling over onto TV and radio. Also, Peters Ustinov and Jones had enjoyed success with their own radio show, *In All Directions*, back in the early fifties. For each episode they entirely improvised a narrative starring their spiv characters Morris and Dudley Grosvenor, which was then edited down into a half-hour by comedy gurus Frank Muir and Denis Norden. Besides which, all panel games contained some degree of on-the-spot wise cracking.

However, the idea of providing a show in the Prune vein without a carefully worked-out script was not an enticing one for the rest of the *Cambridge Circus* alumni. Of course, Graeme and David couldn't put their plans into operation without the rest of the team on board, and the first person that had to be canvassed was Garden's long-standing writing partner and co-founder of Radio Prune, Bill Oddie. He explained the new concept to Bill, who was not instantly slayed by the idea. 'I do remember my attitude was, "Oh great, so you've managed to cut us out of the bloody writing fees, have you?" I was quite sarky about it, saying, "Wait a minute, you've given them a cheaper version of *ISIRTA*, because there's no script fees" – maybe Graeme was copping for a large origination fee, but I very much doubt it.' Nevertheless, Graeme persevered, and convinced his partner that entertaining the Prune crowd on an ad hoc basis was better than abandoning them altogether.

He then moved on to their fellow Goodie, Tim Brooke-Taylor. Luckily, Tim was a lot easier to convince when the 'improvised Prune show' idea was pitched – his one other project at the time was taking over Olivia Newton-John's role in a Scandinavian-funded Cliff Richard vehicle, *The Case* (no, this is true). 'Cliff was very good to work with,' he insists. 'Thanks to his encouragement I found myself dancing on a table in Sweden and singing his hits – his encouragement was in the form of alcohol. Sadly, the best comedy bits were cut out in the edit, but once again I was able to appear in drag . . .'

John and Jo would of course complete the Teams, as and when needed, with the three Goodies being more or less permanent competitors. John's star was still in the ascendant, but he was busy enough with his own radio projects, earning bits and bobs for shows such as *David Frost at the Phonogram* and through recording pilots, that it was no great favour for him to pitch in with his old colleagues and mess about on the radio waves – after all, he was the one who eschewed rehearsal and openly rejigged scripts to suit himself, so now he'd have the chance to vie for laughs on his own terms. Similarly, Jo had more than held her own off-script in the past, so it would be unthinkable not to ask her to join in the fun now.

In the Chair
So the whole Prune gang was tentatively up for the new challenge, but Hatch knew that the toughest job lay ahead. He had learned that the real secret for a comedy panel game that has legs is to find the perfect Chairman – the all-powerful sage who sits in the centre of the competitors and referees every contest, keeping guests in check, doling out challenges and points, and knitting the whole show together. A game with a fascinating, fruitful concept and a great team of writers and panellists can founder if the Chairman doesn't fit the bill. But if your show is not only deliberately devoid of rules and structure, but also completely improvised, who the hell can you find to fill that central chair? Who would be the person to take charge of that all-important symbol of power, the car hooter, or horn? Hatch was the natural head prefect of the bunch in the sketch show, but although the logical person to become Chairman, he demurred. 'What I wanted was for David to produce it,' confirms Graeme, 'and I said in the pitch to him that I didn't think it would work if somebody from the show was in the Chair, because we'd lose their talents as panellists. And also it would be better if the Chair was not our friend, so they could be severe and give us tasks to perform and mark us and fill that rather schoolmasterly role.'

While Graeme was waxing lyrical about the free-form jazz-style comic riffing that would define the new show, the name of a likely candidate popped into both his, and Hatch's head. 'I don't remember which of us said it,' admitted David, 'but I sort of remember the context was that what we already had was a scripted show, like a composed piece of music. And the notion was we should go actually off-piste, and not have words written down, but invent it. And the equivalent to the composed piece of music was jazz. And I think it was from that kind of conversation that his name emerged in the air over that third pint. I think we said it together and then realised how clever we both were.' The two were jazz fans and, naturally, avid radio listeners, so perhaps the same name did occur to Graeme and David simultaneously. Hatch would recall, 'Our choice of Humphrey Lyttelton as Chairman is the major factor, in my view, of the series running for thirty-five years.'

Humphrey Richard Adeane Lyttelton
Born: 23 May 1921, Eton, Berkshire
Educated: Eton College; Camberwell Art School

Jazzman, trumpeter, toff, socialist, calligrapher, cartoonist, satirist, humanist, broadcaster, birdwatcher and word-botcher ... Humph's extraordinary life story by now has become something of a modern folk tale, and no brief biography can do his story justice. But to summarise ... the only son of an Eton housemaster of aristocratic descent (somewhere in line for the Viscountcy Cobham and the Barony Lyttelton), he grew up surrounded by sisters and nannies, except for his cousin Anthony, almost a surrogate brother. There's the development of his musical fascination from an appreciation for military music, sloping off from the Eton cricketing outing with his mother to buy his first ever trumpet at the age of ten, early band formations at school, a growing love for jazz ... There's Humph's political baptism while working at Port Talbot steelworks, making the privileged Eton boy a lifelong 'romantic socialist'. Then the Second World War butts in – Humph the second lieutenant in the Grenadier Guards striding out onto the beach at Salerno with gun in one hand and trumpet in the other – and swiftly after, invalidation back to Blighty, and the tragic news of Anthony's death in action.

Then there's the famed recording of Humph trumpeting from a wheelbarrow on the BBC broadcast of the VE Day celebrations, before the young musician began mixing his art studies at Camberwell with live jazz shows. He landed a job at the *Daily Mail* back when it was a newspaper thanks to his jazz colleague Wally 'Trogg' Fawkes, and the two penned their satirical comic strip *Flook* by day and made post-war London swing by night. Soon he was releasing records and was hailed by his all-time hero Louis Armstrong as the best trumpet player in England ('That cat in England that swings his ass off!'). Humph became one of the biggest names in British jazz, even if his one chart hit, 'Bad Penny Blues', is mainly remembered for being pinched by Paul McCartney.

Suffice it to say that by the time Humph signed up for *Clue*, he had already released dozens of albums, played his horn all around the world, presented his own weekly *Best of Jazz* show on Radio 2 since 1967, and had a number of books published. He was an icon already.

But behind it all, Humph took pride in his role as a husband and father. His first marriage to Pat Braithwaite gave him one daughter, and a second daughter and two sons were born to Humph and his second wife Jill Richardson, who died in 2006. After an operation at Barnet Hospital to repair an aortic aneurysm, Humph died in June 2008, surrounded by friends and family. He had no OBE, but was not short of offers.

In his 2006 collection of anecdotes and life lessons *It Just Occurred to Me*, Lyttelton peppers the text with self-composed adages, to live your life by (should you want to), attributed to his chosen alterego, Chairman Humph. The very first of these is: 'Whatever assignment you are offered, say "yes" first and learn about it afterwards.' And it was this policy which guided the jazzman to jump on board when David Hatch pitched the *Clue* project to him in 1971. After all, it was only a pilot, one of many, and they hardly ever came to anything. Lyttelton had at this point built up a very good reputation as a witty and erudite broadcaster (as well as a gifted cartoonist and celebrated musician) thanks to his Radio 2 show *The Best Of Jazz*, which first aired in 1967 – but he had also already earned a few bob on Radio 4 panel games and plenty of pilots. An evening filling the Chairman's seat at the Playhouse Theatre seemed to be just one more pleasurable sidejob to his main career.

When the Lyttelton name was out of the bag, Graeme left it to the boss to make the crucial phone call. Humph recalls it as a far from difficult negotiation: 'David Hatch said, "We're doing a pilot." And I said, "Oh, yes?" and he said, "Will you do it?"' And I said, "Yes, of course I will" – because you used to get a fee of a couple of hundred quid! And the pilots, in my memory, used to waft upstairs to the upper echelons where they made big decisions, and then they'd be flushed down the plughole. So I thought this would be the same! So I went up and did the pilot, and that was the end of it.'

Humph himself appreciated the close ties between jazz and comic riffing, and even presented a radio programme on the subject in 2004, *Swing When You're Laughing*, which identified the rich dualities of jazz prowess and humour through artists such as Cab Calloway, Spikes Jones and Milligan, Marty Feldman, Dudley Moore, Lenny Bruce and Woody Allen. 'In the history of jazz, music and comedy have grown up together and appear like a double act in every chapter, from early New Orleans through powerhouse swing and be-bop and even avant garde. In music, happily, nothing has become old hat. In cities throughout the world the old and the new can be heard coexisting at any time. And behind the music, there's always been laughter.'

But beyond his jazz credentials, there was just something perfect about Humph being in charge of the proceedings – socialist or not, he was a true toff among the middle-class oiks, his long graceful frame towering above the panellists, more than tall enough to stare down John Cleese in a mood, but always perfectly detached, effortlessly superior. Already being ancient at fifty, there was no question of any of the Prune gang daring to trifle with Humph, or they would get a hefty size-thirteen up the rear end. Hatch confirms: 'It needed a father figure, I mean it was a bit like Ken Horne used to be on *Twenty Questions*, that sort of gravitas. A large figure who could hold these wild young things together.' *Twenty Questions* was another well-bedded radio

panel game which would end up being spoofed and recycled throughout *Clue*,
not least in the regular round 'Paranoia', in which one Team would have an
affliction or kink (they're in love with Mrs Thatcher, or afraid that the King's
Singers are going to kill them), and they would have to find out what it was
by questioning their opponents. Humph admitted that, without realising it,
he was to an extent channelling Horne's gravitas when he took the Chair, as
a great admirer of *Beyond Our Ken* and so on, but *Clue's* current producer Jon
Naismith identified a crucial distinction. 'I heard him describe one of his role
models as being Kenneth Horne . . . And there was something of, you know,
the patrician posh guy amid a bunch of comedians. But it was slightly different
to Kenneth Horne, because Kenneth Horne was, you thought, a sort of voice
of sanity, that he could possibly redeem the chaos in some way. Whereas,
with Humphrey, he was the source of the chaos.' Ultimately, Humph's vast
array of interests and abilities made any one virtue impossible to pinpoint as
the reason for him being perfect casting.

Therefore, it was under Lyttelton's already ambivalent eye, with Hatch in
the producer's chair and *ISIRTA* maestro Dave Lee on piano that the first teams
of Tim Brooke-Taylor and Bill Oddie versus Graeme Garden and Jo Kendall
faced off on 16 November 1971. The fact that the programme was planned as
a Prune placebo was underlined by the eventual name of the experiment: *I'm
Sorry They're At It Again*. As it had been over a year since *ISIRTA* had finished
broadcasting, there was an audibly excited fan-club contingent in the Audience for that first try-out evening, and they were treated to a far more Music
Hall-style show than the one that has survived to this day. In the opening, the
show was described sneeringly as 'a panel game', but the rest of the introductory announcement was bawled out in the voice of a cockney barker:

ANNOUNCER: ... With Dave Lee at the pianoforte and 'Umphrey
                  Lyttelton in the chair! I thank you!' (*Applause.*)
HL: And thank you too. Hello, and welcome to an unlikely
                  panel game in which the four contestants are invited
                  to make utter fools of themselves, for which I shall
                  give them points, and then we can all take the money
                  and go home. In the unlikely event of them giving us
                  any money. The two Teams are – on my left Graeme
                  Garden & Jo Kendall, versus Tim Brooke-Taylor &
                  Bill Oddie. (*Applause.*)
BO: So far, so good!
JK: Now can we go?
HL: I shall be explaining the rules as we go on, which
                  won't make very much difference. So, seconds away,

> round one. Round one – using the word in the widest
> possible sense – is a musical round. Each Team has
> the words of a well-known song which I'm going to
> ask them to sing to the wrong tune.

BO: Oh, blimey.

TBT: I can't sing to the RIGHT tune!

Yes, that very first game in that very first pilot proved to be the single most obscure and inexplicable round of all – 'One Song to the Tune of Another'. Humph would continue to try to find ways of getting the impenetrable rules for this musical monstrosity across to the Teams as the years went by, but to this day none of them can quite put their finger on what the game entails. Still, those first joint efforts at 'Three Blind Mice' to the tune of 'Old Man River' from Graeme & Jo, and 'Sing a Song of Sixpence' to 'These Foolish Things' from Bill & Tim went down well, in the words of Lyttelton, 'reducing the Audience to tears'. The Teams also had access to hooters, duck-calls, whistles and all sorts of traditional noise-makers to augment their singing and continue the bedlam of the Prune recordings.

For the crowd this wasn't just *ISIRTA*, it was *ISIRTA* without a safety net, and the excitement is still audible in the surviving recording. But the reaction isn't just down to *ISIRTA* fandom. It's remarkable to recall just how rare improvised comedy was in those days, at least to a British audience who would be unlikely to have even heard of Chicago's Second City comedy troupe. It often seems as if these early seventies audiences, in the days before *Whose Line Is It Anyway?* and improv comedy clubs, find it almost impossible to believe that any performer can come up with something sharp or pithy without a script. Just the slightest offhand wisecrack is greeted with the kind of delighted applause and gasps of surprise that the more exotic sideshow freaks must have received a hundred years earlier as the curtains were pulled back.

And a good thing too, because, as can be clearly seen from the first two interjections from the players in the extract above, no one on that first try-out panel was feeling confident about going in front of that Audience and making them laugh without a script – except maybe Graeme, the one responsible for landing them all in this comedic mess, who sat in his corner quietly planning his next laugh. 'I can remember everyone sitting around sweating, during the recording of the pilot,' admitted Humph, who was flying by the seat of his pants himself. The sheer terror experienced by Tim, Jo and especially Bill is easy to trace in the nervous giggling that fills the pilot. 'I heard the pilot recently,' admitted Graeme. 'It was one of those that was discovered in a skip when the BBC had an amnesty, and said, "Anyone got any pilot recordings?" This was one that they found. It doesn't actually sound too bad, it was just that desperation that we would hear sometimes ... I think, the Audience miss that now, we don't do it quite so much. We used to do "Ad-lib Poem", which Tim, I know, used to absolutely hate, and none of us enjoyed it that much. You could hear the adrenalin, you could hear the sweat ... The more sadistic members of the Audience used to enjoy that very much.'

Bill freely admits that from the very start, ad-libbing on this scale was anathema to him. 'Nobody was terribly used to improvisational humour, you know? It's now a cliché, everybody does it, but at the time I wasn't comfortable, I have to admit. I don't know if Tim and Graeme were comfortable. I was surprised when I heard it back not too long ago – somebody sent me the first one, and I thought it would be absolute agony. But I played it back and thought it wasn't that bad at all actually, it was fine, but I didn't enjoy it, it was simple as that.'

Oddie's right, that first episode is far from a disaster – perhaps due to some careful editing on Hatch's part, but also thanks to the simplicity of the games. The beauty of the 'One Song to the Tune of Another' format was that it didn't actually require any on-the-spot gag creation, and the idea was merrily extended to most of the other games in that first episode. There's the round in which the Teams replay a scene from *Doctor Finlay's Casebook* or *Till Death Us Do Part*, but with different accents, German, Chinese or Australian ('G'day, cobblers!' and all). There were also the other musical rounds, in which Tim & Bill sang 'Hello Dolly' as chickens while Graeme & Jo had a go at 'The Sound of Music' as sheep. (Though the least said about one quickly abandoned round in which the Teams had to 'la' a song *on one note* and make the opposition somehow guess what it was, the better.) The care with which the improvisers were set up with handy comical supports is best summed up by the fact that Graeme gets to do his tried and tested Eddie Waring impression within twenty minutes of the first show starting.

But, to be fair, there were moments of genuine improvisation on offer, a couple of spots where the performers *really* had to sweat for their fees. As well as faltering ad-libbed calypsos, the Teams were given a scene, a pair of characters and a trio of objects, all suggested by the opposition, around which they had to improvise a sketch within a strict time limit. Tim & Bill were told to recreate a TV chat show featuring Long John Silver, which mentions a kangaroo, nude ladies and a tin-opener. The whine of the traditional Frost impression was inevitable:

TBT: Hello, super and wonderful ... No, please keep applauding. Marvellous, hello, super ... I've got some wonderful guests tonight, I've got Julie Felix – but not on the show. There are several great guests, but first of all I'd like to introduce you ...

(*Giggles.*) God I'm rich . . . Give a big introduction to Mr Short . . . um, no, where are my notes? Where's that researcher? Shoot that researcher, he's done all the work, shoot him! I'd like to introduce that wonderful, warm human being, Mr Long John Silver!

BO: Good evening, I am Long John Silver. I know I may not look like Long John Silver, I may in fact have two legs . . . but if you've got a minute, I'll make it more authentic. Have you got that saw? Thank you. (*Makes sawing noises.*) HAHAR, JIMLAD!

TBT: . . . Super. Can I call you John, or Jack or . . . ?

BO: Call me Long-Johns, me father worked in underpants!

TBT: And what a mess he made of that. Thank you, Long John, and . . . (*Humph rings the bell.*) And I'd like to ask you why you've got that kangaroo on your shoulder? (*Bell rings, Dave Lee starts playing exit music.*) And the next thing I'd like to ask . . .

BO: 'Tis not a kangaroo, 'tis a parrot and he's hopping mad!

TBT: Yes I'm sure he is. And the next question I was going to ask is . . . (*Bell rings again*) when you're on a desert island do you see . . . ?

HL: Erm, I'm sorry . . . (*Rings bell repeatedly.*)

TBT: . . . Many nude ladies . . . ?

BO: I think we're being stopped.

GG: He's unstoppable, you should know that!

For that display, and for failing to keep to the two-minute rule, Tim Brooke-Taylor was penalised, 'minus a mark for total insubordination'. Humph was clearly setting out to be a hard quizmaster . . .

After a few more games of astoundingly deliberate inanity, that first try-out Antidote to Panel Games staggered to an end with Humph's final marks revealing an eleven all draw for the teams, and a muted 'Meanwhile, from me, goodnight', from the host. It wasn't really an earth-shattering comedy moment, this first game without rules but with plenty of puns. However, the Audience clearly caught the drift of Garden's new venture and subsequently drifted happily out of the theatre – the show may not have had the polished anarchy of Radio Prune, but was still enjoyably barking mad.

Hatch, Humph and especially the Teams, meanwhile, limped over to the Sherlock Holmes, and ordered six very, *very* stiff drinks, which were knocked back with trembling hands. Even cool customer Graeme called the pilot a 'hair-raising' experience – which, by his standards, equates to an earth-shattering disaster. His co-panellists went further, with 'Never, *ever* again!' the general consensus – in fact, Tim Brooke-Taylor insists that he found himself repeating the phrase after every single *Clue* recording for the next forty years, as a kind of superstition. By no means the least perturbed figure in the Sherlock Holmes that night was Hatch himself, who had to edit the whole meandering recording down to a usable half-hour. He was not confident of success. Still, they'd given it a go, for old times' sake, and he promised to do what he could. Somebody called out, 'David, what do you think, do you think it'll ever get broadcast?' And the great man was quoted as replying to all, 'Well, possibly, but only on Boxing Day, after lunch, when everyone's pissed.'

Sadly, in a regrettable mirroring of the *Just a Minute* pilot debacle, Hatch was *not* confident of *I'm Sorry They're at it Again*'s chances of making it to a series. 'What I worried more about *I'm Sorry* than ever I did about *Just a Minute*, was how sustainable it was, because Graeme had injected an awful lot of ideas for rounds into it, and one didn't know what sort of mileage they had, and what other new ideas there could be to insert round about programme three or four . . . One wondered whether we'd make thirteen. I suppose that was my worry.' Nevertheless, he spent over twenty hours carefully cutting together a pared-down half-hour from that evening's painful silliness, before it was apologetically played to the Radio 4 bosses. Despite his hard work, Hatch candidly admitted to the head of Radio 4, Tony Whitby, that it was probably unbroadcastable. Whitby sat back and mused on the shambolic thirty minutes of party games and giggling that he'd just heard and, the hero of the hour, he threw Hatch's uncharacteristic pessimism back in his face. 'I like it, we'll have it on!'

The Pilot Gets Its Wings

In a kind of daze, then, work began on the first series of this Antidote to Panel Games at the start of 1972. Graeme commented, 'The problem was that no one had any idea of what the show was supposed to be and thought it was a big mistake – and many listeners agreed! The BBC produced an "Audience Research Report" on the pilot, and although a few of those canvassed thought this "delightful new show", with its "off the cuff humour" was "a winner!", the reaction was, to say the least, mixed. Some thought the Teams, while "trying too hard", had "done their best", others commented "idiotic rubbish, I was embarrassed for the Teams." And "this dismal effort is no good to anybody". What seems to have tipped the balance was Humph's chairmanship, which was universally admired: "excellent", "exceptionally fine", and "an inspired choice". So the series came back, again and again . . .' No one could have been more surprised that the pilot had been accepted for a full run than the Chairman. Humph simply hadn't bargained for a whole dozen episodes of the programme, and when the news came through, he was in a quandary. 'The following February, the message suddenly came – "They've picked up on the programme, can you do it?" And . . . I'd already got band jobs in.'

Humph wasn't the only one caught on the hop. Thanks to other calls on his time as the BBC show-establisher extraordinaire, David Hatch was forced by his superiors to excuse himself from producing duty for the full series, drafting in his *ISIRTA* co-producer (and Footlights secretary at the time Garden was president) John Cassels to call the shots now the format had been fixed and the series set in motion. This was a bit of a blow, but everyone else from the pilot was free to take part, and Cleese also scribbled a couple of dates in his diary. Graeme and John Cassels pieced together a roster of rudimentary silly games on an enormous drawing board and the Playhouse was booked for a run of recordings in the spring, the Teams recording two episodes in succession. This double shift did nothing to alleviate the nerves, and in these early days it proved a massive challenge to squeeze out two cogent half-hours in one night. It was live, it was chaotic, and it was crucial to have a Chairman who would be able to guide the rambling rounds towards a logical conclusion, and still maintain an air of anarchy.

Humph had shown that he was the ideal man for the job, but it proved impossible to match his free evenings with all of the recording dates. He agreed to take part in the three recordings that weren't double-booked, and it was while driving to the Playhouse for one of these evenings that his whole approach to the show became set in stone. The pilot he took for a gamble had been taken up for a series, and now he had time to repent at leisure. 'I remember driving in, thinking, "I don't know what I'm going to do on this!" And in desperation I just decided to express how I felt at the time, which was that I've got a perfectly good career playing the trumpet, broadcasting about jazz, what am I doing here?' This desire to be somewhere else – usually that legendary impending gig in Hull that he would start to worry about missing when rounds seemed to go on for hours – would set Humph in good stead for years to come. But as for the three other recording dates that would make up this series, Humph could only give his apologies, but they would have to find someone else.

Barry Charles Cryer
Born: 23 March 1935, Leeds
Educated: Leeds Grammar School; Leeds University
It comes as a surprise to many that Barry is a Yorkshireman, but it was in Leeds that the younger of the two Cryer boys was born and brought up. His father Carl died when Barry was very small, but Carl's Masonic background was some help to a single mother bringing up her boys alone. Despite the

lack of showbiz blood in the family, Barry was fixated on the lure of the greasepaint from a very early age, and as well as gaining experience behind the scenes he eagerly accepted his first assignment, working at the Leeds City Varieties theatre, while he was putting together the university revue. Having spent more time playing jazz and cracking jokes than studying, he wisely left academia behind, and followed his burgeoning comic career, relocating to London and the hard life of a Windmill comedian at the age of twenty-two. From here, he graduated to writing revues, and was lucky to get a job writing and performing at Danny La Rue's legendary nightclub just off Oxford Street, before *Beyond the Fringe* changed revue forever.

From Danny's club, Barry was invited to write for David Frost, setting the ball rolling which resulted in an awesome list of comic legends who would be grateful for Barry's scripts over the years – the Two Ronnies, Kenny Everett, Morecambe & Wise, Richard Pryor, Tommy Cooper, Dave Allen, Bob Hope, Frankie Howerd and many more. No one else in the comedy world can even begin to challenge that level of experience and the sheer weight of anecdotage that Barry's years as a writer have given him. But the performing bug has never left him, and besides *Hello, Cheeky* and presenting shows like *Joker's Wild*, the similar panel game *Cryer's Crackers* and *The Stand-Up Show*, Barry's popped up in comedy classics like *The Rutles: All You Need is Cash*, played a musical Robert Maxwell in the West End, and even deigned to make a guest appearance in *The Goodies*. As well as belonging to all sorts of entertainment brethren such as the Grand Order of the Water Rats and being one of the country's leading after-dinner speakers, Barry remains a regular at the Edinburgh Festival, most recently touring a musical show with Ronnie Golden.

It was at Danny's club that he met and fell in love with the resident singer Terry Donovan and, despite the severe eczema which he was prone to at that stage giving him the appearance of the Invisible Man, she eventually agreed to his proposal. They have been married for nearly fifty years and have three sons, Tony, David and Bob, a daughter Jacqui, and a fine collection of grandchildren.

Barry Cryer received his OBE for general funniness in 2001. He is the United Kingdom's greatest living comedy guru.

Barry Cryer was a regular voice on all sorts of radio shows both before and after he joined the *Clue* gang, debuting in sound on the talent show *Search for a Star* while he was a stagehand in Leeds, and going on to have names on his CV like *You Should Ask, Wit's End, The Impressionists, Sounds Familiar, Late Joys* and the sitcom *Sam and Janet*, with Joan Sims. His career in radio stretched back to Nicholas Parsons' attempt to bring the satire boom to BBC Radio in 1966, in a show called *Listen to this Space*. He even had a pilot for his own radio show, *Tom, Dick and Barry*, a year later, though what this entailed he can't quite recall: 'Bob Oliver-Rogers, a producer I worked with way back who's no longer with us, he pitched me for a show for Radio 2, and that may have been it. It's bizarre, but he said "They've turned it down, Baz, because they say you're too old for Radio 2." And this was in the seventies! And I said, "Does the name Jimmy Young ring any bells with them?"'

More to the point, his most high-profile performing work had been as chairman of Yorkshire TV's *Joker's Wild*, which was created by his great friend and writing partner Ray Cameron, with Mike King, in 1969. Cryer would mediate between two teams of stand-up comics, whose job would be to tell endless gags, and reach the punchline before one of their opponents buzzed in and got there first – 'Ashtrays in shot, smoke drifting across the camera . . . I'm a smoker still, but it still gives me a jolt to see all this merry smoking going on.' The art of telling a gag without being interrupted by someone who's got a funnier one is also of course the basic gist of the *Clue* game 'Tag Wrestling', which formed a solid part of many shows right from the first episode, before finally being put to pasture in 1992. This epic – and genuinely off-the-cuff – scuffle for a punchline, described by Humph often as his favourite round (and equally often as his most hated) presented each Team with their own punchline to work towards – 'The spaceship landed safely, proving porridge is inflammable in a leap year' or 'So the choir went home and we could see our knees again just over the top of the roof', for example. They then had to tell the shaggiest of shaggy-dog stories, desperately trying to find a way in which those lines could be even the least bit funny. Humph would of course sound his hooter at the optimum comedic moment, leaving the tag-team gag-teller gasping with frustration, so close to a genuine joke, while the opposition got their chance to storm forwards to the predestined woofer. It made for guaranteed white-knuckle stuff, as long as Humph managed to stay awake.

Joker's Wild was the slightly slicker rendition of this marathon round of *Clue*, and in the TV show's eight series before time was called in 1974, Cryer maintained some form of order between legends like Arthur Askey, Les Dawson, Ted Ray, and even Rolf Harris. There was also, rather fittingly, an appearance from John Cleese, and Tim became something of a regular towards the end. Despite his great friendship with Les Dawson, Cleese was not comfortable on the show, Barry recalls: 'I always addressed him as "Mr Cleese". We travelled up on a train – Ted Ray, Arthur Askey, all these luminaries, on the breakfast train from King's Cross. And of course, they never stopped talking, swapping jokes and everything. And John sat across the aisle . . . not rudely, but he was deluged with this chat, and he sat with his hands over his ears reading a Penguin. And I said to him, "Do it on the show!" So he did it on *Joker's Wild*, he was reading a book throughout. And I would go, "Mr Cleese?" – and a brilliant touch, he'd put a bookmark in, close the book and say, "YES!?" "Mr Cleese, the subject is Mothers-in-Law." "WHAT?" "Mothers-in-Law, Mr Cleese!" And the other comics loved it. John was very apprehensive, he said, "I shouldn't be doing this, they're all comics . . .""

Barry, Tim and John went right back to the old *Frost Report* days. Spooling back to 1966, David Frost organised a meeting of his entire stable of gag-meisters, in a Methodist hall just off Baker Street. This auspicious occasion saw the meeting of Cryer with all of the Pythons bar Terry Gilliam, as well as Brooke-Taylor (who had brought his friend Eric Idle into the team in the first place), Marty Feldman, Dick Vosburgh, David Nobbs and many more. From this starting point came Barry's involvement with *At Last the 1948 Show* and a long writing career with Graham Chapman, writing over fifty half-hours including the only slightly mad Ronnie Corbett vehicle *No, That's Me Over There* and plenty of *Doctor* episodes for Humphrey Barclay. As one of the hardest working warm-up men in the business, Barry had also kept the audience ticking over for the agonising duration of the Cleese/Brooke-Taylor special *How to Irritate People*. The protracted recording for the show lived up to its name, and only a comic of Cryer's magnitude could prevent the studio audience's irritation leading to a mass walkout. As the exhausted rabble finally got their freedom, Cleese, Brooke-Taylor and the cast carried Barry to the bar at shoulder height, the hero of the hour.

Slightly less memorably for anyone but himself, Barry had also met Humphrey Lyttelton when the great jazzman played Leeds while Cryer was in his first (and last) year as an English student at Leeds University in 1955. Barry well remembers asking his trumpeting hero for an autograph as a nervous young jazz fan, and star of his own university jazz band: 'I was singing with the university jazz band in Leeds and Humph was a mere thirty-four, goatee beard and sideburns, and he came to play . . . Typical courtesy, he came over and said hello to me, and I thought, "Ooh, it's him!" And then I floated away on a pink cloud, he said, "I heard you singing with the band," and then with an enchanting smile he said, "It wasn't difficult – you're quite loud." He always remembers us meeting but he didn't remember the year, and in 2005 I said to him, "It's our anniversary, dear," and he said, "What? What are you talking about?" I said, "Fifty years." "Oh, my God."' One trembling auto-graph hunter is much the same as the next, so it would be many years before Barry made any impression on Humph – but, like the rest of the Teams – Tim's first memory being that he danced to Lyttelton tunes as a teenager in Buxton – Barry had been a Humph admirer for a long time before he signed up for *Clue*.

Despite his experience as a game-show Chairman and friendship with the team, there was still a definite feeling that Barry was dropped in at the deep end with the first recording of this brand-new series, mediating between the same Teams as in the pilot. His different approach to the Chairman's job is neatly encapsulated in his introduction:

BC: Hello! It says here. Despite a warning from Humphrey Lyttelton, I agreed to take the Chair for this programme, but he'll be back later in the series when he's fully recovered. It says here that the two'm teams are on the one hand – the two'm teams, it's a word I've invented, a grave statement (*Audience groans*) – on the one hand, Graeme 'Oh Come On In, Maud' Garden and Jo 'Hello, Dear, Do You Want to Be Naughty?' Kendall, and opposing them, Tim 'By a Babbling' Brooke-Taylor and Bill 'I'm an Aesthete, Mush!' Oddie!

With Cryer's years of experience at the sharp end of comedy, he was clearly a safe pair of hands for the show, and the all-important ability to be pleased with any reaction from the Audience – be it a groan or a giggle – was so clearly already embedded in Barry that he could have strolled into the *I'm Sorry I'll Read That Again* team at any point in the sixties and not have looked out of place, even without a degree from Cambridge. True, he did commit the cardinal sin of not taking the game as seriously as Humph – one of his own ideas for a round was to ask all competitors for a fiver each, and to penalise them for refusal. He also tended to be far more lenient than Humph, who instantly commanded respect from the unruly players of the games. John Cleese habitually referred to the jazz legend as 'Uncle Humph', usually when protesting at unfair treatment or insisting that he had a note from his mother that let him off doing any singing rounds.

Barry, though, was quick to take pity on the poor sweating extemporisers – and particularly Tim Brooke-Taylor, who knew how to milk the Audience's sympathy down to the last drop. True, on one early occasion, when Tim entirely failed to come up with a last line for a calypso song, Barry was quick to offer him 'more salt for your wound?' by providing a running commentary on Tim's agony, as Dave Lee completed the song unaccompanied.

Conversely, when Uncle Humph was back, there was no messing around, with the rules thoroughly adhered to, and harsh penalties for failure:

HL: Well, I can hardly bring myself to say it, so great is the excitement, but that round puts John & Graeme in the lead with 15, against 14 from Tim & Bill. And we come to a round which is called 'Singing Relay' – one player from each Team starts off a song, and he and his partner must sing a duet, but each player singing alternate words. Any player which falters, or messes up the game, is banished from the BBC for life. And not only that, but 108 points go to the other side. Or two, whichever is the greater.

So Barry was a definite boon when it came to keeping the Audience tickled – introducing an early game called 'Pick Up Song' by assuring the Teams that 'This round is going to be played entirely in the nude, and judged by the volume of the Audience's laughter . . .' Incidentally, 'Pick Up Song' doesn't mean the gramophone-based round, which was first known as 'Singalong', but a round in which a player had to sing a snatch of a song, and end on a word or syllable which the next player would have to locate in a different song, and so on (if you think this sounds complicated, be assured we have barely glimpsed the tip of the iceberg). This early 'Pick Up Song' usually involved desperate players making up a snatch of music that contained the requested word, only to insist that it *was* a genuine song, even if they had written it themselves the evening before. In Cleese's case, this was also accompanied by the forlorn appeal 'You have to be kind to me, I don't LIKE music!' Despite his crawling to the Chairman, John's brief time on *Clue* revealed an unbeaten flair for sulks and tantrums – he even caused a massive problem when one round wasn't going his way by tipping a full glass of water over the microphone in protest. Even Humph had his hands full with Otto, so Barry never stood a chance.

Having a brain stuffed to the rafters with enough gags to fill several Bob Monkhouse scrapbooks is not enough when dealing with a gang of trouble-makers like the Radio Prune gang, and Barry's ability to keep order would be tested beyond all limits by the introduction of an old *ISIRTA* tradition, which would go on to be the defining denouement for decades to come.

Early Arrival
. . . They're At It Again became *. . . I Haven't a Clue* for the full series, making a much needed further break from the original sketch show – after all, with such an ever-changing roster of talent, it wouldn't be clear who 'They' were, especially if this new show was going to run for more than a couple of series. Despite the continuation of the *I'm Sorry* prefix though, *I'm Sorry I Haven't a Clue* never went out of its way to refer back to many of the traditions of *I'm Sorry I'll Read That Again* – a real distinction had to be made from the world of gibbon-stuffing, OBEs, ferrets and rhubarb tarts. The odd reference still cropped up in the early days – a sprat thrown to the Audience to elicit a cheer, or to help the Teams feel more comfortable – but these moments are rare. Admittedly, when in trouble, Tim knew that a Lady Constance impres-

sion was always his wild card in these first programmes. Similarly, if even the slightest chance of crowbarring Eddie Waring into a show cropped up, Graeme could be relied on to gladly take it. One particular ideal opportunity came with the game 'Commentators', in which the teams were called upon to lend a breathless commentary to the most asinine of activities, such as putting up a deckchair or doing raffia work. As ever, the Waring warbling is impossible to capture in text . . . 'and that's all you're getting!'

These few back references aside, there was one tradition of *ISIRTA* which would not only be continued in the new show, but would go on to define the whole programme – unashamedly ramshackle, torturously punning, and very difficult either to stop or to replace: the 'Late Arrivals' at whatever Society Ball the Chairman nominated each week. This was lifted entirely from the Prune Play of the Week, and in fact it's tempting to imagine the brainstorming for the scripted late arrivals in *ISIRTA* providing the spark for *Clue* in the first place. Come each Sunday at the Playhouse, it wasn't rare for everyone to pitch in 'unusual or amusing' names for some poor wretch to reel off. This punishment frequently fell to John, that confirmed naysayer of punnery, to deliver in his most snarling manner – although Graeme or Tim also often drew the short straw and had to face the Audience, delivering the succeeding names of each painfully titled party goer in increasingly strangulated or bellowing tones, to a barracking of giggles and groans.

As the conclusion to each episode of *Clue*, the Late Arrivals became far more riotous than they ever were in any Prune Play. Starting them off was easy enough, as the Chairman announced the Ball and put his feet up for a long snooze – but ending the final round often proved impossible, outside of the editing suite. Even a Chairman as strict and respected as Humph had no power to prevent late Late Arrivals spilling out long after he'd uttered the decisive words 'Well, that's all from us!' Dave Lee would try and stop the flow of facetious wordplay with a desperate play-out number on the piano, but that never worked either – at the end of the show, with everything to play for, each contestant knew that just one humdinger of a Late Arrival could tip the balance, and it was rare that they'd stop before their offerings had been exhausted (along with Humph, the producer, the Audience and the listeners). There was always room to fit in one more 'Please would you welcome, Mr and Mrs . . .' or 'It's cabaret time! Introducing . . .' or 'All the way from Papua New Guinea . . .' or 'Snap your garters with ribald mirth for . . .' or perhaps the more realistic 'Please suspend your critical faculties for . . .'

And the names that followed were designed to test the patience of an ice-lolly-stick manufacturer, be it Glad Rags and Leo Tard turning up for the Tailors' Ball, or those stragglers at the Mechanics' Ball, Mr and Mrs Drover and their son Alan . . . It was the incessant outpouring of tiebreak-busting puns, indeed, that made poor Quizmaster Cryer finally throw up his hands and bellow 'I resign!' after his attempts to bring the show to a close had come to nothing. Humph, of course, eventually got the hang of silencing them in his own way:

> HL: Ladies and gentlemen, kindly SHUT UP! For Mr and Mrs N'Why-I-Must-Interrupt-Is-Because-We've-Overstepped-the-Bounds-of-Decency-and-Also-It's-the-Last-of-the-Series, and their daughter Theresa N'Why-I-Must-Interrupted-Is-Because-We've-Overstepped-the-Bounds-of-Decency-and-Also-It's-the-Last-of-The-Series . . .

Whether each winning pun proved to be a howler or a barnstormer wasn't important, getting a response from the Audience was all that mattered – and if there wasn't any response from them at all, that in itself would elicit a delayed ripple of giggles en masse, as the stunned gagster stuttered apologies or excuses or, in the worst cases, threatened suicide. This suicidal desperation became a special ploy of Barry's, such as in one round called 'Translations', in which Humph suggested that as 'Skill with a foreign tongue will always help you get on abroad', the Teams should come up with some translations of their own:

> BC: 'Hara Kiri' . . . that's an opera singer who was educated at public school . . . *Harrah*-Kiri . . . Te Kanawa . . . *Harrow*. Public school. New Zealand opera singer . . . Who wasn't educated at Harrow at all, that was just for the purposes of the joke . . . And I wish I was dead.
>
> HL: That brings us to our last round . . .

There's always been a sliding scale of joke approval, from all-out groaning, to stumbling silence and self-deprecating apology, to polite titters. Next came the distinction of a line receiving an 'applau' – the most modest of claps from one Audience member. Then came the guffaws, the cheers, and the optimum result, gut-wrenching, breathless laughter that could last minutes, all down to one perfectly delivered piece of filth from Humph. Any one of the above was grist to the mill, though. This ability to get a reaction from good gags, bad gags and indifferent gags was a win-win-win set-up, and the same arrangement would stick for decades. In the show, Humph would wait until the first game had been played before alerting the Teams as to the theme of the Ball, and they would have the intervening twenty-odd minutes to compile their guest list . . .

Mock Ad Hoc

. . . Except, of course, they'd usually already decided the theme themselves, in the pub before the show, and had sat around batting names back and forth for ages before the recording started, making sure that everyone was fully armed with a zinger or two. The generally ad-lib nature of the show certainly lent an edge of hysteria to the performances, with the otherwise quick-witted Kendall and especially Oddie giggly to a fault throughout their appearances, but to the listener at home there was an infectious suggestion that everyone was having a good time. However, the terrifying experience of going out with literally no idea of what they were going to come up with had remained with Graeme since the pilot recording, and he vowed not to let it happen again. The show had to be live, unpredictable and enjoyably tatty of course, but from series one onwards Garden would be experimenting, trying to come up with solid ideas that could be prepared in advance, and give the Teams something to fall back on should the muse be irritatingly thin on the ground when the 'record' button was pressed.

'In the series I did, I felt that all the bits that worked weren't ad-libbed at all,' confirms Oddie. 'Without a doubt, they were written in the pub before the show, so you went along to the pub for, say, two o'clock, and then spent two hours in the dressing room, writing. And it *was* writing, in a way that wasn't much different from writing the actual *ISIRTA* scripts – we were doing "Late Arrivals" and that sort of thing. And I remember saying to Graeme, "I'm sorry, but what we seem to be doing now is giving them a free script! And the only bits that work are the bits we're writing!" I think that was the case, then, much more than it then became.'

John Lloyd, himself practically a professor of panel games, is keen to point out that using prepared material wasn't a new thing when *Clue* first came along, 'There was a wonderful show of the late sixties and seventies called *My Word* which had Frank Muir and Denis Norden in it. It was a word panel game-cum-quiz, and very very good. And at the front of the show the Chairman used to say "I'm going to now give Frank and Denis each a well-known phrase or saying" – "People in glass houses shouldn't throw stones", or whatever – "And at the end of the programme I'm going to ask them to give the explanation as to how this phrase came about." And the best bit of the programme always was this brilliant monologue from the two of them, full of fantastic gags – which I, as a naive teenager, thought they sort of literally had scribbled down on napkins during the course of the half-hour, but of course they hadn't, in the least. I think what they probably did was wrote the thing first and then told the Chairman what they were going to say.'

So there's no secret about this mix of instant wit and prepared jokes. Nearly thirty years ago, in Roger Wilmut's *From Fringe to Flying Circus*, Graeme said: 'In the first series it was all virtually ad-libbed – that was my mistake, and since, we've all learned a bit about doing panel games. We know the audience like it a) because you appear to be witty, and b) because you appear to be put "on the spot" and have to sweat ... Anyone who thinks, "That wasn't done on the spot!" is probably right in their assumptions; but I'd hate them to think that any of the ones we *have* done on the spot were prepared! We can write better stuff than that!'

The tradition of sharing all the best lines out fairly among the Teams under-lines one of *Clue*'s strengths throughout fifty series of panel-game spoofing: a complete absence, or even positive disdain for, competition. *Clue* is all about laughter, not one-upmanship or competing in any way but ironically, and for the show to work, everybody has to look good. Unlike *Joker's Wild* or modern games like *Never Mind the Buzzcocks*, there's no winner in *Clue* – or rather, everyone's a winner. Comedians can be the most viciously back-stabbing, competitive people in the world when they get together, topping gags, spoiling punchlines, heckling ... none of that's welcome in this sedate club. Admit-tedly the players of the game can get incredibly snide and angry in the show, but it's all part of the game – nobody was going to be hung up to dry, and if there's any problem with one player failing to come up with anything for a round, between Barry, Graeme and Tim, there are bound to be a few spare rib-ticklers lying around which they can have for free, with pleasure. Barry cheerfully admits, 'I've benefited enormously from that – "You do that one, Baz" – though I like to repay the bargain, obviously ...' Genuine competi-tion is anathema to *Clue* – and selfishness, ambition and superiority are always the object of the show's satire.

Although the balance of prepared and unprepared material has been redressed considerably in the years since Graeme's admission, it's always been crucial to the show's success that the best kind of comedy anarchy actually comes from seasoned performers who know what they're doing – and who don't have to perform under the kind of pressure that causes hours of wet retching before a show. Because, although these early shows have an infec-tiously giggly tone to them, the giggles were hiding not just nerves from some quarters, but abject misery. Quite apart from enjoying the challenge, the edge of hysteria came from genuine terror, as Garden recalls: 'Bill and John Cleese oddly enough hated the lack of structure and script. Bill used to throw up before the recordings he did.'

'We're Not Playing Any More!'

Despite Oddie's misgivings about preparing so much material, the genuinely improvised stuff was twisting the poor writer into knots, twice a night every Sunday evening. 'I really wasn't enjoying it. I do remember the total sense of relief when I actually said, "I'm sorry, I don't want to do any more of these, it's just making me feel sick every day." I'm sure there was more than one occasion when I swore during rehearsals, or even the recording, saying, "I'm sorry, I really *haven't* got a fucking clue . . ." And profanity was not so easy to come by in those days! It would be fine now, I'm sure *I'm Sorry I Haven't a Fucking Clue* would be a good title.'

Both John Cleese and Jo Kendall sport themselves admirably in their episodes. Kendall's eagerness to get a laugh in often resulted in streams of saucy verbal incontinence which it's impossible to dislike, even if the boys talked over her all the time, and even occasionally stole her gags on mic. As for Cleese, he seemed in many ways more himself, and more at ease verbally jousting with his old college pals, than in any other show he recorded. In many ways all the gang was doing in *Clue* was passing the time in much the same way that they would waste evenings in the Footlights clubroom in Petty Cury – trading daft jokes and singing silly songs. Often Cleese's particular brand of laconic sarcasm was to the fore, sniping at Tim for his Late Arrival at the Medical Ball (Mr and Mrs Sthetic and their daughter Annie), with 'What about Pa Thetic?' But as a *Clue* panellist, John Otto Cleese sung and squeaked and sulked and laughed along with the gang in an almost embarrassingly easy way which is otherwise absent from his huge body of comic work.

But Cleese's penchant for meticulously structured pre-planned humour made the *Clue* format ultimately anathema to him, and he and Kendall eventually stepped out of the *I'm Sorry* story for a final time after only one series. Humph announced the final score for the maiden series, after thirteen weeks – 'William and Mary 1,184, Robert and Elizabeth 308. Making Sid and Enid the overall winners' – and Jo and John called it a day, citing terminally frayed nerves. 'I sympathised with John,' admits Oddie, 'I may have lasted a bit longer, but I'm sure we felt the same, "this isn't something I enjoy".' Nevertheless, despite his misgivings, Bill tried to keep up with Tim and Graeme for a second run of *Clue* recordings the following spring – even if a third regular contestant was going to have to be found to fill the fourth seat, alongside Graeme Garden.

There was never really any question as to who it would be, just as there was no question as to who would be the one and only Chairman. Barry Cryer and Humphrey Lyttelton were never really competing for the job – as Barry says today: 'The show didn't make much of an impact when it started, but it had a rebirth, and the Great Lyttelton and I both – auditioned is an insulting word for him – we both 'did' Chairman. I always say it's the one time in my life I was delighted somebody else got the job because I remember thinking, "No, it's *got* to be Lyttelton".'

With Humph happy to make time in his schedule for *Clue* for the fore-seeable future, by rights Barry's job would have been over if Jo and John had wanted to carry on. Thankfully, his availability, friendship with the gang, and – most importantly of all – supreme powers as a gagsmith, meant that Barry was welcomed into the team without a second thought. Garden and Cassels knew that reliability was a crucial virtue when forming a solid regular group for radio, and Barry had spent the last decade building up just such a repu-tation for dependable mirth-making. He could have no better referee than the godfather of radio comedy Denis Norden, who confirmed, 'There's an old showbiz line about the producer saying, "I don't want it good, I want it Monday!" Barry was the one who always did it for Monday. *And* good.' And so, with Barry signed up to play rather than referee, Humph officially took up that legendary symbol of his superiority, the Chairman's horn – a grand intricate motor-car hooter, which lit up when hooting – and it alternated with his more accustomed, musical horn for the rest of his life.

The second run of *Clue* featured Barry and the Goodies in every episode, and the tradition of rustling up bankable gags in the pub before an optional bout of Olympic vomiting and an evening's double recording at the Play-house, or the BBC Radio Theatre just off the Strand, was now firmly entrenched. But if the challenge of entertaining the masses with off-the-cuff witticisms, parlour games and terrible singing wasn't enough to force Bill to call it a day and save his central nervous system, the scene that awaited the gang when they arrived at the Playhouse one Sunday in March 1973 may have been the last straw.

Graeme explains: 'Just before we arrived, a bomb went off round the corner in Scotland Yard, and as we walked to the theatre we saw the streets were covered in broken glass . . .' There had been an IRA bomb attack, and although it would be good to say that the Teams refused to let terrorism stand in the way of laughter, the entire area was temporarily sealed off, and the recording had to be cancelled. As producer John Cassels, Humph, Tim, Graeme, Bill and Barry hung around the theatre arranging plans for a replacement recording, they noticed a large suitcase sitting suspiciously in the corner of the foyer. Graeme asked the BBC doorman whose it was. 'That's all right,' he was assured, 'it belongs to a foreign lady and I'm keeping an eye on it for her.'

The whole gang ripped open the door and pelted down the road in a flash, only stopping when they finally managed to flag down a taxi. 'Where to?' said the driver. 'TO THE COUNTRY!' yelled Graeme, and they sped away. Whether the foreign lady was reunited with her holiday luggage we will never know.

Between grumpiness at the lack of a writing fee, terror at the need to extemporise not one but two half-hour comedy shows a night, the copious regurgitation that came from pre-show nerves and now the nerve-jangling experience of walking into the middle of a terrorist attack, Bill was, finally, out. It was a huge gesture to admit defeat, when his two *Goodies* co-stars were determined to plough on with the show, but with one last round of the Astronomers' Ball (for which he offered 'Racing in, a nice collection of stars, Mr and Mrs Dromeda and their daughter Anne Dromeda . . . and their pet, the great bear . . . and their dog, Star . . .'), Bill Oddie said his goodbyes to everyone, told Tim and Graeme that he'd see them soon to prepare for the fourth series of their TV show, and made his exit from the *I'm Sorry* story for good. Tim muses today, 'It was fairly extraordinary that he became so nervous, I thought that was my role! Jo was missed too, she added a much needed female presence and was a sharp wit.'

With his subsequent career as the nation's favourite birdwatcher earning him legions of fans and indeed an OBE, does he regret not fighting past his nerves and remaining a regular panellist? 'Ironically, I have to say, *now* I would enjoy it, but I've never been asked, so there you go. I don't know why, but at some stage five or six years ago I suddenly discovered that I was perfectly happy doing long-term improvisation. I think I made some comment a year or two ago, "You'll be having Max Bygraves on before you have me on, by the sound of it." I think I let it be known that I wouldn't mind, but I've never been asked.'

'I think John and Bill were OK when they could be bothered with it,' muses Garden, 'but I think they both found it hard to go along with the premise . . . and would draw the Audience's attention too much to the fact that it was rubbish.'

10

The Winning Formula

John, Jo and Bill weren't really walking out of the *I'm Sorry* story of course, because very soon after striking any further *Clue* recording dates out of their diaries, they were back at the Playhouse recording the very final series of *I'm Sorry I'll Read That Again*. Naturally, there was no way they could get through a whole series of Radio Prune self-indulgence without mentioning the Antidote to Panel Games experiment – Graeme's pet project was pilloried within five minutes of the first episode, when our gang of ragamuffins try and sneak their way back onto BBC Radio without the DG noticing, and are instantly discovered by the man himself.

JC: Three years ago I vowed that you lot would never work for the BBC again, and you keep trying to wheedle your way back, don't you?

BO: I haven't wheedled, sir!

JC: You think I don't notice? Who did that rotten despicable clever-dick so-called quiz show, hmm?

JK: Oh, I rather like *Twenty Questions* . . .

JC: Not that, not that. *I'm Sorry I Haven't a Script* or something, that was you, wasn't it? Yes, yes, it was the title that gave it away. You didn't fool me. Call that a panel game? Don't make me laugh.

BO: We didn't.

But it wasn't until the end of the next summer, in 1974, that Graeme and John Cassels knew for sure that Bill was officially out of the game, and they would have to find a new permanent line-up for the third series. Barry and Tim were raring for more, but there was an empty seat waiting to be filled by someone with bags of the requisite nerves of steel – and, as Garden has it, 'a large helping of "what the hell"' – required to make it through two sessions of semi-improvised stupidity a night.

A Large Helping of 'What the Hell'

In between these barely scripted shenanigans, Tim and Barry were having a whale of a time with jokes old and older in *Hello, Cheeky*. Despite the (trad) nature of so much of the humour in the shows, it attracted such a following that ITV commissioned two series of a television version in 1976 – which sadly were such a flop that it even earned a drubbing from Bill and Graeme in an episode of *The Goodies*. Tim explains today that 'The shame with the television is that obviously when you're doing very quick characters, you have to get into a costume or a hat or something very, very quickly, and on the television they never saw us moving from one to the other, so they just saw somebody appearing on the screen, probably with a hat or a wig or something slightly crooked, whereas what I'd wanted was a long shot so you can see the problems, and that's part of the fun of somebody getting there on time to do the character, and it just didn't really work on television, it was a shame. But it was good fun on radio. Solid, corny, good fun.'

It seems that sound broadcasting was by now the true home of corny fun, so Tim and Barry returned to what they knew best, and continued with the radio version of the show right up until the end of the decade. With Hatch still producing, *Hello, Cheeky* managed to keep the spirit of Prune alive over five series, a couple of panto-style Christmas specials, and two specially recorded commercial LPs entitled *The Least Worst of Hello, Cheeky* and the musical album *The Seedy Sound of Hello, Cheeky*. But it wasn't just *ISIRTA* that was channelled by the show, much *Clue* humour was inevitably to the fore as well, and the Antidote to Panel Games owes a lot to the scripted efforts of Junkin, Brooke-Taylor and Cryer. 'Meanwhile, not a thousand miles from Crewe Junction . . .'

JJ: And now, a look ahead at tonight's programmes. Here is a brief excerpt from tonight's play.

BC: *MY NOSE!*

JJ: More of that later tonight on BBC1. On the other channel, there's a big sugar cube with '2' painted on it going round and round and round. This is a repeat of a sugar cube shown earlier this week.

TBT: On ITV, there's a load of rubbish.

BC: There is a BBC3, but only dogs can hear it.

JJ: So for any dogs viewing later tonight, here are the programmes.

TBT: Seven o'clock, *The Magic Houndabout* followed by *Take Your Peke*. Then *Top of the Pups* with the Setters and Mongrel Jerry with their new hit 'A Little Whelp from My Friends'.

BC: Then Kenneth Kennel will be reading the canine o'clock news,
       followed by *Today in Parliament* with Conrad Vos-Bark.

JJ: International cabaret stars Shirley Basset and Tom Bones singing
       selections from *Fiddler on the Woof* and *Hello, Collie!*

The loose pun-riffing that punctuates *Hello, Cheeky* found its way easily
into *Clue*'s games – the link above pretty much called itself 'Dog Breeders'
Radio Times' in one edition of the show thirty years later, although the star
of *Top of the Pups* had by then been updated to 'Good Boy, Slim'. It wasn't
just the 'Late Arrivals' that opened the pun floodgates in *Clue*; throughout
the years endless excuses for creaking wordplay have been introduced into
the game, with 'Radio Times' being a good example – an edition of the magazine released at the time of the Nativity, for example, would boast shows like
Have I Got Jews for You, *Down Jaweh*, and *Three Wise Men and a Baby*. That
last offering could also be placed under the title of 'Film Clubs' – almost as
many professions and general categories of society have had their own film
clubs and indeed book clubs and songbooks as they've had society balls. The
Cheese Makers' Film Club would be showing *The Guns of Mascarpone* and
Fromage To Eternity, while you could save a fortune on *Great Exaggerations* or
The Little Book of Clam by joining the Fishermen's Book Club, and so on. Few
shows would have the cheek to roll these puns out, and perhaps there were
only ever three of note that really had the nerve – *I'm Sorry I'll Read That
Again*, *Hello, Cheeky* and *I'm Sorry I Haven't a Clue*.

With Tim and Barry enjoying the pleasures of scripted punnery with John
Junkin in *Hello, Cheeky*, then, it would have seemed the obvious move to
bring John in to the quiz show to fill Bill's boots – his quick-wittedness and
mastery of idle saucy silliness more than qualified him for the job. But there
was another well-known radio voice in the vicinity who had all the right
spaces in his diary – a pioneering satirist, cricket enthusiast, inimitable
cartoonist and comic actor who somehow never seemed to be fully engaged
with any of these pursuits, allowing others to step over him to achieve real
acclaim, while he happily ploughed his own furrow.

Willie Rushton was making quite a regular income from broadcasting his
barking Chelsea tones over the radio waves long before Oddie created a
vacancy on *Clue*, being a regular booking for many pilots and shows, with
Just a Minute, *What's It All About?*, *Fair Deal*, *The Impressionists* and *Pro's &
Cons* all featuring the Rushton voice – although his standing with the producer
of this last programme (a con-trick-based panel game presented by Shaw
Taylor) was dented when he simply forgot to turn up for the recording on at
least one occasion. However, he would never forget at least to *turn up* for
Clue, and the existing players of the game welcomed the nonchalant satirist

into the fold in August 1974. *I'm Sorry I Haven't a Clue* was finding its feet, and it had only taken twenty-odd episodes to get there . . .

William George Rushton
Born: 18 August 1937, Chelsea
Educated: Shrewsbury School, Shropshire
The offspring of a reserved English publisher and a vivacious red-headed Welsh girl, the unique package that was Willie Rushton was delivered to his well-to-do parents in 1937, only one day before the birth of his great friend and collaborator Richard Ingrams. At Shrewsbury School, it was with Ingrams and fellow pupils Christopher Booker and Paul Foot that Willie first dipped his toe into humour, when they all worked on a spoof of the school magazine, *The Salopian*, called *The Wallopian*. While his friends all went off to Oxford and the like after national service, he told them they were mad, and that a commercial satirical magazine held the secret of success for them all.

Perhaps it was Rushton's confidence in what was to become *Private Eye* that prevented him from bothering very much with his education or the army – he famously flunked his biology exam by answering the question 'What is this?', attached to a mysterious substance in a test tube, with the single word 'Disgusting', and walked out of the exam hall. He ended up as a solicitor's clerk, doggedly sending off his brilliant cartoons to *Punch*, until *Private Eye* changed everything in 1961.

In the eye of the storm of the satire boom, Willie crafted the look of every issue of the magazine, both before and after Peter Cook took on the mantle of Lord Gnome, and remained an integral part of the staff for the rest of his life. It wasn't long before Willie's singular wit and eccentric appearance landed him a job on the *TW3* team, notably performing his Cook-inspired Macmillan impression. A multiple career as celebrated satirical cartoonist, wit and comic actor beckoned. Also of course a comic author, he became a beloved story-teller on *Jackanory*, a regular face on panel games of all description, and made memorable appearances in movies and shows from *Monte Carlo or Bust* to *Up Pompeii!*

While presenting a pub-based sixties entertainment show called *Stars & Garters*, Willie met his wife, the Australian actress Arlene Dorgan, and became stepfather to her two sons. This necessitated a new regular life in Australia, where he became friendly with Tony Hancock just in time to have the task of taking his ashes back to the UK, proudly telling customs officers exactly who was in his flask as he passed through. He and Arlene had a son, Toby, in 1970. The Rushtons also shared their lives with numerous cats, and Willie listed his hobbies as 'gaining weight, losing weight, and parking'.

Willie died in 1996, entirely unfestooned with OBEs.

No Such Thing as a Free Willie

As with Barry, the roots of Willie's links to the rest of the team seem to be lost in the mists of time – though the furthest back was probably travelling through the states of America with Tim in the *TW3* tour, of which Tim still has fond memories. 'In San Francisco we had too much to drink and found it difficult to climb the hills on the way to the venue. Willie would take two paces forward and three back whilst singing "I Left My Heart in San Francisco". When I suggested that he might be a bit tipsy onstage he tore my suit jacket from top to bottom – thirty years later we were still laughing about it.' Willie had also been a part of the original line-up for the television incarnation of that show, and with Barry a senior scribe on *The Frost Report*, Cryer and Rushton managed to ascertain that they must have met in the sixties 'somewhere round the back of David Frost'; but how Willie actually came to be nominated to fill Oddie's still warm seat is hard to say.

A great big ball of sarcastic wit wrapped up in affable Englishness, with a voice like the crustiest of vintage port (a distinctive quality which would be destined to make him as essential a part of celebrity quiz shows like *Blankety Blank*, *Through the Keyhole* and *Celebrity Squares* as garish neon buzzers, a Ronnie Hazlehurst theme tune, or Terry Wogan's silly little microphone), Rushton's apparently effortless input instantly gelled. He hit the ground running with a sterling first appearance on *Clue*, including the memorable Late Arrival at the Booksellers' Ball, 'Adjust your raiment, pray . . . for Mr and Mrs Jonathan Cape, and their son the Great S. Cape . . .' It should be added, however, this was an uncharacteristic show of willing from Willie, who would go on to become known for his complete ambivalence to the final round of punning. The idea was of course that only Humph took time out for the 'Late Arrivals', but Willie also decided that it was an ideal opportunity to put his feet up after half an hour's improv, his voice often conspicuous by its absence in most final rounds, causing his poor partner Tim to whimper 'Are you there, Willie?' on many occasions. Sometimes Willie even asked to leave early, to be excused punning duty.

Willie's wonderful laissez-faire attitude was perhaps most perfectly displayed in a round of the perennial *Clue* favourite, 'Paranoia' (basically a slightly more offensive version of *Twenty Questions*). Over the years the Teams would be blighted with some form of physical or mental problem which only their opposition, the Audience and the Mystery Voice who clued in the listeners at home would know, and they would be forced to desperately guess what was up with them – whether it was worshipping Jason Donovan, or appearing in *Crossroads* (to which Tim prophetically proclaimed 'I wouldn't mind that . . .'), a fear that they were going to be murdered by the Dagenham Girl Pipers, or that Barry is Michael Parkinson and Graeme is David Frost ('God, you know how to hurt a man!'). The afflicted had to ask questions to find out the problem, depending on the Audience to give them encouragement, at Humph's signal: 'Audience, you can clap, if you like, if they're getting warm . . . or you're getting cold.' But on the occasion that Tim and Willie's afflic-tion was that Tim was totally invisible and couldn't be heard, Willie's shining indifference to the silly game was revealed for all to see, as his partner's numerous and increasingly high-pitched attempts to find out what ailed them fell on deaf ears, with Barry and Graeme only able to answer to Willie . . . and Willie remaining absolutely silent, clearly thinking of something else and enjoying Tim's evident desperation.

Despite (or indeed, because of) these in-character bouts of idleness, with Willie Rushton's arrival a solid, happy team was established that would keep *Clue* entertaining listeners for the next twenty-odd years of unbroken silliness, which could be summed up with Humph's intro to the very first programme with the new line-up: 'I'd like to welcome you to another series of encounters with verbal wit and brilliance, but never mind, you can't win 'em all . . .'

The fourth series was only a short run, being six episodes rather than the usual twelve, but in his final stint as producer, Cassels was really beginning to hone the show into a format far closer to the modern game. The broadcast was now always introduced as the 'Antidote to Panel Games', and closed with the dismissive words '. . . were given silly things to do by Humphrey Lyttelton'. In fact, perhaps the biggest sign that there was still some way to go for the show was that Humph was still blatantly awarding points for every round – not very sensibly, admittedly, but with a regularity that just sounds wrong today.

There were still a few hangovers from *ISIRTA*, as well. A brand-new game that seemed to perfectly encapsulate the facetious approach to parlour games was christened 'Sound Charades' – taking a game that relied entirely on mime and broadcasting it in sound only was an inspired decision. When the game first appeared it was closer to the original charades, and allowed the Teams to break down the name of each film, play, song or book into its separate words, or even use the 'sounds like' option if need be. But they soon discovered that it was far funnier (and also quicker) to try and do the 'whole thing' in one short sketch. The back reference to Radio Prune came in a round in which that infamous favourite of Radio Goodies, 'A Walk in the Black Forest' was conveyed as 'Just listen to the trees whispering, "How de do dere, honey?"' – a guaranteed guffaw from the Audience, and instant recognition from Graeme on the opposing team, naturally followed. A less potentially offen-sive clue was offered when *Pride and Prejudice* was given away by Graeme's roar 'I'm very sorry, but I CAN'T STAND LIONS!' Only a devoted cat lover could take umbrage at that.

When the next series came round in the summer of '75, Cassels' job was inherited by that other talented protégé of Hatch's, Simon Brett of Stepney, gaining crucial experience before the launch of *The Burkiss Way* the following year. He agrees that Cassels had left him a strong show, far tighter and slicker than the desperate improvisation that dogged the earlier series. 'By the time I did it, the show was quite established. John Cassels started it, and I just had my turn, as it were . . . *Just a Minute* got passed round quite a lot among the young producers, and I did that too, and I think *I'm Sorry* came that way. In the early days it was very sort of random, and very hit-and-miss. And it began to get a bit more structure – I think John started that, but I remember we had a meeting before the series started and just talked through some rounds, and introduced some new ones, and began to give it more structure before we actually started the recordings. You know, sitting round the table, throwing ideas in. I don't think I can claim any round as completely my own. But there was the joining two film names together, that sort of thing.'

This last new game was billed as 'Double Feature', and it became a solid part of the show, introducing decades of similar punning takes on movie titles such as the combined remake of *Ben Hur* and *Get Carter* to create *Get Hur*, or *Room at the Top*, *Barbarella* and *Custer's Last Stand*, making *Roobarb and Custard*, or Willie's insistence that 'They're making a punk version of *Separate Tables* called *I Spit In Your Gravy* . . .' The game would survive well into the nineties, allowing Tim to sail very close to the winds of public decency with the double salvo of mixing '*Fu Man Chu*, *The Lion King* and *For the Love of Ada*, to produce *Fu King Ada* . . .' (Cue the sound of an entire Audience gasping as one.) 'It's like handing in your notice, really . . . On the grounds of taste, the makers of *The Big Country* have decided not to combine with anyone, but if they did, Oliver Reed would be the star.'

Despite this game, and the odd bit of tweaking, Brett insists that the show wasn't really designed to be a great training ground for young producers at the time: 'I'm very pleased to have my name on it, but it was the least producing I think I ever did. Because there'd be a call for three o'clock or something, and you'd say hello and have a cup of tea, and then they'd go off into corners and work out their ad-libs. Then at about six you'd do a sound-check, and then go off for a drink, do the recording . . . And then the editing was quite self-dictating in a way, so it wasn't really a producer's job, you know, it was all coming from them.'

The Musical Chair

However, one major decision made by the new boss would have far-reaching repercussions. Brett's first job as producer was to fill yet another vacancy on the *Clue* staff – and the last one for another two decades. Having outlasted his musical collaborator Bill Oddie by one short series, Dave Lee made one more attempt to keep time with the rebellious teams in 1974, before finally moving on to continue his successful career as maestro on several BBC shows, and leaving the *I'm Sorry* story for good – or at least until the 1989 *ISIRTA* reunion. Lee's job as resident pianist was far from an easy one, mixing musical genres, fitting his playing to the often radically 'distinctive' singing styles of the Teams, and all this while under the gaze of Humphrey Lyttelton, a genuine icon of British music. Perhaps Willie Rushton's absolute inability to sing with even the vaguest idea of timing or rhythm had been the last straw, but Lee declared himself out, and someone with the same awesome mastery of the pianoforte would have to be recruited before the recordings began in June.

That other stalwart of *ISIRTA* music, Leon Cohen, had sat in for Lee on one occasion, but in the event, Brett was incredibly quick in finding just the right person to fill Dave Lee's piano stool – a keen, young piano-playing prodigy with a short but distinguished career had been discovered, and duly signed up . . . that is unless you asked Humphrey Lyttelton's opinion of course, as he would claim that Brett simply didn't bother, and brought in Colin Sell instead.

Colin Sell
Born: 1 December 1948, Purley, Surrey
Educated: Bristol University
Brought up in Croydon, Colin was inspired to take musical lessons from his grandmother's playing of the old standards on the family piano. Despite his aptitude and a passion for jazz, Colin never studied music, receiving a BA in Spanish and Latin American Studies from Bristol University in 1971. Bristol did, however, provide an entry into musical revue and the Edinburgh Festival, where he would be spotted by producer Simon Brett.

When not being abused by Humph at *Clue* recordings, Colin has forged a reputation as a skilled accompanist and musical improviser, working with the Comedy Store and the RSC. He has also composed and performed extensively for the theatre, and for radio, scoring many plays for the BBC World Service Drama Department. When not doing this, or *Clue*, or accompanying Barry on one of his tours, Colin is Head of Music at the East 15 Acting School, Essex. He really deserves an OBE.

The jokes about Colin Sell's musical prowess that would come to litter every episode of *Clue* simply wouldn't work if he wasn't just a proficient pianist, but a brilliant one. Despite not having a music degree – 'My musical quali-fications are Grade VI piano, which just shows how you can be mediocre and still grow up to be insulted by the finest trumpeter in the country' – Colin

Sell had developed his own brand of comedic orchestration, having been inspired at a young age by Dudley Moore's straddling of the worlds of music and comedy. 'The revue area of Bristol Uni was especially strong,' he recalls, 'and we started taking material to the Edinburgh Fringe. After I graduated I continued to write for Bristol Uni revues in Edinburgh, and it would have been in either 1973 or 1974 that Simon Brett spotted me. Edinburgh Fringe in those days was crowded, but not as badly as now, and people really did do talent-spotting. In '74 Simon phoned me, we met for a drink, and he told me he liked what I did but had nothing to offer me at that point. A couple of weeks later he phoned again and told me he'd been given *Clue* to produce. I hadn't heard it, so he sent me a tape . . .'

Despite not having picked up on this funky new Antidote to Panel Games scene, Sell was knocked out by the comic company that he was now keeping, as a relatively green twenty-something: 'Simon took my breath away when he offered me *Clue*; the people involved were my icons, not least of all Humph. I did my first series, and was convinced my nerves had translated themselves into my playing and I'd never be asked back. But I was, series after series, and got to know the Teams, all of whom were charming to me from the start. I think they were (and are) as nervous as I, and sensed a kindred spirit.'

And so the impressionable young curly-mopped accompanist took his place, at a respectful distance behind the sainted Chairman's back, and embarked on a part-time career that would ultimately make him one of the most widely known ivory-ticklers in the country. Like so many of the institutions that join together to create the *Clue* chemistry, Sell's place on the team took some time to bed in. At first, Humph was positively protective of the new boy, warning him in one show that 'the Musicians' Union rate includes danger money and a pension for premature old age', and even giving the pianist a generous helping of points for his playing at times, just to put the Teams' noses out of joint. But it wasn't long before his rightful role as musical dogs-body would come into play and, in addition to the constant brickbats (such as 'Colin's musical influences are Middle Eastern in origin. Mainly Shi-ite', or 'Colin Sell, one of the finest musicians of the day. Of course, when night comes, something seems to desert him . . .'), the brave musician would have his work cut out keeping up with the players of *Clue*, sitting quietly at the back of every show, like a docile Dormouse at the Mad Hatter's Tea Party, ready to play when prodded.

'Everybody says, "It must be awful being insulted like that," and of course it's not. First of all, Humph and I were the best of friends, and secondly, just to be mentioned at all by that man was wonderful, so it didn't matter in the slightest . . . It upped my profile, in a loony kind of way.' Humph claimed that the infamous, torrid Taylor-and-Burton-style relationship between the two of them began on one of the rare occasions when the youngster Sell spoke out of turn, denting the pride of the presiding Chairman. This came in the staggeringly pointless musical round entitled 'Fourth Bridge', in which the Teams were called upon to sing songs . . . but omitting every fourth word.

HL: Let's start with you, Tim and Willie . . .

WR: What would you like us to sing, Humph?

HL: Well . . . if they'd put it on my card, I'd be able to tell you.

WR: I wonder if the Mystery Voice knows?

CS: (*Off mic.*) May I make a suggestion?

WR: Colin's got a suggestion!

BC: Colin SPEAKS!

CS: How about 'I've Got Rhythm', Humph?

HL: *Did anybody ask you?* Tim and Willie, will you sing 'I've Got Rhythm'?
   They do so, omitting every fourth word. The Audience show their appreciation.

BC: That was the rhythm method! You know it makes sense.

HL: Couple of minor errors I detected in there, so that rules you out . . .

TBT: That was the piano though.

HL: Now, Colin Sell, have you any ideas as to what I should ask Graeme and Barry to sing?

CS (*Off mic.*) How about 'Leaning on a Lamp Post', Humph? Or indeed, singing it?

TBT: Ooh, you'll be in trouble now, Colin!

BC: One in a row!

HL: Just for that I'll turn that suggestion down. And so we go onto . . .

Despite the veneration which Lyttelton inspired right from the start, he never forgot the slight, and the slightest questioning of his awesome powers of adjudication could lead to sulks of epic proportions. 'Since then,' admitted Humph, 'it's gone on to the extent that his mother, according to him, once said to him, "Why do you let that dreadful man speak to you like that?"' The treatment Colin was to receive from his musical master over the decades was, however, warranted – never undermine the Chairman.

Having acknowledged the fact that managing to keep up with the panel's singing was a supremely difficult challenge, that's not to say that they were tone deaf. Willie *did* have an almost preternatural ignorance of timing and rhythm, but his voice itself was a treat, if it came in at the right time – his very own hit single 'Neasden', written for *Private Eye*, is a classic. Those revue hoofers Tim and Graeme obviously spent their time in the Hit Parade in the 1970s, egged on by Oddie – besides which, Graeme plays the banjo and a few other instruments, and they can both hold a tune. Barry, however, is often picked out as having the finest set of musical vocal cords on the show, with a rawness that comes from decades of smoking menthol, ideal for belting out Elvis Presley numbers. Plus, he has the distinction of being the only member of the team to have had a number one in Finland. In 1957, when the young Cryer had barely got a toe on the bottom rung of the showbiz ladder, he was taken on by the manager of Frankie Vaughan, who at the time was the UK's greatest weapon in the war against Elvis. Vaughan and Cryer became good friends, and Barry was booked to do his stint in the pop world, as one of an endless stream of unlikely young male hopefuls in the fifties such as Jimmy Young (who at the time would have been thirty-six). Cryer did a sterling job recording the British version of 'The Purple People Eater', an American hit about a horrendous abomination of nature that starts a rock 'n' roll band. For contractual reasons, Sheb Wooley's original couldn't be released in Finland, and so Barry Cryer spent three weeks as the King of Finnish Pop, before quitting his musical career while he was ahead – or rather, safely containing his musical career within the games of *I'm Sorry I Haven't a Clue*.

Another popular musical round was, and remains, 'Just a Minim', a form of tribute to Hatch's radio hit, which first joined the roster of *Clue* games in 1982. Its primary purpose was of course to allow Humph to launch a blistering attack on the one panel-game chairman who dared to claim a level of immortality comparable to his own – Nicholas Parsons, 'who, I hear, is regarded as a bit of a cult'. But the challenge of singing a song 'without hesitation, repetition, repetition, lobster or deviation' has also guaranteed the round plenty of airplay over the years, with specifically lyric-poor songs chosen to optimise rough and tumble. As with the spoken version of the game, the best fun is usually had by letting the singer – often Graeme – run with a song without any intention of interrupting, so they fumble on in the most embarrassing way possible. The need to grope for off-the-cuff musical synonyms has seen such great perversions of popular tunes as Willie Rushton's take on the Ray Charles classic 'Hit the Road Jack', which emerged as '*On yer bike, Jim, and never return, not at all, not in March, April, December . . . GET OUT OF HERE, BASIL! AND THAT'S THE END OF IT!*'

Being a busy, buzz-reliant round, 'Just a Minim' has also given plenty of opportunity for the Chairman to belittle Colin – 'Do remember that excessive buzzing is likely to drone out the music provided by Colin Sell. Another good way is with a pneumatic drill.' But as barely a single round of the game has ever been played without the Teams getting completely lost in a song,

Sell usually has to step in to keep things in order – which of course is guaranteed to test the Lyttelton patience, as in one round featuring young upstart Stephen Fry, one of several *Clue* players to become infamous for a complete and apologetic inability to croak even in the most meagrely musical way:

HL: OK, well, it says here, 'If this round ends quickly, you might like to try it again.' Do you want to try it again?

CS: Yeah.

HL: Oh, let's!

SF: Oh yes, please.

HL: This time, it's the song 'One Man Went To Mow' – Colin!

CS: (*Starts to play, and* stops.) Who's starting, Humph?

HL: Oh, you say. You've taken over the bloody show.

CS: OK – Stephen!

BC: *You swine!*

I Woke Up This Morning . . .

However, especially for those sadistic listeners who like the Teams to sweat for their cheers, there has always been one musical round which towers above every other – 'The Blues'. Someone as tuneless as Stephen Fry can usually be heard groaning piteously whenever a singing round is announced, but the few rounds which require genuine on-the-spot construction of rhyme and metre have always inspired players of all kinds of musical ability to whine and wheedle and provide Humph with notes from their mother. 'The Blues' round was one such game, certainly when it first appeared right back in the first series. Judged, according to Humph, on 'appositeness and ethnic feel', the creation of such a simple, four-line twelve-bar style of song seemed ideally suited to unscripted giggles, but even the maestro Oddie tied himself up in knots trying to provide the goods at first. The default opening line 'I woke up this morning . . .' became an instant thorn in the Teams' sides, being so predictable an opening that a hundred-point penalty was introduced for starting that way – even if the replacement 'I woke up this afternoon' wasn't much better.

Games like 'The Blues' were at the centre of the move to preparing material, just to avoid the complete, embarrassing silence which could result if the Teams were given the theme of their improvised song on the spot – what mattered most was that it was *funny*, never mind how the laughs were arrived at. Graeme has always admitted, 'If you've got to make up, say, a calypso, it's almost impossible to do that on the spot, and so you spend an hour or so beforehand writing it. If you have to make up a poem as it goes along, that is *just* possible, but you have to sweat!'

Some variety was introduced to the round by expanding the genres to include madrigals and, of course, calypso, which had first popped up in the pilot. The calypso was perhaps the most obvious song style for improvisation, since the days when Lance Percival would strum his guitar before the *TW3* audience, incorporating any of the crowd's suggestions into a tropical topical tune with an apparently lightning wit. This didn't really solve the 'I woke up this morning' conundrum, however, as calypsos were difficult to begin without singing 'I saw (someone or other) the other day . . .' while madrigals (or 'Mad Wriggles', as the round was briefly known) tended to kick off with 'As I stepped out one May morning . . .' It didn't prevent some classics finding their way into the show, such as the Humph Madrigal which featured all the players, and elicited the response from the Chairman: 'You don't seriously expect any marks for that, do you . . . ?'

> *When I went out one evening to a Humphrey Lyttelton gig,*
> *I knew I'd come to the wrong place, for the audience was quite big.*
> *So I went round to the Gents next door, downcast and sad at heart,*
> *And there stood Humph with his horn in his hand . . .*
> *Saying 'Thank God, now we can start.'*

There was also the Mary Whitehouse Calypso from Tim and Willie that allowed them to have a pop at public enemy number one:

> *I saw Mary Whitehouse the other day,*
> *She appeared to be in the family way,*
> *How she got like that cannot be repeated,*
> *But it must have been the result of an (expletive deleted).*

Tim's struggle against the horn-rimmed president of the National Viewers' and Listeners' Association while in *The Goodies* is well documented, while Willie actually composed an entire book, The *Filth Amendment*, in answer to her busybody movement. Published in 1981, this slim volume, subtitled 'Rushton Against Sextremes', contained not only dozens of Willie's masterly cartoons depicting all sorts of historical sexual depravity, but a superb, intelligent and incredibly funny rebuttal of everything that Mrs Whitehouse stood for. He proves quite logically and intelligently that the censors are foolishly fighting a losing battle – not because 'the dangers of sex' are spreading in society, but because humans have been so massively obsessed with rumpy-pumpy since the Dawn of Man that it's not a new danger – in fact, he reasoned, it's positively boring.

The single most groanworthy round, however, was the 'Ad-lib Poem' – if the Teams had written these in advance, then their palpable agony and dithering and moaning every time the game was played was the stamp of incredible acting skills. For years, Humph would toss out a first line guaranteed to put the first poet in an impossibly filthy position, such as 'My lady fair revealed to me a lovely pair of pistols . . .' and then, without fail, would happily tune out for the proceeding five minutes as Barry, Graeme, Tim and Willie desperately floundered through a world of metre, scansion and rhyme. Once or twice Humph would sound his hooter or ring his bell and the improviser would be gratefully relieved of the burden of composition. Whether this challenge resulted in any verse worthy of inclusion in the canon of English literature is open to debate:

> *My love, she is a handsome lass, and Herbert is her name.*
> *She's not a lot to look at, but you must admit she's game.*
> *She lives in Billericay, where she makes apple pies . . .*
> *There's not a lot of truth in this, in fact it's a pack of lies.*
> *I'd rather tell you summat else, summat else I'll tell,*
> *About this witch that lived in't woods, and used to cast a spell.*
> *It was a spell that did involve frogs, newts and taddlypools,*
> *You've probably heard tell of her, her name is Scaddlypools . . .*

. . . but the consensus is likely to be 'Not really, no'. The pleasure of the round, for both Humph and the Audience, was in watching the Teams squirm and stumble as they versified – perhaps affecting a Pam Ayres voice for inspiration, or a northern burr for a 'Lion and Albert'-style Marriott Edgar approach. There was even one round entirely devoted to that renowned Scottish poet William McGonagall, whose epic messes were perhaps the Teams' greatest inspiration, when it came to quality of rhyming and scansion. Players took eager pleasure in setting the next poet up with the most impossible lines (while risking the threat of completing the painful rhymes themselves if Humph chose not to intervene on time), and bellowing 'Scansion!' or 'Metre, Tim, metre!' if the current odesmith was in trouble. Tim often tried to play his joker to excuse himself from 'Ad-lib Poem', and admits today 'I can still hear myself squeaking in agony when the rhyme and metre, never mind the jokes, wouldn't come. It certainly wasn't the money that made us return; maybe we thought if we didn't return then someone like Rolf Harris might slip into our chairs.'

Swanee, How I Love You!

Thankfully, musical rounds didn't always depend on improvising lyrics – the Teams have always had the opportunity to show off their instrumental talents

as well. Quite early on, attempts were made to find a round which would set
the Teams the task of playing a song with no need for any musical skills at
all, imaginatively entitled 'Playing Tunes on Instruments They Can't Play'.
Ear-splitting early attempts included Bill Oddie scraping away at a violin, but
it was decided that there was a limit as to what a Radio 4 audience were
willing to put up with. The instrument accompanying Bill, however, showed
more promise. The swanee whistle is a friend to all frustrated musicians,
offering musical noises for those with the ability to blow and move their hand
up and down a bit. The origins of the piston-based instrument are unsure,
but the basic concept seems to be African, stretching back at least to the
eighteenth century, when they were used as bird-callers for hunting. They
first began to take off musically in the 1920s, when none other than Humphrey
Lyttelton's idol, Louis Armstrong, sometimes briefly switched over to swanee
flute from trumpet when playing with his band, the Hot 5. Despite this, to
British ears the swanee whistle will always be evocative of the dialogue from
Oliver Postgate and Peter Firmin's children's classic, *The Clangers*.

With the violin ditched, the next attempt to use the swanee whistle in
the game involved having the Teams try to play a song blindfold, passing the
instrument between each other when directed. This only lasted for a couple
of rounds, partly due to the players' disgust at the amount of spit it required
them to share – and also because Willie actually broke their only whistle
during the first attempt. It wasn't until the dawn of the nineties that the
perfect accompanying instrument would be found for the swanee whistle within
the world of *Clue* – the kazoo being the one universally recognisable musical
instrument which required even less talent to play. Another 'instrument' of
African origin, dating back centuries, the kazoo requires that the instrument-
alist merely grunts into the mouthpiece for the jolliest of rasping tones to
blare out. Only the most musically challenged Jeremy Hardy could fail to play
it – if you can hum, you can play the kazoo. Technically, this makes the
instrument a mirliton, or membranophone. In practice, it often makes it a
public nuisance.

Nevertheless, 'Swanee Kazoo' was finally launched, the hugely popular game
which 'combines the heady rasp of the kazoo with the ethereal ululation of
the swanee whistle, instruments both originating in the Deep South of America,
where they were much favoured on Mississippi steamboats such as the *Robert
E. Lee* and the *Ulysses S. Grant*, before arriving in this *Rubbish E. Game*'. It's
astonishing how the mix of musical raspberries and what sounds like a highly
confused Clanger can be so laugh-out-loud funny time and again, without a
single word being spoken. It's perhaps the purest form of musical comedy –
and, only very occasionally, it can achieve some level of musical accom-
plishment, with Barry & Graeme's tender reworking of 'Chanson d'Amour' a

definite highlight. Graeme says, 'I was looking for a musical round using instruments that were easy to get a sound out of, but difficult to play beautifully. The kazoo always sounds daft, and the swanee whistle is almost impossible to play a recognisable tune on. They are very distinctive too, so on radio you can easily tell them apart. The voices of Barry and Willie were very suited to the kazoo, so Tim and I ended up on the swanees.' Humph may have claimed that the combination of swanee and kazoo 'went together like a horse and marriage', but his lifelong obsession with every kind of musical instrument means that he knew they were onto a winner – and, after all, Humph's very first band of any kind was a swanee whistle and kazoo band arranged by an undermaster called Charlie Sheepshanks at Sunningdale Preparatory School in the 1930s. Listening to the Teams whistling and raspberrying away must have felt like old times.

The real height of musical discord, on the other hand, came with a now abandoned game which allowed Colin his chance to get his own back on everybody. 'The Bad-Tempered Klavier' simply challenged the Teams to see how far they could get through a song when accompanied by a musician who is tone-deaf and incompetent – 'in other words, Colin Sell'. The vindictive pianist had a ball thumping away mercilessly at the keyboard, changing key at random and mixing in any piece of musical sadism he could to put the singers off, and make the worst noise imaginable. It may come as a shock to regular listeners to learn that this round delivered undoubtedly the absolute eardrum-splitting nadir of *Clue* music way back in the pre-Jeremy Hardy days of 1989, when Stephen Fry and Graeme Garden were charged with the task of keeping up with Colin's bad-tempered performance of 'The Lambeth Walk', from *Me and My Gal*. Even though Fry's writing of the book for that musical made his fortune, the combination of his sadly diabolic trilling with Colin's catastrophic skipping between gentle tea-dance notes and Russian experimental chord-hammerings created a nightmarish din which couldn't ever be replicated, and the round was retired soon after. 'I miss some of the musical rounds we used to do,' admits Colin, '"Bad-Tempered Klavier", for instance, always went well – but I think Jon's feeling is that the show needs anchorpoints, and whenever "One Song to the Tune of Another" or "Swanee Kazoo" are announced they are invariably greeted by roars of approval from the Audience, as if greeting an old friend. So I don't argue.'

The choice of songs featuring in *Clue* over its four decades has also obviously helped define the show, with many old-time tunes cropping up again and again – 'The Laughing Policeman', 'My Old Man's a Dustman', *Goodies* favourites 'Anything You Can Do' and 'Land of Hope and Glory', 'I've Got a Lovely Bunch of Coconuts', 'Mairzy Doats and Dozy Doats', 'I'm a Blue Toothbrush, You're a Pink Toothbrush', 'Gilly Gilly Ossenfeffer Katzenellen

Bogen by the Sea', and ancient numbers stretching right back to the *ISIRTA* songbook, such as the 'soupy, sentimental' Victorian hit 'Come into the Garden, Maud':

> *Come into the garden, Maud,*
> *For the black bat, night, has flown,*
> *Come into the garden, Maud,*
> *I am here at the gate alone;*
> *And the woodbine spices are wafted abroad,*
> *And the musk of the rose is blown.*

The ominous lyricism of Tennyson's poem lends itself perfectly to 'One Song to the Tune of Another', preferably when twinned with unsuitable tunes such as 'Chitty Chitty Bang Bang' or 'The Teddy Bears' Picnic', but as a lyric that has featured in *I'm Sorry* since the early sixties, any reference to it is always worth making. Graeme says, 'We wanted to use songs that most people would know, whatever their age, and the old Music Hall-type songs you would still hear on the radio. People would be aware of the standards, but not everybody would know the lyrics to the latest chart sounds.'

But if we're talking about real Radio Prune throwbacks, the ultimate example is the game 'Censored Songs', which took Bill's original Dirty Songbook idea and ran with it, and it still occasionally surfaces to this day, four decades after Oddie realised that the idea had legs, and 'could work for anything'. Perhaps that may be overstating the game's scope somewhat, but the Colin-backed live renditions, complete with on-the-spot expurgation from the Teams, has made it impossible to hear some songs ever again without thinking the most filthy of thoughts. *Clue* has recycled some of them from the original *ISIRTA* outings, notably Tom Jones and Rolf Harris medleys, but over the years many different tunes have been given the 'nudge, nudge' treatment, with even apparently innocent children's songs such as 'Puff the Magic Dragon' and 'Rudolph the Red-Nosed Reindeer' being revealed to be positively disgusting, if you use your imagination.

The Meme Team

It's probably been noted that this history of *I'm Sorry I Haven't a Clue* is already swinging wildly around in time, from the seventies to the nineties, and back again. This is because, with the full line-up finally established by the mid-seventies, there's such a strong continuity throughout the twenty-two years the Team was together that any random episode can crop up on BBC Radio 7 and it would be very difficult to estimate the year of its original broadcast. Topical references can occasionally give the game away, but like some form of Radio 4 Antidote to Panel Games version of P. G. Wodehouse's infamous typewriter (or if you must, Trigger's broom in *Only Fools and Horses*), *I'm Sorry I Haven't a Clue* has changed only imperceptibly, bit by bit, until, over the years, the show has taken on at least three distinct forms. And it's this incarnation, the endless battle between Tim & Willie and Barry & Graeme, invigilated by Humphrey Lyttelton, with Colin Sell on the piano, which will always be the classic formula.

With the soundscape of the show so key, it must have been clear to Graeme and Simon Brett that Willie's voice was definitely the missing piece of the puzzle that made up the winning formula. Fittingly for a show like *Clue* (there is no show like *Clue*), this is probably best illustrated by listening to the Teams' laughs, each of which is greatly distinctive. Oddly for a man of his stature, Willie's laugh was a high and fluting guffaw, rather like a countess who has just won a game of croquet. Graeme's throaty chuckle was a far rarer sound, but clearly distinguishable from Tim's hiccuping (and often insistent) giggle, and had added value due to Graeme's usual composure. Barry Cryer, of course, has often been described as having the best laugh in the business, with a Sid Jamesesque bray that could be seen as the ultimate confirmation of a joke's funniness – just as the gagsmith Cryer's cry of 'That's it!' in approval of an untoppable gag, was always the last word. Humph recalled, 'On my travels around the country wearing my musician's hat ... Perhaps the commonest question is "Does Barry enjoy the show as much as he sounds?" I can't answer that, since it's my job as Chairman to see that everyone enjoys it as little as possible. But, short of a seizure, I can think of no other explanation for that laugh. "Cluck" is the word that springs to mind, but it's quite inadequate. Hen-like, yes, but a hen that has had a brief, injudicious but fertile liaison with an ostrich and is now paying the excruciating price.'

The biggest giggler of them all, though, was Humph himself. Well, certainly in terms of uncontrollability, once a gag had started him sniggering. 'When you hear him giggling,' says Tim, 'that's when you know the real Humph.'

The balance of the Teams was also evidence of a perfect blend – although it has to be said that if the show really had contained an element of competitiveness, it would have been an incredibly unfair game. On our right, Graeme – the man who actually created the game, and Barry – the King of the Punchline, both raring to go and often spoiling for a fight. On Humph's right, the other two – Willie ready to get back to the pub from the start of the second round, and poor old Tim, the Audience's pet since the *ISIRTA* days, trying to play his joker and wring every drop of sympathy out of the Chairman. When it comes to killer instinct, the latter Team was buggered, but luckily Tim and Willie always just about had the edge when it came to lovability.

At no stage could the *Clue* team know how long the show would continue to be a part of the Radio 4 schedules, but with the years stretching out before them, there was plenty of time to establish running gags that would run further than any other quip or joke has ever travelled, fermenting series by series. 'Although at first it wasn't as popular as it became later,' says Graeme, 'we kind of knew we were doing something different and unique, and it was quite exciting – like bungee jumping for radio.'

When the line-up was established of course, they were all spring chickens, or at least *summer* chickens. Colin may have been the baby, but Tim and Graeme were only just hitting their mid-thirties, Barry had just hit forty and Willie had a couple of years to go to reach that milestone, and the joint schoolboy caperings of this rabble were kept in check by the old man, Humphrey, who joined up at fifty and had reached the positively geriatric age of fifty-three by the time the team was complete. With the powers that be at the BBC so notoriously difficult to please, the odds of such a shambolic piece of radio entertainment surviving the scheduler's whims for too long was unlikely, so until the game was up, Graeme decided, they may as well carry on regardless and have some fun.

And yet the show continued – they were getting away with it, year on year, and it was like *the BBC hadn't noticed!* In fact, the show had caught on well enough that a specially compiled book of highlights was published in 1980, by Robson Books.

As Graeme Garden once said in a round of 'Complete Quotes', 'Some men have only one book in them. Others . . . don't indulge in that practice.' Each member of the *Clue* team has a respectable roster of books to their name – Humph published his first autobiography, *I Play As I Please*, when he was only thirty-three, and followed it up with several more publications over the years, notably his music books, including the *Best of Jazz* series. Graeme's first novel, the spy-thriller spoof *The Seventh Man* (detailing the bland adventures of an insufferably boring paper-clip pusher from MI5 who gets slightly embroiled in the Philby/Burgess/Maclean defection) was published in 1981, with a tie-in to his historical TV series, *A Sense of the Past*, and a treasury of medical humour, *The Best Medicine*, following a couple of years later. *The Skylighters*, a children's book, was published by Methuen in 1988, and the year before saw the release of *Graeme Garden's Compendium of Very Silly Games*:

Why do people play games? Games have been played throughout recorded history – certainly throughout the recorded history of games. And all authorities on the subject are agreed on at least one point: that games have been played almost exclusively by players. There are games of every shape and length, games for fun, games for profit, stimulating games, tedious games, games of excess, games of moderation, outdoor games, indoor games, Buddhist games, dangerous games, vegetarian games, games of literacy, games of chance, games of stealth – in a word, all sorts of games.

This slim volume then offers a whole cavalcade of inane ways of wasting time and disturbing children, such as the fascinating sounding 'Grandmother's Hat' – a game for seven to 136 players: 'Grandmother is sent out of the room. The players then select one person to be the "Grandmother's hat". The selected player then stands on a chair behind the door and, when Grandmother is called to reenter, jumps on her head and perches there. All the other players shout "Oh! Look at Grandmother's hat!" and make suitable comments . . . (If no Grandmother is available, any elderly and frail person will do.)'

Goodies books aside, Tim's publishing history is briefer, with two volumes on sport, *Tim Brooke Taylor's Golf Bag* and *Cricket Box*, and *Rule Britannia*, a humorous look at Englishness that played on Tim's patriotic *Goodies* persona. Its subjects include the history of etiquette, Empire, and so on – with one handy extract being relevant here, where Tim quotes an old tome on the subject of a gentleman's conversation, which should 'avoid tedious narratives, eschew quotations from foreign languages, and avoid pedantry generally. Punning is a low and offensive habit; and when jokes are made, others should be left to laugh at them', which Tim admits 'sounds like good advice for a newcomer to a radio panel game'.

Willie, on the other hand, was by far the most fecund author of the bunch, and of course a prolific cartoonist. Beginning his career with *William Rushton's Dirty Book* in 1964, he followed this up with many *Private Eye* books and other satirical works like *The Filth Amendment* and its EU-examining stablemate, *The Reluctant Euro*. A few years after Graeme's novel, Willie also had a poke at the spy thriller, in the very silly *Spy Thatcher* and there were, in addition, many typically daft and facetious books on sports from his beloved cricket to pig-sticking, a book on gardening, and armfuls of children's books like *The Incredible Cottage* and *Humphrey: The Nine Lives of the Number Ten Cat*. Then there was his sort of magnum opus, *Superpig*, the bizarrely practical guidebook for the modern bachelor which was basically his answer to Shirley Conran's *Superwoman*. It boasted such headings as 'What to Do With a Sudden Chicken' and 'Jazzing Up Your Jaded Underwear', and a true world-beater of an introductory paragraph, which it would have been wonderful to steal for this book:

I would simply say that this book in no way intends to be complete. You can look up 'Grouse – How To Kick To Death in Bedroom Slippers' in the index and find not a mention. On the other hand look up

'Grouse – How to Cook in the Accepted Manner' and you won't find a word about that either. At the same time if you *have* savaged one of these poor beasts and are eager to get your teeth around it, you can always buy a cheap paperback on 'How To Cook Grouse'.

And then there was this neat little early *Clue* book, filled with 'Unexpurgated highlights', with memorable poems, jokes and silliness from the first eight years of the show, adorned with visions of the gang at the height of their hairiness, hanging about Mornington Crescent station. The contents of the book, despite being festooned with brilliant original cartoons from Humph, Willie and Graeme, didn't quite transfer the fun of the shows to print success-fully, being mainly straight transcripts of random rounds – as the suitably curmudgeonly introductory 'Disclaimer' disclaims, 'When the idea of doing a book first came up it was felt that there might be some problems in presenting a set of games which had been largely suitable for radio. But these fears proved unjustified when the book turned out to be as scrappy and unintelligible as everyone hoped.' Nevertheless, today it's a definite collector's item.

The book had been pieced together with the aid of newbie producer Geoffrey Perkins, who took over the job from Simon Brett in the summer of 1978. The Oxford graduate was seen as a wireless whizz-kid at the time, and only a couple of years after joining BBC Radio he was hard at work on *The Hitchhiker's Guide to the Galaxy*. Perhaps taking his turn at producing this silly game for middle-aged men was to be a comparable holiday from arranging the sound of a billion singing androids or the audio fallout from an inter-galactic space war. 'It was one of those shows that I'd been a huge fan of, and the notion that two years later you were going to be producing it was extra-ordinary to me, so that was a huge treat, really,' he admitted. Just like Brett before him, Perkins was expected to hit the ground running: 'I pretty much went in cold. I can't even remember having a proper handover, but I knew the programme very well, and so there were a whole load of games that I knew I wanted to go with, and then I also decided, in that naive way, being rather young, "Let's try a lot of completely new games and see how they go", as well.'

The Game's Afoot
One particular wish of Perkins' was to encourage the number of utterly point-less rounds – the moments of pure facetious whimsy that would wind up the listeners at home, leaving them wondering what they were missing by not being able to see the Teams at work. There was 'Murder in the Dark', in which Colin played sinister music as all the lights were dimmed, and a scream rang out. It turned out just to be Humph reacting to Colin's playing, but

Willie was still left wondering, 'I know this is only radio, but should Tim be bleeding?' Then there was the Yard of Ale competition, which Willie won without any trouble at all (whereas Tim sipped his throughout the evening), plenty of rounds of 'Hide-and-Seek' (one in which the whole Audience had to hide, but they were quickly located), and then there was the 'Bang Bang Relay'. This required the Teams to blow up a paper bag, run around their partner, and then burst it, before the other did the same. Tim lost this game, but claimed he was handicapped, having further to run than Barry or Graeme.

There was also the long-forgotten round 'Wobbling Bunnies'. The whole panel was geed up to take part in this intriguing-sounding parlour game, but week on week Humph ran out of time, the game was postponed, and the Audience and listeners were left disappointed. They were as eager as the listener at home to know, what did 'Wobbling Bunnies' constitute? Were real bunnies involved? How would points be scored? By the very last episode of 1981, at last Humph managed to find time to include the infamous round, and put everyone out of their misery, with a show of expert play which saw Tim lose by falling over after only twenty-one seconds. Of course, amid all the giggling and activity, the listener at home was left none the wiser as to what 'Wobbling Bunnies' actually *was*, but all these years later, none other than Graeme Garden can reveal that the game itself was 'an awesome challenge'. So there you are.

Perhaps the reason 'Wobbling Bunnies' was so quickly forgotten was that Geoffrey Perkins' time as *Clue* producer introduced a far more memorable round. The one conviction Perkins arrived on the show with was 'I decided I wanted to play a complete non-game. I talked to the rest of the cast, and the notion was just that you pretended that it was real, and had lots of rules, but it didn't . . . I think probably that was one element that I did bring in a bit, which was that there were quite a lot of things that you simply couldn't do on radio. And therefore it seemed a very good reason to do it, on that show. They relied entirely on lying, really.' Having one single regular round which basically acted as the whole *I'm Sorry I Haven't a Clue* concept in microcosm (meaningless and silly, but presented entirely as a deadly serious challenge) was a very strong idea, and it just so happened that the Teams had precisely the right format in mind already.

From day one, much of *Clue* had its roots in the pub. It was first discussed in a pub, many of its rounds were dreamt up within dashing distance of a bar, and often in these early days it paid to be drunk while listening. Before and afterwards the crew would always congregate in the Sherlock Holmes or the Captain's Cabin to run through games and jokes – and yes, although Humph would joke about the Teams coming 'through snow, rain and the pub to get here' within the show, they often really would be tough to shift out of the snug and onto the stage. Tim would be the first to begin to worry about getting in front of the microphone in time and in good shape, and was usually the main ally of any anxious young producer when it came to calling time and getting down to work. In addition, both Barry and even Doctor Graeme were heavy smokers back in those days, although Graeme gave up in the late eighties (and then again in the early 2000s). Humph refused to fraternise with them when they lit up, and got into the habit of waving from a safe distance before shows rather than joining the Teams, to preserve his all-important lung capacity – as well as getting his own smoke-free dressing room. Right up until the nineties, the Teams could even smoke onstage, and the sound of ashtrays and lighters occasionally permeate the early shows as Barry and Graeme puffed their way through the games.

Back in the days before 24-hour-smoke-free boozing, when licensing laws still strictly prohibited hostelries serving alcohol in the afternoons and closing time was punctual and usually incontestable, Barry, Willie and co. knew all the watering holes in the capital where one could get a skinful out of hours. One such handy bolt-hole was Gerry's Drinking Club, in Soho, where they repaired one evening. Without meaning to suggest that unduly Herculean amounts of alcohol had been consumed by everyone on this occasion, it's hard to say exactly who was there that night. However, Tim is a likely candidate, maybe with Barry but definitely John Junkin, an ITV producer called Pat Johns, and Tim also nominates Bunny May and David Clime as part of the party. There was definitely one unnamed 'joiner' as well – somebody who had tagged along with the drinking party uninvited, and was by all reports causing a certain amount of neck pain.

Perhaps the journey to Gerry's on the London Underground, staring up at Harry Beck's iconic tube map on the way to Soho Square (and all those silly names, rich with innuendo – Shepherd's Bush, Cockfosters, Turnham Green, Wapping and of course Finsbury Park, which those of an anagrammatic bent will know better as Crappy Rubsniff), had initially inspired whoever it was to start playing the game, but it seemed an ideal way to shake off the joiner. While the unwelcome guest went to the Gents someone (Willie Rushton claimed it was John Junkin) decided to start playing a game, and egged on the others to jump in on the act in all seriousness. It didn't really matter what they said to play their 'move', as long as it sounded convincing.

This kind of made-up, deliberately confusing game was also a Garden/Oddie speciality, with a scene in the 1982 *Goodies* episode 'Holidays' centring on Tim and Graeme deliberately bamboozling Bill with a highly complicated card game called 'Spat':

INT.   *HOLIDAY COTTAGE. NIGHT.*

GG: ... Tell you what, let's play Spat!

TBT: Spat!

BO: Ohh! Spat! Oh why didn't you say? Spat eh, we're gonna play Spat ... What the hell's Spat?

TBT: Graeme knows, don't you?

GG: Certainly ...
           Tim deals one card each.

GG: Right, I start. Eight of hearts.

TBT: Queen of diamonds.

BO: Two of clubs.

GG/TBT: RATBAG! (*Bill jumps.*)

TBT: Oh I'm sorry, we should have explained. Two of clubs, you shout 'Ratbag' to win.

GG: Right? Got the idea?

TBT: Two of clubs, 'Ratbag' to win.
           Graeme deals one card to Tim, Bill then himself.

GG: Right, off you go.

TBT: Jack of hearts.

BO: Six of spades.

GG: Two of clubs.

BO: RATBAG!
           Graeme and Tim throw cups of tea in Bill's face.

GG/TBT: SHUT YER FACE!
           Bill, looking resentful and wary, begins to deal.

BO: Two. (*Then deals to himself.*) Three!
           Graeme and Tim slap Bill's head repeatedly.

GG/TBT: Spat spat spat spat spat spat spat!

BO: Oi!

TBT: Dealer in Prig invokes Spat!

BO: But I've got an ace!
           Graeme and Tim both intake breath, pull revolvers out of their pockets and point them at Bill.

GG/TBT: Ooooh Grand Spat!
           Bill covers his face with his arms and backs away.

BO: No no no, get off! This is a rotten game this is!

TBT: It's a great game, stop spoiling our fun!

All this naturally drives Bill up the wall, but a few years earlier at Gerry's Drinking Club the plan had worked for real, as the hapless toilet-goer returned to the gathering, and found them all embarking on some bizarre test of mental agility, like spoken chess, with each participant clearly playing a move, strategically trying to reach some unknown goal. According to legend, the interloper then tried to join in, but his every attempt to make a move was mercilessly mocked and logically damned by the others – was he an amateur? Didn't he know the rules? Had he never even heard of the game they were playing? Whatever it was . . .

The feeling of power that comes from making up the rules of a game as you go along was obviously an effective one, so when Barry, Willie, Tim and Graeme got to chat with their new young producer and heard his call for a new confusing non-game that they could play every week, they remembered that recent evening at Gerry's with John Junkin, and began to play that game for him. Geoffrey agreed that it seemed exactly the kind of pointlessly complicated apparently real trivial pursuit that he wanted to fit into the show.

In the end, however, they all ditched the 'non-game' idea entirely as far too cliquey and obtuse, and decided instead to revive that most well loved and ancient of intellectual pastimes, Mornington Crescent.

11

Mornington Crescent on the Diagonal

Even the most gormless of students of the game of Mornington Crescent will be aware that its true origins are lost in the fog of time. The earliest signs of the game taking its hold on civilisation can be gleaned from Roman mosaics from the second century, which depict a very basic layout of the game then known as 'Maledonium Lunatus' – a stunning archaeological find which was excavated by Professor Barry Cunliffe in the last century. After the exit of the legions, the game was then reintroduced to Britain by Brother Chalfont, a sixth-century monk who first spread the Received Rules among the Britons. His work would have been forgotten were it not for Chalfont's champion, the sixteenth-century bishop Hugh Latimer. In the interim the game had been referenced in the Bayeux Tapestry and *The Canterbury Tales* and played a large part in the cataloguing of place names in the Domesday Book, but with the rules finally laid down by Henry VIII's Act of Six Articles, Tudor Court Rules became sacrosanct in British law, and Latimer was burned at the stake for popularising Chalfont's doctrine.

Nearly one hundred years later the game reached new heights of popularity and clarity thanks to the publication of the very first *Old Twonk's Mornington Crescent Almanac* by Tobias Twonk in 1621. It was this annual guidebook, still in good health today, that first enraptured the young Lord Knaresborough, Hugh de Montague Smythe-d'Arrison-Smythe, whose flair and skill on the amateur Mornington Crescent circuit in Regency England made him a true icon of the game. His introduction of the rule of Nidd formed the basis of the most popular variation on the game, Knaresborough's Rules. In turn, it's universally undisputed that Knaresborough was the hero of Hugo Granville Korpoise Smith, the 87th Marquess of Turberry, who at last defined the Original Modern Rules of the game in 1863. It is the game as played by Turberry Rules that everybody is familiar with today, and they form the basis of that indispensable work on the game, *Mornington Crescent: Rules and Origins*, the magnum opus of author and noted Mornington Crescent academic N. F. Stovold.

The tricky subject of the derivation of the name 'Mornington Crescent' has been the cause of centuries of violent debate, but clearly all of the current theories are nonsense. However, as the name in some form has existed since Norman times, it's clear that it was the merest coincidence that in the 1820s Wellington's brother, the Earl of Mornington, was honoured with a crescent-shaped street erected in his name, on a greenfield site to the north of London, in Camden Town. On 22 June 1907, a London Underground station was opened nearby which took the same name, and thus players of Mornington Crescent have ever since naturally linked the game to the station itself. Even the *Clue* team agree that the true home of the game is that unprepossessing tube station in an obscure corner of Camden.

Despite the centuries of popularity among both the cognoscenti and the hoi polloi that Mornington Crescent has enjoyed, it is true that when Geoffrey Perkins first included a round in *I'm Sorry I Haven't a Clue* in the late seventies, the game had become so sidelined in the public consciousness that the more ignorant listeners could conceivably have been all but unaware of Mornington Crescent's history at the time. Matches were still regularly covered by the BBC Sports Department of course, but both the professional and amateur leagues had become elitist, and almost wilfully obscure (no surprise for a tradition that has in the past been connected with the Knights Templar). Unbeknown to Perkins and the Teams, they were about to do the game a greater service than even Lord Knaresborough himself, popularising the peerless pastime more successfully than anyone else in history.

When the pilot round was first played, Perkins had to admit that he wasn't sure if even the Chairman himself was au fait with the game's rules, and made special efforts to drill Humph in what was expected of him, as the adjudicator. 'I'd been trying to meet up and have a talk with Humphrey about how we were going to do this, and we kept having these lunch meetings which kept being rearranged, and then eventually the plan was that he was going to turn up an hour and a half before the show and we'd go and do stuff. But he actually turned up about quarter of an hour before the show, and I remember coming down the stairs with him, into the studio, trying just to explain this game, and the rules and so on, and nothing seemed to be going in. And I thought, "Oh my God, he's gaga!" This was back in 1978! And of course he was anything but, it was just his manner.'

Little did Perkins know that Humph was to all intents and purposes a Mornington Crescent grand master. Indeed, in 1951 the young jazz star took the crown of World Amateur Champion, beating the reigning champion Heinz Kipf in the final in Helsinki. A rare pre-match interview with Richard Dimbleby survives, with one fascinating detail worth repeating:

RD: It was rather touching to see this year's championships opened by a child – six-year-old Timothy Brooke-Taylor of Buxton. Viewers will have seen you exchanging words with him at the end of the ceremony. Can you remember what you said to him that should have reduced him to tears in that way?

HL: I told Timothy I saw a great future for him playing the game for 28 years or more on a light-hearted BBC wireless programme. It's a pity the boy didn't get the joke, but then I don't suppose jokes will be his thing either.

Young Humph went on to denounce the role of adjudicating Chairman in Mornington Crescent as a miserable fate: 'Frankly, it doesn't appeal to me – it's a thankless task open only to over-the-hill, talentless, egotistical failures who gain nothing but abuse from both players and the audience alike. Goodness, I'd almost be better off taking up the trumpet.' But sadly, with the ailing super-sport introduced to the world of *Clue*, Humph was stymied. Despite being recognised as perhaps the finest player of modern times, he was prevented from ever taking part in another official championship, due to his new status as Chairman, and was doomed to spend decades invigilating bouts between groups of relative amateurs, playing what he described with venom as 'frivolous' Mornington Crescent. He admitted to taking the game seriously: 'People always come up to me when I'm signing CDs or whatever and will say: "What are the rules of Mornington Crescent?" I say: "You're talking about a game that is on the level of chess, bridge, mah-jong. You wouldn't ask me to explain the rules of bridge while I was doing something else, so why Mornington Crescent?"'

However, when the game debuted, Humph was unaware of how its popularity would affect his career.

HL: ... We go on to the next game, which is an old favourite, and I know a lot of you like to join in with this one at home, Mornington Crescent. No special rules come in to play in this particular round, so we'll start now with you, Tim Brooke-Taylor.

TBT: Mm. Er, Neasden High Street.

BC: ... Goodge Street.

WR: Ah ... Cromwell Road.

GG: Oh! (*Hits table*.) Dollis Hill.

BC: Good lad.

TBT: ... The Strand.

BC: Mornington Crescent!

HL: Yes!

GG: *Yes!*

WR: Swine!

TBT: Actually, is that right, because –

BC: Yes.

HL: Yes, Barry definitely wins that game … (*Audience reluctantly applaud.*)

GG: Yes, *come on!* Well deserved.

HL: The Audience recognising brilliant play when they see it …

That very first round, played in the summer of 1978, received a minimal Audience response, but by the end of the series, just the announcement of another Mornington Crescent contest would be greeted by roars of approval. The game's rehabilitation was under way.

Not that this was down to the prowess of the players, if the truth be told. They were but amateurs at this stage, and it would take thirty years for them to become truly world class at the game, though Barry modestly admits today, 'I'm on a par. We're all experienced players, I wouldn't put myself above or below any of the others, we're all tuned in.' Graeme has always seemed to be perhaps the most confident of the *Clue* stalwarts in the Mornington Crescent arena. Just as championship chess (another popular game) relies as much on psychological warfare as the ability to strategically move chesspieces, Mornington Crescent is a battle of minds, and endless swotting up on the rules and natural strategic flair can mean nothing if your move isn't made with supreme confidence. Graeme, the Quiet Man, is rarely heard to challenge an adjudication or fret about a move, he simply states his intentions and leans back with a grin. On the other hand, he hardly ever wins. Willie was equally ballsy and, as ever, nonchalant, as a player – and enjoyed far more success. Barry Cryer is the John McEnroe of *Clue*, sniping at Humph's judgement if it holds him in Nidd or sets him up for a parallel trumping. His main contender in these Mornington Crescent fights has always been, of course, Tim. Poor Tim's dithering, pedantic and confused approach to every stage of the game often caused even his partner Willie to pluck his beard with exasperation and disdain and damn his luck at being saddled with such a partner. And yet, the scoreboard proves, Tim's cautious exactitude and regular crawling to the Chairman have seen him all right over the years, and he remains, in Mornington Crescent terms, one of the highest scoring players in the world.

Humph, the Teams and Geoffrey Perkins were astonished to discover just how badly the fine game's popularity with the British public had deteriorated. Letters started flooding in to Perkins' office like never before in the history of *Clue*, all wanting to know what the hell it was all about, and how one actually plays Mornington Crescent. Perkins tried at first to reply to each one, but ultimately he was forced to write a special announcement for the Radio 4 continuity announcer to read after the show. 'Many listeners have asked for the rules to the popular family game, Mornington Crescent. Well, unfortunately, there are so many variants of the game that it's impossible to go into them in detail. But if you remember that it's basically just the game that we all used to play when we were children, you won't go far wrong.'

'We got quite a lot of letters. Interesting thing about Radio 4, because when I did *Hitchhiker's* there was a point where theoretically the audience figures were like 0.1 or something, but I was getting about twenty-five to thirty letters a day, about the show. And *I'm Sorry I Haven't a Clue* is the same thing really. You get a lot of response.' Perkins recalled that there were often three stages of letter – a first epistle saying 'I'm sorry, I really don't understand this game,' which earned the stock reply; a second letter along the lines of 'When we were children? No, I'm really sorry, I've talked to lots of my friends, nobody remembers it . . .' to which Perkins replied, 'I'm sorry, I can't explain the rules, it would make *War and Peace* look like a footnote,' and pointed them towards Stovold's fine guidebook. But then often a third letter received from the same correspondent would read, 'I must complain because in the episode last broadcast you went transverse using yellow from Bond Street to Old King's Road . . .'

The game is simple – employ strategic moves to get to Mornington Crescent. First one there's the winner. At last, it seemed, the Listening Plenty got it, and rediscovered the pleasures of a game that had dazzled and thrilled their forebears for generations. *I'm Sorry I Haven't a Clue* staged regular listener competitions, with the first prize for the winning move 'Marble Arch' being won by a Marcus Platt of Holloway. Humph beamed, 'He wins an *I'm Sorry I Haven't a Clue* book, if he sends in the price of £1.95, or £2.24 with postage.' Humph also allowed Audience members to dare to come up on stage and play alongside the Teams. By this point the recordings for *Clue* had been shifted to a lunchtime hour, and the schoolboy contingent in the crowds at the Paris Studios was evident in the laughter in every episode, which started to sound like it was sampled from *Crackerjack*. Allegedly half the Audience was made up of school children, and the other half of middle-aged women on their lunchbreak, eating their sandwiches as the Teams worked extra hard for their laughs. One lunchtime a headmaster from a nearby school received an absolutely colossal cheer from his pupils in the Audience, after his dismal performance had lost him his game of Mornington Crescent. An early star of Celebrity Mornington Crescent was Alec Guinness, but he didn't say much.

As *Clue* continued, there were many splendid celebrations of the game that was now back on everybody's lips. A fascinating two-part *Everyman's*

Guide to Mornington Crescent was broadcast over the Christmas period of 1984, introduced by Raymond Baxter. Sadly the second part, which dealt strictly with the rules of the game, has been wiped from the BBC Archives, but the first episode boasted an expansive history of the game's origins, which brought us one of Willie Rushton's finest hours, in a reconstruction of a classic Victorian pop song, *I'm Lord Mornington Crescent*, which in its day resounded throughout Music Halls up and down the country:

> *I'm Lord Mornington Crescent, I'm extremely unpleasant,*
> *I dress up in ladies' attire;*
> *Then leap from the closet with a cry of 'How was it?'*
> *And invariably pee in the fire.*
> *I'm Cres! Cres! In Mummy's own dress,*
> *I walk up Pall Mall night and day,*
> *Almost everyone knows me, as Cynthia or Rosemary,*
> *I'm Lord Mornington Crescent, hooray!*

This classic crowd-pleaser not only popularised the game, but also furthered understanding of transvestisism in those buttoned-up times.

It may come as a shock that, the Teams having done their bit to reinstate the game in popular consciousness, Perkins' final series of *Clue* tried to abandon Mornington Crescent altogether. But by popular demand it simply had to remain a cornerstone of every recording for the show, and Humph and co. realised that now they would be inextricably connected to the cult of Mornington Crescent for evermore. Even when the government temporarily banned the playing of the game (due to legal complications arriving from an American attempt to purchase the tube station itself), the Teams were undaunted, and played by passing pieces of paper around with their moves written on them. The takeover thankfully never happened, but that wasn't the end of troubles for the game – when the Underground station was threatened with closure in the 1990s, the *Clue* stars became figureheads for the campaign to keep it open, and were actually invited to participate in the grand reopening in 1998. Humph proudly boasted, 'Mornington Crescent is a distinguished underground station because it's a listed building and it's also had a ludicrous career. Trains only used to stop on Fridays or something . . . We went down and posed for photographs when it was re-opened after a long period of refurbishment. It was a big thing and we all smiled at the camera and picked up a nice comfortable fee . . . and it was closed within the week. I was told it was because they had installed one of those lifts where you go in one way and come out the opposite way but they hadn't realised that the opposite way went into a solid brick wall.'

The Decade Horribilis

Of course, Mornington Crescent had been an unqualified success, but Perkins had his share of disasters while in the producer's chair as well. 'There were quite a few rounds we tried to play with mixed results. Once we played a round which never went out, which was called "Break a Man's Arm". And it was based on the idea that if you talked to somebody about swans, at some point they would be prone to say "They've got really strong wings, they can break a man's arm with a single blow" – that being the phrase that you then want them to say. But the problem is, in a quiz where actually people like to be funny relatively often, it's a bit tricky. And when we played this round, Barry I think got a bit nervous after about a minute of there not being any laughs in it, and people trying to guess, so he started to just make funny remarks, which were all great . . . Until eventually, everybody just lost sight of what they were doing, the Audience were completely bemused, and this round went on for about twenty minutes! I can remember Tim pleading, "Just please, tell us what you want us to say!" I almost put it out because it was like an utter antidote to a proper comic round. But it was too . : . completely unfunny.'

In a way this aborted round was salvaged eventually with a game called 'Party Bores', in which one team had to have an incredibly interesting occupation or characteristic – such as being one of Michael Palin's film crew, or working for the Mafia – but then had to remain as boring as they possibly could.

GG: Must be a terribly exciting life. Are you on the run the whole time?

WR: If you think it's exciting, to go into work in a suit and a black homburg carrying a little briefcase containing the tools of your trade . . . it's very, very dull.

BC: But death is always around the corner, surely?

WR: Oh, yeah . . .

TBT: Well, yes, you may think so, but you never know, do you?

WR: What's exciting about that? Lying on your back, doing nothing, not even breathing, for eternity.

BC: But the pressure's on you, I mean, to do the job you're supposed to do, which is pretty terrifying.

TBT: That's true if you're selling insurance . . . I'd love to sell insurance, the thrill of meeting people . . . that stay alive.

This game in turn gave birth to 'Good Morning Radio', or, latterly, 'This Morning with Barry & Graeme', in which one Team of presenters had to interview fascinating stars without allowing the level of banality in their show to drop one iota. One golden round of this also clinched regular returning characters for Tim & Willie:

HL: It's time now to find out who'll be taking the couch on BGTV, with your hosts Barry and Graeme.

GG: Good morning! And, well, over the years, on the couch we've had . . . a lot of fun, actually.

BC: And then the guests came in.

GG: Yeah. And this morning we're very privileged to have Her Majesty the Queen and Princess Margaret.

TBT: Good morning!

WR: Morning! And to all my people, good morning!

TBT: And to all my sister's people, morning!

WR: Us are well, thank you.

GG: Ma'ams . . . I'm sorry to interrupt, but before we get to the makeover . . .

BC: Your Majesty, has your facial hair ever caused you embarrassment in public?

WR: I once grew a fourteen-inch beard just for the hell of it . . . it doesn't show on the stamps at all!

So even the biggest disasters in *Clue* can have redeeming qualities. But after four years, three series, numerous specials and a book, Perkins' time on *Clue* was up. It's not that writing and performing in *Radio Active* would have taken up too much of his time, but he recalled that it was just natural for producers to be kept on their toes. 'To be honest I think it was David Hatch having the understandable notion that producers should be moved around between programmes. It was probably a combination of *Hitchhiker's* and *Radio Active* and various other things, and David just saying. "I think you should move on and do something else now." I would quite happily still be doing it now! It was a huge laugh to do.'

In order to keep things fresh Hatch had brought in Paul Mayhew-Archer, a keen young Cambridge graduate fresh from producing *Radio Active*, to take the reins. But the boss was certainly pleased with how Perkins had upped the madness of *Clue* in his time, and was characteristically supportive of him in his Mornington Crescent campaign. 'David Hatch had just taken over as Head of Radio Comedy,' remembered Perkins, 'so I gave him the cut of the first programme – presumably so he could check that I hadn't absolutely wrecked the thing. And he came into my office and said, "Very funny. This round 'Mornington Crescent' . . ." And I said, "Yeeees . . .?" "Well, how many programmes are you going to play it in?" Assuming that he was basically saying "Well, you could get away with this once, but don't do it again", I said, "Well, I don't know, we might play a few more . . ." And he said, "I think you should play it in every single programme."'

Besides his role in *Radio Active* and *KYTV*, Perkins was to repay Hatch's trust in him by helming some of the best TV comedy throughout the eighties and onwards before his tragic and senseless death in 2008, not least *Harry Enfield's Television Programme*, *Spitting Image*, *The Fast Show*, *Father Ted*, *Big Train*, *How Do You Want Me?* and Arthur Mathews' one-series wonder *Hippies* – but if it wasn't for Hatch's policy of rotating protégés, he would never have left *I'm Sorry I Haven't a Clue*. In the period when he was leaving, he believed the players of the game were facing pretty dark times. 'Tim and Graeme and Willie were all in a slightly odd position at the point I was doing the show, in that *The Goodies* was finishing, and they were a bit regarded as the children's version of *Python,* which was very unfair. Willie had just had several television pilots which hadn't happened . . . And *Not the Nine O'Clock News* had just come along, which for them was like a new generation of people suddenly coming through, and I remember Willie being pretty annoyed about the fact that they were doing lots of playing around with film footage, and he'd done a pilot about two years earlier where he'd done a lot of that, and they'd made him cut it all out, and absolutely wouldn't back it, and he was quite cross about that. So they were feeling like a slightly lost comic generation. But still wonderfully funny, in this show.' Barry was also coming close to feeling the chill as a scriptwriter, as a new generation of writer-performers began to make their mark on British comedy, and had no need for a jobbing gagster.

With Tim, Graeme and Bill Oddie all going their separate ways after *The Goodies*' brief stay at LWT, the early eighties really seemed like a watershed for everyone – both Bill and Graeme had divorced from their first wives and remarried, with Graeme symbolically leaving behind his home in Cricklewood for a rural dwelling in Oxfordshire. As for their professional lives, many solo TV projects came and went – Bill entertaining the kids in *Saturday Banana*, Graeme giving his medical background an exercise by presenting *Body Matters*, Tim beginning his career in sitcom and so on, although the trio would regroup on radio to provide the voices for a revival of *Billy Bunter* in the early nineties. But *Clue* remained the one constant, and this fun little side project on radio was beginning to appear a lot more important to their careers. They might have to fight tooth and nail to keep their profiles high on television – even going to the length of appearing in *You Must Be the Husband* – but at least Tim and Graeme still had *Clue* to attend to, several recordings a year, and it was still bloody good fun.

Radio panel games had also moved forward, however. Fresh from reinvigorating *Just a Minute* by perfecting a new style of editing, tightening up shows pause-by-pause rather than just cutting out flabby rounds, John Lloyd, pre-*Not the Nine O'Clock News*, had launched *The News Quiz* in 1977. The first pilot – *Keep Taking the Tabloids* – was not to his taste, he admits, partly because of the presence of *Clue* on Radio 4, undercutting some of the more twee existing shows. 'One of the things that was wrong with the pilot – it had Gyles Brandreth and Nicholas Parsons, and slightly the same old suspects. And you knew that wouldn't have survived, because the whole point of *Clue* is that it's called the Antidote to Panel Games, and it's taking the piss out of tired old shows of that kind. Even then it seemed old-fashioned, that sort of sense of humour, and what I did, I came along and said no, I want it to be sharp and modern and I want people you've never heard of. I think it was the first real radio that Richard Ingrams did. And Clive James, and Alan Coren and Barry Norman, so it was a different kind of generation, much more informed and fresh and kind of edgy.' Lloyd and Perkins also both worked on a radio game show that pre-dated the satirical panel game. In 1976, fresh from *Week Ending* and *The Burkiss Way*, Nigel Rees had the idea to launch a show based on quotations, called *Quote Unquote*. Some say the programme continues through to this day.

Perhaps the increased importance of *Clue* in the wake of the changes in television comedy is what led to Humph and the Teams' demanding of a few improvements throughout the eighties. For a start, whenever a round required a secret answer to be relayed to the listeners, the show had always had its Mystery Voice – an uncredited announcement from some BBC employee, veiled in secrecy. It may interest some to know that one announcer during Perkins' time was a young Moira Stuart, but otherwise, the Mystery Voice itself was to be an enigma always. The one time that Tim plucked up the courage to ask, 'Who is the Mystery Voice, by the way?' Humph shot back, 'That's another round.' Humph also added in a later show, 'He's asked us not to reveal his identity.' '. . . And we respect Lord Lucan's privacy,' agreed Barry. Tim liked to pre-empt the Mystery Voice wherever possible, intoning 'Swedish Gangbang. Swedish Gangbang . . .' before the round had even got under way.

But when it came to letting the studio Audience know the answer to a round in advance, the punters had to make do with a blackboard and chalk, and Humph often got very testy waiting for the poor producer to wipe it clean for the next round. Perkins remembers that the new boy was traditionally expected to put up with a great deal from these old lags when they started their job. 'They must have loved getting new producers coming on the show, because they'd say, "How about the Gardeners' Ball?" And you'd say, "You haven't done that before?" "No." "But I distinctly remember –"

"No, never done that before." So they could recycle everything all over again! They liked that a lot.'

Paul Mayhew-Archer was treated no differently, one of his first jobs being to find a replacement for the old blackboard. He certainly excelled himself, providing the game's first ever computerised scoreboard, an awesome piece of processing power for 1982, which must surely have upped the show's budget by an astronomical amount. By the time the equipment had been upgraded to a laser display board in the nineties, and Humph was able to proudly proclaim 'Your title is now being scrolled in pixellated Technicolor across our newly upgraded touch-sensitive high-resolution, virtual reality-style visual display board', the costs must have been beyond belief for a mere radio panel game, but it was clearly good use of licence payers' money. Garden admits, 'It has its own budget – in fact, it has its own BBC Department devoted to it. We're not the only show that uses it, but we're the only one that mentions it . . .'

Mayhew-Archer did perhaps try to play with the format a little too much for some, however. A decade's 'Late Arrivals' and society balls had, in his opinion, put the bottom of the barrel within scraping distance, and for his second season he tried to consign the tradition of ending with the blaring announcements to the dustbin. In its place, he suggested an almost identical roster of punning names on a theme that Humph could take at random from the Yellow Pages, and the Teams would make up suitable names for that section's adverts. Willie could be heard harrumphing a little, Tim completely misconstrued the nature of the new round on air, Humph clearly wasn't interested enough to enforce the producer's designs, and the round quickly melted back into the old *ISIRTA*-inspired rave-up ending. Some traditions are very hard to lay to rest.

Samantha
Born: Twentieth century
Of course a lady is entitled to her secrets, and the fact that Samantha's orphanage burned down shortly after she did her GCSEs means that much documentation of her early life is non-existent anyway. Beset by paparazzi as she unrelentingly is, Samantha has even jealously guarded her original surname, having legally changed her name at sixteen to merely 'Samantha', in the mould of Cher, or Swampy. We do know that Samantha has devoted herself to glamour since she was a teenager, but – as well as her arduous work on *Clue*, almost charitable work from Samantha's point of view – she also has a wide range of hobbies, including bee keeping, French polishing, IT, opera tuition, gourmet cookery, riding, fishing and, of course, caring for the elderly. She lives in London, with Sven, and nobody asks any questions.

Bring on the Girl

Scoring was very much high on Paul Mayhew-Archer's agenda throughout the eighties. Humph had long complained of the arduous task of keeping score on *I'm Sorry I Haven't a Clue* – even if he never actually gave any scores out, it was obviously felt that they should be *kept*. He also recalled, 'I said: well, this is an opportunity to satirise and pour scorn on the Chairman/scorer relationship. You know, "Give us a twirl" and all that.' And so the producer was sent out into the streets of London to find the Chairman a suitable assistant, someone to sit on his left hand and keep their eyes on the Teams' points. Someone to lend the show a little class.

'Samantha has been giving us a hand for longer than it would be gallant to say,' Graeme recalls. 'Our producer at the time spotted her while working behind the bar at the BBC Club (he often served there in between producing jobs). She came in one night and ordered a Double Entendre, so he gave her one. Later he made her an offer and after thinking about it long and hard she took up the position.'

Despite the decade being the absolute zenith of political correctness in British culture and society, the eighties was also a golden era for the Page Three Girl. The topless glamour phenomenon piloted and championed by the *Sun* had been around since 1970, but when diminutive popular 'stunnah' Samantha Fox crossed over from revealing her breasts in black-and-white newsprint to having her own pop career and ZX Spectrum Strip Poker game (and of course disastrously co-presenting the Brit Awards with Mick Fleetwood), it proved to be a renaissance time for the 'dolly-bird' – Linda Lusardi had already branched out from Page Three and, like Maria Whittaker, forged her own successful multimedia career in Fox's wake back in the days when Katie 'Jordan' Price was still chasing the boys in the playground. Many young women at the time were realising just how far an attractive girl could get if she used her sexuality, and no doubt many of them were disappointed with how far their exposure got them. Perhaps our very own Samantha could have suffered a similarly seedy fate when she embarked on her own career in glamour modelling, if she hadn't been welcomed into the supportive clique of doting sugar daddies that made up the *Clue* team.

It wasn't until the second episode of the twelfth series, back in the summer of 1985, that Mayhew-Archer's protégée was first mentioned, and then only in the most casual manner, as she lent the Teams a hand in one of their few strenuous rounds in thirty-five years.

HL: Today's contest is called 'Squat Thrusts', and we want to see how many of these painful and rather unsavoury movements they can do. Because of Barry's personal problem we're going to let him do his behind a screen.

BC: God bless you. Every day of this career's been a bonus, you know.

HL: And our lady scorer is going to accompany him. Did I tell you at home that we have a lady scorer? It's been eleven years now I've been trying to get a lady scorer like all the other Chairmen have sitting next to them – give her an actual round of applause . . . *Colin plays a pretty tune, the Audience applaud.*

HL: Right, ducky, if you'd go back there with Barry. Right, you ready? Off you go, Teams, start – now!

After a few minutes of incessant panting and slapping and occasional counting, Willie won the contest with 118 squat thrusts ('The squat may have gone, but the thrust's still there!'), and the 'lady scorer' returned to her silent duty. It wasn't until the next show that Humph decided that someone so delightful and helpful should be given full credit, and indeed a warm hand at the start of every programme – Humph even introduced her as 'The person you've all come to see . . .' and the Audience were never left unsatisfied. The cult of the 'Lovely Samantha' was established, and for over twenty years she would man the abacus and have an intimate view of the Teams' every playful chestnut. Which makes her an extremely lucky woman.

The arrival of the show's first regular female presence, after over a decade, re-poses the question of *I'm Sorry*'s political incorrectness. As with *I'm Sorry I'll Read That Again*, accusations of racism or homophobia can be quite comfortably laughed out of court from the start – if anything the Teams were ahead of their time in terms of political correctness in those areas. One double feature of 'Sound Charades' in 1981 featured some regrettable 'Ching Chong Chinaman' voices employed to suggest *I Am Curious Yellow* and *The Chinese Detective*; but Graeme's cautious reaction to Tim & Willie's performance: 'Something "yellow" must be in the title . . .' – was answered by Tim, 'If you're a racialist, yes.' Very early on, the gang decided that they didn't need to stoop to 'How de do dere, honey?' material, and similarly Tim was glad to have escaped the pressure to camp it up constantly. Homosexuality was never an issue – two of Barry's greatest collaborators, Graham Chapman and Kenny Everett, were gay after all.

Clue was always very keen to display a politically correct attitude, as Humph once stated in the show, 'Like Barry Cryer's trousers, political correctness has had rather a bad press recently. So I've decided we're going to bring it into the programme, so from now on I will of course be referred to as "Chairperson", Samantha will be "sexually challenged" . . . something to look forward to for her, no doubt. And the Teams will be known as "differently entertaining."' However, on the subject of how this crusty old gentleman's club came off in the face of gender politics, it's hard to be quite so dismissive of any charge of chauvinism, at least in the early days. The Teams' treatment of the 'tottering totter' when she first started keeping the scores was, they agree with no small amount of shame, regrettably caveman-like. Although she usually only got the one mention per show, she was greeted with wolf whistles and leers and even cries of 'Jelly on a plate!' or 'We welcome her back . . . but not as much as we welcome her front!' or 'The girl who puts Dolly Parton in the shade, not to mention half the population of Nashville Tennessee'. Humph was forced to admit, 'I've had any number of letters accusing me of sexism for constantly referring to the "lovely Samantha", so let's try another tack. Here's the woman with a face like the northward view of a southbound duck . . .' Of course, Samantha being Samantha, she took it all on the chin. But it would be many years before she came out from under her bushel, and began to give as good as she got.

Despite the show debuting with a regular female extemporiser in the form of Jo Kendall, *Clue* is undeniably a testosterone-fuelled arena. In those early days the presence of such a glamorous woman undeniably brought out the extra-bawdy in the Teams, and accusations of the show turning into a men's club were unavoidable – as Sandi Toksvig noted in her first appearance, 'It's too thrilling to join the long list of women who've been on this show . . .' But Barry Cryer insists, on the contrary: 'We want more women, but we have no luck. Sandi Toksvig and, God bless her, Linda Smith both did it. Victoria Wood told me she records the show, but she won't do it. She likes it all cut and dried and scripted. She says she couldn't handle all the pissing about. I did *Chain Reaction* with Jo Brand, and she blatantly said on the recording she'd like a go, so we're going to lock her in to do it.' Tim adds, 'I've always been very keen to get females on board. A lot of women comedians have felt they need to be very aggressive in the stand-up world and this isn't right for the show. Maddeningly,' he concludes, 'Victoria Wood had agreed to do one of the shows we didn't do in 2008.'

It's not as if Britain has ever been short of funny female performers, but the problem with *Clue* is that, for all that it's a supportive, uncompetitive arena, the brand of humour is mainly of a kind of quick-fire gag-slinging nature, mixed with a boozy silliness, which is far more prevalent in male performers. The witty comic actresses that have excelled in shows like *Just a Minute* – Sheila Hancock, Wendy Richard and so on – bring great value to the shows they've appeared on, but the rate of joke-telling in *Clue* wouldn't quite have fitted their talents. Perhaps it's another throwback to the old-time Music Hall tradition, in which the men led the proceedings and performed the sketches while the women were on the whole restricted to singing love songs (albeit bawdy ones). But there is a killer attitude to firing out awful puns, with each comic trying to top the others with each successive painful gag, that's a rare commodity in our comediennes – and worth all the more when a female performer has it in spades.

But the gang have, as Barry says, striven to even out the balance of the sexes in *Clue*, and indeed the most regular guest performer on the show back in the nineties and beyond was that chirpy veteran from Humphrey Barclay's *Do Not Adjust Your Set* troupe, Denise Coffey. 'We'd known Denise a long time,' says Graeme, 'since the *Do Not Adjust Your Set* days, although we hadn't worked with her on that. And we were very fond of her, she's a very funny person. She doesn't tend to do much comedy now, I think she's a painter.' And it wasn't just Denise; although the regular line-up is the one that everyone remembers, there has been a whole army of gagsmiths that have made special appearances on the show, right from the days when Willie's arrival completed the default team. *Clue* had always been an open challenge to comic performers of all kinds, so if any one of the main team were in any way indisposed, there wasn't any trouble finding a funny cove with that 'what the hell' attitude to make a special appearance for a couple of shows.

John Junkin

Born John Francis Junkin in Ealing in 1930, John's first break came at the start of the sixties, as an actor with Joan Littlewood's Stratford East Theatre Workshop, and the Royal Court Theatre – four years later he found fame as the Mal Evans character Shake in The Beatles' movie debut *A Hard Day's Night*. Becoming a much-in-demand comedy writer as well as a performer, Junkin's major vehicle was probably *Hello, Cheeky*, but he also cropped up in *Marty*, *The Avengers*, *Inspector Morse*, and was a regular in *EastEnders* – perhaps his last notable role before he died of lung cancer in 2006. He was a fine Mornington Crescent player.

Jonathan Lynn

The Bath-born Lynn studied law at Pembroke College, Cambridge, like Tim Brooke-Taylor and John Cleese, but as a contemporary of Graeme's he was very lucky to be promoted to the *Cambridge Circus* cast. Gaining performing experience in *Twice a Fortnight* and *The Liver Birds*, it was the move to writing that spelled Lynn's biggest success, when work on Video Arts projects led to collaboration with Antony Jay, and *Yes Minister* was born. Subsequently, Lynn has become a well-respected Hollywood movie director, helming crime caper *Clue*, *Nuns on the Run*, *The Whole Nine Yards* and *My Cousin Vinny*. He lives in Los Angeles.

Denise Coffey

Aldershot, 1936 was the place and time of Coffey's first ever appearance, and in the ensuing seventy-plus years she has appeared on stage, screen, radio, and worked as a theatre director in Canada and the UK. She started her career in rep in Edinburgh, but soon turned the right heads as one of the core *Do Not Adjust Your Set* team, and remained much in demand as a comic performer for over forty years and a familiar face from a wide range of classic children's programmes. Now retired, she lives in Brighton, exploring her artistic bent.

Mike Harding

Mancunian war baby Michael Harding tried his hand at many things – dustman, road-digger, teacher, factory worker and bus conductor being just a few blind alleys – before taking an English degree at the University of Manchester. It wasn't until he began performing comedy in folk clubs in the seventies that his talents really began to get him noticed. Dubbed the Rochdale Cowboy, Mike released over twenty albums over the following twenty years, and dozens of books humorous, poetic and informative. As well as being a successful playwright, he also deserves laurels for writing the theme tune to *Dangermouse.* He's presented Radio 2's flagship folk programme since 1999.

Kenny Everett

He was born Maurice Cole in Seaforth, Merseyside in 1944, but by 1962, after a thoroughly misunderstood youth (including being kicked out of junior seminary for nicking communion wine), Maurice had become a fully-fledged Kenny Everett, an irrepressible, multi-talented, groundbreaking radio broadcaster. At just eighteen he turned down a BBC offer for the exciting world of pirate radio, until the forming of Radio 1 finally gave Kenny his ideal canvas – creating finely wrought, insane radio entertainment was his true métier. His popularity led to a similarly innovative (and very saucy) TV comedy career, much of it co-scripted by Barry Cryer. The TV work had already run its course and Everett was back in his radio element on Capital Radio when he came out in 1989, admitting to the world that his private life had been every bit as exuberant and decadent as his on-screen antics. Having been part of the gay scene since long before Aids awareness was even a possibility, however, he left Capital in 1994 due to ill health, and died the following April. Everett will always be remembered as a true pioneer of sonic comedy.

Stephen Fry

Between his birth in Hampstead in 1957 and his current life split between Norfolk and the capital, Stephen John Fry has fitted in more achievement, more creativity and more experience than most of us could manage in several incarnations. A comedy writer and performer of genius thanks to the likes of *Blackadder, A Bit of Fry & Laurie, Jeeves & Wooster* and *QI*, a respected actor in everything from movies like *Peter's Friends* and *Wilde* to his own TV series, *Kingdom*, a celebrated novelist, screenwriter, essayist and podcaster, a

Footlighter, an ex-offender, an ex-addict, a TV presenter, documentary-maker, gadget freak, raconteur, wit and, not least, a fine preparer of cocktails. Stephen also directed his first motion picture, *Bright Young Things*, in 2003.

Bill Tidy

Born in Tranmere in 1933, Bill Tidy is one of the UK's most celebrated cartoonists, seeing his efforts in print both before and after leaving the army, in 1955. Quickly establishing himself on a freelance basis, by the sixties Tidy's cartoons were doing a rare trade in the *Mirror* and the *Daily Sketch*, and he soon became a regular contributor to *Private Eye*. One of the co-founders of The Cartoonists' Association – and eventually the President of the Lord's Taverners Charity – Tidy's reputation as not just an artist but a wit grew as he became a regular voice/face on radio and television during the seventies. In 2000 he accepted the MBE, and still works very hard illustrating, writing and cartooning – but not at weekends.

Paul Merton

Born on 9 July 1957, a family trip to the circus for little Paul Martin triggered a lifelong adoration for comedy, and by his teens he was recording every comedy show he could, to learn off by heart. His own comedy career took a long time to get going, an ungraded CSE in metalwork only getting him as far as a job at the Tooting Employment Office, before an experiment in 1982, taking to the stage at the Comedy Store, gave him the confidence to join Equity, changing his name to Merton in the process. Despite an early cameo in *The Young Ones* and lots of live improv work, there were years of struggle and a case of hepatitis A, before the right vehicle was found for comedy stardom. *Whose Line is it Anyway?* got him the job on *Have I Got News For You*, and panel game immortality was his. He has also had his own inventive sketch show, acted in *One Foot In The Grave* and *An Evening With Gary Lineker*, written several books, and presented travel programmes. He is also a patron of the Bristol Silent Comedy Festival, along with Tim, Graeme and Neil Innes.

Tony Hawks

Christened Antony Hawksworth in Brighton in 1960, Tony would probably not have shortened his name if he knew how often he would end up getting mixed up with the US skateboarder Tony Hawk. The injustice of this is carried out by just how more amusing his career has been than his American counterpart. On leaving Brighton College in 1978, Hawks' original plans verged on serious music, but soon his separate life as a stand-up was taking precedence, and the two joined together in the formation of Morris Minor and The Majors.

A popular warm-up artist, Tony started making memorable appearances on shows he worked on, such as *Red Dwarf* and *A Bit of Fry & Laurie*, before *The Brain Drain* brought his humour centre stage. As well as his television career, Tony has had great success as a writer, notably with the best-selling *Round Ireland with a Fridge*, but also *Playing the Moldovans at Tennis* and his attempt to get Norman Wisdom to number one in Albania, *One Hit Wonderland*.

Jeremy Hardy

On 17 July 1961, the socialist stand-up comedian Jeremy Hardy was born, to a grateful Mr and Mrs Hardy, of Aldershot. He attended Farnham College before studying modern history and politics at the University of Southampton. As the eighties dawned Hardy rapidly became a regular figure at comedy benefits – the cardigan-wearing worrier with shades of political fervour – and in 1988 he won the Perrier Award. As one of the first of the Comedy Store Players, Jeremy met and married his first wife American comedienne Kit Hollerbach, with whom he has one daughter. Jeremy has an enviable roster of TV credits, teaming up with Jack Dee for *Jack & Jeremy's Real Lives*, Team Captain on *If I Ruled the World* and a scene-stealing cameo in *Blackadder Goes Forth* – but it's for his work on Radio 4 that he's most rightly celebrated, with *Jeremy Hardy Speaks to the Nation* a recognised classic, and pitch-perfect participation in panel games, especially *The News Quiz*, which is just one outlet for his brand of satirical comment (although he was fired as a *Guardian* columnist for being too left-wing).

Stand-Ins, Stand-Ups and Stand-Offs

It would be indelicate in the extreme to specify the wide array of ailments and bodily disasters that have befallen our heroes over the decades, even if the previous extract made it rather clear the agony Barry Cryer has suffered at times (and Humph was always keen to rub it in – 'Incidentally, many keen followers of this programme will be wondering why our fourth regular of many years, Barry Cryer, is absent from the series so far. Barry is, I'm sorry to say, off sick with a complaint which good taste and the spectre of Lord Reith forbids me to specify . . . But if you're listening, Barry, get well soon. I hope you're sitting comfortably, but I doubt it.'). One specific ailment worth noting is Willie Rushton's diabetes, which he was always voluble about from the first time it was diagnosed at the start of the eighties, as it forced him to forgo that great pleasure in life, the Booze. A true lover and connoisseur of the bar room and all the alcoholic fluids contained therein from an early age, Willie even ruminated on the title 'Through a Glass Brightly' for his autobiography, had he written one. But with the arrival of diabetes he sadly had to give up the plonk for good, and lost a considerable amount of weight as a result. He didn't like to complain, admitting later in life that 'Diabetes has done me nothing but good, really'.

But this aside, the roster of illnesses includes gout, eczema, the inevitable haemorrhoids and Humph once claimed 'Graeme Garden has gone down with Hong Kong flu' (though Tim insisted that should have been 'Hong Kong Flo'). Garden was a trooper though, even turning up to a recording despite an attack of Bell's palsy, a mild but incapacitating condition which hampered his attempts to pronounce his plosive consonants, P's and B's – in which case, he noted, 'it was a bit sick of them to call it Bell's palsy'.

But if any of the panel really couldn't make it to a recording, word was sent out to friends and colleagues, and the first stand-in player was that comic natural and Mornington Crescent champion, John Junkin. He stood in for an absent Tim in only the fourth series, at Colin Sell's second ever recording. His *Hello, Cheeky* training made him a sharp, ruthless player of the game, and a great contrast to his temporary partner Willie, who was glad to merrily coast along and let the temp do all the hard work. Junkin went on to make several appearances up to the mid-eighties, but Tim's old *Cambridge Circus* friend Jonathan Lynn only joined in with one recording – not that he wasn't as witty as the rest, but as Tim's partner it was unfortunate that their voices were so similar, and as his appearance pre-dated *Yes Minister* by only a year or so, he was too busy anyway. His appearance on the show in 1978 coincided with his directing of the play *The Unvarnished Truth*, which ran in the West End that September, reuniting Tim and Graeme with Jo Kendall for the first time in five years. In a way Lynn added to the show indirectly with the *Yes Minister*-inspired 'Political Jargon' game, in which the Teams had to find a Sir Humphrey Appleby-style permutation of popular sayings, such as 'Any person who reacts least immediately to an amusement situation will in addition exhibit an ongoing response for the greatest period of time'. And eventually this was opened up to all sorts of 'Jargon' rounds – when a builder says 'Don't worry, you won't know we're there,' they mean 'We won't be there', and so on.

Lynn was in good company as a one-off guest, as Barry roped in his friend the legendary Kenny Everett to play *Clue* just the once, in 1985, while Graeme was laid up with Flo. It was quite fitting that Kenny's one appearance was also the first ever show to namecheck the Lovely Samantha, as he and Barry (his collaborator since the late seventies), would have been working on the third outing for his BBC sketch series *The Kenny Everett Television Show* at the time – with Barry also working with producer Ray Cameron on a HBO sketch show with the same team, *Assaulted Nuts*, which was Tim Brooke-Taylor's last expedition into sketch comedy. The starring role in both shows for Cleo Rocos as a saucy lingerie-wearing busty sidekick was probably the closest television equivalent to Samantha that can be imagined, and perhaps

Samantha herself could have moonlighted as a member of Kenny's steamy dance troupe Hot Gossip.

As if any further links between Everett and *Clue* were needed, Rushton was a regular on Kenny's TV programme (the two had appeared together in a 1972 show, *Up Sunday*), playing a disciple of Everett's fake Indian mystic while the crew (including Barry) can be heard giggling in the background. And then who could forget the sketches in which the popular choreographer and performer Lionel Blair was strung up half naked on the walls of a dungeon, being whipped by Kenny and loving every minute of it? This popular strand of Kenny's show would not be the only time that anyone would have the gall to suggest that poor Lionel had any form of sexual perversion. Rushton also got to embody the Spirit of Christmas Present in the Cryer co-written *Kenny Everett's Christmas Carol* in 1985, succeeded on-screen by Peter Cook's Spirit of Christmas Yet to Come, replete with migraine-inducing eighties video effects.

Two other stand-ins around this time were the Mancunian folk-singer, poet and Radio 2 stalwart, Mike Harding, and Bill Tidy, the Merseyside cartoonist whose work for *Private Eye* and collaborations with John Junkin (not to mention devotion to the cricketing charity the Lord's Taverners, also supported by Tim and Willie) gave him plenty of links to the team. Both had impeccable comic credentials, and sported themselves well when sitting in for any of the *Clue* regulars throughout the eighties. As well as winning Mornington Crescent at his first attempt, Harding upped the satire in the shows, guessing that the link between 'Snakes, doors, teeth and mountains' in the 'Connection Quiz' was that 'They've all been privatised by Mrs Thatcher'. His folk sensibility also came in handy in a politically flavoured 'Mad Wriggle' shared with Willie, during those heady days of philandering Cabinet Ministers:

> As I rode out one May morning, in 1983,
> A bailiff came up with a paternity suit, and said 'this be for thee',
> I said it's Peter J, or perhaps mayhap it could be Cecil P,
> I'd even put money on Prince Charles, but the blood test proved it was me . . .

Garden says: 'I was a terrific fan of Bill Tidy's cartoons, and he was as off the wall as Willie – maybe it was a cartoon thing – with his gags and strangeness. I mean, he used to make me laugh even when the Audience would sit in stunned silence. And Mike Harding was fun too, coming from the folky circuit, as did Max Boyce when we were in Wales.' Tidy, who managed to get laughs just from repeating the word 'omelette', also featured in a doubly strange episode in 1991, in which there were no Goodies present at all. While Bill sat alongside Barry Cryer, the most popular early guest of all, Denise Coffey, was paired with Willie. Coffey made an impressive ten appearances between 1979 and 1997, and proved that she was more than a match for the boys, setting her opponents up with impossible rhymes in 'Ad-Lib Poem' and chiding 'You've been to university, it shouldn't be beyond you . . .' and getting in as many anti-Tory jibes as anyone, such as in the round 'Good News Bad News' which featured almost weekly for decades. Barry's Good News suggestion that Thatcher was going to resign was answered by Denise: 'The bad news is she's going to resign herself to being prime minister for the next five years.' 'She did lots,' remembers Graeme, 'and that's because we did like having the female voice and it was a struggle even more than it is now to find funny female people to do those shows – especially the more post-satirical, non-sitcom comedy personality. Denise was great fun, she was one of the lads, mucked in and did very funny voices, opened up a whole new range of situations we could play by having a girl there.' She may have occasionally had her pigtails pulled during games of 'Musical Chairs' and the like, but Denise Coffey made the most appearances over the longest period of time of any *Clue* guest.

But another reason for celebrating Coffey's stints was that they inspired the hiring of another member of the *I'm Sorry I Haven't a Clue* family. Just like the Teams, Samantha couldn't always be relied on to make it to every single recording, and when she was offered a role in a low-budget movie 'for private release' in 1991, a temporary replacement had to be found. The agency that provided Samantha had sent along other equally obliging lasses in the past – a mysterious beauty named Monica filled in for one session around the time that Jeffrey Archer got in a spot of bother in connection with an escort named Monica Coghlan, and in another barrage of Conservative-baiting, the Tory Party special of *Clue* in 1990 was scored by a totally unsuitable and far from sexy woman called Margaret (Samantha having been involved in a riding accident).

However, due to 'a bit of a mix-up at the agency', the show featuring Coffey and Tidy was the first to be graced by the presence of the 'Very Lovely Sven'. The rise of the male striptease troupe the Chippendales at the start of the nineties had been a boon to the buff young Swede's career, and in between dancing assignments, he was always glad of a little something extra in his pocket. A stranger to our shores, he was welcomed with, if not open arms, then certainly a friendly handshake by the Teams – and Denise made sure to extract all the pleasure she could from the unexpected turning of the tables, cooing to the shy young Scandinavian and admiring his rippling muscles in between rounds. Although never a serious replacement for Samantha, Sven became a firm friend of the Teams and indeed of Samantha herself, who was glad to have a fellow scorer who knew what it was like to be judged by looks alone, when both of them had such hidden intellectual depths. Sven was not only invited to accompany Samantha in a few recordings (funded by the Teams themselves), he was even allowed to bring along his special friend Björn for one evening, providing they didn't put the Teams off their game in any way. More disruptively, in the late nineties when *The Full Monty* inspired a downturn in popularity for male strippers who were fit and toned, he even brought along all his old Chippendale friends to a *Clue* recording, they having formed a choral society, the Queen's Singers. For one show only they were invited to sing the scores in between rounds and, like both Samantha and Sven before them, they really did manage to transport the show to new highs of cultural sophistication.

The Young Ones

This band of witty contemporaries that joined the Teams of course fitted in perfectly, but it would be wrong to assume that the *Clue* veterans were huddling among players of their own age, using their relative obscurity on Radio 4 to hide from the surge of young comics that were taking over TV and changing British comedy forever. Tim and Graeme may have started their radio careers as the Voice of Youth, whooping it up on the Wonder Show, but their ungraceful march into middle age wasn't marked by a grain of resentment towards younger comics – besides the odd reference in some games to Alexei Sayle's penchant for swearing, *Clue* generally carried on as normal despite the reported revolution in comedy that was going on outside the Paris Theatre. But if anything, the Teams were eager to involve the best and brightest of the new-wave performers, if they felt up to the challenge of joining in the fun of playing the Antidote to Panel Games.

At this time it was still the received opinion that 'alternative' comics saw everyone that had gone before as bloated mother-in-law haters, and all the traditional comics hated the young whippersnappers, who seemed to do nothing new but swear too much. In the mid-eighties, Barry Cryer was invited onto a late-night discussion show on Central TV, to debate the perceived gulf between the Old Guard and the Bright Young Things. He recalls bumping into young Ben Elton in the Gents, and being warned by an anonymous member of the crew that the producers were planning an outright battle of the clowns that night, and praying for a real bust-up on-air. Neither Ben nor Barry saw much logic in this, and when the show finally got under way – with Cryer, *Goon* originator Michael Bentine and writer Neil Shand batting for the old school, and Elton, John Lloyd and Stephen Fry on the other side, a charming love-in and meeting of minds commenced that must have had the production team crying with frustration. There was no divide between the groups at all, and it was clear that any number of the so-called alternative crowd would excel behind the microphones on *Clue* – many of them had been listening for years, after all.

And so it was, at the offensively young age of only twenty-seven, that Stephen Fry made his *Clue* debut, in the summer of 1986. He can't recall the exact genesis of his involvement, but feels it may have been 'thanks to Barry's haemorrhoids, as I remember. What could be more appropriate, that Barry had some sort of unfortunate operation he had to undergo, and they very sweetly got in touch with me and asked. It was of course like all my Christmases coming at once, I could not believe it . . . and it was in the great old days when it was at the Paris in Lower Regent Street, and the tradition of going and having a drink in the pub afterwards, the Captain's Cabin . . . I certainly don't remember schmoozing for the part in any way. I had been to a couple of Radio 4 LE Christmas parties, and I may without knowing it have said something complimentary about *Clue* to somebody, and they may have thought, "How nice, he likes it . . ." For whatever reason they thought it would be appropriate, it was incredibly good fun, and I remember just being blown away by the pleasure of it.' He also recalls the idiocy of the supposed enmity between comic factions. 'It was right at the height of that time when there was this completely false divide between what were known as "alternative comedians", and whatever the opposite was. And although I was by no means an alternative comedian, maybe they thought I was safe because I was also, like two of them, from Cambridge Footlights. I remember Barry Cryer coming up with an absolute cracker – I said to him that maybe he thought I was an alternative comedian, and he said "Do you know the difference between alternative comedians and regular comedians? Alternative comedians don't play golf." Because in the end, there was no ideological difference really, no difference of technique, or anything. There was a different audience, I think it was as simple as that . . . Anyway, the point is I was deeply welcomed, and I enjoyed myself enormously.'

In fact, Stephen fitted so comfortably in with the rest of the players of the game that he remained closely connected with the show for the next two decades or more, appearing more than a dozen times and only coming short of being a full-time regular thanks to his inhuman workload, as British comedy's leading polymath. His first appearance was such a joy that in return he invited one of the Team to guest star in his own radio sketch show in 1988. In the first episode of *Saturday Night Fry*, Stephen plays a scientist who invents a Dr Jekyll-style chemical called Floric 19, and finds himself turning into a female alter ego, Jenny Flemisto, as played by Emma Thompson. The chemical's surprise side effect comes at the end of this long sci-fi sketch, when our hero(ine) is facing off against their nemesis, another scientist played by Hugh Laurie with an appalling American accent that was never going to get him anywhere:

ET: What? How did you . . . Nobody could have interfered with my broadcast projection like that – no one! Unless . . .

HL: Unless they had taken Floric 19 too? Yes! You've met your match Jenny Flemisto! Meet –

<u>GRAMS:</u> <u>Dramatic sting.</u>

BC: Barry Cryer!

ET: But you – that is, I . . .

BC: Following the instructions on your lab tapes I formulated the serum and injected myself with it.

ET: Why that is – you – I . . .

BC: Instead of turning into a woman I turned into Barry Cryer. I may have left out some vital ingredient but don't underestimate me. I am packed with strange powers. Amongst my supernatural gifts I have the remarkable ability to find something suggestive and naughty in anything you say.

ET: But that's extraordinary!

BC: Extraordinary? At my age, it's a miracle!

ET: But it's horrifying!

BC: It is horrifying, isn't it? I'll put it away. There, you see what I mean? A lewd ambiguity for every occasion . . .

ET: You can keep this up indefinitely?

BC: Are you sure you want me to answer that?

Youngsters looking to get in on the action in *Clue* were liable to be patronised, at least indirectly – Fry's debut show began with Humph's disclaimer: 'This week we have on our Teams a complete novice, someone who knows nothing about the games we play . . . Tim Brooke-Taylor.' But Fry was to be the first of many, even if it took another five years before the game was graced with the presence of a true master of the comedy panel game – Paul Merton. Despite setting out on his comedy career at the same time as Fry, Elton and the Comic Strip alumni, Merton didn't really begin to make any impression on the general public until he became a regular on the Channel 4 improvisation show *Whose Line Is It Anyway?*. But the roots of that show, which is still showing to great acclaim in the United States, brings us back to Fry's radio career, and one of the closest competitors that *I'm Sorry I Haven't a Clue* has ever come up against.

In 1987, immediately prior to Fry's arrangement of his friends around the microphone to perform *Saturday Night Fry*, the producer of that show Dan Patterson (along with collaborator Mark Leveson), had hired the up-and-coming wit to be a regular on their new radio game show which, like *Clue*, would feature a Chairman and four funny off-the-cuff performers. Unlike

Clue, however, *Whose Line Is It Anyway*'s selling point would be the entirely improvised nature of the show, with the audience providing suggestions for each round. Improvisation had grown in popularity throughout the eighties, with Kit Hollerbach and Mike Myers (an American and a Scouse-Canadian from Chicago's Second City improv troupe) arriving in Blighty to help set up the Comedy Store Players in the eponymous London comedy club in 1985 – or at least to turn the Brit comics on to improv. Jim Sweeney and Steve Steen had been running improv shows for a while, but the American game-based format really saw the comic form take off. Three English aspiring comics – Paul Merton, Dave Cohen and ex-Footlights president Neil Mullarkey – quickly got into the swing of the tried-and-tested improv games that Kit and Mike had brought over with them, and a tradition was set that would continue to the present day, with regular Sunday-night rounds of silly ad hoc games that nobody ever wins. Among the guest improvisers in these early days was a painfully young Tony Hawks, who had toured with Merton when he was still known by his real name of Paul Martin, and in the coming years other performers would join the gang – Footlighters Richard Vranch and Sandi Toksvig, plus Sweeney, Steen, Josie Lawrence, Lee Simpson and, briefly, Jeremy Hardy, who convinced Hollerbach to stay in the UK by marrying her. 'It put it on the map,' Hardy says. 'British comedians obviously didn't know that stuff, and it was Kit who produced that format and those games. I was in it for about a year, and joined permanently after Mike had gone to America to work on *Saturday Night Live* – which was after Edinburgh '86 I think. Mike had to go to America to become famous, but I used to guest with them before and I'd worked with Mike, which was great, it was brilliant working with him.'

However, although most of this group would be the real fuel of the TV incarnation of *Whose Line*, Patterson and Leveson's pilot series was peopled by a mixture of Oxbridge and theatre talents, featuring John Sessions as Fry's regular co-player and Footlights star Clive Anderson in the Chair, with Hugh Laurie, John Bird, Jan Ravens, Griff Rhys Jones, plus young lovers Lenny Henry and Dawn French. The tone of the series was witty but with none of the rambunctiousness of *Clue*, or the Music Hall-inspired background. The scoring system was almost as ad hoc, although there was a weekly winner, and it was every improviser for him or herself. Many of the games had actually been heard years earlier in *Clue*, such as scenes that had to react to different music, 'Every Other Line' – in which one performer had to follow a script as their partner extemporised the other half of the dialogue – and so on. In fact, so little was done to differentiate from *Clue* that they even snatched Humph's plaything from him – Colin Sell was on the piano for the whole radio run. 'We did only one series,' Colin remembers, 'Dan got me in to provide musical help, but since none of the team was willing to impro any songs I was surplus to requirements. John Sessions in particular was reluctant to sing, as was – and still is – dear old Stephen. When the show went to TV they got in various people who took on singing, Josie Lawrence, for instance, who's unbelievable at making up a song and following a suggestive accompaniment – I've worked with her a lot at the Comedy Store in London – and the musician was Richard Vranch. Richard, with whom I've also worked at the Store and is a good mate of mine, is as clever a comedian as he is a muso; he plays guitar as well as piano, and can do just any style to perfection. He deserved the TV series.' It's bemusing how underused a talented chap like Colin is in *Whose Line* – his one reason for earning his pay cheque being a little background music, on about one round per programme. Humph must have been hugely jealous of Colin.

Jimmy Mulville appeared in two of the radio shows, and was no doubt admirably eyeing up the set-up that Patterson and Leveson had created, as they rapidly received an offer to record a TV pilot for Channel 4 from his new production company, Hat Trick. Although it seemed a risk after only six episodes on Radio 4, it fitted the duo's designs perfectly. They weren't interested in stepping on *Clue*'s toes, but constrained to sound-only improvisation, of course they were going to clash. Given the visual element – plus a timely trip to the Comedy Store – they were finally able to find their own voice and create one of the most fruitful sources of TV comedy of the nineties. Graeme Garden himself even put in an appearance in the rudimentary first series, and was one of the first hosts in the legendary game 'Party Quirks'.

Paul Merton was soon to establish himself as one of the true stars of *Whose Line Is It Anyway?*, and indeed of Hat Trick Productions, which went into panel-game overload as the decade unfolded. Merton had form, of course. In the late eighties, he had personally written in to the then producer of *Just a Minute* requesting to be given the chance to play the game, having been a fan since his radio-addicted youth. In the wake of the loss of that game's star, Kenneth Williams, Merton got his chance, and filled the verbal vacuum admirably. At the same time, his work with the Comedy Store Players had led to a radio series, *The Big Fun Show*, which also featured Julian Clary and the aspiring warm-up Tony Hawks, who was about to get to number four in the charts with his Morris Minor and the Majors hit, 'Stutter Rap (No Sleep 'Til Bedtime)'. Meanwhile, having scooped up *Whose Line*, Hat Trick were looking for a TV answer to *The News Quiz*, and the great producer Harry Thompson snapped up Merton for *Have I Got News For You* right from the first pilot in 1990. Despite creating his own brilliant sketch series with old mate John Irwin, *Paul Merton – The Series*, it was as a panel-game maestro bar none that Merton's career would truly take off. Barry Cryer himself says that Paul 'brought being a panellist to the level of an art form'. His brand of deadpan lunacy and fine trade in facetiousness would make him an admirable addition to the *Clue* stable, and he was called up to stand in for Willie back in 1991 – proceeding to win Mornington Crescent at only his first attempt (as would so many debut players, oddly enough). Merton was the perfect example of a new breed of inveterate improvisers to whom firing out quick-fire gags came naturally – so different to the tremblingly nervous approach that had driven the first couple of series of *Clue*. And of course, he knew how to slip in a running gag:

HL: Our first round is entitled 'Official Sponsor', and it takes as its subject the ever increasing role of advertising in the world of entertainment and sport. As an unashamed lover of public service broadcasting, I bitterly resent the creeping commercialism that's seen so many of our great artistic and sporting events taken over by the brand names of one product or another; it really makes me sick to the stomach ... Which is why I take Rennies, for instant relief. OK, Teams, I'd like you please to provide some titles of well-known shows, programmes or sporting events that have suffered from overzealous sponsorship. Barry, I'd like you to start, please.

BC: ... 'News At Tennant's'.

PM: Um ... 'Bring Me the Head and Shoulders of Alfredo Garcia'?

GG: One from the Duchess of York, 'Budgens the Helicopter'.

TBT: 'Prisoner Cell Block Preparation H'.

BC: 'The Four-X Files.'

GG: 'Audi They Do That?'

TBT: 'Lillets Spend the Night Together'.

PM: 'Gardeners' World of Leather' ...

With reference to *Bring Me the Head of Alfredo Garcia*, Graeme Garden first name-dropped the title of this Sam Peckinpah road-trip movie in 1992, suggesting 'Bring Me the Bread of Alfredo Garcia' for 'Bakers' Film Club'. The film itself is the epitome of obscurity, and what it's actually about is irrelevant. For reasons barely known to himself, the title just proved to be irresistible pun material to Graeme – 'Hedge', 'Hod', 'Veg', 'Vest', any replacement for 'head' could be crowbarred in to great approval. Tim and Fred Macaulay even chose it as a 'Sound Charade', before Garden put the cap on the whole thing with the killer line for the plot-ending game 'Last Episodes': 'I've Brought You the Head of Alfredo Garcia . . .' There were no rules against anyone else on the panel pitching in with a reference to the movie though, and Merton survived the pun-poaching to become the most regular guest in the show for much of the early nineties, allowing Graeme to suggest the following ditty in the game 'Greetings Cards':

TBT: On Your Circumcision . . . Not a big seller, but . . .
       It's the time for one small cut – well done on your circumcision!
       I only have one tiny but – I think you've made the wrong decision.
GG: I've got one to Tim Brooke-Taylor on his return to this
       show.
TBT: Why do I think I don't want this one?
GG: *The Audience are glad to see you back, of that I'm pretty certain.*
       When you came on, they all stood up and shouted, 'Where's Paul
       Merton?!'
TBT: Ha ha ha!
WR: . . . Good question, that.

Merton would make a return to radio improvisation with his Comedy Store Players pals in 1993 with their improvised historical saga *The Masterson Inheritance*, and in doing so they found the perfect way to get the laugh-out-loud inventive atmosphere of their live shows across on radio, but without infringing on the *Clue* copyright.

Merton's radio co-star Tony Hawks wouldn't follow him onto the *Clue* panel for another four years, standing in for Tim at the Hackney Empire, when he got to accompany himself singing 'Stutter Rap' in a round of 'Pick Up Song'. Merton's fellow Comedy Store Players Neil Mullarkey and Sandi Toksvig, however, didn't get the call to sign up for duty until after 1996. By the time Tony debuted in 1995, he had already proved his flair as a comedy panellist with two seasons of another Hat Trick show devised by Patterson and Leveson, *The Brain Drain*.

Dan Patterson remained with Radio 4 for only a brief while after the launch of the *Whose Line* TV series, but it was long enough for him to make it up to Graeme for poaching Colin Sell by producing Graeme and Barry's first joint sketch venture, *The Long Hot Satsuma*. In 1989, at the same time as he was putting together the *ISIRTA* reunion with Bill, Graeme got together with Barry (plus Patterson, Martin Booth and co-performer Paul B. Davies) to write and compile the first direct sketch descendant of *ISIRTA* and *Hello, Cheeky* in over a decade. Barry and Graeme led the show, ably abetted by legendary comic actress Alison Steadman and *Who Dares Wins* star Julia Hills. A sound-effect-heavy tapestry of spoofs and skits, *The Long Hot Satsuma* was a far more risqué entertainment than its forebears, despite having a similar format, with the gang appearing as themselves in between the gag-heavy interweaving sketches:

GRAMS: <u>Classical sting.</u>
BC: Graeme?
GG: Yeah?
BC: You having your vasectomy done privately?
GG: God, I hope so!

There's a sketch starring Graeme as a filthy costermonger undertaker which easily rivals its *Monty Python* equivalent for sheer sickness and bravado, and despite only making six shows, *The Long Hot Satsuma* stands up as a skilfully made dose of modern radio comedy, from two old hands in the game easily capable of taking on anything that the new comedy generations could throw at them.

Patterson's move into TV improvisation had given him the chance to leave radio behind, and so his next project, *The Brain Drain*, would debut on BBC2 in 1992. Basically a comic version of *Question Time*, Jimmy Mulville ended up in the Chairman role, with Tony Hawks a regular and three other comics forming one panel accepting questions from the audience – in fact, many clearly specifically written questions, allowed the panel to play regular rounds that were more than familiar to fans of *Clue*. The game 'Sounds Peculiar' had been a cornerstone of most *Clue* shows since the late seventies, as its reliance on sound effects made perfect use of the medium. A very silly version of the Barry Took nostalgia quiz *Sounds Familiar* (which transferred to TV as Denis Norden's *Looks Familiar*), 'Sounds Peculiar' featured carefully created ludicrous sound-effect collages which the panel would then have to identify – so the sound of a loo flushing with typing in the background was suggestive of 'Nigel Rees working on his next book', a leafy falling noise followed by a Tarzan wail could be 'Jane falling off the vine and grabbing at the nearest thing handy', or complete silence could be identified as 'Harpo Marx and Marcel Marceau discussing the plot of Jeffrey Archer's latest novel'. Any panellist who managed to get the answer right was invited to have a look in Humph's little box, so they were always keen to solve the mystery. Despite having the arguable benefit of cameras present, this radio-centric game was included without alteration in *The Brain Drain*, and rounds like 'Names for books that would never sell' certainly ring rather loud bells too. *The Brain Drain*'s loose comedic format and self-abusive spirit made comparisons with *Clue* impossible to avoid.

Tony Hawks, however, shone on the programme, fending off bullying brickbats from the other panellists in a highly Brooke-Tayloresque way and comfortably developing his own brand of observational daftness alongside familiar Hat Trick faces like Sandi Toksvig, Paul Merton and Andy Hamilton, not to mention his eventual co-regular Jo Brand, plus Craig Ferguson, Dawn

French, Angus Deayton and, in one of his last TV appearances, Les Dawson, who used his wealth of experience on similar gag-based quiz shows going right back to *Joker's Wild* to wipe the floor with all the other panellists without breaking a sweat.

The final player of *Clue* to be a special guest – once again filling in for Tim – was one of the original Comedy Store Players, Jeremy Hardy – who had also put in an appearance on *The Brain Drain*. Jon Naismith recalls, 'Jeremy wrote a rather candid letter, saying that he'd taken stock of his career and he really felt he'd like to devote more time to radio and he was a huge fan of *I'm Sorry I Haven't a Clue*, could he be on it? Few people have been humble enough to actually write in and ask.'

Hardy did an excellent job on his debut in 1995, more than keeping up with the Teams when it came to firing out gags, but when Colin first struck up the opening chords of 'Scarborough Fair' for Hardy to sing the lyrics of 'Kung Fu Fighting', Humph and the Teams were agape. This was something new to *I'm Sorry I Haven't a Clue*. Something unique. Something . . . horrible. 'I smell points, there!' noted Willie, and Hardy's musical career was launched.

The New Boys

These later stand-in sessions of course only came once the nineties were well under way, but a few *Clue* producers had come and gone by then. Paul Mayhew-Archer, that first flame of Samantha's, bowed out in 1986 after four years, and has continued to be the producing genius behind all the radio shows featuring his great friend Andy Hamilton, as well as a successful writer, penning many an episode of *The Vicar of Dibley* and mainstream fare like *My Hero* and *My Family*. Paul Spencer took over for a year or two before moving into commercial television, and Jon Magnusson also had only a brief stay – he now produces much of Graham Norton's TV work, as well as *Bremner, Bird & Fortune*. The show had long had a reputation among radio comedy producers as being tantamount to a non-job, with Graeme and co. all there to steer the good ship *Clue* their way, no matter what the producer did. Certainly, having survived two decades of audio tomfoolery, *Clue* remained fundamentally the same ragbag of silly games and ideas that Hatch and Garden had cooked up all those years ago. Magnusson's first ever show, at the turn of the nineties, rather said it all right from Humph's introduction: 'Hello and welcome to a brand-new series of *I'm Sorry I Haven't a Clue*, the show that does for comedy. It's a new year now and a new decade, so we're all looking forward to new faces, fresh ideas and startling originality. But while we're waiting, let me introduce the Teams . . .'

So despite respected names like Brett and Perkins thriving in the role in the past, it seemed that *Clue* was not seen as the kind of show on which any young producer could make their mark. One fresh young candidate whose name was potentially kicked around was Armando Iannucci, but his reason for resisting the lure of *Clue* was very different: 'I did say to Jonathan James-Moore who was head of the department that I didn't want to produce it – I just wanted to stay a listener! I didn't really want to know what they were like, or how they made it, or if one of them was really grumpy ... I didn't want the joy of listening to it to be spoiled by knowing what it was like. And so the only time I've seen them live is as a member of the Audience – I went to a recording of it, and that's enough ... I don't want to get too close to that. I still think it's great, it just cheers me up.'

Iannucci couldn't be blamed for wanting to remain ignorant of the show's secret formula. It's incredible, given an archive of all-but every episode of *Clue* to dip into, over fifty series, that any random show will manage almost without fail to reduce the listener to a giggling twit at least once – which is more than most comedy shows that have run for a tenth of the time can claim. Entering into the fraternity of *Clue* listeners means surrendering yourself to the sheer pleasure of laughter, be it from an unexpected sliver of satire, a mind-stretching non sequitur, or the kind of knob gag that Chaucer was probably tempted to drop for being old hat. Of course, to a melancholy minority, such arguably cliquey silliness could be open to criticism, no matter how out of place any kind of deconstruction would be when it comes to the free-form rib-tickling offered by *Clue*.

It seemed like one such moment of censure had arrived in 1991 when the first episode of Iannucci and Chris Morris' news spoof *On the Hour* featured a mocked-up trailer for *I'm Sorry I Haven't a Clue*, sniping at the likes of the 'Gargling' round, by having 'the Teams' sing a song using only the words 'bottom' and 'counterpane'. Steve Coogan and Patrick Marber were the ones sending up the Teams, but in putting the spoof together, Iannucci did splice in one crucial element of real footage of the show. 'I did tell Barry Cryer that I actually used his laugh – just because I found his laugh very, very infectious. So I thought it would be quite nice to pinch it and use it in *On the Hour*.' Militant *Clue* fans (should such a strange being exist) might be forgiven for taking offence at having their heroes pilloried, but Iannucci has since insisted that the sketch was completely affectionate – how could it not be, given his reasons for turning down any offer to work on the show? And Barry says, 'The spoof was funny, I loved it. It's a compliment to have the piss taken out of you, especially by something like *On the Hour*.' Graeme, on the other hand, adds 'The spoof didn't bother me because I didn't hear it. I really liked *On the Hour*, though. I look forward to its fiftieth series.'

Swipes such as *On the Hour*'s, no matter how velvety the gloved fist, do show that *Clue* needs a surgeon's hand on the tiller, with a razor-sharp eye on the programme's quality, carefully walking a tightrope over a dangerous pit of smugness (and avoiding mixed metaphors like the plague). By 1991, the job had been taken less seriously than perhaps it needed to be, and maybe standards had dropped a little. Games like 'Fourth Bridge' and the 'Gargling' round did veer towards the kind of tiresome pointlessness that Iannucci and Morris considered fit for ridicule. It was funny to hear Willie dribbling water all over himself if you loved the show, but there was always that fine line between silliness and self-indulgence, and new blood was needed to get the Teams back on track as they entered their third decade. As Cryer attests: 'We've had quite a few producers through the years, and one or two of them, they hardly did anything. They owned up later on to saying "Oh these old farts, they run this show. I don't have to do anything but just turn up and record it . . ." When Jon came in, his predecessor didn't help him at all, so he came in cold. It didn't show, but he did say he was somewhat apprehensive of taking it over. But very early on we realised he had real input, and we *wanted* input, we didn't want to be sitting there smugly with the producer just . . . sat there!'

When he joined the *Clue* team for his first series in the late summer of 1991, Jon Naismith was not even especially enamoured of the show. 'I'd not really listened to *ISIRTA* and though I enjoyed *Clue* I wasn't a great fan. I think this helped as I didn't feel constrained about altering things. I took over the show around the time that the *On the Hour* spoof went out – I seem to recall they were making fun of the "Gargling" round. I never liked the round myself and we've never done it since. It may have been Herring or Lee or someone who wrote that, rather than Armando, but there was a truth in it. You know, when it's just pointless . . . I love the show, and I wince when I listen back to those things because I just think there has to be a seam of wit. Even in a nonsense round, like "Name That Barcode", there has to be a logic that will run through it. I believe that people who listen to Radio 4 want a comedy that is a cut above the average, that is sharp. And I felt occasionally *I'm Sorry I Haven't a Clue* had just been . . . a bit lazy, really.'

Gifted with the bemusing task of keeping this twenty-year-old Antidote to Panel Games ticking over, young Naismith was not one to follow the obvious producer's path of allowing the Teams to run the show without demur, and wait for a more hands-on job to come along. One of his first decisions was to continue the influx of younger talent, when the opportunity arose, giving Hardy and Hawks their debuts, as well as booking Fry and Merton for more.

Farting About
Around this time, the downturn of comic opportunity being offered to Cryer and Rushton finally caused one of them to leap to desperate measures. As

Barry recalled: 'Willie and I were discussing how the world was changing. Both of us, to say the least, had been around for some years, and we realised that TV was concentrating on younger performers . . . Will, the great pragmatist, said we should get off our arses and try to create our own work. The previous year, with Colin, Graeme, juggler Pierre Hollins and singer Christine Pilgrim, we had put together an evening in aid of the Spinal Injuries Association, with which we toured the country. *Two Old Farts in the Night* was created from this, minus Graeme and Pierre, who had other commitments.'

This jolly evening's entertainment, hosted by the unlikely double act in exquisite evening wear, took in the Edinburgh Festival and a tour of the provinces and ended up at the Hackney Empire in 1994 during its initial run – although Barry and Willie would continue touring, on and off. With Colin in his dicky at the piano and Barry's daughter Jacqueline as the show's chanteuse, *Two Old Farts in the Night* was a refined hour of ribaldry, as laid-back and rough around the edges as the stars themselves. Both being solo performers at heart, the general idea was that Barry and Willie would entertain the punters in tandem, strolling on to take the reins when the other one was ready for a convenience break. Only very rarely did they overlap:

BC: Where've you been?
WR: Waiting for my bimbo to dry.
BC: Fair enough.
WR: I'm afraid the papers will be full of it tomorrow.
BC: What?
WR: Crap. I'm afraid that *The News of the World* are onto me – they're going to do something of a splash on me. The Matron at the Frith Street Massage Bar and Bouncy Castle has blown, among other things, the gaff. My wife was very good. She said 'I shall stand beside you, darling, throughout this whole beastly business'. And then I realised she wasn't talking to me . . .

Indeed, they were so laid-back that they gave Colin his own solo spot, performing his song 'The Boys in the Band', as well as backing up Barry's performance as US evangelist the Reverend Ricotta Limeswold, calling upon the faithful to praise 'Cheeses'. Willie voiced his concerns about striking out as a stand-up in advanced middle age while actually onstage: 'Cryer knows every joke ever committed, I don't know any at all . . . In fact, if you say "jokes" to me, a chill hand touches my bowels. Well, a warm hand nowadays, as we all know, is prohibitively expensive. I am actually joke-blind . . . People tell me a joke, it goes in one ear and out the other. Specialists call it quipslexia.' But despite his withering disclaimers, the show was a clear hit. Years later Barry would recall Willie's time as one of the Two Farts: 'He loved the theatre more than anything else and, during the seven years that we did the show, I watched him blossom and grow, as I lost the will to live waiting in the dressing room for him to finish. No matter – he was funny. As Richard Ingrams said, he never changed but seemed to get better all the time.'

The nineties was in a way the start of a renaissance for Graeme and Tim as well, perhaps inspired by the *ISIRTA* reunion in 1989 (and a growing army of support for the re-evaluation of *The Goodies*, the sheer popularity of which in the funky seventies made it a cert for derision throughout the slick eighties), and it was good to see the *I'm Sorry* legacy still getting away with the same old loose silliness after nearly twenty series.

Incidentally, the disparity of the number of *Clue* series is down to the fact that for the first fifteen years, there had on average been one long series of ten to twelve shows every year, but in Jon Magnusson's time shorter series had started to creep in, and Naismith was insistent that a new format of two six-part series a year, every late spring and autumn, was the ideal. 'It just needed commitment, and so one of the first things I did was to stop these long series – producers don't usually have the time to keep the quality up with that number of shows, no matter how dedicated they are. So I said, "Look, we'll still do your twelve programmes a year but we need it split into two." When you've got a long-running show, people's commitment can waver, so if we double-record and we've only got six in a series, that's only three recordings. And I'm very keen also that we never have less than a two-week gap between recordings, and that means people are always quite pleased to see each other! And that's another great advantage *Clue* has – the guys really get on, enjoy each other's company, and enjoy the show. You see the cast of *Just a Minute*, and many of them appear to hate each other's guts . . .'

However, when the twenty-first anniversary of the first show came round, Graeme Garden was adamant that no special celebration should happen to mark the occasion, because in the new Birt-led BBC such an event would have been the perfect excuse to pension off what was easily seen as an ailing brand of radio comedy. Humph even mentioned a special message that the programme received from the Director General during one round of 'Greetings Cards': '"To *I'm Sorry I Haven't a Clue*. Get Better Soon, love John Birt". How kind,' Humph smiled. 'I think there was a certain amount of paranoia in the air,' says Graeme, 'because James Boyle was Head of Radio 4 at the time, and there was a rather sort of Maoist regime cutting off the grey hairs . . . I think Tim, as I recall, was particularly paranoid.'

Was the show in danger of being pensioned off? Perhaps it seemed an ill omen that Humph lost his legendary totem of authority, the Chairman's Hooter, at this time – Samantha headed up 'The Campaign for the Safe Return of Humph's Hooter', but their efforts were unsuccessful, and Humph just ended up getting a new one.

If *I'm Sorry I Haven't A Clue* was going to be able to keep on going throughout the decade, Jon Naismith would have to put the cluttered *Clue* house in order, take stock of what had gone before in the name of *I'm Sorry*, and build a bigger and stronger show for the nineties. But until the new boy had got a handle on his awesome responsibilities, if they were going to keep getting away with this one ridiculous extended joke, the Teams had to bide their time.

12

Beyond a Joke

'A Harry Potter wannabe' is how Barry Cryer has been known to refer to his esteemed producer when the microphones are off, and if that's how the eternally youthful (thanks to the company he keeps) Jon Naismith is described today, how much like a schoolboy must he have seemed back in 1991 when the 25-year-old first blinked through his spectacles at his unruly aged charges and laid out his plans for *I'm Sorry I Haven't a Clue*? It wasn't the easiest billet for any producer, but for a kid like Naismith it was a mighty challenge: 'It was traditional to meet in the Captain's Cabin, and then my great effort was to try to shift them from the Captain's Cabin to the Paris Studio, where they prepared the things at their desks. And they much preferred being in the pub. My big ally was Tim, who would say "Oh, I really think we ought to be getting on, we've got a lot to get through . . ."' However, he soon managed to flex his muscles a little. 'We've always had producers who were quite keen to put their stamp on the programme,' says Graeme. 'Jon Naismith has now been doing it for over fifteen years. And before every series he calls us in for a very serious meeting, and unless each one of us comes up with half a dozen ideas for new rounds, he's very disappointed, and we get our knuckles rapped.' Jon confirms: 'I think it would be fair to say that Graeme and I have devised the bulk of the new rounds played during my tenure as producer, though Iain has come up with some good ideas, as have Tim and Barry. Barry was responsible for the one-off round "Spot the Ostrich" which I imagine was scrawled in desperation on his cigarette packet prior to a meeting to discuss new rounds and to his surprise was met with approval.' Barry concurs: 'That was a one-off, yes, and "Guess the Barcode" was mine, and you'd only play those once. They're novelties. For "Spot the Ostrich", Humph gave a long, ridiculous intro, and then said, "Open the cage!" and you heard the bars sliding back, and I said, "There he is!" And there was applause, and Humph said, "Barry wins that," and I said, "Humph, I have to own up . . . I've played this before." And that was it.'

Although like two of his new colleagues Naismith was a public-school boy and a Footlights man (graduating in 1988 alongside Mel Giedroyc, Simon Munnery and Tom Hollander), Graeme says, 'He didn't seem anything special, and it took him a while to get things up and running. But he was very effective and agreeable, and he was obviously meticulous. He was a good producer from the start, but he didn't put his stamp on the show until a good series in, when things started really beginning to hum.' 'The show when I took it over was I think very much junior to *The News Quiz* and *Just a Minute*, certainly in terms of popularity,' insists Naismith, 'It was "the rather eccentric one" that fitted in with those. In my opinion it wasn't as good as it could have been . . .'

In the season immediately before Jon's arrival one big change had been effected in the show, with Jon Magnusson managing the trick of convincing the Teams to do without the traditional barrage of punnery that attended the 'Late Arrivals' at the Society Balls. Rushton had progressed from putting his feet up to let the other players squirm their way through the tenuous announcements, to loudly disowning the whole round, as the groans rang out and the silence descended, and Humph looked towards Willie expectantly. 'I've been trying to cut this bit for years, you know I don't like it!' he roared, going on to fill the gap with 'Where's that nice Announcer? I like it when he comes on . . . I've been looking forward to him for about the last five minutes. They play the nice music, Pom-po-pom! ". . . given silly things to do by Humphrey Lyttelton", and the Audience go mad . . .' When Naismith came along, he too agreed that they'd done everything they could with the Balls, and had to move on. But though Willie got his wish, there was something rather disappointing about the show not having a pun-jamboree ending. They tried to fill the gap with 'Limericks', which was always one of the most fertile ways of generating laughs with very little work, and beat wading through an 'Ad-Lib Poem' any day.

The origins of the limerick are hotly debated, but poetry scholars tend to be insistent that the centuries-old folk verse form was *always* designed specifically for the creation of the filthiest of bawdy jokes. The rhythm and rhyming scheme make suggestibility irresistible, and as a *Clue* round it was a guaranteed success. With Humph suggesting a fecund first line ('At Tesco's, with Earth, Wind and Fire . . .' or 'One evening while playing at whist . . .') and four more lines for the Teams to chip in, it's no wonder that the *Clue* limericks were a constant treat right from the first series:

> *I'm Sorry I Haven't a Clue,*
> *So tell me, just what would you do?*
> *We haven't much time,*
> *So I'll say it in mime . . .*
> *Oh I see, very well – same to you!*

However, as a finale they lacked the growing mania of the pun marathons, and only a couple of series after Jon took over, the Balls were back. But, each member of the panel having explored almost every punning-name avenue in existence over the previous two decades, Naismith introduced other formats for the finale – the Book Clubs, Songbooks, Film Clubs and so on which certain societies patronised when they weren't attending Balls. And it worked a treat, keeping the long tradition of painful punning alive while apparently offering something new – the perfect producer's trick.

As well as looking at new ways of keeping the twenty-year-old show fresh, Jon Naismith began the task of overseeing the long-overdue release of a range of *I'm Sorry I Haven't a Clue* BBC cassettes. Starting with the first volume in 1993, the extra work put in by Naismith combing the archives for the very best moments (or at least back to the mid-eighties – the BBC's archives didn't even stretch much further than the late seventies) made each volume of *Clue* released on cassette especially dense with laughter, of course, and provided yet another tempting starting point for listeners to be lured into the supposed '*Clue* clique'. By the time they were into their third or fourth volume, the *Clue* compilations were easily the biggest sellers in the BBC Audio Collection – people were being palpably sucked in to the cult.

This was a boon because, after all, how do you pick up on all the in-jokes and tried-and-tested traditions of a show like *Clue* (if indeed there could be another show like *Clue*)? Finding out why the hell a Scotsman saying 'Ah, Hamish!' is funny, or who Samantha is, or why nobody's scoring any points, is rather like trying to find the end of a roll of Sellotape. To enter into this world does take a little effort, as Barry Cryer admits: 'We're not complacent, we just hope it doesn't sound indulgent. Because it's a show you've got to listen to more than once. I think anybody listening to it for the first time might get quite baffled and irritated, like, "What's going on?" But by the process of absorption . . .'

The Hot Ticket
It's hardly surprising that so many millions of listeners signed up for this process of absorption, with the introduction of youngish popular performers luring in a more youthful listenership than before. Also, more people were becoming aware of *I'm Sorry I Haven't a Clue* as a live experience at this point, since the early nineties saw the show moving out of the capital and beginning to follow the *Just A Minute* route of putting on shows all round the provinces. Jon Magnusson had produced one evening at the Brighton Comedy Festival in his last series, and in the past there had been freak record-ings in unusual theatres such as the Barbican or Middlesex Hospital (at the invitation of the students), but the Teams enjoyed the Brighton experience

so much that a year or so into Naismith's reign the show's metropolitan roots would be torn up, allowing Graeme and the gang to enjoy the experience of playing in some of the finest theatres (acoustics permitting) around the British Isles – with the beautiful buildings of Frank Matcham a preference. Graeme is also open about another boon that came from moving further afield. 'It's not patronising to say that the audiences outside of London are very pleased to see a show that they know well coming out and seeing them. There were other shows – *Have a Go* in the old days was all about touring, they used to go to factories and places and ask a local audience to come up onstage and ask some questions, and Wilfred Pickles would have Mabel at the table with her sixpence prize or whatever it was . . . and Violet Carson at the piano!'

From Brighton, then, they visited Tim's home town of Buxton, Graeme's neighbourhood in Oxford, the Edinburgh Fringe Festival, Stratford-upon-Avon, Chester, Harrogate, the Theatre Royal in Bath, and many more were to follow. Barry and Willie had played the Theatre Royal on their *Two Old Farts* tour, and became aware of the legend at that theatre of the ghostly butterfly – it brought good fortune to a company if it was seen fluttering through a rehearsal, but everyone in the show would be damned if a dead butterfly was discovered. 'Willie acquired a butterfly in a glass case. As I told the audience the saga, Willie walked on behind me displaying the case to the audience, shouting, "Got the bugger!" After the show, one of the stage crew took me to one side. "Never mock the butterfly," he said . . .' However, it was when *Clue* reached nearby Cheltenham that the police had to be called in, when an irate ticket holder was refused entry.

Of course, there's a grand tradition of TV and radio recordings being free, a generous amount of tickets being sent out to those who express an interest, and mainly these days through the internet. But the sudden surge of interest in *Clue* in the early nineties, triggered by the break from London recordings, demanded a change. As Stephen Fry recalled, 'According to Jon Naismith what really helped was when they decided to charge for admission to the theatres. It's a psychological thing, it's not that they want to make any money out of it, because they don't. But beforehand, when it was free, people moaned incredibly about not being able to get in. And they'd say, "You don't understand, I've driven down from Dundee!" And Jon said, "Well, you don't understand, it is literally full. There is nowhere for you to go without breaking the law, and there is a fire officer standing there." "Yes, but you've got to let me in!" "We *can't*! We literally cannot . . ." Whereas the moment you pay for it, nobody's going to drive down from Dundee to a sold-out theatre when the tickets have been bought . . . Somehow it also meant that the atmosphere was better, oddly enough. You'd think it'd be more fun if it was free.'

Spending cold hard cash on radio recordings was unheard of. The fact that tickets were hot enough to be actually sold in each opulent theatre the Teams visited obviously increased interest further, and before long blagging your way into a two-recording evening of *Clue* when it reached your region had become a game of chance – you had to get in there quick before it sold out. But once you were in, you knew you were in for a good time. It's no wonder that there's a certain smugness attached to those accepted into cliques, when you see the wreaths of smiles adorning those who get to make up the crowd for a *Clue* recording. The flipside of this is the uniquely friendly, warm atmosphere created by thousands of 'insiders', all ready to share the experience of being part of the mob – young and old, male and female, all groaning as one at the same old puns.

Apart from the times when they will cheer together, and be simmered down into a stomach-achingly painful broth of helpless laughter together, and holler 'PRIZES!' as one, it would seem that these *Clue* patrons have little in common. Stephen Fry feels differently, however, from his vantage point behind the microphone: 'There's always that sense that the core audience for *Clue* is a kind of student. A kind of old-fashioned sixties student, almost the kind that could get away with wearing a college scarf, and possibly even have a beard. And he's there with his girlfriend, and he's funny and charming, but he's not a drug-taker and he's not a thrower of stones at windows. He's not a terrible swot, but nor is he a complete rebel. It's very interesting, I suppose it is the embryonic Radio 4 audience . . . Maybe that's just my imagination, but that's how I picture them. Of course when you actually do it, we did one at the Coliseum, which was gigantic, there were thousands and thousands of people there, I think it was one of the biggest audiences they'd ever had. And I was looking at them and thinking, "would I know that was a *Clue* Audience?" And somehow I would, I don't know what it was . . . It was very pleasing.' Rob Brydon has not played the game as much as Stephen, but agrees. 'Audiences are often disparate – the extreme example of that would be somewhere like a Jongleurs comedy club, you know, hen parties and lots of different groups. *Clue* is as far from that as I think it's possible to be. Everybody is of one mind, and that's what you want, as a performer, you want the Audience to be one entity.'

One in the Eye for British Tourism

The nationwide recordings had another happy consequence. There's no question of course that Humph had always been a crucial part of the set-up, the Chairperson par excellence. But besides introducing the Teams and the games and complaining about the whole damn experience in his own way for the previous two decades, Jon Naismith realised that the great man was being underused in every episode of *Clue*. He'd open the show with a withering show of contempt for what his announcements were about to wreak on the listening few, perhaps throwing in a grumble as to how he would be free of it all 'if I could get the negatives . . .' and of course to take issue with the script: 'I wish they wouldn't put "I'd like you to . . ." in this script. I have to read it in a voice vibrant with sincerity, it gets harder every week.' But now they were in a different part of the country every couple of episodes, Humph was called upon to introduce the shows more fully – and doing so in a serious manner was of course out of the question.

At one recording, Humph mentions 'the university town of Cambridge, where our very own Tim Brooke-Taylor got a very respectable 2-2. And I'm glad to say he's wearing it tonight.' When the show reached the Cambridge Arts Theatre, Humph went further: 'I understand that our own Graeme Garden and Tim Brooke-Taylor were undergraduates here before being discovered. Luckily the graduates escaped in the confusion of the police raid and no charges were brought.' In no time at all Humph's insane but scholarly introductions to each show became a solid tradition, and the perfect way to ease into a half-hour of punning perversity, 'the sound of time wasting'. Jon Naismith had no intention of crafting these speeches for the Chairman though, and he called in the services of some of the best scribes working in radio, including Cambridge alumnus Steve Punt, and *Guardian* columnist Peter Bradshaw plus Rob Colley, and the late Debbie Barham – although two writers stood out. 'When I started, I got on Robert Fraser-Steele and Iain, who I knew from *The News Quiz*. Bob is a brilliant writer, he writes for Jonathan Ross and is really at the top of his game. The two of them were just a breathtaking combination, I don't think the links on *The News Quiz* have ever been as good since the two of them wrote for – well, it was Barry Took then. But they were two very different people. Fraser was young, he'd just recently graduated, and Iain was older, and he'd taken early retirement from Shell. So he had grounding in the world, and was financially secure in a way that Fraser wasn't – and Bob Fraser-Steele went into telly and found himself earning tons, and had no desire to return, whereas Iain was happy. It became clear after a while that no one was going to equal Iain's contributions, and he was so committed to the show that I gave him the gig on his own.'

It wasn't until 1996, after quite a few series of toil at the smut-face, that the Sidcup-born suit turned gagsmith Iain Pattinson would become the first writer to receive his own specific 'programme consultant' credit at the end of every show – but giving him the job is a decision that Naismith has never regretted, and indeed his predecessor Geoffrey Perkins called the hiring of Pattinson Naismith's 'masterstroke'. Jon says, 'It has been one of the most selfless decisions I've had to make in my life, to not write for Humphrey. Such was his mastery of delivery that he could make even an average script seem good. I think my scripts were every bit as good as any other producer who worked on the shows, but that wasn't quite the point. The fact is that the show is labour-intensive, and you need someone to concentrate on both the rounds and writing the material. I found it just became very hard work. But of course I loved people coming up to me and saying, "Oh really, do you write those lines? How fantastic! You must be some genius!" and of course all of that I've handed over to Iain . . .'

Humph's intros were astounding comic monologues that Pattinson spent enormous amounts of time carefully constructing to suit his elderly avatar down to the ground. 'I think it's probably A. J. P. Taylor I've got at the back of my mind, delivering a lecture, which is complete and utter nonsense, but sounds as if you could be doing your degree based on it . . .' admits Pattinson. 'A lot of it is just silly jokes, which because Humphrey delivers them in that style, they're much funnier.' His ability to get away with such startlingly risky gags via the sheer curmudgeonly lovability of Humph was perfectly demonstrated at the 1999 recording in Nottingham, home of the Center Parcs holiday resort:

HL: You find us today at the Theatre Royal in Nottingham, a fine city with a fascinating history. The legendary people's hero Robin Hood spent his life nearby. He famously, on his deathbed, shot an arrow from his bow asking that wherever in Sherwood Forest that arrow should land, there he should be laid to rest, and the whole area covered with an enormous plastic bubble for visitors to ride bikes in. It's well documented in official records that the city's original name was 'Snottingham', or 'Home of Snots', but when the Normans came, they couldn't pronounce the letter 'S', so decreed the town be called 'Nottingham' or the 'Home of Notts'. It's easy to understand why this change was resisted so fiercely by the people of Scunthorpe.

As well as these glimpses of Humph's Britain, every opening monologue had to end with a damning introduction for the Teams, the 'four most available', 'not able' performers in the land. 'Incidentally the management have asked me to draw the Audience's attention to the several rough-looking spiv-types previously seen loitering outside the theatre trying to flog tickets for the show at extortionate prices. They are on my left, Barry Cryer and Graeme Garden . . .'

Iain Pattinson would become the source of so much of *I'm Sorry I Haven't a Clue*'s greatness over the next decade and more, that it's irresistible to note the parallel with Morecambe & Wise and Eddie Braben. The nation's favourite double act had been doing very well for themselves for decades,

'That cat from England that blows his ass off', as Louis would have it.
(And didn't he have it?)

Mornington Crescent underground station, London NW1. First one there's the winner.

Graeme Garden, Barry Cryer, Tim Brooke-Taylor and Willie Rushton were given silly things to do by Humphrey Lyttelton, with Colin Sell setting some of them to music, for over twenty years.

The Twenty-first Century Boys, 'We looked after the jokes in their old age, now they can look after us in ours.'

On your left, Jeremy Hardy & Tim Brooke-Taylor with Colin in the giggling corner.

The Great Chairman and 'Harry Potter wannabe' Jon Naismith dispute re-takes.

And on Humph's left, Graeme Garden and Barry Cryer perform another classic
to bring tears to your eyes.

Programme Consultant Iain Pattinson arrives just in time to supply extra gags for
Barry and Tony Hawks' conversation.

'I just had the most awful night-marish dream. A bunch of old men were pointlessly listing London placenames ...' The whole extended family at the Lyric Theatre for *Humph In Wonderland*, December 2007.

Humph and the Teams on stage at the Hammersmith Apollo,
prepared to face their biggest crowd ever.

Backstage at the Apollo: Sex & Cough-Sweets & Rock 'n' Roll.
Many thanks to Samantha for taking this photograph.

'There was something magical about that evening …'
Hammersmith Apollo, London 2008.

with their own TV shows, attempts at movie stardom and successful live cabaret, all mainly written for them by Sid Hills and Dick Green. But it was only when Ken Dodd's gag-man Eddie Braben took over their scripts and reformed them into the adored duo of the BBC *Morecambe & Wise Show* – the rubbish little playwright show-off and his daft macho buddy – that they became officially the nation's favourites. Their shows that united millions at Christmas all started off with one poor Scouser sat at a type-writer on his own, slowly going mad trying to keep up the impossibly high standard, and not disappoint the fans. And that's just what Pattinson has done for *Clue*, rather than accept the higher salaries offered him by TV producers. Jon Naismith prefers to liken the link between Humph and Iain to the legendary fusion of Tony Hancock with Galton and Simpson – but either way Pattinson's words emerging from Lyttelton's mouth has brought us comedy more than fit to be mentioned alongside these greats. 'As a professional gag writer,' Pattinson says, 'to be chosen to write for Humphrey Lyttelton on *I'm Sorry I Haven't a Clue* was like being chosen to play football for England (except when they were good), to win the British Grand Prix, to score the winning run in the best Test Match ever – it's that equivalent. Plenty of times I've been at the odd BBC function, people have come to find me, to say, "I just wanted to meet someone who writes for Humphrey Lyttelton." To hear Humph reading your script, and then to hear that fantastic Audience reaction, is something that other gag writers would kill for. I first noticed, with the first few shows I wrote – I didn't get to the recording and I heard my script coming out on the radio, and it seemed to be about three times funnier than I thought it was on the page. And I have to say, up until that point (I'd been writing for four or five years then), it had generally been the other way round.'

Iain wasn't the first 'programme consultant' by any means, but he was different – he hadn't been in Footlights, for a start. Graeme notes, 'Some of the writers used to turn up now and again, but Iain became a fixture. He would come in the afternoon before the recording with ideas as well as everybody on the Teams, and help out then as well. He became much more integral to the team.' Jon and Iain already had a wealth of experience of comedy and quiz shows between them, and working together, they very quickly managed to take everything that the previous producers of the show had worked into the *Clue* hotchpotch and rejuvenate, twist and otherwise remould each running gag into a new form, wringing every drop of comedy potential out of each round and introduction, right up to the newly embroidered farewells. Where once Humph was happy to just drawl 'From me, it's goodbye', Pattinson would create wonderfully elaborate valedictions in the name of Fate and Eternity, Hope and Disappointment, as well as very silly announcements like 'Well, with Mickey Mouse's hand pointing upwards, and Goofy's tail pointing downwards . . . I realise my Rolex is a fake. And also that it's the end of the show . . .' The old Humphrey Barclay trick of not letting any part of the show slack on the gag-rate was performed to perfection, and soon the bits in between games were anticipated by the Audience with at least an equal excitement to the rounds themselves.

Once established as an indispensable part of the team, Iain was especially lucky to be taken into the confidence of Samantha. For years she had remained silent, only occasionally meriting a mention from the Teams, but when Iain and Humph realised what a fascinating, eventful life the beauty lived, the show reached new heights of hilarity. As the constant search for female talent continued, Naismith also saw Samantha's more active role as a good way to put sexism to bed. 'I remember when we took over the show we used to get quite a few letters accusing us of sexist references to Samantha. It was quite true that before my time there were several references to her breast size. However, since we discovered she's a raving nymphomaniac we've not had a single complaint.'

That's as maybe, but Humph remained insistent that the biographical bon mots that Samantha permitted him to relay to the Audience were entirely innocent. *I'm Sorry I Haven't a Clue* has always had a thick throbbing streak of bawdiness, with double entendres aplenty, just like *ISIRTA* – but the filthy minds of the Audiences as the nineties wore on would prove exasperating to the Chairman. And the Teams were no better – he couldn't even say 'Lest you go on for too long, I'd remind you that Samantha's on the lookout, and I've got the horn' without Willie observing that 'He seems such a nice old man!' 'They always do!' Barry would tut in disapproval, but poor old Humph had no responsibility for the way his barely voluntary reading of the script was twisted by filthy minds.

If you take, for instance, the jolly titbit 'Incidentally, exciting news! Samantha tells me she's expecting a visit from a film producer in her dressing room after the show, with news of a part he's been holding for her. He seems sure she's going to make it big!' then you can see just what a harmless, simple instance of support for the scorer that is, when written on the page. But somehow Humph's delivery could give the wrong impression and create an explosion of shocked hilarity that often took several minutes to dispel. Lyttelton of course had no idea that what he was saying could be misconstrued – 'That's my story,' he insisted, 'and I'm sticking to it.' Instead, he would seem genuinely puzzled at the huge response that would come from a nugget like 'Samantha says when it comes to criminals, there's nothing she finds more satisfying than hardened ones being put away by the yard.' Only once in the show's history did he actually cotton on, when the fact that 'Earlier Samantha went down to the Gramophone Library to choose the Teams' records. While she was there, the kindly old archivist usually asks Samantha to do some routine maintenance tasks for him, including checking the ancient sound equipment. This week it was cleaning off some rust, replacing record needles, and attending to a stiff knob on his list of tasks. It was quite a long one, so she asked if he didn't mind her sitting on it for a while . . .' elicited an unusually dirty and elongated guffaw from the Audience. Humph gazed around at the helpless mirth, crying out 'What?' with his usual pained expression. 'Oh, I *see!*' he finally cried, and upbraided the crowd with an outraged 'Filthy beasts!' delivered through gritted teeth.

Singalong-a-Clue
This last observation of course came from the intro to the round 'Pick Up Song', which debuted in 1976, right back in Simon Brett's day – although, as has been observed, at first it was known as 'Singalong'. The names got switched in the early nineties, but the challenge of having the panellists accompany a genuine song track, dropping out the sound for an agonising period of time, and then bringing it back to see if the singer is 'within a gnat's crotchet' or 'a cheesy quaver' of the original, has always been a crowd-pleaser – with the added bonus, for Humph, that it didn't require any participation from Colin Sell. Although the round still caused him agonies, and he could be heard to bleat, 'I'd got out of the habit of prayer until I had to sit here waiting for that damn tape to come back in . . .'

This was yet another game which asked for no quick thinking on the part of the player, a willingness to appear stupid being all that was needed. Perhaps it begged for a modicum of skill – Willie's early attempt to sing along to 'The Girl from Ipanema' fell foul of his usual rhythm problems, and there was a lot more than a gnat's crotchet of lag when the music came back in, meriting the chastisement 'I've just done that bit, you silly bitch!' from Rushton. But he soon got into the swing of it, especially once Naismith had promoted the occasional round to pride of place in the 'One Song to the Tune of Another' slot. 'Pick Up Song' became an excuse for the most excessively ragged renditions of standards and pop hits, with cries of 'Your glasses, please!' usually bellowed out by Cryer as the singer reached for the high notes (especially on a drunken anthem like 'Danny Boy'), before the crowd simply roared their approval at the sign of the slightest synchronicity when the gramophone recording returned. 'What would you do if they actually came back in time with the music?' asked Humph, disapprovingly, 'Orgasm, I should think.'

It was Samantha's job to visit the BBC Gramophone Archives and seek out the desired tunes, which ranged from classical opera right up to Tim's buoyant delivery of Althea and Donna's 'Uptown Top Ranking', and modern tunes like

'Teenage Dirtbag' and 'Because I Got High'. Even Colin got a look-in once or twice, vamping wildly and jazzily when Tchaikovsky's Piano Concerto No. 1 in B-Flat Minor faded out, only to receive an enormous ovation for coming in bang on the right note. 'This is the worst moment of my life,' whimpered the Chairman. Samantha, being the cordial soul that she is, made a lot of friends down in the archives, as Humph was keen to relate: 'DJ Samantha has completed her customary research down in the Gramophone Archives. As the kindly old archivists can't get out much these days, Samantha sells them light snacks and confectionary. Initially they were shocked by her prices, so she offers selected discounts. There's been nothing off Mars bars, but they were delighted to see Samantha's Snickers come down at a price they could afford.'

The latest news from Samantha wasn't the only reason that 'Pick Up Song' became a crowd-pleaser. Naismith and Pattinson began to introduce prizes right out of the 'Unnovations' catalogue for the best performance (ranging from Loyd Grossman Linguaphone cassettes, Dalek bread, a Dusty Bin Laden, semi-precious scones, cordless pyjamas, a leather-bound cow or rechargeable battery hen, to 'the very latest in transcendental furnishing, an occasional table' or 'two weeks on a luxury lino') and the duo also provided an extra chance for the Audience to butt in. As in the Playhouse days, the Audience has always been a crucial ingredient, whether it was cheering the announcement of a favourite round, groaning at an obvious howler or applauding when a guessing Team is warm (or often, still extremely cold).

'Pick Up Song', then, was always a good moment for the mob to join in, when the spirit took them, clapping or even singing along in encouragement (and usually steering the singer way off course in the process). However, Humph's script soon required him to encourage further Audience participation – whether he liked it or not. Never being one for catchphrases, Humph threw in a side swipe at the king of them, Bruce Forsyth, just as a one-off: 'What do points mean?' And of course, the Pavlovian response roared back at the stage – 'PRIZES!'

In an echo of the disdain shown by the staff of Radio Prune at the excessive volume of the Audience, *Clue*'s voluble crowd could often take Humph and the Teams by surprise. 'Zeig Heil!' shouted Barry at the Nuremberg Rally-esque reception they were getting as early as 1975, and although Humph echoed this consternation at the rabble's noise, the new call-and-response slot gave him plenty of opportunity to mess with the crowd. 'Yes, well done,' he would patronise them after another 'PRIZES!' moment. 'Now let's try another one – HEIL HITLER!' or 'I just got 1,200 people making complete prats of themselves . . . a very intoxicating feeling. Tonight Plymouth, tomorrow the world!' What power he had at his fingertips, the whole Audience putty in his hands and eager to repeat anything he told them to. 'What do points mean? – GATWICK AIRPORT!' was obediently called back at the Chairman on one occasion. 'Do you know what you just said?' Humph replied with disgust. However, the Audience knew their limit:

HL: Points mean . . . operation devices to divert trains so they don't crash into each other, what do points mean?

AUDIENCE: PRIZES!?

HL: OK, you play your game and I'll play mine.

'Pick Up Song' obviously caught on with the public, as before long it was making a regular appearance on the Mike Smith-fronted panel game *That's Showbusiness*, which spread its cheesiness onto Saturday teatimes on BBC1 from 1989. The basic idea was still gaining ratings of some kind in the twenty-first century, with cheap formats such as *Don't Forget the Lyrics*, presented by Shane Richie on Sky One, recycling much the same concept. But despite casting the irrepressible Kenny Everett as Team Captain in the first series, opposite Gloria Hunniford, the blandness of *That's Showbusiness* made the game-cribbing a little hard to bear.

HL: Now we go on to a very entertaining game which I came across while watching the recent television series *That's Showbusiness*, with Mike Smith. In it people sing along to a song they're given, and the song is then faded out. The object is for them to be in time with the music when it's faded back again . . . Brilliant. I don't know where they get their ideas from . . .

BC: Humph, the producer of that television show's Christian name is Nick.

HL: Ah, that explains it all . . . To somebody. Not me.

Another boot was got in when Humph introduced a relatively new round, 'Hitler's Diaries', in which 'Teams should take turns to read extracts from the private diaries of famous people, either still living, or appearing on *That's Showbusiness* . . .'

It's Only TV, But . . .

That's Showbusiness ended up running in some form for several years, but in the nineties the real boom in panel games came in the shape of usually post-watershed high-concept comedy vehicles for the stars of *Whose Line Is It Anyway?*, all trying to compete with the massive success of *Have I Got News For You*. Whether it was Rory McGrath looking uncomfortable on the garish set of *A Word in Your Era* (introducing a trio of comics playing historical characters justifying their immortality), Tony Slattery invigilating two teams' battle to see who knows the most about etiquette in *P's and Q's* or medicine in *Tibs and Fibs*, Nick Hancock questioning *Question of Sport's* comedy content with *They Think It's All Over*, Tony Hawks playing Chairman between Alan Davies and Fred Macaulay for advertising panel game *The Best Show in the World . . . Probably* or any of the other multifarious, tenuous comedy game shows (with or without Tony Slattery in them), the decade was drenched in a tidal wave of humorous gameplay. The 'money for old rope' road-to-Damascus realisation that Graeme had back at the turn of the seventies was by now apparently one of the central creeds of the independent TV companies that were fuelling British comedy. He agrees. 'I think the show gave rise to a whole lot of . . . I don't know, postmodern panel games. Everything, from *Have I Got News* and *Never Mind the Buzzcocks* and all those, you know, *They Think It's All Over*, they're all similarly based – you get some funny people on the panel and then give them what appears to be a straight game to play, but actually it's there as a platform for them to bounce off and do their gags . . . before plunging to the earth!'

Loose gag-based celebrity shows in the mould of *Joker's Wild* or Lenny Bennett's *Punchlines* still popped up occasionally as well, notably Jonathan Ross keeping order between Bob Monkhouse and Frank Skinner in *Gag Tag*. Then there was Julian Clary mincing through *Sticky Moments* on Channel 4, and taking on Phill Jupitus with Ross again in the chair for *It's Only TV But I Like It* (a Jon Naismith Production at one time), or Jupitus with Mark Lamarr or Simon Anstell and Sean Hughes or Bill Bailey in the music quiz *Never Mind the Buzzcocks*, still running after more than a dozen years . . . The list is very long, twisted, tangled and exhaustive – and no matter how the panellists pretend otherwise, the game (and scoring of points) in all these shows was, and remains, irrelevant.

With so many others getting in on the game, perhaps it was wrong for the *I'm Sorry I Haven't a Clue* team ever to make any attempt to cross over to television. The fuss of make-up and lights and autocues and warm-ups and God knows what else a transference required will always seem alien to the *I'm Sorry* spirit. What, after all, was the point in risking a move of media when you're already one of the greatest radio shows of all time? But try it they did. And they even outlined their motives in an in-show limerick in 1994:

> When turning on BBC2,
> I thought, 'They need something brand new.
> Something witty and funny,
> That doesn't cost money.
> Why not Sorry I Haven't A Clue?

When the gang was approached by ex-producer Paul Spencer to attempt a pilot of the show for Central TV (where he was now Head of Comedy), Barry and Graeme were up for the challenge, there wasn't exactly a mutiny or much of a whoop of delight from Humph or Tim, but Willie was particularly adamant that it was a fruitless project. As Barry recalls: 'Willie jumped both ways, he said "It'll never work, it's pure radio," and then he enjoyed it. But he said, "We'll do six tellies and it'll kill the radio show," which was quite a shrewd remark, actually.' Jon Naismith was in agreement – 'I've never thought a TV version of the show was a good idea, because I think it would look ordinary on TV whereas as a radio show it's clearly extraordinary' – but he let them get on with it. After all, no format was more suited to sound-only than *Clue*'s big sister, *Just a Minute*, and that perennial favourite was transferred to TV on more than one occasion for both cosy daytime BBC1 and late-night ITV, both times with Nicholas Parsons still on board, plus regulars Peter Jones and Clement Freud, our own Barry Cryer, Tony Hawks, Linda Smith and many more – although Paul Merton eschewed both series. Besides an on-screen countdown, the odd crowbarred-in visual subject, and a rather desperately garish last stab featuring Dale Winton and Tony Slattery as Team Captains, *Just a Minute* remained much the same on both its TV runs, and the transfers never really took off. There was even a TV version of *Quote Unquote* after a fashion, *Don't Quote Me* being presented by none other than Geoffrey Perkins.

So Spencer and Garden knew they had their work cut out to make *Clue* work on-screen. As Harry Hill might say, so much of *Clue*'s humour relies on 'the power of suggestion', that to replace the mental image of a long-suffering Humph dealing with the inanity of his situation with the reality, was a risky business. Still, they managed to win Willie round, at least for a pilot, and the full line-up (with the glaring omission of Colin at the piano) turned up at the Nottingham studios to give it a whirl. Barry shrugs, 'We had all sorts of grandiose ideas as to how to do it on telly, but we did it quite simply as a filmed radio show . . .'

'We tried to put some visual games in,' Graeme protests, 'like, there was a glass-fronted box and you had to put your hands in and sort of feel something, and tell what it was.' This was a souped-up version of the forgotten *Clue* round 'Feelies', in which the mystery objects often turned out to be along the lines of a sausage and two plums. '. . . And it didn't work!' he admits with a sigh. 'There were maybe two, three visual-type games which just for some reason didn't work at all. So there was virtually no point in making it for television, the one real televisual element was not adding anything . . . It was tricky because Humph was reading his cards, and that's the image we all have of him, he delivers his line, looks up and gets the Audience reaction. But on television it somehow didn't work, and he didn't feel he'd be competent with a teleprompt machine.'

The Central heads were keen to give the show a try if some of the regulars were replaced with younger stars, of the Fry/Merton variety, but Barry quite rightly remembers 'We said, "No, it's our show, at least start with us! And then we can go into the guest thing, you know" . . . So it all fizzled out, and nothing happened. And I think it was all for the best!'

Not that there weren't plenty of other TV projects for them all – Willie was the default panel member supporting David Frost on *Through the Keyhole* and *The Ultra Quiz*, Tim had presented *Britain's Got Talent* forerunner *The Fame Game* for Granada in 1985 (allegedly featuring very young efforts from Harry Enfield and John Sparkes) and *Qd – The Master Game* on Channel 4 in 1991, while Barry, as well as being a regular in Dictionary Corner on *Countdown*, had been quizmaster on shows as diverse as *Crosswits*, *Those Wonderful TV Times* and *Music Match*, a BBC1 show from 1987 in which he kept order over Willie's Team Captain, ruthlessly trying to trounce his nemesis Liza Goddard in the musical knowledge stakes. Graeme, as well as presenting 1977's *Tell Me More* and 1989's *Tell the Truth* (*Child's Play*-esque and *What's My Line*-ish formats respectively), also took over Bernard Cribbins's running of the far more *Clue*-like kids' show *Star Turn* on BBC1 at the turn of the eighties. But perhaps the most exciting sounding TV *Clue*-alike remains long forgotten, and Graeme co-starred in it with Willie. 'There was a strange show Willie and I did down in Southampton for one of those southern TV companies in the eighties or late seventies, and I think it was called *Ask a Silly Answer*. Terry Wogan was in the chair, and one team was Willie and Alfred Marks, and the other team was me and Spike Milligan. And there were two girls who were Page Three Girls from the *Sun*, who were referred to as Bob and Alf . . . and I think it was kind of an attempt to do *Clue* on television . . . I can remember nothing about the show, what we had to do.' If a team as stellar as that could provide no comedy worth remembering, then it's clear just how next to impossible it is to make a TV Antidote to Panel Games work, so it's no wonder that there was only one attempt to play *Clue* in front of the cameras.

Besides, by 1995 a rough pilot which had featured in the BBC2 special evening of programming *At Home With Vic & Bob* in 1993 had become Reeves & Mortimer's breakthrough quiz vehicle *Shooting Stars*, without doubt the most confusing, obtuse and hilarious antidote to panel games that TV has seen. This senseless bulldozering of all the rules of panel games (in which questions like 'Macaulay Culkin is a child, but can you name an adult?' or 'Who's a cheeky boy then?' were probably about as close to a real quiz show as the series got) is certainly Jon Naismith's nomination for the nearest TV has ever managed to get to the madness of *Clue*. 'I think *Shooting Stars* was the purest of imitators, because it just took the piss out of a panel show. It had no proper score, it had no proper rounds, it took the piss out of the guests, nothing mattered. It probably took *Clue's* sort of ironic panel game thing to the very limits, but it very much followed in its footsteps.'

Unlike *Clue*, though, the humour of *Shooting Stars* came almost exclusively from the presenters themselves – plus Matt Lucas as the great big baby George Dawes, a horrendous anti-Samantha keeping Team Captains Mark Lamarr (or Will Self, or Jack Dee) and Ulrika-ka-ka Jonsson's scores while banging away on the drums – and decidedly not from the celebrity panellists, who were best advised to play the game as seriously as they could and try and get through to the end. Nevertheless, both Tim and Bill Oddie took the bait and managed to keep up with the Reeves & Mortimer brand of lunacy, just about. To those who never experienced the cries of 'Eranu' and 'Uvavu', the spectacle of the Dove From Above and all the other myriad mental elements that made up *Shooting Stars*, Tim Brooke-Taylor's cheery introduction (delivered as the guest slowly and disconsolately rotated on a pitiful platform) can be only the slightest taster of its humour: 'Gormless Tim is often mistaken for Latino tennis hulk, Andre Agassi – in fact he's so preposterously handsome that he is often forced to hang olives on his pecker, to fend off his armies of lustful female admirers.'

From Rhyl with Love
Listening again to the decades of *Clue* recordings, one of the most striking realisations is just how many of the traditions of the modern show started off a lot earlier than is generally believed. Over the years there have been plenty of running gags that have come and gone – for the first decade or so, for instance, Joan Collins was namechecked in every other show, as a kind of Lady Constance-gone-wrong figure, movies like *The Bitch* and *The Stud* giving her a reputation for grotty salaciousness that the Teams were quick to condemn with mock-moralising – there was nothing she wouldn't do. One round of the game 'Find a Date in the Diary on which Everyone Can Make the Next Recording' featured Willie's excuse: 'I can't make the 7th, I'm taking a sexual assault course at the Joan Collins Adventure Playground ...' and for the Newsagents' Ball, Graeme announced: 'Here comes Joan Collins. She's got a *Mail on Sunday*, two *Mirrors* and an *Observer* ...' The sad side story to this mockery is that when Humph first became established as the most swinging horn-blower in post-war London, allegedly his number-one fan was a besotted teenage Joan Collins, who would make googly eyes at her jazz-playing idol every night he played. How different things could have been for them both ...

Luckily for Collins, times changed – in their later years the Teams were more likely to make jokes about Jordan or Posh Spice or Anne Widdecombe

– and the motif was dropped. Each producer, as well as Graeme and the Teams, had to start each series with a good knowledge of which old favourites were going to resurface and which were best left on the shelf, and Jon and Iain were very careful about choosing the traditions that they wanted to continue – not that it was always by choice. For instance, during the eighties, although the heaving postbags that Geoffrey Perkins used to get concerning Mornington Crescent had shrunk in size somewhat, there was always at least one insistent correspondent fighting to be heard among the avalanche of mail. It wasn't unusual for Humph to read out the odd letter from fans and fools on-air, and indeed past Mornington Crescent competitions had been held with the listeners via post. But after years of persistence, it wasn't until the very last show of 1990, nearly Christmas time, that Humph read out the very first letter . . . 'From a Mrs Trellis, of North Wales, who writes, "I think your Mornington Crescent Elevator Reconstruction Fund is a noble cause, and it has my full support." Well, that's just typical of the many thousands of letters we receive each week . . . from Mrs Trellis.' She was clearly very happy to have finally been given some recognition, because lo and behold, there she was again at the end of the following series, doing her bit for the 'C.S.R.H.H.': 'Very sorry to hear about the loss of your hooter – have you thought about looking down the back of my cooker? I always lose things back there.'

Naismith must have been bemused at the colossal postbag that came with his new job, and the sheer weight of them postmarked 'North Wales', because he didn't twig and allow any more of Mrs Trellis' letters to be read out on-air until he was a couple of series into his tenure, where it was revealed that her Fantasy Mornington Crescent line-up would consist of Bruce Willis, Tom Cruise, Richard Gere and Graeme Garden. Who was this woman? She claimed to be a fan of *I'm Sorry I Haven't a Clue*, but she never once got the Chairman's name right.

HL: 'Dear Ned, Wonderful, marvellous, extraordinary, remarkable . . . are just four of the many words on page 93 of my new Thesaurus. Yours sincerely, truly, faithfully, Mrs Trellis. P.S. How about some signed photographs?' Well, thank you, Mrs Trellis, they're very nice.

If we sift through the paperchain of clues which *Clue*'s ultimate fan – a sort of female Angus Prune – has left over nearly twenty years of obsessive letter-writing, we remain none the wiser. She is once described as 'holidaying in Rhyl', and yet she has also claimed to be the head of the Rhyl and District Naturalists' Mornington Crescent Society, passing on the tip 'Tits like

Coconuts! . . . but sparrows prefer breadcrumbs'. Elsewhere she is identified as 'Endeavour Trellis', and there are whispers of her being a kind of Mornington Crescent savant. But the North Wales telephone directory contains no Endeavour Trellis (the Christian name may be a red herring), and only three Trellises in the Rhyl district. When contacted, one of these claimed not to have a radio at all, one was a businessman who lived alone, and the third spoke only in Welsh (although it was gleaned that the partner of the apparently enraged man who answered could not come to the phone as she was at the post office with her forklift truck, picking up stamps).

An Autumn Almanac

With this precise chemistry of hoary old gags and hoary new gags created and strung out by themselves, Naismith and Pattinson provided the strongest framework for the Teams to play in that they'd had for years. Reaching, or indeed, soaring past retirement age, and with their children growing up, and having children of their own, the side job that this bunch of elder statesmen had been sharing over three decades became an ever more important date in the diary, six trips to a fine British town or city a year, still getting away with their silly games up and down the land.

The Teams often travelled to each venue separately – Barry, having admirably lived for seven decades without ever taking a driving test, often came by rail; Humph without fail made his own way to recordings in his old Volvo, no matter how long the journey may be, right up to the fiftieth series. In 1994, the comedian and political activist Mark Thomas wrote an extensive celebratory article on Barry for the *Mail on Sunday* (of all publications), and in this celebration Humph made it clear that the Team were very happily sliding into old age together, and took some time to appraise his unruly charges: 'Barry's greatest asset is that he enjoys himself. In *I'm Sorry I Haven't a Clue*, you can always hear him roaring with laughter. The Audience love that. Everybody on the show contributes something special. Graeme Garden has the dry wit, Tim Brooke-Taylor is the one the Audience sympathises with. Willie Rushton offers the satirical humour. And Barry, I always say, is the mortar of the show, its cement. He has a gag for every occasion. I must say he wouldn't be a bad person to be marooned on a desert island with. Never a dull moment, for the first fifteen years . . .'

Until Jon Naismith took over the show, there was a decidedly ad hoc feel to every half-hour broadcast in the name of *Clue*, the listener never really knowing when each well-loved game would crop up. Somehow, Naismith's decision to form a solid, predictable line-up made for a more enjoyable, crowd-pleasing show. The first half would kick off with a warm-up round of punning (maybe 'Cost-Cutters' or 'Wuthering Hillocks', which debuted in the eighties and saw the Teams suggesting cut-price entertainments such as *Only Horses*, *A Dance to the Music of Tim*, *The Tetchy Sink*, *The Concise Oxford Word*, or Bruce Willis in *Stub Your Toe Hard*), followed inevitably by 'One Song to the Tune of Another', and usually ending on a 'Complete Quotes'-style quiz.

Then, after the interval, the second show recorded would put 'Pick Up Song' in the musical spot, generally followed by the big Mornington Crescent match (preceded very often by a flurry of 'Historical Headlines' such as Garden's Arthurian headline for *The Times* 'WHO GETS SEAT AT ROUND TABLE? "IT'S A LOTTERY", SAYS CAMELOT BOSS', Barry's 1066 nomination for the *Daily Mail*, 'ILLEGAL IMMIGRANTS SWARM INTO HASTINGS' or the *Sun* featuring Macbeth's death with 'PHEW, WHAT A SCOTCHMAN!' plus of course endless *Guardian* misprints) and ending on a different 'Complete Quotes'-alike game where the Teams had to pre-empt the nub of 'Handy Hints', or guess how Humph's choice of local proverbs could end, such as in the following extract with Tony Hawks in Plymouth, where Humph, not terribly tolerant of superstition at the best of times, really lost it:

HL: Tony, according to a Devon custom, how might a man find a girl-friend with the use of a snail?

TH: I don't know, but if it works I'll be well pissed off. I've just spent thirty grand on a Porsche.

HL: The answer is that you take a snail from a gooseberry bush and place it in some ashes.

TH: I want to meet the women in this part of the world.

HL: No, the letter it makes in the ash will be the name of your lover . . . What a load of tosh!

HL: Graeme again, complete the following rhyme, recited by Devon girls in front of a bowl of . . . (*Long pause, as he tries to control himself.*) I tell you, I can't get out of this county quick enough! – Graeme again, complete the following rhyme, recited by Devon girls in front of a bowl of water . . . (*giggling*) with the letters of the alphabet in it. 'I place my shoes in the letter T, in the hope . . .'

GG: '. . . I'll pass English GCSE.'

HL: Well, it's really, 'My true love I shall see.' . . . What does it mean, Tony, if a shrew passes over your foot in Shaftesbury?

TH: You get shafted in Shrewsbury.

HL: I'm afraid the answer is you'll walk with a limp for the rest of your life.

BC: With a limp what?

The solid structure of the shows seemed to heighten the Audience's expec-
tation for each old favourite, and every returning game began to get bigger
and better cheers as the years went by. There wasn't a trace of doubt left that
I'm Sorry I Haven't a Clue didn't just belong on radio rather than TV, it was
finally, after years of skulking round the back of the bike-sheds of Radio 4,
the funniest, most loved show on the air.

Having always been broadcast in rotation with *The News Quiz* on
Saturdays at lunchtime, before a Monday-evening repeat, the arrival of James
Boyle as Head of Radio 4 in the nineties signalled what felt like a dramatic
change for *Clue*, as it now debuted on Mondays with a Sunday-lunchtime
repeat. As Jon recalls, 'It changed for not a bad reason – James Boyle wanted
to have satire on Fridays, which is a pretty good idea in itself. So we were
moved from Saturdays, to Sunday repeats.' As with any Radio 4 scheduling
change, *Clue*'s move to the Monday night 6.30 p.m. slot had caused consternation at first, but it turned out to be the ideal spot for the jewels in the
station's crown, with *Just a Minute* alternating with *Clue*, and then *Quote
Unquote* stepping into *The News Quiz* slot to fill the gap. Sadly, this meant
that millions of *Radio Times*-less readers tuning in for a laugh were often
disappointed by the discovery of a very cosy literary quotation quiz, and
although most of the gang and even Humph himself had guested on *Quote
Unquote* in the past, Nigel Rees's show was to come in for a real kicking over
the years in *Clue* – such as Humph's description of it as the programme 'which
we all find, quote unquote, amusing'. Or indeed, his admission 'I heard a very
funny joke at the end of *Quote Unquote* last week . . . they said they have a
"Listen Again" facility. Good one, Nigel!'

'We've had some great fun at *Quote Unquote*'s expense,' admits Naismith.
'But to be honest it's not its fault – it's a quiz show, it's not a comedy show!
It doesn't belong in that slot.'

I'm Sorry I Haven't a Clue on the other hand flourished on Monday evenings,
and became the jewel of the three programmes in that time slot, never needing
any introduction, beyond 'This is Radio 4', launching right into 'The Schickel
Shamble', to the delight of millions. Humph's introduction to the 1995
Christmas special, 'Now when I think back on what a year 1995 has been for
this programme, all that comes to mind is award after award. But I'm pleased
to say that Matron has granted the Teams a day release . . .' was disingenuous
– by this point the Teams had picked up the Sony Gold Award for Radio
Comedy for the first time – and then a British Comedy Award.

'It was a nice surprise,' admits Graeme, 'I think we'd all won awards for
various things in the past anyway, and were aware that awards can sometimes
be a double-edged sword – sometimes if you win an award you don't work
again for the next three years. I think we took it in the spirit in which it was

offered, but we didn't go overboard. Everyone who gets an award says it doesn't really mean anything, "we keep it in the lavatory" and stuff like that, but I think that's a bit mean-spirited really. It's a bit rude to the other people who were up for the award if you diss it the minute you're given it. They could quite rightfully come up to you afterwards and say, "If you don't want it, I'll have it!"' Perhaps a more meaningful appreciation had already been shown in 1992, when estate agent Stephanie Slater was abducted and imprisoned in a coffin by Michael Sams. After her horrific ordeal she announced that the one sign of hope she had throughout was the sound of laughter coming from the radio, as the Teams batted old jokes about. Talk about the power of laughter.

After four years in the role, Jon Naismith could undoubtedly have given himself a pat on the back and moved on to his great TV career at this point, but the idea never really entered his head. 'Onwards and upwards' was always his motto, and he had no intention of resting on his laurels and letting *Clue* slacken the pace. These 'old farts' had beaten the young comics at the Sony Awards, and the show could only get better and better as each irreplaceable part of the chemistry matured, ripened and improved. The brainwave of having young tykes like Merton and Hardy stepping in had of course helped the show find a bigger following than ever before, luring in those who hitherto would never have made the time to tune in to Radio 4 at the end of a day's slog. Cryer and Rushton especially sparked brilliantly off the younger guest panellists, but with the inevitable return of the Prodigal Regular, the true line-up – those four time-weathered veterans who had totted up enough hours of casual wisecracking and saucy extemporisation to schedule several days of continuous badinage – was always intact at the end of each series, to greater cheers than even in the previous year.

The Last Will Testament

The second series of 1996 had been a blast, taking the Teams to Liverpool (the city named after Carla Lane sitcom *The Liver Birds*, but so nearly named 'It-Ain't-Half-Hot-Mum-erpool'), Northampton (described as 'The Naples of the Midlands', or at least as often as Naples is described as 'The Northampton of Lombardy'), and ending up at the Cambridge Arts Theatre. They'd had an unbroken run of the whole gang being together for every recording, and were on a roll. In Northampton, they'd kicked back with a random game of 'Trivial Hirsutes' – the popular board game about hairiness which called for extensive dice-rattling. Of course, it was just another excuse for showing up the lunacy of board games – just as in the past they'd played Monopoly with a real dog as a counter, and Chance cards reading 'You are caught short during the second act of the London Palladium. Miss a turn.'

Stephen Fry once wrote, 'It was *homo ludens* who first rose to take his place above the other creatures, not *homo sapiens*,' arguing that games-playing was 'one of mankind's best and most distinctive instincts'. But for a man who has filled most of his career with silly games of all kinds, Graeme Garden is not a fan of trivial pastimes. Far from being the kind of party guest who insists that everyone congregates for a jovial bout of charades or blind man's buff, he sighs, 'I'm not a great games player. I think *Clue* is not a show for people who like games, because it's an annoying send-up of games, saying how stupid people are to give themselves bizarre rules and then try to follow them . . . I must admit that as a kid my heart would sink when they announced it was time for games. I can play a game and enjoy it, but like a lot of families, every Christmas we'd buy a board game – some new game would be in the shops, and you'd play it once. Or possibly not even once, you'd get halfway through it and then eventually everyone gets tired of, sort of, finding the seven jewels that you have to take to the pyramid before the cobra strikes . . . I think, on balance, games are more disappointing than satisfying.'

The Cambridge show had been a particular barnstormer. The Teams had given 'Unhelpful Advice' to those who are getting married (Willie suggesting 'It's not enough to say "I'm going down the pub". You've got to say "I'm going down the pub *darling*. Here's the Hoover"'), announced the 'Late Arrivals' at the Undertakers' Ball, and compiled an exhaustive list of programmes to be featured on 'Children's Channel 4'. Humph advised them that 'It'll help to have in mind an image of childish innocence tinged with sinister corruption . . . so think "Andi Peters"', and so they came up with *Chitty Chitty Gang Bang*, *101 Reservoir Dalmatians* (directed by Quentin Dandyandbeano), *Electric Blue Peter*, *Bill and Ben Behaving Badly*, *Muffin' the Mule*, *Postman Pat Always Rings Twice*, *Jackanorgy*, *Last Tango in Trumpton*, *Swallows and Amorous Nuns*, and the topper, from Willie, *Lust William*. Besides singing the words of 'Y.M.C.A.' to 'Greensleeves', Willie also managed to give the most note-perfect 'Pick Up Song' performance of his career, getting 'Rawhide' bang on the crotchet, and there was more singing to be done when he and Tim all but closed the show with their rendition of their alter egos Her Majesty the Queen and Princess Margaret singing the Beverley Sisters classic 'Sisters'.

But once Humph had noticed that it was time to go, 'As the short-sighted rhino of Time attempts to mount the VW Beetle of Eternity, and the rubber glove of Hope gets lost in the Aberdeen Angus of Destiny . . .' the Teams headed off for their usual convivial after-show slap-up feed. Willie, however, usually the most eager of the bunch to take command of the festivities and get the first round in, gave his apologies and just headed off to the hotel for an early night. This was almost unheard of, but he'd explained to the rest of the gang that he'd been feeling a little off colour and his wife had compelled him to submit himself to a doctor's poking and prodding, resulting in a summons to the hospital not long after the recording to 'have my bloody plumbing sorted'. He'd already made his apologies to Barry that he'd have to perform as 'One Old Fart in the Night' for a while, but he made it clear to everyone that it was but a hiccup, and they wished him goodnight and went their separate ways.

Looking back, it almost seems as if the early to mid nineties was the epicentre of a cruel exodus of comic legends from the land of the living. Maybe it began with the double blow of losing Frankie Howerd and Benny Hill in one weekend in 1992, followed all too swiftly by Les Dawson, then Peter Cook at the start of 1995 . . . but it feels rather like the last blow came one dark December night in 1996 when news leaked out that Willie Rushton had died on the operating table while undergoing triple bypass heart surgery. Despite the warning they'd had, it came as a shock to every one of his fellow players of *Clue* – in fact, to everyone. Willie was just one of those forces of nature, the Bacchanalian figure par excellence, a great, galumphing Lord of Misrule whose loss could only be seen as a ridiculous mistake. Sadly, his great friend Peter Cook had been just such a larger than life, irrepressible force, another performer whose comic genius was positively *needed* by his friends and fans, and who should have been firing out wisecracks year after year until he got his Telegram from the Queen – and he too had proven all too mortal.

The sadness of Willie's death was keenly felt up and down the country – not just thanks to *Clue*, but for thousands of *Private Eye* subscribers, and to children who had grown up with his readings of *Winnie-the-Pooh* or *Asterix* or providing the voice for the insane plasticine cartoon *Trap Door*. The sadness of missing the great man's cartoons, his occasional TV appearance, the possibility of a further iteration of *Two Old Farts in the Night* and the simple knowledge that he was in the world is one thing – but the situation that arose from his eccentric absence was a rare and unpleasant one, experienced only by the longest running shows. Could it survive? Was the programme, and all it represented, strong enough to overcome the loss of such an unbelievably crucial ingredient? Or – gulp – would *I'm Sorry I Haven't a Clue* stop at twenty-eight seasons?

The Rushton family insisted that Willie's last show was broadcast as normal, and it went out only three days after the sad news, with an introduction from *TW3* mastermind and close friend, Ned Sherrin:

> On two public occasions since Willie's death, all people have wanted
> to ask me about has been Will . . . He watched the world and its follies
> with such a sharp, intelligent and observant eye. Had he not, he would

not have been the great cartoonist and insightful caricaturist that he was. Willie was both one of nature's toffs and the people's champion. He grew funnier and funnier as a witty, life-enhancing English eccentric. And never did his spontaneous comic genius flourish more splendidly than on *I'm Sorry I Haven't a Clue*. Enjoy his last contribution to the programme, as wholeheartedly as Willie enjoyed recording it.

As for the future of the show – it was just too early to say. Humph after all was well into his seventies, and Jon had already been on the show longer than most of his predecessors, and tradition dictated a change – or an ending. For the meantime, though, the mourning of Willie's loss was going to be a full-time occupation. Cricket had always been of the utmost importance to Will – not only did he illustrate a book co-authored by Fred Trueman and Eric Morecambe, *The Thoughts of Trueman Now*, he also frequently played hookey from *Clue* between 1986 and 1993 by playing Team Captain opposite Tim Rice in the Brian Johnston-chaired radio panel game *Trivia Test Match* (a thoroughly confusing quiz in the form of a cricket match, with guests including Paul Merton and Stephen Fry), so it was fitting that his ashes should be buried under the boundary at that cricketing mecca, the Oval. His memorial service at the Actors' Church, St Paul's in Covent Garden, was partly arranged by Barry – and was, in his words, 'a riot. Endless laughs. David Kernan sang a hymn to fornication written by Will, and his son Toby read a piece Will had written about the birth of cricket. Humphrey's band played. The word "celebration" was never more apt.' After the tributes and the tears, the congregation joined together to sing Willie's *Private Eye* anthem 'Neasden' and play along on kazoos, before Humph's band led the mourners through the streets of Covent Garden in a traditional New Orleans procession. As the kazoos played, Graeme recalls catching the eye of fellow mourner Peter O'Toole and them both giggling at the suitable absurdity of it all, before he lost all trace of the procession. 'We didn't know where they'd gone. The instruction was "Follow the band", but there was no sign of them ... so Naismith and I went to the pub and had a drink for Willie.' A further tribute came when the Teams returned to Mornington Crescent for its grand re-opening in 1998 – or rather, it came four years later when a plaque bearing Willie's name was unveiled, clearly visible on the wall just before you reach the escalators, to be seen by millions of commuters and confused tourists for years to come.

But could the show go on? The *Clue* team had the whole of winter to come to their decision, and they did seriously consider canning the programme there and then. After twenty-odd years of Rushton's singularly effortless wit being knitted into very nearly every show, it was almost unthinkable to try to carry on, with public opinion in favour of a respectful cancellation.

However, ultimately the show *had* to go on, at Willie's own bequest. It was like a scene from *Henry VIII*, with the great king laid low and his advisors huddled around debating the fate of the kingdom. Archbishop Tim Brooke-Taylor had visited the patient not long before his operation, and they had discussed the seemingly endless quality of the game that they had only kicked off for a laugh all those years ago. He looked at his old team-mate and, thinking over their two long decades of playing silly games together, sighed, 'How long can this go on?' Willie thought for a moment, before thoughtfully intoning, 'Oh, I think it can go on for as long as Humph's still around,' to which Tim sagely nodded.

Jon Naismith attests, 'Willie adored the show, though he would never have admitted his affection – at least I thought he never would before he was interviewed by a crew from *Look East* before what turned out to be his last recording at the Cambridge Arts Theatre. He waxed lyrical about *Clue* – said it contained more jokes than any other show on radio or TV. I was quite taken aback. He was so thrilled when we won a British Comedy Award as well as the Sony Gold in the same year . . . There's always a danger that just "doing silly things" runs the risk of being rather pointless and twee. Willie added a hint of sharper humour to offset what occasionally was in danger of being a bit saccharine.'

But Willie's wishes were clear – with or without him, there would always be a desperate need for one song to be sung to the tune of another, for the 'Late Arrivals' to be announced, and for Mornington Crescent to be played in the public arena.

Willie's throne lay empty, and there was no pretender among the legion of players who could possibly fill his sizeable space. They would have to leave the 'guest spot' open for the time being at least – Jon Naismith's history as a guest booker at comedy club Jongleurs meant that he had an eye for the funniest people for the job – but however they managed the transition, *Clue* would never be the same again. No one person could ever have embodied the cocktail of satire, facetious silliness and positively horizontal nonchalance that summed up *I'm Sorry I Haven't a Clue*, like William George Rushton. The Antidote to Panel Games had had its ups and downs, but it made no claims to be a piece of flawlessly crafted comedy – for the *Clue* veterans, it was just their wireless playground, a unique home of conviviality and laughter, and thank heavens Willie had been there to join them in the game. Perhaps Barry Cryer put it best: 'Willie Rushton once observed that he had had enough of erratic geniuses and temperamental prima donnas and that all he wanted from life was to be with people he liked and laugh a lot. I'll drink to that.'

13

Sort of Organic

It's unknown whether some insanely superstitious member of the crew smuggled in a fluttering butterfly for the first *Clue* recording *sans* Willie, a few months after his passing, but Rushton's old colleagues certainly did the great man proud that night at the Theatre Royal, Bath – as was clear when the first episode of series 29 was broadcast on 7 June 1997. Paul Merton was the first comic to dare to test the now permanently vacant seat next to Tim, and the series was completed by Denise Coffey in Brighton and Stephen Fry in Canterbury. Sadly this was to be the last outing for Denise after years of brilliant ribaldry – but there was a whole host of talented types banging at the door waiting to be let in, keen to sew the *Clue* badge on their comedy uniforms. 'I think everybody enters the spirit of it,' says Fry, 'and it's helped by the fact that I suppose we've been listening to it since we were children.'

Mornington Crescent: The Next Generation

Like an intensified version of the virgin listener picking up on the show's running gags, hearing how a fresh contestant copes with their debut performance on *Clue* is always intriguing – discovering how smoothly they spark off the regulars, wondering how they'll fare in their first nationally broadcast round of Mornington Crescent – it becomes another reason to tune in. The new influx, as Barry agreed, gave the show 'a new lease of life. Because you can't replace Willie, he's a one-off, so you don't even try. It's sort of organic, you don't realise it's happening, but it is changing through the years. We don't analyse it, but we know it's been happening . . .'

The change of set-up was a big moment for Tim, as well. 'Willie Rushton was the alpha-male of the group, no question about that,' says Jon Naismith. 'I observed them working together when we prepared the shows, and Willie's decision went really, I think everyone respected him enormously. And I think Tim was very much the sort of junior party in that relationship. Tim is like me, he's more of a worrier, he'll think "Is that right? Are we finished there?", whereas Willie would just go "That's enough, yup! That'll do" and it would all be done.' Having spent years cultivating a deliberately wimpy (but eminently lovable) persona, Tim the elder statesman now found himself blooming in an avuncular role, charged with taking each new player under his wing, and in doing so, he got to play mentor to some of the finest comic performers of recent times. 'I think we've all evolved a bit,' he agrees. 'I know I've changed. I used to be the scared, "playing for sympathy one", but that's more in the background waiting to be called on if absolutely necessary – and sometimes it is absolutely necessary.'

Neil Innes

Born in Essex in 1944, Neil Innes is one of the most legendary living legends alive, his 'Seventh Python' label doing no justice to his achievements in both music and comedy. His collaborations with Viv Stanshall from the day they helped form The Bonzo Dog Doo-Dah Band at Goldsmiths School of Art at the start of the sixties would guarantee him immortality alone. However, The Bonzos' overlappings with The Beatles, Innes' further collaborations with Eric Idle in *Rutland Weekend Television* and *The Rutles* and solo work as a musician and creator of lost classic *The Innes Book of Records* lifts Neil to an altogether loftier plain, no matter how uncomfortable he may feel up there. Neil has three sons and grandchildren, and continues to tour, perform and record in multiple combinations and guises.

Sandi Toksvig

Despite being born in Copenhagen in 1958, Sandi's father's work as a foreign correspondent meant that she and her brother and sister had a globetrotting childhood before settling in the UK. At Cambridge Toksvig took part in the first ever all-women Footlights revue, while also winning prizes for outstanding intellectual achievement, studying law, archaeology and anthropology – which naturally led to a career in Saturday-morning kids' television. But while Sandi was becoming known as Ethel in *Number 73*, she was performing at night with the Comedy Store Players, and soon appearances on *Whose Line* and *HIGNFY* allowed Sandi to become fully established as a comedian – not to mention children's author, travel writer, actress, columnist and political commentator. Sandi has three children with her ex-partner Peta, and lives in Surrey. Since 2006, Sandi has made the chair of *The News Quiz* her own.

Neil Mullarkey

The Footlights president in 1984, Neil Mullarkey's early comedy career featured three different double acts, teaming up with Nick Hancock, Tony Hawks and Mike Myers, in succession. This final duo went all the way to a hit show at the Edinburgh Fringe, before Myers returned to Canada (Neil has subsequently made two cameos in *Austin Powers* movies). One of the central members of the Comedy Store Players, Mullarkey has remained a committed improviser, still regularly performing at Edinburgh and around the world, and he was the presenter of the Radio 4 historical panel game *Missed Demeanours.*

Max Boyce

Born in 1945, Maxwell Boyce is an ex-coal miner and rugby enthusiast whose performance of folk songs like 'Hen Wlad fy Nhadau' at an eisteddfod led to a recording career, with an album called *Caneuon Amrywiol.* Boyce is Welsh. Although already a popular singer and comic in folk and rugby clubs throughout Wales, it took a failed appearance on *Opportunity Knocks* in 1973 to pique the interest of EMI, and then the whole of the UK, when his second album for them, *We All Had Doctors' Papers,* became the only comedy album ever to reach the top of the UK album charts. Max still performs to huge crowds today, and has never left his home town of Glynneath, where he has a wife and children. He received the MBE in 2000.

Fred Macaulay

Born in Perth in 1956, Fred was already thirty-two when he first dipped his toe into the comedy world, having graduated from the University of Dundee with an accounting degree in 1978, and spent a decade balancing books. An early splash at the 'So You Think You're Funny' competition at Glasgow's Mayfest led to more and more offers of work as a stand-up and warm-up, and after five years he went fully professional. A regular on panel games, Fred has also presented the morning show on BBC Radio Scotland for over a decade, and is married with three children.

Phill Jupitus

Jupitus (his real name, anglicised from the Hungarian) is famous for his Essex roots, but was actually born on the Isle of Wight, in 1962. Having dropped out of college to work, like Merton, at his local job centre, Phill spent as much time as possible cartooning and writing political poetry. Finally, taking the name Porky the Poet, he began performing his work and supporting local bands, ending up as part of the Red Wedge tour with fellow Barking boy Billy Bragg. Working in the music business eventually took second place to his comedy, and he's been a regular on *Never Mind the Buzzcocks* for over a decade. Still based in Essex where he has a wife and two daughters, Phill is perhaps one of the busiest comics in the country, as well as a radio DJ and musician, touring with The Bonzos reunion band.

Andy Hamilton

Contrary to popular prejudice, Andy is not a mythical being, even though at his birth (in Fulham, in 1954) it was noted that he had six fingers on one hand – which may make him slightly magical. He's certainly been involved both as a writer and a performer with some of the finest comedy of the last thirty years, being spotted as part of a CULES show at Edinburgh in the seventies and shunted straight onto *Week Ending* to learn his craft. His greatest success may have been co-creating the topical sitcom *Drop the Dead Donkey* with Guy Jenkin, but other shows bearing his stamp include *Outnumbered* and *Bob and Margaret* for television and *The Million Pound Radio Show*, *Old Harry's Game* and *Revolting People* on Radio 4. He, his wife Libby and their three children live in Wimbledon.

Jack Dee

James Andrew Innes Dee was born in Orpington in 1962, although the Dees relocated to Winchester when Jack was just a boy, the youngest of three. Leaving college, Dee's plan to attend drama school was rejected in favour of a far more sensible career in catering, and several years of waiting, restaurant managing and heavy drinking led Jack to the ultimate desperate act: in 1986 he took to the stage on an open-mic night at the Comedy Store. Having caught the bug, Dee's distinctively sour style of deadpan comedy eventually made him one of the biggest names in stand-up by the start of the nineties. Sell-out tours, stand-up shows like *Live at the Apollo*, John Smith's ads, winning *Celebrity Big Brother* back when it still seemed like a good idea, straight-acting roles and his own sitcom, *Lead Balloon*, have kept Jack busy ever since. He is married to Jane, and they have two daughters and two sons.

Bill Bailey

Keynsham in Somerset saw the creation of Mark Bailey in 1964, an only child of the local GP and a complete swot at everything at King Edward's School. It was only as puberty kicked in that his musical training led to rebellion and rock 'n' roll – although he still passed his music A-level with flying colours. Being dubbed 'Bill' by his mates at school, it was under this moniker that he began to find work, after years of musical and theatrical procrastination. First becoming known as half of the musical duo the Rubber Bishops, Bill stepped out as a solo stand-up in 1995, with his hit show *Cosmic Jam*. Ever since, his brand of dazed stoner silliness and inspired musicality have made him one of the nation's favourite comics, as well as a gifted comic actor. A huge *Star Trek* fan, Bill and his wife named their first son Dax.

Harry Hill

Of course Dr Matthew Hall is not the only qualified medical practitioner to forge a comedy career, but he may be the most unlikely. Born in Woking in 1964, Hall qualified in 1988, but found he got more of a kick from performing in medical revues, and in the double act the Hall Brothers. Finding his Harry Hill persona, he was crowned Best Newcomer in Edinburgh in 1992, and despite his wildly silly act, he went on to win over viewers young and old on *Saturday Live*. Sell-out tours, Radio 4 show *Fruit Corner* and its Channel 4 adaptation, hilarious books like *Flight From Deathrow* and *Tim the Tiny Horse*, regular appearances on David Letterman's show, and of course his own much-loved *TV Burp* series have made him one of the most popular comics in the UK. He and his wife, the artist Magda Archer, have three little ones.

Linda Smith

Linda Smith's journey to becoming the nation's favourite female satirist was a long one. Born in Erith in Kent in 1958, Linda began her career in comedy in Sheffield, where she studied English and drama at university, and was also heavily involved in socialist politics, producing and performing in many benefits. She won the Hackney Empire New Act of the Year in 1987, but it was several years before she found her métier on Radio 4. Her senselessly early death, from ovarian cancer in 2006, has robbed us of one of the finest satirical minds of British comedy.

Ross Noble

Cramlington-born Ross Markham Noble may have only turned thirty-three on 5 June 2009, but he has already been voted tenth best stand-up of all time in one of those Channel 4 polls. He's achieved this despite never plumping for any TV vehicle or turning to acting, and being dyslexic. A comedy fan since infancy, he was a street performer and clown before the stand-up style he began honing at fifteen got him noticed. His loose improvisatory style has resulted in a stream of popular tours and DVDs, and his own Radio 4 show, *Ross Noble Goes Global*. He is married, and lives in Melbourne, Australia.

Rob Brydon

Although the first many would have seen of Robert Brydon Jones was his cameo as an unfortunate traffic warden in *Lock, Stock & Two Smoking Barrels*, by then he had endless years of radio and voiceover work behind him, yet ached to be a comedian. Born in Swansea in 1965, he attended drama school in Cardiff, but moved into radio before graduation, and began honing his talent for impressionism. The route from Toilet Duck advertising to successful comic came when he created the character of lonely optimist Keith Barrett alongside Hugo Blick. He has three children from his first marriage, and became wed again, to Claire Holland, in 2006.

Denise Coffey wasn't the only regular to drift away from the show, as Paul Merton, once the most recurrent stand-in player, also completed his last game in 1997. His fellow original Comedy Store Player, Neil Mullarkey, only made one appearance that same series, despite providing an embarrassingly huge amount of laughs – but a third member of the Players, Sandi Toksvig, was clearly a keeper from the start. From her debut show at the end of series 30, the lone female player picked up the torch from Coffey and ran with it, making sure to take the piss out of *Clue*'s unfortunate 'Boys' Own Club' mentality from the start ('It was during the war!' protested Barry, 'They were all in the factories!').

Being anything but a 'token woman', if anyone was going to take the boys on at their own game, it was Sandi. She found her niche, over on the 'naughty schoolboy' side of the panel, and soon established a reputation as the Queen of the Gigglers, which, in combination with both Tim and Humph in full giggling mode, made for many extensive edits on Naismith's part. According to Graeme: 'When they all go at the same time it can take up to fifteen minutes to calm them down again . . .'

Her helpless appreciation of Humph's gags highlighted another of the pleasures of having a wide pool of guest performers – the added array of laughs that made up the audio landscape of the show. Added to the main team was Toksvig's and Hardy's unstoppable sniggering, Fry's much imitated bray, Merton's hacking laugh . . . even the genuine mirth of the deadpan Jack Dee is unmistakably audible in his shows, no matter how he tried to rein it in. One of the golden rules of so much of comedy is *not* to laugh at your own jokes, but in *Clue*, that rule is joyously discarded. After all, says Barry, 'I'm laughing because if you want something doing well, do it yourself . . .'

There's no denying though that Sandi was definitely 'one of the lads' once she became established on the show. Her sexuality is of course irrelevant to her humour, but from her earliest TV appearances, Toksvig has always had a unique tomboyish nature that seems to circumvent any of the usual prejudices against funny women. Linda Smith, on the other hand, never seemed to have compromised on her femininity at all, and established herself as the most loved voice on Radio 4 comedy, even being voted 'Wittiest Living Person' by listeners in 2002. Not that she didn't have to fight for the honour – in his emotional memoir, *Driving Miss Smith*, Linda's partner Warren Lakin recalls the frustration she experienced trying to break in to Radio 4 comedy, Linda's natural home, due to the perceived difficulty of having not just a woman, but one with a working-class accent, on the BBC Home Service (anyone who finds it hard to believe that listeners in this day and age could be so backward as to harbour such prejudices has clearly never opened a Radio 4 mailbag). For her own Radio 4 show, *A Brief History of Time Wasting*, Linda even wrote: 'There are two things women just can't do – open jars and appear on light-hearted Radio 4 panel games.'

In the end, Linda lowered herself to write a letter applying for a spot on *The News Quiz* to the show's producer, and from there, like so many other performers, she earned her right to step up to the oche for *I'm Sorry I Haven't a Clue*, debuting in 2001 in Sheffield, the city where she began her comedy career. Graeme recalls that ultimately she was notably fearless as a player but 'The only time she showed any nerves was the first time she appeared on the show and took Jon aside and said she was a bit worried about Mornington Crescent, and could he give her any tips on how to play without making herself look a fool? And he said, "No, just play it, and the Audience will decide whether you're playing well or not." And she was brilliant!' In fact, she won Mornington Crescent on only her second attempt. But Linda wasn't alone in feeling the heat when becoming part of this bizarre comic cult; from Oddie onwards it's a scary prospect – John Lloyd even settles the guests on his twenty-first-century panel game for enquiring minds, *QI*, by reassuring them that 'It's a lot less scary than *Clue*!' Jon Naismith has nursed the best of them through their nerves, but admits, 'I'm always surprised when guests are frightened before appearing on *Clue*. I remember Stephen Fry being terrified before a recording at Canterbury . . . I asked Jo Brand to appear, and she said she was so frightened at the prospect she'd need time to think about it. I've always thought we're such a friendly, unthreatening show. But I guess people are scared being the "new bug" in front of a large Audience who are all fans of the show.'

Her initial nerves forgotten, Linda played a blinder on both of her *Clue* appearances. She and Jeremy Hardy went way back together as politically motivated comics, and she paid a fitting tribute to her old colleague when performing one of the *Clue* highlights – singing 'Psycho Killer' to the tune of Renée & Renato's 'Save Your Love', with the disclaimer 'I'll have a go, but as a singer, I'm no Jeremy Hardy . . .'

The traditional problem of finding women who can play *Clue* to a high standard added yet another layer of sadness to the tragedy of Linda's death from cancer in 2006, just as the public were beginning to get an inkling of how funny she was. For her published tribute, *I Think the Nurses are Stealing my Clothes*, Barry wrote a heartfelt poem, and, originally nervous of sitting next to Smith, afraid that her sharp tongue would take over proceedings (he wasn't to know that the producer of *The News Quiz* tended to build the show around her in the edit, as everything she said was of such a high

standard), Tim saluted Linda as 'the ideal mixed doubles partner'. Jon
Naismith also pays tribute: 'Linda was a phenomenal loss to radio comedy.
The years of unfulfilled potential, of galvanising more women onto shows like
Clue, *Just a Minute* and *The News Quiz*. So, so sad. A brilliant, charming,
kind person.'

Let's Make Up and Be Friendly

'They have nothing in common, they blend in but no two of them are alike,'
insists Barry, but the rest of the new guests were overwhelmingly of a younger
generation (or two) than Tim, Graeme and Barry. However, as Cryer had
insisted back in the eighties, as long as they're funny, there is no real difference between comic generations. And of course, younger performers meant
younger, bigger, even rowdier crowds. Colin Sell reflects, 'We certainly get a
broader age range nowadays – even many of my students know I do the show,
whereas formerly they didn't.'

When Cramlington-born 'sonic waffler' Ross Noble made his first appearance at the age of twenty-six, he could easily have been one of the Teams'
younger sons, but his free-wheeling nonsense fitted in perfectly with the tone
of the show. Harry Hill similarly is a performer who has created his own
wonderful comedic world, of disturbing puppets, badger parades, meat-chop
worship and kitsch references very much in the mould of Reeves & Mortimer.
Despite bringing his brand of lunacy to the world's attention via the obscurer
corners of Radio 4 and Channel 4, Hill, with and without his infamous cat
friend Stouffer, managed the near-impossible by bringing together every
extreme of comedy fan, from the most hardcore comedy anorak to the most
casual Jim Davidson lover, all united in the enormous viewing figures for his
award-winning prime-time ITV show, *TV Burp* – proving that no matter how
odd he can be, there's something universal about Hill's humour, which makes
him ideal for *Clue*. He also knows how to use a running gag better than
anybody. Not that he wasn't nervous of taking part – he almost went to bits
during his maiden Mornington Crescent outing:

> HH: I'm actually close to tears.
> GG: Can we get him his little cat puppet, to cheer him up?
> HH: It's not a puppet, don't spoilt it for the band.

Nevertheless, when Uncle Tim staked his claim to Mornington Crescent in
that show, he insisted that it was 'Thanks entirely to Harry!'

As a contemporary of Tim and Graeme, the comedy music legend Neil
Innes was an exception to the age-gap rule. He helped out in 1997 when, as
Humph announced, 'Listeners will be shocked to hear that regular pianist

Colin Sell was double-booked this evening. However, after an acrimonious row, and the threat of legal action, the other show reluctantly conceded defeat and agreed to take him.' It's clearly not a job for a musical novice, keeping up with *Clue* singers under Humph's watchful eye, and although others had played the piano for *Clue* before – Matthew Scott, David Firman, Tim and Barry's *Hello, Cheeky* maestro Denis King – Humph pointed out that Neil's awesome career with The Bonzos, The Pythons, The Rutles and as a solo artist were 'But a small sample of the successes that put Neil where he is today. Standing in for Colin Sell.'

As with any of the guests that would come to enrich *I'm Sorry I Haven't a Clue*, Innes' appearance made the most of his talents, and he was even called upon to do a 'Pick Up Song' rendition of his Paul McCartney-produced 'medley of hit', 'I'm the Urban Spaceman':

HL: Now, I can't tell you how nice it is to be here with someone else with a decent Top Twenty hit under their belt. Neil, I'd like you to finish by accompanying yourself, singing –

TBT: Only one?

HL: Only one what?

TBT: Top Twenty hit?

HL: No, two. Counting me.

TBT: Oh . . . It's just that Graeme and I have four, that's all.

BC: Ooh, handbag, handbag . . .

HL: I did say 'decent Top Twenty hit'.

TBT: . . . Fair enough.

Just as they had a kinship with *ISIRTA*, as the world's leading purveyors of that wonderful genre 'British Rubbish', The Bonzo Dog Band are unquestionably the musical cousins of the *Clue* brethren, and share so much of the same philosophy when it comes to booze, silliness, jazz, Music Hall and, of course, filth. So it was a perfect repayment of the honour of Innes' guesting on Colin's stool when the band's 2007 reunion album contained a very trad track entitled 'Mornington Crescent', by Innes' co-producer Mickey Simmonds:

Are you the one who called Leicester Square?
Well I don't think that was very fair . . .
Are you the one that tried to Turnham Green?
Well they saw through you, and they know where you've been!
The way you carry on and on is so incessant,
The atmosphere that you create is so unpleasant,
You're harder to understand than Mornington Crescent!

The Innes connections were cemented by his appearing alongside Graeme Garden on the 'well-seasoned' Radio 4 sketch show *The Right Time*, which ran from 2001 to 2004. The buoyant sexagenarian-and-upwards sketch show was originally set to prominently feature Barry, but once the pilot gave way to a full series he sadly wasn't able to make the recordings. By this time however Graeme was already set to join him and went ahead with the show, both performing and writing sketches for the first time in over a decade. *The Right Time* was aided greatly by the creation of a very convivial atmosphere at the Drill Hall radio theatre, with live music from Innes and Ronnie Golden which added to the overall audio aura of a great night out. Neil and Graeme were joined in the first couple of series by Eleanor Bron, Clive Swift, Paula Wilcox and *Spitting Image*'s Roger Blake, and although the show could be dismissed as relatively cosy, it represented the troupe's generation as savvy, sexy and every bit as dysfunctional as the young tykes of shows like *Man Stroke Woman* – and in turn, went some way towards refuting the lie that sketch comedy is 'a young man's game', as if comics should cease being comical when the menopause arrives.

One of Innes' few competitors as a comedy maestro also graced Willie's chair on one occasion, when Bill Bailey made a guest appearance in Hastings in 2002. As well as injecting his own brilliant brand of slightly damaged whimsy into the proceedings (giving the 'Unhelpful Advice' to tourists that in Britain 'the hedgehog is sacred' and so on), Bailey's musical leanings were acknowledged in a debut round which signalled the start of a new emphasis on sound effects in *Clue*. The fun of improvising radio sound effects went way back to the second series. It wasn't until the start of the next century that Jon Naismith introduced a little box of tricks that would allow the Teams to provide their own sound effects at will – a recipe for bedlam. Historically, any sound effects required for *Clue* would be played in from the recording gallery or the Outside Broadcast van parked round the back of the theatre (the producer would often explain to the Audience that the evening's recording would start the second that the sound technician had finished serving the last hot dog), but, recalls Naismith, 'A brilliant sound engineer in TV called Laurie Taylor tipped me off about a great piece of kit comprising a small twenty-key pad linked to a minidisc machine which allowed the user to trigger off twenty different sound samples at the press of a button.' The doohickeys were given their first real airing in a round dubbed 'DIY Soap Opera' – or 'Medical Drama', or 'Costume Drama' and so on – allowing the guests to flex their thespian skills while providing the necessary SFX at will via the hotkeys. This idea even extended to a spoof of the award-winning series *Life on Mars*, in which, Humph explained, 'a chap goes into a deep coma at the beginning of the series and keeps waking up to find himself in 1973 . . . they've stolen my life!' Bill Bailey was given the extra task of providing music in the very first *Archers*-inspired drama, in his role as the village of Umbrage's church organist, Blind Lemon Watkins.

Soon the new sound-effect technology was making its way into other games, revolutionising Mornington Crescent by pitting the Teams against a 'Deep Blue'-style computer, or, infamously, playing the whole game via a talkative satellite-navigation system with a crush on a particular guest player:

HL:	In a bid to speed things up I have this week provided you each with the latest satellite-navigation technology. So if you'd please programme into your satnav boxes a route from Liverpool Street to Mornington Crescent which takes account of Montague's Second Stationery ruling . . . I'd like you to start, please, Tim.
TBT:	From Liverpool Street, yes?
HL:	That's what I said five minutes ago.
TBT:	Let me just, er, set it up . . .
SATNAV:	*Turn right after two hundred yards.*
TBT:	Well, that's helpful. I think that takes me into Goodge Street.
BC:	Goodge? Goodge. Well, let me see . . .
SATNAV:	*You've got the map upside down.*
BC:	Oh, great. So clever.
SATNAV:	*Shut up and let me concentrate.*
BC:	OK, OK . . .
SATNAV:	*Have you never played this game before?*
BC:	Shut up, you. Bethnal Green!
GG:	Yep, yep, that's good.
JH:	Erm, Turnpike Lane.
SATNAV:	*That was fantastic play, Jeremy.*
JH:	Thank you very much indeed.
SATNAV:	*I love you, Jeremy.*

To Play The King

Bill Bailey also had the distinction of being the one and only player of *Clue* to have also guested on perhaps the most flagrant attempt to ape *Clue*'s success on radio. It's little wonder that there have been plenty of shows which cut to the chase by presenting their own briefless antidotes to panel games, when there are so few opportunities available to try and gain access to the exclusive *Clue* club. Graeme explains the selection process: 'All the Team members discuss possible guests with the producer, but Tim has the ultimate say, as he has to work with the guest on his Team. As we only have six recording days in a year and therefore room for six guests, we find there are now too many super guests we would love to come back, but we can't fit them into our schedule, and new guests are always more than welcome too. So there's a very long list of people we would like to invite or invite back.' Tim confirms: 'I suggest people I'd like to take part and Jon always runs suggestions by me. If I'm not keen then the guest doesn't appear. I'm keen that Sean Lock is a guest sometime, but he always seems to be working. I'm also pushing for Sue Perkins . . .' On the subject of his dream *Clue* partner, he says, 'Assuming I can pick from the past then Willie Rushton would be top of the list followed closely by Peter Cook. I reckon Hugh Laurie would be pretty useful. The guests I really like are the ones who don't think they're worthy – Jack Dee is a classic example and of course he was more than worthy.'

With these restrictions making the available 'pissing about on Radio 4' time incredibly limited, one gang of gifted comics who could easily have done well at *Clue* were instead rounded up by *Black Books* co-writers Kevin Cecil and Andy Riley, with producer David Tyler, for the very silly panel game *King Stupid* in 1999. Presented by Footlighter William Vandyck, the guests, as well as being from a different generation to the *Clue* stalwarts, were also more likely to be writers and stand-ups than all-round entertainers, and there was no pianist standing by for musical games. The whole programme was like a half-hour of bizarre corporate brainstorming sessions, every contestant for him or herself. The players were challenged to come up with new toy products, fake traffic reports, wildlife commentaries, futuristic predictions for the year 2000 (made in the late summer of 1999), and even New Commandments ('Thou shalt not lie with Michael Winner' being a given).

Jon Naismith couldn't help but see the similarities when the new show was launched: 'It was *Clue* for young people, but . . . you know, not as good, I don't think . . . You remember the more bizarre things on it, but a lot of it was just doing the same things, "Come up with titles for this, that and the other . . ."
I personally thought its funniest manifestation was with William Vandyck hosting it, I thought he was really good, and I can't imagine why they dropped him, he was a really original, interesting voice.' After just one series, a huge amount of complaints from Radio 4 listeners necessitated a considerable over-haul for the show, with another Footlighter, the aforementioned Sue Perkins, taking over the Chair (Vandyck continued writing, but otherwise returned to his life as a practising barrister) and the name changed to *The 99p Challenge* – the idea being that games were rewarded with pence and the winning contestant would get the chance to gamble their winnings on a final game which could net them the eponymous cost of an ice cream. 'There were some complaints because they thought it meant "Fucking Stupid",' Naismith

continues, 'and I didn't think it did, it was "King of the Stupid People". I don't think it mattered . . . Changing the name was just facile, and people need to know when you ignore listeners' complaints and when you don't.'

. Throughout its five series, up until 2004, *King Stupid*/*The 99p Challenge* boasted some of the greatest names of modern comedy, including regulars Armando Iannucci and Simon Pegg, plus Peter Baynham, Richard Herring, Jack Docherty, Morwenna Banks, Peter Serafinowicz, Nick Frost and many more, all coming up with the silliest part-scripted jokes. Although puns were legion, the jokes were generally of a more specifically absurdist, post-*Brass Eye* brand of humour. However, as a self-deprecating quizless quiz show, its debt to *Clue* is unmistakeable:

PERKINS: If you noticed the recent General Election – and let's face it, 60 per cent of you didn't – you'll have noticed that whenever David Dimbleby said 'We're going over to the count now', and we saw all the candidates lined up, there was a big banner behind them for whatever town it was, with slogans trying to get you to go there. Slogans like 'Gateshead – Our Flashy New Bridge Works, You Southern Ape-Monkeys!' and 'Liverpool – The Beatles Come From Here, Did We Mention That?' So, contestants, do we have any other straplines for cities? Starting with you, Simon.

SP: Um, yes. 'Essex – The Garage of England.'

AI: 'York – So Good They Named It Once.'

BB: . . . 'Hartlepool – We Hanged A Monkey Once By Mistake But Now We're Committed To Urban Renewal . . .'

SP: . . . 'Glasgow – Birthplace of Stabbing.'

AI: . . . I'd just like to say I'm from Glasgow, and when you said it was the Birthplace of Stabbing, I presume you were referring to Sir Ronan Stabbing, the distinguished Scottish author?

SP: Yeah, of course I was.

AI: Who was also the first person to stab someone.

Over five series, the youthful antidote to panel games provided many great laughs, somehow managing to pull off the trick of being a lazier show than its inspiration, with the silliest half-thought-through jingles and ideas thrown in purely for the amusement of the panel. Perhaps it would still be chugging along now, if some of its main stars hadn't moved on to Hollywood. But Iannucci puts up no struggle when faced with the suggestion that *King Stupid*/*The 99p Challenge* was heavily influenced by the elder piss-taking panel game. 'I'm sure it was, it certainly felt like it was a kind of . . . young person's, non-jazz-playing *I'm Sorry I Haven't a Clue*. I think it was conceived to bring a younger audience to that sort of thing.' Even renowned supporter of newer acts Cryer has to laugh: 'They ripped us off . . . It isn't exactly mysterious where some panel games get some of their ideas from. But they come and go. *They* might grow organically if one survived and became something of their own. But if they seem derivative, they just shrivel away and disappear.'

Humph and His Merrie Band

The pleasure of inducting suitable new comics into the exclusive club coincided neatly with *Clue*'s continued and expanding tours up and down the British Isles. Humph, his loyal band of jesters, and the new apprentice marched on Edinburgh many times, almost regulars at the festival, but it was in Glasgow that native wit Fred Macaulay made his first appearance on *Clue* in 1999. Regarding Samantha, he announced, 'Can I just say, this is the first time I've been on this show, and I had no idea she was so pretty.' 'You'll learn . . .' replied Humph, without a beat. Drawing up in Wales that very same series for a show at the New Theatre, Cardiff, the entourage was welcomed into the court of Max Boyce. Graeme recalls, 'That was interesting, when we did the show with Max Boyce – he came to the hotel beforehand, and was treated like the Second Coming of Christ in the bar, with people coming up to him jabbering in Welsh and touching the hem of his garment! It was wonderful.' By this time it was a surprise to see a comic closer to the Teams' age join the fray, but Boyce earned his rapturous welcome from the home crowd admirably, while Barry took his chance to crowbar in a syllable-perfect 'Llanfairpwllgwyngyllgogerychwyrndrobwllllantysiliogogogoch', to enormous cheers.

The Teams' arrival in Dublin however, saw the debut appearance from the very English Jack Dee. Paul Merton of course was one decidedly deadpan comic who had flourished on *Clue*, but no one – bar perhaps Humph himself – could contend with Dee's sour-faced persona. True to form, he took an awful lot of convincing to go on the show as well. 'I've been listening for as long as I can remember, and I was once asked by someone at the BBC which radio shows would I like to be on, and I said in answer to this, "There's one show that I *never* want to appear on, and that is *I'm Sorry I Haven't a Clue*." And my reason for this was that it was so *great* that I wouldn't want my own voice to spoil it. Which it would. I didn't explain that reason to the bloke at the BBC, he just went away feeling rather offended, as he happened to be the producer . . .' As a dedicated gagwriter, Dee wasn't especially used to the real ad hoc nature of the show at the time, but his one-time double-act partner Jeremy Hardy believes Dee's doggedness works in his favour. 'Jack Dee's very good on it. He comes armed to the teeth with very good gags – if there's a round that's prepared, like the list rounds or Uxbridge English Dictionary, which you always know is going to come up, Jack will have loads of those, he's a real workhorse in that way.'

Jack's reluctance to become a panel-show regular was also clear when his role as Team Captain on Naismith's *It's Only TV But I Like It* was taken over by an absolute quiz show fiend, Phill Jupitus, for the second series. Jupitus has appeared with aplomb on so many panel games over the years, if he had never appeared on *Clue*, it would almost seem remiss, and his ample frame comfortably filled Willie's space, albeit on just a few occasions. In his first show in 1999, Humph admitted, 'As our special guest today is Phill Jupitus, we all agreed it would be a terrible waste if we didn't bother to come up with a new round to demonstrate his unique talent. Still, there you are, that's life.' Being welcomed in as a *Clue* panellist and an adopted member of The Bonzos is a double distinction that Jupitus shares with his hero, Stephen Fry.

Probably the final stalwart of the regular guests was Andy Hamilton who, coming from the same radio panel-game stable as Hardy, Smith and Toksvig – all integral to the popularity of *The News Quiz* – seems to fit in with the old-timers every bit as well as the other 'bankers'. Plus, as a Cambridge graduate and long-time collaborator with Paul Mayhew-Archer, there was a certain inevitability about Hamilton's distinctive voice and tireless gag-slinging becoming part of the *Clue* casserole. He was such a dependable joke machine he became a go-to man for those few emergency shows when one of the regulars was indisposed – when Tim was absent for the last show of 2007 in Peterborough, Andy and Jack were up against the toughest duo in comedy, Graeme and Barry. Despite the veterans' years of extra experience, they were well-matched adversaries, as can be seen from the new game, 'Catalogue Complaints' – Cryer and Garden being unsatisfied with their mail-order brides:

GG: The next one I got from you I was disappointed with. She allegedly come from Bangkok, and she was supposed to be a titled Lady – the widow of Lord Boy, I assumed. She was full of surprises, she was.

JD: Well, it depends how you fill in the form. I mean, did you tick her box?

GG: Not on the first date, no, but I mean . . .

AH: Also, it has to be said that we've had complaints.

JD: It's true, we have had quite a lot of complaints.

AH: Complaints – from the girls. About you two.

BC: What?

AH: Mental cruelty. Dragging them around radio shows, trying out jokes on them . . .

JD: Some of these shows in the middle of nowhere.

AH: Towns, you know, no one would ever want to go . . .

BC: Mr Brooke-Taylor was a client of yours, was he not? At one point?

GG: Yeah, they sent him to me. He was my third . . . Best of the lot, actually.

Jack Dee's long-standing reluctance to join the Team could possibly also have been linked to his undeniable choral dyslexia. An ability to sing is of course not a must for any of the _Clue_ guests – it helps, but in such a convivial atmosphere any old noise tends to do. Yet while Jack and Sandi, and obviously Stephen, have vocal cords cursed by Lucifer himself (and all have given Colin Sell sleepless nights), as has been hinted at hitherto, Jeremy Hardy is somehow different. Stephen Fry may claim to be literally tone-deaf, but it's in Hardy's willingness to have a damn good stab at singing that his popularity lies. Fry says, 'Jeremy Hardy is bolder than I am at singing loudly. I sing badly but am deeply ashamed, and just mumble, whereas he really goes for it. And I really admire him for that. And how dare Rob Brydon sing so well? What is it about being Welsh? It's just ridiculous!'

'I really do try, sometimes to my own detriment,' Hardy admits. 'I remember trying to do "Sexual Healing" in Southport, and trying to do it really well, because I wanted to get it right. And I've always somewhat resented the fact that people like that I sing so badly!' The points that Willie smelled right from Hardy's first number soon transformed into voluble adoration from the Audience. 'And finally, Jeremy . . . words laden with doom!' Humph would intone, during each 'Pick Up Song', and already a ripple of anticipation would travel through the crowd. 'Occasionally I do sing in tune – when I did "Heaven Knows I'm Miserable Now", apparently that was in tune. I think it's a bit like when people have a stutter, but if they're in character they lose it – if I'm in character I can sing in tune. Sometimes. But the problem is I can't tell if I'm in tune or not, so it wanders in and out. Even now, occasionally I'll wander into tune and the others get very worried, thinking "that's the golden goose gone" . . . I got Humph's book and I went straight to the index and looked up my name, and all he said was that it was very strange that I couldn't sing a note in tune and yet on the kazoo I was pitch perfect. But I took it as a great compliment from Humph, because he was of course a musician.' As Fry suggests above, the arrival of the last new performer to be welcomed into the club, Rob Brydon, only underlined the infamous dodginess of Hardy's singalongs – the desperately keen, theatrically educated Welshman's exuberant renditions of Tom Jones numbers were almost as funny for their aplomb as Jeremy's were for their ramshackle nature.

The realisation that the age-old trick of repetition leading to warm recognition could continue with a tight crew of gifted guests was a blessing for the show's new phase, Cryer says. 'Jeremy Hardy is triumphantly proud of being an abysmal singer, and we play on that. It all becomes part of the pattern, it just evolves. It's a rich field now, because most of them are used to improvising, they're not set in their ways. Plenty can cope with it. I can't give you a list, but Jon Naismith keeps from time to time mentioning somebody and they say "Oh, I love the show but no, I couldn't do it." I'm sure they could.' Graeme is also aware of the expanding cast's worth. 'The stable of regular guests is indeed awesome, and we feel bad that we can only have three guests per series. Rob Brydon was an excellent new addition, and there are many others that we would like to do the show . . .'

Never Mind the TV

As the TV panel-game boom continued, Graeme especially cropped up on several shows, looking terribly medical and elegant behind the desk of *Have I Got News For You* on more than one occasion. But it was at the suggestion of TV producer and format deviser Richard Osmond that he found a permanent spot, on the political BBC2 panel game *If I Ruled the World*. This timely reaction to the arrival of Blair's New Labour government featured chairperson Clive Anderson in the role of dogged political interviewer, doing all he could to catch out Graeme, as the fusty head of the Blue Party, and his arch-rival Jeremy Hardy, the slick leader of the Red Party. Piloted in 1997 with a first series the following February, this show featured a number of inspired rounds designed to test the players' smarminess and suitability for government, and best of all, the audience really did get their chance to vote on which team was the winner at the end of every show.

It was because of this show that Hardy became such a mainstay of *I'm Sorry I Haven't a Clue*. Having only made one appearance, filling in for the absent Brooke-Taylor, Jeremy hadn't been invited back on, and Tim still wasn't sure about the satirist fitting in. 'I think Tim had to be persuaded that I'd be a good person to be on it, and what persuaded him was that in the first series of *If I Ruled the World* we had Tim on as a guest, which I think was Graeme's idea, for Tim to meet me, and to convince him that I'd be good on *Clue* . . . It was a strange mixture of acting and improv. I was supposed to be a Labour politician, and Graeme was supposed to be a Tory, but we didn't have to stay completely in character if we wanted to sort of shamelessly do gags. We had some good guests on there, we had some nightmarish guests, but it was great fun.'

It's no wonder Tim saw Jeremy at his best when he accompanied him as one of the Red Party, as both Garden and Hardy excelled in their roles on the show. However, Tim definitely had the necessary political bullshit down to a T from his first utterance on his episode: 'Who among us can put their hands up and say they have never slaughtered a goat at midnight and then pasted the blood over the naked body of Jean from Accounts? I know I have, I know you have, and Graeme does very little else . . .' Although many other guests all helped to make it top-drawer television, including Rebecca Front, Will Self, John Sergeant, Richard Wilson, Pauline McLynn and *Clue* stalwarts Fred Macaulay, Andy Hamilton and Tony Hawks (who even stood in for Hardy as Deputy Leader of the Red Party for one episode), Brooke-Taylor's one appearance was a definite highlight.

As well as rounds in which Graeme or Jeremy had to be interviewed by Anderson while obeying insane pager alerts from their spin doctors, or coming up with last-minute vote-grabbing pledges (such as reducing the size of NHS waiting lists by writing really small, or simply, 'Nicky Campbell's head on a stick!'), one brilliantly fertile regular round was 'I Couldn't Disagree More', in which one of the leaders was called upon to take issue with any opinion fired at them.

TBT: No one wants to see Jim Davidson running the country.

GG: No, I couldn't disagree more. This idea's far too complex, the words 'running the country' are superfluous.

JH: Well, it is our firm belief that the Pope is Catholic.

GG: I couldn't disagree more. The word 'Catholic' means 'all-embracing', and the Pope embraces very few people; he's never embraced me. You've seen him snog a couple of airport runways but that's about it.

CA: We're not getting onto bears and woods are we?

It could be argued that the strictly themed format of *If I Ruled the World* never made it the kind of show that could withstand endless series year after year, but viewed today it's of such a high quality that the premature cancellation of the show in 1999 after only two series still bears all the hallmarks of a major error – not least when it's the kind of panel game that today's BBC4 audience would eat up with a spoon. The decision to axe the show came from BBC2 controller Jane Root, who allegedly accepted it was a great show, but it 'didn't fit in with her idea of the direction BBC2 should be headed'. Goodies fans will be well aware of the ex-BBC2 controller's name, as the woman who vowed that *The Goodies* would never be repeated on the BBC, despite its years of successful repeats in Australia and other parts of the world, and growing popularity on video and (At Last!), on DVD. None of the Goodies were too subtle in their affront to this treatment (especially if their grousing elicited a laugh and a cheer). The thorny issue even cropped up in another unforgettable

Clue sound-effects round, 'Don't Kids Ask the Silliest Questions?', in which a decidedly creepy child's voice (actually provided by a precocious four-year-old from the Sylvia Young School) interrogated the Teams endlessly, eventually causing Humph to cry out 'Come back, Herod, all is forgiven!'

CHILD: *How are babies made?*

GG: Well, a stork flies out of the gooseberry bush, and Daddy is so amazed he doesn't notice the milkman nipping in the back door.

CHILD: *Why did my cat die?*

JH: Well, your cat didn't exactly die, it went to live with Jesus – who has a small flat under the compost heap.

HL: Tim, let's see if you can answer this baffling question.

CHILD: *Why aren't The Goodies on any more?*
(*Audience cheer.*)

TBT: Now that's the first sensible question you've asked.

CHILD: *Why?*

TBT: Well, we've been trying to get at the root cause of this, um, but you'll be pleased to know that there is a DVD available for Christmas.

CHILD: *Why?*

TBT: Because there's such a demand for it.

CHILD: *Why?*

TBT: Because it's such a great show and it's so reasonably priced.

CHILD: *What a load of rubbish.*

HL: I'm rather warming to that kid.

CHILD: *What a load of rubbish . . . What are those people laughing at?*

HL: I don't know.

CHILD: *Why?*

HL: You're asking the wrong person.

Despite the early bath for *If I Ruled the World*, it is remembered fondly by many, and not least those who worked on it. 'It was one of the few things I've done on TV that I thought really worked, and that I thought I was good in!' Hardy says, 'There aren't many other things that I've been in that I've really felt that great about. Quite a bit of *Mock the Week* is ripped off from *If I Ruled the World*, which is a shame, because I think ours was a better show.' The idea was also semi-recycled by the comedy debating quiz *Argumental*, which runs on the Dave channel. Graeme adds, 'Funnily enough my son is living in Sweden at the moment and *If I Ruled the World* is their top comedy show. It's called *Parliament*.'

Tim and Graeme did return to our screens in quiz mode thanks to another game devised by Richard Osmond, *Beat the Nation*, which appeared in the snoozy daytime *Fifteen to One* slot on Channel 4 in 2004. This was a test to find the cleverest person in the land (presumably out of those without gainful employment) using statistics of how 1,000 surveyed members of the public had answered a question as a yardstick for the studio contestants. The idea was that Tim would take the 'good cop' role of indulging in the politest of light banter with the contestants, while Graeme played 'bad cop', asking the more difficult questions and keeping order. However, many claimed that the ex-Goodies (paired up for the first time on British TV since they were deemed 'two nice young men' on *Broaden Your Mind* nearly forty years earlier) were actually playing 'nice cop' and 'much nicer cop', and the show only lasted for one series. With that experiment halted, Tim and Graeme had nothing to fall back on but the most successful, universally adored radio comedy show that had ever existed. Sometimes life is tough.

The Antidote to Panel Games

It's little wonder that *I'm Sorry I Haven't a Clue* has so thoroughly mocked other game shows throughout its history. It is, after all, the antidote to the existing quizzes, so they're fair game. 'Just a Minim' and the digs at *Quote Unquote* go without saying, but a ridiculous version of *Call My Bluff* was also played for years –via the game 'Daffy Definitions'.

> HL: These are all from Webster's Dictionary, therefore these are all proper words. Or as proper words as ever get into Webster's Dictionary. John Cleese, your word is . . .
>
> JC: Who has ever met Mr Webster? He may be a practical joker on an immense scale! . . . I'm having it put in my contract from now on, 'No Webster!'

Call My Bluff was Humph's favourite game in the old Robert Robinson days, as it was the only *Clue* round on which he stood to gain some points for himself, being the guesser. The listener of course had to trust the Chairman on whether he was right in selecting the correct definition out of the four fatuous offerings from the Teams, as we couldn't see whether the chosen card had 'Bluff' written on it or not. By the nineties, the real *Call My Bluff* had returned to greatness on daytime BBC1, with Bob Holness, Alan Coren and Sandi Toksvig in charge, and an array of *Clue* regulars appearing –Tim and Graeme were even on the same show, still on opposing teams.

On the subject of definitions, perhaps the most celebrated of the new batch of games dreamt up by the Teams was 'New Definitions', which soon blossomed into the authoritative *Uxbridge English Dictionary*. This game took a well-known word and redefined it in such a way that it was impossible to look at it in the same way ever again. The punning style wasn't new of course, but having actually *defined* the 'alternative definition' joke forevermore as coming from the *UED* is a testament to the popularity of *Clue*. It became another game that was irresistible to try yourself, at home or in the pub, when conversation ebbed – define, say, 'Hurricane' as 'A go-faster walking stick', and soon the challenge becomes contagious. 'Here's one more for Uxbridge . . .' became the cry, and once the game was established as the unchanging opening round to every recording (or every post-interval recording), all of the guests got their chance to add to the punning lexicon. Once the gag was out, it all seemed so obvious – 'Humpty Dumpty: One who is humped and dumped' – but all of the guests had their chance to add to the punning lexicon, and all too often the original gag-teller would be forgotten, so here are a number of entries from every player of the game. Right from the start, Humph wasn't confident in its success, naturally:

HL: Many words we use today have a meaning which is quite different from the original. For example, the word 'terrific', as in 'This game is a terrific one', clearly means 'really good'. But it used to mean 'instilling terror', and it still can, given a subtle change of context. For example, if I say 'This game is a terrific waste of my, and everybody else's, bloody time and always will be', the original meaning becomes all too apparent. So let's hear a selection of new meanings which the Teams have spotted for us . . .

JH: Dictator: a humorously shaped root vegetable.

BC: Colonnade: a fizzy enema.

GG: Gurgle: to steal a ventriloquist's dummy.

TBT: Snuff box: a coffin.

LS: Hustle-bustle: nineteenth-century kerb-crawler.

ST: Propane: people who are into S & M.

TH: Diarrhoea: an unattractive bottom.

PJ: Condominium: a birth-control device made from metal.

AH: Egret: an apology sent by computer.

SF: Rectitude: the angle at which a thermometer should be inserted.

BB: Napkin: one of the tiny sleep imps.

HH: Telepathy: when you can't be bothered to turn over the TV.

RN: Slippery: a bit like a slipper.

JD: Cathartic: when the bag freezes.

RB: Arson: to sit.

Instantly, it seemed somehow impossible that the *Uxbridge English Dictionary* had only been around since the start of the twenty-first century, with Jeremy Hardy offering the first entry, as seen above, in 2001. The round has been richly rewarding, already inspiring two published volumes of definitions. The *Clue* publishing stable had been ever growing since Naismith's first audio releases had shown that there was a hungry Audience out there, and *The Almost Totally Complete I'm Sorry I Haven't a Clue* was the first attempt to capture the show in print since Perkins's modest volume nineteen years earlier. Its glossy design went a lot further in translating the gags to print throughout (Paul Merton's suggestion for an invitation to the Legal Cannabis Campaign Dinner and Dance, '"Please arrive promptly at . . ." Oh hang on, the edge of the card's been torn off!' being presented with a perfect roach-shaped tear), plus there were the great Pattinson-led Humph monologues to print this time. There have also been two scholarly works on Mornington Crescent, *The Little Book of Mornington Crescent* and *Stovold's Mornington Crescent Almanac*, and the first release of them all, 1998's charming Limerick collection, released in tribute to Willie and bursting with not just prime poetry, but illustrations making full use of the cartooning talents of the whole Team – Rushton, Lyttelton and Garden each having their own distinctive, masterly style.

Barry had also squeezed in a couple of volumes of anecdotes by this time as well, and, like every *Clue* book, they found their way into the show itself one way or another – not that it was advertising in any way, of course. That's illegal:

HL: Now, Teams, browsing in my local bookshop recently, I noticed a new title called *The Almost Complete I'm Sorry I Haven't a Clue*, which looks unbeatable value at only £9.99. And I got to thinking, with the growth of the internet as a provider of intellectual stimulus, there's a real danger that such traditional books will go out of fashion. There are still occasions on which only a real substantial volume by an author such as *(intake of breath)* Jeffrey Archer will do. Try propping up a table leg with a Pentium processor . . . With the promotion of book-reading for pleasure very much in mind, we're going to play a game called 'Opening Lines'. Earlier I provided the Teams with a brief resumé of a book title, and from that information they've provided what they think may be the opening lines. The book is *You Won't Believe This, But* . . . No, not the Vanessa Feltz story, it's in fact the autobiography of our own Barry Cryer. To give you some assistance in imagining how Barry might have started his work, here's how he modestly describes it on the jacket cover: 'In this highly entertaining look at a career spanning stand-up days in the Windmill Theatre in the fifties, to his cult status with today's young audience . . . (*tittering throughout the theatre*) Barry brings together a wealth of showbiz anecdotes revealing his world at the forefront of British comedy.' OK, Teams, your suggestions for first lines for Barry's book. Phill, what have you got?

PJ: 'It was the best of haircuts, it was the worst of haircuts . . .'

TBT: 'These two nuns and a Scotsman walked into a pub. And I thought, "Hey what a great idea for a career! Going into pubs . . ."'

Returning to the subject of TV mockery, but still in a wordplay vein, there was the occasion on which the Teams played *Countdown*, with the chosen letters GGGGZVQYG eliciting Willie's complaint 'I suppose it's too late to ask for a vowel, is it?' and *Through the Keyhole* was another early TV show that came in for a real drubbing (despite the grocery bills paid by Willie over the years from being a regular on the real thing). Naismith and Pattinson, however, ramped up the spoofs of existing shows as the nineties gave way to the noughties, and massive quiz show successes like *Who Wants to Be a Millionaire* and *Weakest Link* began to rule the TV schedules. Indeed, Anne Robinson would soon take her rightful place alongside Joan Collins, Jeffrey Archer and Anne Widdecombe as one of the show's favourite figures of derision – Humph once referring to her marital woes which were filling the tabloids: 'There are strong rumours that she's met someone else. And who's the lucky man? Mr Robinson.' Even non-quizzes like *Dragons' Den* and *Hell's Kitchen* have been pilloried, with reality shows like *The Apprentice* providing inspiration for one of the special trails recorded to herald the return of the show:

VOICE-OVER: Humphrey Lyttelton is a self-made man who appears to have lost the instructions.

HL: Jeremy, sing Jenni Murray to the tune of Sue Lawley!

JH: What?

HL: Not quick enough. You're fired.

VOICE-OVER: Two teams of hopeful young pensioners compete to become Humphrey's Apprentice, complete with a two-figure salary and their own company cardigan.

HL: Barry, Graeme and Tim – you're fired. Colin? You're a lightweight. You're fired too. And you lot, what are you gawping at? You're all fired.

GG: Er, that was the Audience.

HL: Hm. Shifty-looking pair.

Mocking our modern celebrity culture became more and more important to the programme as the years went by, with *Hello!* magazine a favourite target, and indeed 'Complete Quotes' soon expanded to become 'A Day In The Life', altering interviews given by the likes of Posh Spice. However, an attempt to play 'Complete Quotes' using speeches given by George W. Bush proved something of a washout, when a full quote, from a speech given in Seganor, Michigan, with the president attempting to prove his environmental credentials, was revealed – 'I oppose breaching those dams. I know that . . . human being and fish can co-exist peacefully.' The problem with the round was succinctly pointed out by Brooke-Taylor: '*How can we possibly top him?*'

But it was in 2000 that Anne Robinson, the self-styled Ice Queen of Quiz Shows, was most jubilantly stitched up, when Graeme and Iain collaborated on one momentous compendium of game-show clichés, the 'Quiz of Quizzes'. This round not only managed to get in references to *Brain of Britain*, *Masterchef*, *Play Your Cards Right*, *Family Fortunes*, *Who Wants to Be a Millionaire?*, *Weakest Link*, *Countdown* and more, it also offered a rare chance for the writer himself to make a cameo appearance on the show:

HL: Tim, question or nominate?

TBT: Nominate Graeme.

HL: No, the right answer is 'Nominate Barry'. You lose ten points. Barry, what is the first letter of the word 'aardvark'? Is it A, B, C or D?

BC: Oh, erm . . . Can I go fifty-fifty, Humph?

HL: Right, computer, take away one wrong answer and one right answer. Barry, you have two wrong answers left, which do you go for?

BC: Can I phone a friend?

HL: Oh all right, if you must. Who are you calling?

BC: Um, Iain.

FX: A mobile phone rings, beeps.

IAIN: Hello?

HL: Iain, this is Humphrey Lyttelton from Radio 2's *Best of Jazz*. Now I know you can't see the show . . .

IAIN: Um, yes I can.

HL: Why? Where are you?

IAIN: I'm here, I'm in the Audience!

HL: Well, you were told to switch off your mobiles before the recording, please switch yours off now.

IAIN: Oh, sorry.

HL: Barry.

BC: Iain? Iain, what's the first . . . Iain? Hello? He's gone!

HL: Aardvark, does it begin with C or D? Take your time.

GRAMS: *Who Wants to Be a Millionaire?* rumination music.

BC: I'll ask the audience.

HL: Go on then.

FX: Hundreds and hundreds of mobile phones ring.

HL: No, no, no, switch 'em all off! Barry, you're out of time. But let's see what our survey said.

FX: Family Fortunes 'No' buzzer.

HL: Well, Teams, at the end of that round you've banked a miserable 72p out of a possible £10,000. Who is letting you down? It's time to vote for who you think is the Weakest Link!

FX: Weakest Link dramatic music.

GG: Anne Robinson.

TBT: Anne Robinson.

BC: Anne Robinson.

JH: I'd have to say Anne Robinson as well.

HL: Tim, why Anne Robinson?

TBT: Exactly.

HL: Well, Anne Robinson, you are the Weakest Link, Goodbye!

GRAMS: Brain of Britain exit music.

14

The Purveyor of Blue-Chip Filth

'Our whole effort,' reaffirms Jon Naismith, 'has been to build on and develop the best things about the show, and slowly allow the less good things to fall by the wayside ... One Lionel Blair joke just worked particularly well, and before long he'd become a fixture.' Of all the TV game show piss-takes scattered throughout *Clue*'s history, the most long-running and celebrated must surely be the way that 'Sound Charades' made mincemeat of the cosy ITV daytime charades show *Give Us a Clue* – 'the entertainment show that really is something else' – which ran from 1979 to 1992, under the watchful gaze of Michaels Aspel and Parkinson. However, it's the Team Captains on that game that everyone remembers.

Lionel and Una Get the Horn
The late nineties will always be remembered for the Rise of Blair. This cheesy figure, coming seemingly from nowhere, was soon at the centre of an incredibly popular movement that the British people embraced with rapture. And the funny thing is, Lionel hadn't done *Give Us a Clue* for years when he was first namechecked. At first, the much loved, eternally orange choreographer and theatrical legend was only generally thrown in for a random chuckle, described as 'the dancer and father of the Labour leader, Ramsay MacDonald', but soon other aspects of Lionel's life were brought to light – or rather, yet again, Humph's innocent memories of a classic parlour game show were misconstrued by a shamelessly filth-intoxicated Audience, suggesting scenes that would make a libel lawyer purr with pleasure and upgrade his next holiday.

Whenever Humph introduced the ancient game – 'As you'll remember, in the TV version, the players were not allowed to speak, leading to much mirth and hilarity. Our version operates on similar principles, but with two exceptions – mirth and hilarity . . .' – he tended to reminisce about classic moments, claiming that 'No one who witnessed the event will ever forget the sparkle in Lionel Blair's eye as he received *Free Willy* from Michael Aspel . . . for two minutes!' or perhaps the time the veteran improviser was 'on his knees finishing off *An Officer and A Gentleman*', or 'the occasion he was given *A Town Like Alice*, when he chose to do a silent impression of the author. Such was the performance, Una Stubbs gasped in amazement when she saw Neville Shute in Lionel's face.' To be fair, Una herself was often in Humph's thoughts. 'Fans still speak in hushed tones of the day Una Stubbs, her hands a-blur, managed *Three Men in a Boat* in less than ninety seconds . . .' And these were great commendations from a Chairman of Humph's standing. But of course the Audience took it all the wrong way. As did the panellists – this would be the window for Jupitus or Toksvig to squawk like burning parrots. Only Humph knew the injustice of the double entendres, but thankfully the star of these tales himself never bore a grudge, and is a big fan – besides, he'd been a regular on Kenny Everett's show and accompanied Barry on a biographical radio panel game called *The Name's the Game*, so he knew how to handle a little mockery. When questioned, Lionel Blair insisted: 'I think it's a great show, and I'm very flattered that the show and the Audience take such an interest in me!'

Humph may have repeatedly declared that he was oblivious to any double meanings, but Iain Pattinson certainly knew what he was doing. Back in the *ISIRTA* days the writers managed to get away with 'Martha Farquar' and all sorts of staggering innuendo for the time, but Jon and Iain knew they could probably go a lot further, especially with such a supportive listening fan base out there urging them on. But at the same time, the restrictions of being in the traditionally staid panel-game slot made it a real challenge to push the envelope. 'It didn't help,' says Naismith, 'because I think *Quote Unquote* and so on has an older listenership, it's quite an old-fashioned format and it's a different audience, and I think when *Clue* followed it, we might have had more complaints as a result. We never had many, but *Clue* is on the edge of good taste, and sort of for a younger mentality. There are plenty of older people who love it, but I think you have to be young at heart and broad-minded.'

It wasn't just the dubious phrasing of what Blair, Stubbs and Christopher Biggins used to get up to either, Samantha's hobbies were eliciting ever-larger gasps of disbelief every week too, no matter how innocent they prove to be, on paper:

HL: Samantha is out on a dinner date with a gentleman friend from Moscow, who's brought over caviar and a variety of vodka-based aperitifs. She says he's going to offer her delicious food in their hotel room and then liquor out on the balcony . . .

Samantha tells me she's had to nip out to meet a nice chap who's training her in computer skills. Tonight she's hoping he's going to show her the three-and-a-half-inch floppy he's got in his Mac . . .

As a matter of fact Samantha has started keeping bees, and already has three dozen or so. She says she's got an expert handler coming round to give a demonstration. He'll carefully take out her thirty-eight bees and soon have them flying round his head . . .

And of course the astounding introduction to the round 'Italian Radio Times' which barely managed entendres in duplicate:

HL: Samantha has to go now as she's off to meet her Italian gentleman friend who's taking her out for an ice cream. She says she likes nothing better than to spend the evening licking the nuts off a large Neapolitan.

Jon continues, 'The reason Humphrey was able to get away with so much was because he was a very old, nice, gentle-sounding man! People tend to complain about things because they think they've offended somebody else, rather than being offended personally . . . And context is all. I think the idea of someone of an older generation than just about anyone who's listening coming up with these things kind of provides a safety net. Plus he delivered these lines as if he had no idea what they meant, and I think in some instances he actually didn't! He didn't bother, he just read it out.' The combination of perfectly tuned wordplay, affable innocence and sheer depravity was an immensely powerful brew, its effect on Audience and listener uniquely disarming, reducing all to a shaking, jelly-like mirth.

Bugger Scunthorpe
Having provided so many years of top-drawer radio comedy scripts for *ISIRTA* over the years, Graeme knows just how rare a perfect blend like the marriage of Pattinson's words with Humph's charm really is. 'Iain has written for loads of people but I think he wrote his finest stuff for Humph, the style and the delivery were perfectly attuned. I've tried to write a Pattinson-style intro for the special shows, and it makes you realise how very cleverly and carefully constructed his gags are.' Jack Dee, like every guest, was in awe of the depth of the scripts' double entendres from a ringside seat, and observes, 'Iain Pattinson is a brilliant writer and consistently came up with very, very funny intros and monologues for Humph to do, but what was extraordinary about seeing that process happening, was that I don't think Humph ever questioned a line of it. He'd literally get it, sort of mumble it through to himself by way of rehearsal, and then read it onstage and make it work brilliantly well, and I think part of the magic of that was he simply didn't seem to really care either way. He did care, but he had that great way with his delivery of relaxing

the Audience – because it didn't seem to matter much to Humph whether it was funny or not. And of course that's half the secret. Once you've got the Audience relaxed . . . then you've already got an Audience that are going to enjoy everything an awful lot more.' Soon Humph's rendering of Pattinson's pitch-perfect innuendo earned him the moniker from the press of the Nation's Finest Purveyor of Blue-Chip Filth, a title of which Humph declared himself 'intensely proud', and ruminated about the idea of having a van specially painted with the legend, travelling from town to town doling out sauce.

But smut was one thing. What about the language the Teams started to get away with? Naismith is right – context is everything. When Peter Cook and Dudley Moore were doing unspeakable things to the boundaries of taste as Derek & Clive in the seventies, they were trying their luck in the form of underground recordings – what the teams managed on *Clue* has been every bit as taboo-busting, but in the context of the Home Service. None of the veterans are particularly enamoured of any reliance on swearing to get a laugh, with Graeme particularly more keen on suggestive wordplay than balls-out profanity, but occasionally, when the joke demands it, they've taken big risks. The most eye-opening example of this came in a 'Complete Quotes' round in 1998, in which Barry was played a sample of translation from Saddam Hussein's official spokesman:

GRAMS: 'For it is a right on all of us to carry out the Holy Jihad, the Holy War of Islam, to liberate the Holy . . . the Holy . . .'
BC: . . . HOLY SHIT, HE'S GOT A GUN!

Hearing this moment broadcast on BBC Radio 4 on the Sunday repeat, just as folk around the British Isles were settling down to Sunday lunch, it seemed like a watershed in broadcasting. What other show could have got away with such a stellar four-letter-word at such a time? And, even when hidden under deft layers of wordplay, it's a miracle that moments such as Fry's definition of 'Countryside' as 'To kill Piers Morgan', the infamous 'Scunthorpe' gag, and the sheer abuse of Humph's aside: 'I'm getting fed up with these ridiculous celebrity endorsements. Only the other day I was in the supermarket and I saw a packet of sausages with Antony Worrall Thompson pictured in his kitchen on the packet. Underneath was the wording "Prick with a fork" . . . Rather harsh, I thought . . .' But, unbelievably, such instances elicit far less griping from the real Mrs Trellises of the world than moments like this:

HL: Right, we're going to have a bit of good old-fashioned fun now, with the marvellous game called 'Hunt the Slipper'. Actually, the last time we did this the Teams got rather overexcited because they thought they were going to play 'Hunt the Stripper'. The man who was in to take the paint off our door frames got quite agitated as well. In 'Hunt the Slipper', I'll sit with my eyes closed while the slipper is passed around behind the Teams' backs. After a few seconds' slipper-passing, I shall call out 'Slipper search on!' And then I'll open my eyes. Obviously I will have no idea where the slipper is, but the Teams should keep passing the slipper round secretly, and I shall have to guess who's holding the slipper, and challenge them by pointing and calling out 'Slipper holder!' ... *I'm seventy-eight, for Christ's sake!*

This entirely spontaneous outburst of course brought the house down, and as one of the few times that the cool jazzman ever let the silliness of it all get the better of him, it instantly became a cherished *Clue* moment. But still some people out there decided to complain about the apparent use of blasphemy. 'There are Rules and Regulations, we have a Producers' Guidelines which we have to read, and respond to as producers,' says Naismith. '"Shit" will offend some people, but it's the way it's delivered and it's the quality of the joke. "Christ"' is one of the most controversial things you can say, certainly more so than "shit". We did have some complaints about "Christ", but I referred it – because I thought it was a gloriously funny moment, for fans of Humph it almost seemed like a benchmark in the show's history, that exclamation – and was given permission.'

But the Teams had been openly messing around with religion from the very start of the show, with many games going far beyond the cursory naming of a character from the New Testament. Not one of the *Clue* regulars is in any way religious, with many, Humph included, being fully paid-up humanists – Barry Cryer's family tend towards the Catholic Church, but he has always politely declined to take the sacrament. So it's no wonder that they've all given themselves free rein to come up with, say, 'Biblical Chat-Up Lines':

BC: Hello, I'm Lazarus. Wanna see me rise again?
LS: David, is that a slingshot in your pocket, or ... ?
GG: Look, I don't mind the wailing but if you're going to gnash your teeth ...

Or Graeme's alternative opening for the Book of Genesis: 'In the beginning there was a cosmological expansion of space, time and matter from a gravitational singularity; which came as a bit of a surprise to God.'

However, Tim does admit, 'I'm not a believer, but I tend to avoid religious jokes as they're more trouble than they're worth. Mind you, if I had a good one . . .' Any which way, there was always a third way when it came to dealing with complaints, as Humph discovered when introducing a round of 'Strip Poker': 'We're required to issue a warning that the next section is likely to include scenes of gratuitous nudity. Any listeners liable to be offended who might wish to write letters of complaint are politely asked to turn the volume down now . . . OK, Teams, now we've got rid of that bunch of po-faced whiners, you can start the game.'

By the Beard of Moira Anderson!

Lionel and Una's shenanigans were one reason the crowd greeted 'Sound Charades' so enthusiastically every time it came round, but soon there was another reason. Would they or would they not be getting a visit from the Highlands when it was Graeme and Barry's turn to communicate their Charade? The duo of course had been performing torturous clues together for the round for eons, but they soon discovered that having alter egos who could deliver some of the riper puns they had in mind would be a smart move, and the cornier and more outlandish they were the better. Graeme had been having fun with his Scots ancestry from the very first episode of *Clue*, which contained the first of many spoofs of *Dr Finlay's Casebook*, two kindly medical practitioners and their bleating, kipper-obsessed housemaid Janet having adventures in the Highlands, replete with all the clichés of the area – 'Hoots', 'Jings', and the traditional cry of the stereotypical frugal Scotsman, 'You'll have had your tea . . .' Having Scottish roots of his own, Graeme felt perfectly free to plaster on the clichés with a trowel. 'It's a send-up of stereotypes, the kilt and shortbread image of Scotland, which most Scots find irritating. The world of Hamish and Dougal is the twee Scottish world of the old White Heather Club and tartan egg cosies.'

It may come as a shock to some – perhaps even to Barry and Graeme – to learn that Hamish and Dougal first turned up in all but name in a 1979 Christmas Special, with a prototype performance to give the clue for 'Wee Freak Ings of Orient Are' (the dwarf footballers Jimmy Ing, Frank Ing and so on). This is made all the more remarkable by the fact that John Junkin was sitting in for Barry at the time – and almost forgot to do the accent. Tim got the answer so quickly perhaps it's not surprising that it was another sixteen years until the punning Highlanders returned, in the 1995 Christmas Special.

HL: It's your turn now, Barry, Graeme, and your title's going up on the hologram imager screen, and here's the Mystery Voice for the listeners at home.

MV: *The Queen's Speech. The Queen's Speech.*

HL: Right, what is it, Barry and Graeme?

GG: It's a TV programme.

BC: It's three words. Ahem. Begin . . . Ah, Hamish, nice to have you here for Christmas. You'll have had your dinner.

GG: Oh, well, no, I . . . What?

BC: Would you like to see my hives?

GG: Oh, how very unpleasant.

BC: No no no. No! You misconstrue! Come down the bottom of the garden here and see my jolly swarm.

GG: Oh, the bees, the wee bees.

BC: Yes, they've settled now, bless them, and they're feeding on the honey as usual but – look at her.

GG: Ooh, she's a big one, isn't she?

BC: She's over there. She's got her own wee meal there!

GG: What's that she's eating?

BC: A succulent fruit!

GG: That's a very succulent-looking fruit! (*Audience groan.*)

BC: Anyone comes near that it puts the fear of death in them.

GG: That's her own fruit, then?

BC: You're very observant . . .

GG: This succulent fruit, what do ye call it?

BC: I'd have thought that was obvious, Hamish. (*Applause.*)

HL: Tim and Willie, can I just tell you something? They always tell you on these radio shows that even if you know the answer, to sort of hedge around it a bit . . . or forget it.

Before long the saucy pair were back, briefly appearing under the monikers of Alec and Denzil – but Hamish & Dougal they soon became, a regular fixture. Graeme says that of all of *Clue*'s games, 'I have a soft spot for "Sound Charades" when we get to do Hamish and Dougal – partly because it annoys Tim.' Being thoroughly left out of the corny Scots fun, Tim's withering reactions to Hamish and Dougal's doggerel were never muted – loudly complaining as each skit went on and on, or yawning 'Is it *The Longest Day?*' before his compadres had even got going. When Barry & Graeme launched into their usual 'Och aye the noo!' act in a recording in Glasgow, Tim positively begged them to reconsider, but to no avail. Luckily the locals lapped it up, cheering the Highland reprobates louder than any other crowd.

Soon the cheers that rang in the ears of Graeme and Barry with every other game of 'Sound Charades' presented a clear opportunity to the pair, Graeme confesses, 'They sort of caught on, and we kept doing them. And eventually, we thought, "Well, it's quite fun doing these and we find it quite easy to write some jokes for them, why don't we try and write a whole, long sketch, with a little story, and try and sell that idea for a series?" So we did that, and the first thing we had to decide was which was which, because we'd done them sort of three or five times a year for a long time but we couldn't remember who was Hamish and who was Dougal. So we decided eventually that I would be Dougal and Barry would be Hamish, and that's the way we kept it.' Graeme knows all too well how tempting it can be to give a besotted crowd just what they want, and so it was no surprise when Hamish and Dougal became the stars of the first ever *Clue* spin-off, with a run of fifteen-minute specials over Christmas 2002. Cryer and Garden of course had to expand the world of the aged Highland funsters to create a sitcom around them, but ultimately the series *You'll Have Had Your Tea: The Doings of Hamish & Dougal* had exactly the same pervy punning that had featured in 'Sound Charades', except – bad news for Brooke-Taylor – ten times the length.

It was decided that what Hamish and Dougal needed was a figure to kick off against, an aristocratic laird who would hold the heroes in complete contempt, and Jeremy Hardy further confirmed his place as the first among equals of all *Clue* guests by jumping at the role with glee (even if most episodes did require him to sing, loudly and badly). More than a decade after *The Long Hot Satsuma*, Barry and Graeme had also been hoping to find a way to work once again with Alison Steadman, who now stepped up to the mic to portray the boys' housekeeper, Mrs Margaret Morag Beyoncé Naughtie – an inflated sex hippo not too far removed from Lady Constance De Coverlet herself. However, Barry does admit, 'We always wanted to work with her again, but she wasn't the first Mrs Naughtie – I don't think Alison will mind at all – it was Denise Coffey, who's an old friend, but said, "No, I've retired, I love you all," and that was it. I think it was Jon Naismith who came up with Alison's name, and we said, "Oh, yeah!" And she read it and played it totally differently from the way Denise would have done – very aggressive, and in your face! And we loved it, so that was it, it was very happy the way it turned out.'

As well as the thinly veiled Blue-Chip Filth that always characterised their outings, Hamish and Dougal's new show also bristled with the kind of rug-pulling silly jokes that you can only do on radio (such as 'Pick those feet up! I don't know who they belong to, but they've been here since last night!'), and Cryer and especially Garden had so many years of radio comedy writing behind them that every opportunity offered by the medium was exploited to the full. Sound effects naturally play a huge part. Graeme says, 'I have a bit of a bee in my bonnet – Jon Naismith always goes on at me about how difficult my scripts are to edit because I put in so many sound effects, but I keep telling him, that's what radio is all about! Well, I don't have to tell him, of course ... Because half the fun of radio is creating those pictures. I think a lot of radio comedy – sketch comedy and sitcom – you listen and think, "well, that's just people saying funny things to each other, I'm not really getting much of an idea of what's happening here. I can't *see* anything funny."' Garden ensured that *You'll Have Had Your Tea* was true radio comedy. 'Again, full of visual surprises – you suddenly realise that they're talking to each other in the bath and so on . . . When I say that you get the best pictures on the radio, they're not necessarily the most desirable.'

Live music, another luxury of Graeme's, was also central to the show's charm, with any excuse to make the Laird break into song, and Highland reels incorporating chart hits, provided by a talented young musician called John 'JJ' Garden – also a member of New York dance act the Scissor Sisters live band. Indeed, so proud is JJ's father that he's paid tribute by squeaking his way through two Scissor Sisters tracks during games of 'Pick-Up Song'.

There were three joyously silly series of *You'll Have Had Your Tea*, with the duo getting into silly scrapes with vampires, Nessie and TV-talent show judges. But the most memorable of their adventures was the 2004 Hogmanay Special, broadcast on New Year's Eve itself and running at twice the usual length. The *Clue* roots of the show were celebrated with a guest appearance from the famous celebrity Timothy Brooke-Taylor, playing himself, arriving at the laird's big house for a golf tournament, and meeting the despot's famous servant.

FX: <u>Winds blow, sleighbells jangle.</u>
GG: Hamish, hurry up there! And stop playing with that brass monkey.
FX: <u>Two clanking noises.</u>
BC: Oh, the bells have fallen off!
GG: Oh, never mind, we're here at the Big Hoose. I'll ring the bell.
FX: <u>Doorbell rings. A catastrophic crashing.</u>
BC: Oh, that's fallen off as well!
FX: <u>Door creaks open.</u>
HL: Good afternoon, gentlemen. Don't just stand there shivering – go away!
BC: And who might you be?
HL: I *might* be Geri Halliwell. But in fact I'm His Lairdship's butler, Lyttelton.
JH: Lyttelton? Who is that at the door?
HL: It's me, sir!
JH: Well, come in, for goodness' sake!
HL: Thank you, sir!
FX: <u>Door slams.</u>
GG: Oh, jings!

Lyttelton eventually is forced to grant the eponymous pair admission when they sneak in, behind the guest of honour, Tim.

Neither Hamish nor Dougal turn out to be fans of golf themselves (Cryer has always insisted, 'I don't play golf. I *like* women.'), but they are soon press-ganged into caddying for Tim as he plays a round against the famous seven-foot-tall female golfer Sandi Wedge, played by wee Sandi Toksvig. With Colin taking the huge thespian leap of cameoing as a pianist who ends up being sacrificed in a Wicker Man, and even a guest appearance from presenter of Radio 4's *Today* programme, James Naughtie (arriving to confirm that he is indeed the son of Hamish and Dougal's housekeeper), plus a traditional singalong ending, led by the Laird with his painful rendition of 'Auld Lang Syne', it was a Hogmanay to remember. But this wasn't the only festive special connected to *Clue*, and indeed the whole Hogmanay idea was inspired by the success one year earlier of the first *ISIRTA*-style extended radio panto written by Garden for many years.

God Rest Ye, Merry Gentlemen

Any long-running successful show that *doesn't* in some way have a go at Charles Dickens' *A Christmas Carol* is doing something wrong. *Blackadder, The Flintstones, The Goon Show,* even *Quantum Leap* have all reworked the Scrooge story for festive specials – and *ISIRTA* had already made its own attempt, in 'A Christmas Carrot'. All you really need to make it work is an irascible central character surrounded by jovial merrymakers, all in his thrall. Graeme wasn't going to need to stretch Dickens's prose very far to put together *I'm Sorry I Haven't a Christmas Carol*, which entertained millions over Christmas dinner in 2003.

There had been Christmas broadcasts of the nation's favourite comedy show since the start, often with Humph and, later, Samantha linking clips from the year's shows from the Chairman's Highland retreat ('Every loyal *Clue* listener will imagine my excitement at the BBC's invitation to choose nothing but highlights from twelve programmes. And will understand my disbelief at their wanting a full thirty minutes!'), but the idea of scripting a full Christmas Special with a few gaps for traditional games was a masterstroke of Garden's. Of course the guests flocked to take part, with Fry providing the Dickensian narration, setting the scene of Victorian London, where 'As usual, it is Christmas . . .' in his most caramelised tones. Barry recalls, 'He's so busy these days he hasn't been on our show for a while, but when Jon rang Stephen to ask about *Christmas Carol*, he didn't even say "When?" – he said "Yes!"'

The *Clue Carol* told the tale of Ebenezer Scrumph, his housemaid Samantha, poor downtrodden employee Colin Crotchet, and the night of spectral haunt-ings that shows the miser the error of his ways. Tony played Nephew Fred,

Jeremy filled the role of Marley, naturally the three Spirits of Christmas were portrayed by Barry, Graeme and Tim, and there were parts for Linda, Andy and Sandi too, when they weren't coming up with gags in the games worked into Dickens' plot – 'Pick Up Phonograph', 'Victorian *Radio Times*' (with shows like *Ibiza: Covered, Can't Cook, Don't Have To Cook, Cook Will Cook, It's Only TB But I Like It* and *Crimea Watch*), and of course, in Christmas Past, there was the grand Mornington Crescent Tournament at Toksiwig's Ball.

Scrumph manages to hold on to his withering flintiness throughout the apparitions, until The Ghost of Queen Boadicea (the Spirit of Yet to Come being unavailable due to unforeseen circumstances, allowing Tim a double offering of Lady Constance-isms) shows the unrepentant old man what the future has in store – Nicholas Parsons presenting *Clue*! Not to mention an extended version of *Quote Unquote* and twenty-four-hour rolling *You and Yours*! At last, a changed man, Scrumph invites the whole assembled cast to join him in the traditional game of *I'm Sorry I Haven't a Clue*:

HL: . . . Here beside me, recovered from her recent indisposition, is my assistant Samantha, a fine young lady and a model of propriety. At the piano, we're lucky to have that genius of the keyboard, my good chum Colin Crotchet. Of course no panel game is complete without a collection of the cleverest and most amusing people in the land, and here they are. Now let's play some entertaining games, what larks! I'm looking forward to this hugely.

BC: This isn't going to work.

GG: No, he's being nice!

TBT: Where's the fun in that?

<u>FX:</u>   <u>Bell tolls, chains clank.</u>

JH: Wooo!

HL: Well, hello, Marley! It's so nice to have you back where you belong!

JH: Ebenezer Scrumph . . . you should have paid heed when I tried to warn you – resist the temptation to change your ways! Your career will depend on your being a grumpy old misery guts! It's an image thing.

So the old formula is reinstated, for a 'Swanee Kazoo' finale of 'White Christmas', with Adrian Macintosh and Mick Hutton on drums and bass, and finally Humph joining in on trumpet, showing off his legendary hotlips within *Clue* for only the second time. The panto won the show another Sony Award when the 2004 ceremony rolled around (the second nod having arrived in 2002). The official quote from the judges was 'A stunning cast performing a blistering script – only really possible on radio. An excellent blend ...' It could just as easily be summed up by Dickens' own description of Nephew Fred's Christmas festivities: 'Wonderful party, wonderful games, wonderful unanimity, won-der-ful happiness.'

All Clued Up

It was said a few hundred pages ago that *ISIRTA* worked like a dynamo over its decade of madness, kicking off to a muted reaction and winding up as comedy bedlam, with committed fans roaring their approval of every silly gag. *Clue* has been going for too long to have such a smoothly definable history – as Naismith observes, it's been a bumpy ride. 'I detected a sea-change in Audience reaction at our recording in Harrogate in 1995 – Jeremy Hardy's first show. Before that it was only Mornington Crescent that would get a cheer; at this recording the Audience were much more vocal. I notice that on the first ever show which the BBC Radio Collection have released, the Audience are very enthusiastic – clearly due to the fact it was packed with fans of *ISIRTA*. If you listen to later recordings from the seventies and eighties there's very little in the way of Audience reaction. In fact, the shows have much less energy and atmosphere ...' Since Jon took over, the show hasn't let anything get in its way. Year after year, the Teams have returned – not just to the silly side job that kept them ticking along in previous decades, but to greater and greater ovations, creating hysteria like clockwork at every recording.

It seemed so unthinkable, so silly, that this fill-in panel-game piss-take wasn't just still running in the twenty-first century, but had developed into the most universally adored British Institution on the wireless. They'd had a moment of well-deserved back-slapping with the broadcast of *I'm Sorry I Haven't a Desert Island* in 1999, with favourite rounds chosen by famous fans and guests including noted admirer, Dame Judi Dench. Dame Judi had already proven her devotion to the show by appearing in a 'Celebrity *What's My Line?*' round in Sandi Toksvig's first recording. Where once the Teams would have only pretended that the likes of Sir Alec Guinness were in attendance, this time they had the real deal, with the First Lady of Theatre facing seemingly endless impertinent questions until her affirmative answer to the latter half of Sandi's question 'If you are in a group situation at work, do you tend to command respect from your co-workers, or do they just let you bang on until it's their turn?' revealed to Graeme that she was, indeed, an actress.

Dench shared a memory of listening to the show alongside her late husband the actor Michael Williams which has since become something of a common experience for *Clue* listeners. 'I get very very angry and baity if I can't hear *I'm Sorry I Haven't a Clue*. If I know it's coming up it makes my day ... I remember once driving along the motorway, and Michael and I had tears pouring down our face, I'm afraid we had to go onto the hard shoulder and stop, and say the car had broken down, because we simply weren't driving in a safe way.' If this kind of careless driving was as widespread as people insisted, then the BBC would have been making a great contribution to road safety if they had axed the show, or at least rescheduled it. Even Humph made reference to the phenomenon, when he was interviewed about his status as a radio comedy legend: 'I've made a rule over the years, since 1972, to avoid thinking about it at all costs. I'd get scared if I thought about it. I've never listened to myself on radio. What I like about it is being en route somewhere or other and stopping at traffic lights while the programme's on, and looking along the line and seeing people in cars alongside me, their shoulders shaking with laughter. I love that . . . obviously it's a ball.'

The year that *Clue* received its second Sony was also of course its thirtieth anniversary – 2002 – marked by the April broadcast of a special episode, back at the Playhouse, with Fry filling Willie's throne for the evening, and an Audience packed with the usual ecstatic fans, but also the cream of the extended *Clue* family. Jon Naismith even invited the co-creator to say a few words before 'The Schickel Shamble' crashed in. 'I didn't know David very well,' admits Naismith, 'but I loved and shared his passion. You're unlikely to do anything well if you're not passionate about it. David was passionate about comedy and about radio. When he was MD of Radio I'd occasionally get notes from him asking for tapes of the last series of *ISIHAC* . . . When he died he was described on Radio 4 news as "the man who started *I'm Sorry I Haven't a Clue*". Not the man who was MD of Network Radio or any of his other achievements. He was a huge figure in BBC Radio and it owes him a great debt.'

Back at the thirtieth anniversary show, the Teams and Humph were assembled, and the affable ex-Radio Head took to the stage and quietened down the rabble:

DH: Well, I can see you're as noisy as ever. The history is actually quickly told . . . the idea for *Clue*, like most good programmes, was conceived in a pub. And one day there will be, I'm quite sure, a blue plaque outside the Guinea, saying 'Mornington Crescent was born here'. We wanted a show that was totally trivial, irrelevant and irreverent. And I'm glad to say that that fine principle has been rigorously upheld . . . It is actually remarkable that a programme devoted to being unremittingly silly should have survived so long. Its achievements, I think, are threefold: that anyone called Samantha will always get a second glance, that all foreigners believe that all stations lead to Mornington Crescent, and that careers masters in all schools and universities compel their students to listen, because it demonstrates beyond peradventure that a living can be made talking rubbish, even outside of Parliament. Here endeth the lesson.

And with that dismissal from the boss, on they went, for another year, and another, and another, without Humph, or the Teams, and especially not Jon and Iain, allowing the pace to let up for a minute, series after series. Thirty years and still going strong! At the end of the anniversary show, Humph reflected on the feat of lasting for three decades, and decided that 'To have brought joy and laughter to thousands of listeners ... might at least have been worth a try.'

The specials continued as well, with Andrew Marr presenting a brand new investigation into the unflaggingly popular game of champions, *In Search of Mornington Crescent*, in 2005. The Teams aided the political commentator in his quest to uncover the real rules of the ancient pastime – Marr being one of the poor minority not to have played it as a child. On his journey to master the basics, taking in the game's questionable connections to the Templars, the Freemasons and the Church of Domestic Scientology, Marr took the time to examine Mornington Crescent's history in more depth, from Brother Chalfont to Great Britain's triumph in the five-day series against Australia in 2005. Graeme looked for clues to the game's secret history in the vault at Berwick Abbey, Tim investigated the history of Cromwell's Mornington Crescent-hating Gamefinder General, Matthew Brooke-Taylor (no relation), and Barry was abducted by a shady figure while playing a physical version of the Tudor Rules, moving around Old London Town. The blue-chip nature of the show's fan base was revealed by the keenness of both Dame Judi and Sir Michael Gambon to perform a scene from the lost, then found, Restoration Comedy, Arthur Farquar's *The Bromley-by-Bow Stratagem*, while Antony Worrall Thompson showed no hard feelings over the 'Prick with a fork' incident by recreating a Mornington Crescent-themed recipe, and Marr continued his mission by visiting the BBC's Museum of Morningtonia, which has since burned down.

Perhaps the best example of the seemingly endless growth of the show can be seen in Humphrey Lyttelton's attempts to explain the rules of 'One Song to the Tune of Another' to the Teams after hundreds and hundreds of attempts. Where once a simple explanation of the concept sufficed:

HL: As ever, with these cryptic titles, it'll need some detailed explanation. What I've done, Teams, is to make two selections of songs. The first will be played without the words, or lyrics, leaving just the backing accompaniment, or music. The second selection will also have the words, or lyrics, but they'll be separated from the music, or backing track. Then – and here comes the clever part – what happens next is that the remainder libretto part of the first selection will be matched with the residual tunes of the second list, in a way that puts different backing tracks with contrasting words that weren't originally intended to match. And if you thought that was hard to follow, just wait until you hear Colin Sell's piano accompaniment.

Surely that would clear up the matter once and for all? But no, he'd be back to square one next time round, with an analogy even more helpfully succinct. By now the momentum of the show meant that the odds of getting a ticket to a recording, without being on the official mailing list and being damn quick with a mobile phone and a credit card, were very slim indeed. This was undoubtedly down to the love for the show, but at the same time, the unspoken question hung in the air: 'How long can this go on?'

It's all about Timing, really. *I'm Sorry I Haven't a Clue* is like a practical joke played on the nation, a 'Kick Me' note on the back of the BBC, and the joke just got funnier and funnier the longer it went on. There comes a point with any foolish pleasantry when it seems the joke has run its course – then you realise how ridiculous it is that the joke's still going on and it becomes funny again, funnier still. But at a recording, as both Teams and Audience looked around at each other, basking in the physically debilitating, tear-jerking after-effects of another Samantha anecdote from the Chairman, that one sane, well-ripened man staring innocently out from his umpire's chair, everyone in attendance knew – but would never dare admit as much, even to themselves – that something had to give eventually.

If *ISIRTA* acted like a dynamo, *ISIHAC*'s growth and ripening was like an ever-inflating balloon, brightly-coloured and squeaking fit to burst in front of your face – you don't know how big it can get, or what the snapping point will be, but what fun it is while it lasts!

The older the whole gang became, of course, the more jokes about their decrepitude they could do. This was particularly prevalent any time Humph's usually razor-sharp delivery wandered from the target, allowing Barry especially to take the proverbial mike, chivvying around the elder statesman like a nursing-home carer. In all fairness, Barry was the first to turn the joke on himself whenever he was representing the senior citizen, happily pretending to be gaga when appearing on *Never Mind the Buzzcocks*. When an old-age-themed round cropped up, such as 'Pensioners' Chat-Up Lines' (including 'I want to run my fingers through your hair, so pass it over' and 'Let's lock

Zimmer frames and rattle till we drop!'), Tim was wont to complain to his compadres, 'Do you remember when we used to find these funny?'

Usually, it goes without saying, Humph's asides and monologues were unstoppable forces of nature, such as his tirade against TV adverts for the Royal Mail which triumphantly held up a round of 'Complete Ad Slogans':

HL: 'If I need to write a letter, I'll post it.' What the blazes do they think I'm going to do with a letter? Sellotape it to a carrier pigeon? Actually now I come to think of it that isn't such a bad idea, at least pigeons wouldn't sort out the second-class mail and leave it in a cupboard for a fortnight. At least they wouldn't practise penalty shoot-outs with my Christmas parcels either. And what's more, pigeons don't hang about – I've seen continents shift faster than our postman ... Whoops, I'd better be careful in case the Post Office know where I live!

But occasionally, sat there between the Teams trying to retain his sanity, Humph was known to allow his mind to wander wherever he liked – as long as it wasn't in any realm of sanity, often leaving him sounding like a real-life Totteridge. You couldn't blame the Chairman for indulging in a little mental escapism while the Teams were still playing some game that had continued long after he had lamented that he was never going to make that gig in Hull, causing the sprightly Teams to cry:

TBT: Matron!
BC: The glasses are in your locker, I told you!
JH: He doesn't even know we're here, Barry.
BC: I know, I know ... *Your trumpet went very well at the auction! Mr Kenny Ball got it.*
GG: *He's growing a geranium in it!*
HL: ... I'm just going to pick up Samantha's score. (*Sound of shredding.*)
BC: You've just torn up your pension book now! See what you've done.
HL: And finally, What goes 'Tick tick, woof?'
GG: A dog marking homework.

Poor Humph was often forced to suffer the indignity of recording one or two retakes of fluffed lines after every recording, but he always had the sense to blame them on Naismith's handwriting, which he claimed had to be pinned on a wall and run past to be legible. Any ongoing verbal misfires would be explained away similarly: 'I can't read his writing again ... which is sad, because it's typed.' But as some of the outtakes show, there's no way he would let this affably crumbly old-relic act lose him one iota of his authority as Chairman:

JN: Mornington Crescent . . . there was a printing mistake in the script, it's actually 'website', not 'websit'.

TBT: I thought that was intended.

BC: Yeah, I did.

GG: So did I.

TBT: Made me laugh. (*Audience cheer their agreement.*)

HL: I just read what's here, I don't know.

BC: These bureaucrats . . .

TBT: It sounded like something Humph might not get quite right.

HL: I beg your pardon? Right – *do it again!*

TBT: But you'd only *pretend* not to get it quite right . . .

Humph was just one of those forces of nature who would power on without letting old age ever slow him down. Sandi Toksvig says today, 'I never once thought about his age, it never came up! He was just a boy having a laugh . . . I never saw a single moment when he started to slow down. His manager Susan was always trying to get him to eat a bit more and sit down a bit more, and have a cup of tea, but he would stand and pace around in the green room, and tell us jokes and anecdotes – he was just brimming with vitality.' So, as Graeme defined the spirit of *Clue* himself, What The Hell. Nobody expected Willie to leave the party so early, and the youngest player, Ross Noble, could easily go under a bus tomorrow. And, in fact, as if to put two fingers up to anyone who expected the Chairman to retire timidly, not only would the show go on, but after thirty-five years, *I'm Sorry I Haven't a Clue* – a veteran comedy gang of four men and a pianist with a combined age of well over three hundred – was hitting the road, and going on tour! In that order.

A Radio 4 panel game touring the country in a live, non-recorded commercial show? It was unheard of. Nevertheless, within a week of the 2007 tour's announcement, half of the dates were sold out and a second leg in 2008 became a necessity. Graeme was surprised. 'We knew the radio recordings sold out quickly, but we weren't sure if a stage show which involved people sitting at desks would sell as well with a higher ticket price. We were relieved and delighted when the theatres were full and the Audiences seemed happy with what we had to offer!' As Stephen Fry gasped when he heard the news: 'Eat your heart out, Led Zeppelin!'

15

I'm Sorry, I Must Be Going . . .

It was only fair that a few more of the average two to three million people who tuned in to Radio 4 for each Monday's show or the Sunday repeat should have got an increased chance to get to be part of the *Clue* clique, rather than crossing their fingers and hoping that one of the year's six recordings would be coming near their home town. But at the same time, this wasn't the first time that a live iteration of *Clue* had been mooted. Willie Rushton in particular would often wax lyrical about the possibilities of making a stage show out of the programme, sharing his daydreams of dancing girls and spectacular visual games, most of which were either insanely expensive or simply impossible, and the dreams came to nothing. It wasn't until the show's popularity reached astronomical proportions that Graeme realised that they wouldn't need any dramatic adaptation to wow the fan base – all the crowd wanted was the full experience of seeing Humph and the Teams in action . . . although Barry admits it was a bit of a risk. 'We didn't know what it would be like. We had all sorts of ideas for it, but Jon Naismith boiled it all down and said, "They know what they're coming to see, we must give it to them!" So you know, it's like *Round the Horne Revisited*, onstage, done as t'were.'

On The Road Again
There were no dancing girls, no garishly painted props or scenery for the big Mornington Crescent number, no upgrade for the laser display board – the live show was to be just like a normal recording evening, but with no tape running, no need to keep to a strict thirty-minute running time, and no BBC contract to fulfil (so no fears about offending Radio 4 listeners). Just as with the recordings, the gang made their own way to each town or city, checked into their comfy hotels and rolled along to the venue for a quick soundcheck before repairing to the green room as the happy crowds milled in. Further familiarity came from the choice of Jeremy Hardy to fill the guest slot at every

date. 'We'd talked about the idea of doing a live show for some time,' he remembers. 'It almost seemed a waste not to, because there's such a lot of goodwill out there, so many fans, so many theatres to play, it seemed a fairly natural thing to do. And by the time they decided to do it, I'd become the guest who was on every series, the most regular guest. And I guess for that reason they decided that I should do the tour . . . or possibly because I was more likely to be available than some people. I was really pleased, I jumped at it.' Tim & Jeremy had become such a double act by now that they had even developed a successor to HM the Queen and Princess Margaret, with Brooke-Taylor being upgraded to Monarch accompanied by Hardy's Prince Philip. The live show featured the couple's inimitably offensive rendition of 'Something Stupid' in the game 'Stars in their Ears', plus Barry & Graeme's classic performance of 'Wand'rin' Star', by Lee Marvin and his louchely camp hairdresser.

Of course, Samantha also signed up for the wider exposure, but sadly many dates on the tour presented problems, and some punters were denied the pleasure of seeing her beauty in the flesh, when her naturally charitable nature kept her from actually making it to the theatre. One minute she was having to help an elderly neighbour who had troubles using his stairlift ('She goes in every night to put him on downstairs, and then pulls him off on the landing'), the next she was running late due to the attentions of a grumpy gentleman friend ('Despite being very busy, Samantha says she can always find time to handle his testy calls'). Sometimes even the flimsiest excuse brought poor Jon Naismith running on with a note for the Chairman, explaining that his usually loyal scorer couldn't make it because she was 'off to meet a gentleman friend who's helping her restore some old furniture. She's just purchased an antique chest of drawers which her friend says has suffered from having candles placed on it. Samantha says she's looking forward to stripping her new tallboy while he scrapes the varnish and wax off next to her . . .' But of course, on the nights when she *did* make it to the recording, she was as radiant as ever, more than twenty years after her debut, and still every man's desire.

Even when Samantha was available, though, it wasn't going to be plain sailing, getting this commercial tour off the ground, and the newspapers were quick in reporting that a spat had flared up between the *Clue* Team and their BBC bosses, about who actually owned the show, and had the right to stage it. To some this seemed like the last bid for supremacy from the killjoy corporate bods who had called the shots in *I'm Sorry I'll Read That Again*, bullying Tim and Graeme since the Radio Prune days, and Barry was quick to tell the media at the time: 'We have lined it up with a commercial producer but the sticking point is the name – the BBC won't let us use it. We've been with the show for so long it would be nice to get some financial benefit for it all. We could go on tour as just us and do some similar things in the show but it would confuse the fans. We're thinking of possible alternatives for the name – *I'm Sorry the BBC Hasn't a Clue* is one. But they are being so bloody stingy about this and it may scupper the whole thing.'

However, the story was blown out of all proportion, while the matter was settled pretty rapidly behind closed doors, and in the autumn of 2007 the tour went full steam ahead, with the BBC's full blessing. Far from getting any thrill from 'sticking it to The Man', Graeme Garden today is keen to pay tribute to the Corporation for which he's been working for nearly half a decade, almost since he first started drawing any wage at all. 'The BBC speak of *Clue* very fondly. They took a terrific chance on the show in the first place, and have been happy to stick with it through thick and thin! I don't think for the first few years that it was necessarily a show that was bound to come back the following season, you know, so they've done us a great favour by keeping us going when we were still spending quite a long time finding our feet. I mean, it's always been an amusing show but its longevity and the fact that people know it so well now helps the Audience – you know, the laughter of recognition as much as the laugher of, er . . . hearing comedy. And now it's sort of built up to the mass rally that we enjoy when we go to the provincial theatres . . . So we have to thank the BBC for sticking with it – it paid off in the end!'

The main departure for the Teams was the absence of a necessity to come up with new gags. Where ordinarily they would be sure to have a couple of fresh half-hours in mind, and would reasonably diligently arrive on time to, for instance, listen to that evening's 'Pick Up Song' choice on headphones and try and learn how it went (especially tricky if it's The Streets' 'Dry Your Eyes' and you're sixty-five and have never heard it before), this time they knew what they were doing every night. Hardy continues, 'We had one meeting in the summer about what it should be like, put in lots of ideas and then Graeme went away with Jon and basically devised the show, using the "greatest hits".' Tim adds, 'Though we changed the show nightly, we knew there were certain moments that would always work. Sometimes with the recordings we have that dread feeling that this could be the day when the Audience finally wakes up to the fact that we're just being really silly and not remotely funny.' Actually, the fact that most of the material was well known added an extra layer of mischievous pretence to the proceedings, another twist to the game of playing *I'm Sorry I Haven't a Clue* – some Audience members could prob-ably have recited half of the rounds word for word. Graeme feels that this also played to Humph's strengths. 'I think what happened on tour was that it was more like his jazz, I suppose – he was playing tunes that he was familiar with. The script had been the same for almost every show, but he would find new little ways of delivering it, new moments, new timings, finding a different rhythm in a piece.' Despite being a 'Best of', though, the evenings proceeded as normal, right down to the traditional warm-up by Jon Naismith.

Give 'Em What They Want

Taking the piss out of the producer as they have to get the sensible stuff out of the way – pointing out fire exits, explaining how a radio recording works to the crowd, that the show will begin when Alick out in the hot-dog van presses the play and record buttons together and so on – is an *I'm Sorry* tradition stretching right back to the *ISIRTA* gang taunting Humphrey Barclay on the stage of the Playhouse. But, as an old Footlighter himself, Jon Naismith has always managed to get things off with a chuckle, and collected at least three jokes over his two decades on the show. These include the 'Thora Hird' gag, involving a deep freeze and a large amount of beef, and the joke about two goldfish in a tank (Yes, the 'How do you drive this thing?' one). He was especially pleased many years later to acquire another joke involving illicit threesomes and pensioners, which fitted in nicely with the unbroadcastable theme of the live shows, but needn't detain us here. Not least because no matter how well his jokes went, Jon's patter was sure to be given the thumbs down from his unruly charges when they rambled onto the stage, along with Colin, 'The only ivory-tickler on radio!'

Once the Teams were settled down in their traditional places, water (yes, it is water) decanted before them, cough sweets safely in place, scripts and notes assembled, the time would come for Colin to vamp some entrance chords ('Banging away', as Humph would have it), to herald the arrival of the star of the show in the flesh. Naismith would take centre stage to build up the tension like any good Music Hall barker: 'Ladies and gentlemen, the jazz musician's jazz musician's jazz musician's jazz musician's panel-game chairman . . . *he's still alive* . . . HUMPHREY LYTTELTON!'

Humph then casually, almost regally shuffled his tall, lissom frame onto the stage, script in hand, clad in whatever cardigan he happened to have put on that day and all but wearing slippers (a style referred to as 'post-grunge ironic casual'), raised his hands up towards the rafters, and received a thunderous ovation of a welcome from the thousands in attendance. The broadest grin would stretch across his face as the Teams wiped away mimed tears and bowed at Chairman Humph's magnificence. 'Isn't it remarkable?' Barry would sob. 'Oh, I'm filling up. Everytime he walks on . . . I think "What a miracle."' And then, eventually, once the dust had settled, the Chairman picked up his trusty hooter, and took his place for something like the 370th time, to play *I'm Sorry I Haven't a Clue*.

Tim grins, 'On tour, he suddenly got this gleam in his eye, and he would skip onstage – I said to him, "You're not supposed to be enjoying yourself!" And by the end, it was like he'd shed forty years. I'd like a copy of that Humph.' They'd kick off the first half of the evening's entertainment with a round of the awkwardly titled 'Missed Hits', suggesting cut-price fare like *Perverts of the Caribbean*, *Syphilis in Seattle*, *Being John Craven* and the intriguing-sounding *Edward Fingerhands*, and close the first half with 'Nursery Rhymes', with updates like Graeme's:

> *The North wind doth blow, and we shall have snow,*
> *And what will poor robin do then, poor thing?*
> *He'll sleep in the barn to keep himself warm,*
> *And hide from Bill Oddie, poor thing.*

Then there were the musical games, the 'Complete Quotes', the 'Uxbridge English Dictionary', 'Sound Charades', the entirety of the 'Quiz of Quizzes' . . . but the one game that the Teams most looked forward to on the tour belied any idea of them just parroting the same lines every night.

'Cheddar Gorge' first debuted in the autumn of 1987, 'Just one of the many games derived from famous British landmarks. These include "Tower Bridge", a card game for very tall people, "Winchester Cathedral", which provides the chance to win Chester Cathedral, and of course "Beachy Head", invented by our own Sven when holidaying at Camber Sands . . .' and was one of those silly pastimes which swiftly became too joyfully inane ever to seem scripted. Creating sentences in one-word relays is a promising enough task, with the aim being never to reach a full stop, thus triggering Humph's hooter. But when you have the *Clue* crew trying to top each other and catch out the next player by using the words 'and' or 'yet' (or if you're really sailing close to the wind, interjecting a 'comma' or 'semicolon'), the sheer sportsmanship of 'Cheddar Gorge' generates at least half of the laughter. Who cares that the resultant sentence reads something like: 'I once saw a large but somehow strangely attractive, yet oddly, bizarrely, grotesquely and *horrendously* yet in a deckchair, crabs, lobsters, not only nudists cavorting lewdly over a cliff, who was in wuthering mood – he was once a crab-like person, until one day he decided to try sewage.' . . . when it's the pauses and banter in between the words that really matter? After many years of extracting entertainment out of the basic game, Naismith began to search for different shapes for the gameplay, once setting the Teams the challenge of coming up with a letter to the *Radio Times* (which ultimately read 'Why oh why oh why oh why is the schedule so outstanding and inspired? Many of the listeners are hoping to engage you in some productive debate on enormous matters. Why oh why oh spells . . . something beginning with the letter Y' and as such, was easily up to that magazine's usual standard). Clearly a lot of fun could be had by having the Teams play against each other in letter-writing mode, recreating lost correspondence between legendary or historic characters, and so '84 Chicken Cross Road' was born, in 2005:

BC/GG: Dear . . . abound in Sherwood Forest. I hope you will pop round and see four of them, as we frolic and swing through the afternoon. And after that we could perhaps indulge in a little bit of freemasonry – if you know what I mean. Regards to your good king, and to the lovely wife of your immediate neighbour, Guy of Fawkes. Cheers, must go – ROBIN.

TBT/JH: Dear Robin, I hope that this is the last time I shall have the honour of spitting in your tea! I detest such thieving, frolicking, egalitarianism freemasonry. My father, Tommy, said to me 'Oi, you twat! What the hell are you doing over there in Nottingham while I am stuck here in London? Richard wants to kill all of your slimy, green but attractive (to him, and me) . . .' So what do you think of this letter? Answer on a fax. Which I have invented. Recently. Bye for ever – SHERIFF.

Despite being simplicity itself, and arriving so late in the show's run, no other *Clue* game ever invoked quite so much breathless giggling from both Audience and performer as this one, with the meandering replies from Tim's team, be it from Catherine of Aragon to Henry VIII or Davros to Doctor Who, taking the improvisers by surprise at every turn. The above extracts only work when you realise that most of the spaces in between the words printed involved asides and giggling fits that could take minutes to dispel, while Humph gently snoozed away. There was no way they could have left that game out of the live show, and the unpredictability of it soon became the highlight of every evening, not least for Tim & Jeremy.

There were several nods made towards the live, unrecorded nature of the shows – a double whammy being that the singers for 'One Song to the Tune of Another' and 'Pick Up Song' got their moment in the spotlight out at the mic like real pop stars, and when Jeremy came to give his legendary performances, he could get away with telling the Audience, 'Don't fuck this up for me, Audience – music is my life!' They got to chop and change the songs as they moved around, when they and Colin (and Humph!) got bored of one number they moved on to the next – but it was strictly the Greatest Hits, with the highlight being Tim's joyous Tiny Tim-style delivery of the Smiths'

'Girlfriend in a Coma' to 'Tiptoe Through the Tulips', originally performed on the radio by Tony Hawks.

Graeme also decided to work into the shows a rediscovered love for spot effects which he and Tim had enjoyed as part of the *ISIRTA* short in their recent *Goodies* tour. The round, 'Sound Effects Stories', brought tales to life by bringing on a trolley bursting with traditional sound effects paraphernalia – boxes of gravel, rattles, door handles and so on – and then were systematically ruined by the narrators' false cues, whether it's Barry & Graeme getting irate at Tim & Jeremy's wartime thriller 'Ginger Pulls It Off' . . .

TBT: It was dawn.

BC/GG: *Cock-a-doodle-doo!*

TBT: Yes, Dawn, our hero's fiancée . . .

JH: They were under attack! Squadron leader Ginger Dobbs gave the order, 'Quickly, blow Reveille!'
        Both Barry & Graeme play bugles amateurishly.

JH: 'Thank you, Dawn,' said Wing Commander Reveille . . .

TBT: All at once, the door opened.

GG: *Crrrreeeeeaaaakkk!!!*

TBT: . . . Silently.

. . . or Tim & Jeremy being defeated at every turn by Barry & Graeme's Girl's Own Adventure 'The Secret Three Pull It Off Like Ginger':

GG: The year, 1896. China.
      Tim sings Chinese gamelan music, Jeremy bangs a gong.

GG: . . .Was laid out on the table. At that moment the girls were distracted by the sound of a mobile . . .
      Tim & Jeremy endlessly warble the Nokia tune.

GG: . . . library, which was coming along the road.

TBT: *Brum, brum!*

JH: *Shhh!*

The Teams also made full use of their newfangled hotkeys too, especially for a round which, like so many others in *Clue*, called for Tim & Graeme to display their acting skills, gleaned from *Crossroads* or hospital sitcom *TLC* or, in Graeme's case:

HL: Graeme Garden might be at something of an advantage in this round. He's recently been starring in *Peak Practice*, playing the role of a slightly doddery prematurely ageing doctor . . . That couldn't

have stretched his range much. There was one especially interesting scene where Graeme examined an attractive young woman
wearing only lacy underwear and stockings. Sadly this was cut and
in the final version we see Graeme wearing a white coat instead.

One of the highlights of every live show was Tim's turn as an orgasmic Clanger
performing the diner scene from *When Harry Met Sally*, but in the same round
Barry & Graeme provided a direct link to the roots of the entire 'I'm Sorry'
saga, being another distortion of the famous 'Handbag' scene from *The Importance of Being Earnest*. This iconic scene had been a recurring motif throughout
Clue, but recasting Lady Bracknell and Jack as Darth Vader and Obi-Wan
Kenobi took the biscuit.

The final relatively new game which took pride of place in the stage show
was the crucial ingredient that gave every member of the Audience a chance
to shine. Within the radio show, 'Karaoke-Cokey' set the Audience the task
of humming a well-known tune as close to in unison as possible, and then
set the Teams the far more difficult task of identifying the tune. Staring out
at the eisteddfod-esque humming rabble, Barry would venture, 'It's Beyoncé,
but I don't know which one . . .' For the live show, though, the Teams pulled
out all the stops, and provided every last one of the lucky ticket-holders in
every venue with their very own brightly coloured plastic kazoo, to play the
game in style. The free kazoos added to the excitement of being one of the
crowd, with more than an echo of the party-hooter-filled Audiences for *ISIRTA*.
The many thousands who collected their own *Clue* kazoos certainly appreciated the gesture, forever having a keepsake to remind them of the evening,
with the added bonus that it could provide ever-lasting musical entertainment
utilising, of course, the minimum of talent.

Giddy Giddy Yum Yum

Well, it was a tour, after all, six seasoned pros out on the road – Ipswich one
night, the temptations of Reading the next. They had their riders of course –
plenty of booze in the green room, drugs aplenty (well, cough sweets), and,
surely, there had to be groupies thrown into the mix somewhere. Humph and
the Teams had always taken great pains not to be a disappointment to the fans
loitering around every stage door at the recordings, with Humph in particular
known to suffer all sorts of hardship in all weathers after both *Clue* and jazz
gigs to ensure that he'd signed every book thrust at him. By the time the tour
came round, the crowds milling round the back of each theatre had become
immense, everyone hoping to get a programme signed, or a CD, or even one
of the brand-new, specially created 'Mornington Crescent' or 'Chairman Humph'
T-shirts. One notable omission was the usually dogged Mrs Trellis, who once

again failed to get in touch with her heroes, although Graeme admitted, 'I didn't see her, but Samantha claims she glimpsed her in Tunbridge Wells.'

On the other hand, at most dates, there was a special die hard contingent that wouldn't be content with just a signature and a photo. The Official Goodies Fan Club had been running since 1995, but this was not enough for some, and with the club's lack of emphasis on the tightness of the funky trio's trousers, a splinter group began to congregate regularly in the shadows outside the stage door for most *Clue* dates. The Giddies was established round about the time of the show's sojourn at the Edinburgh Festival in 2006, being a small but dedicated group of twenty-something females from Scotland, England and Australia with but three preoccupations to link them: an insatiable adoration for double entendres wherever they can be found; an all-pervading desire to cuddle their comedy heroes no matter how far they have to travel, and a shared penchant for discussing the shortness of Graeme's shorts in the *Goodies* episode 'Scoutrageous'.

A representative Giddy, who shall be referred to as 'Miss X' (not because she requested anonymity, it's just more fun that way), denies that this is the only appeal, however: 'The appeal spans all spectrums, it's more than just the tightness of the Goodies' trousers, honest. There is something very appealing about a man who can be a perfect gent on the one hand and deliver a line so strewn with smut on the other. Very, very few people could get away with that but the *Clue* chaps all pull it off so well . . . and deliver a good innuendo.' These budding Samanthas never stint in their mission to get their hands on their elder idols. 'We have travelled the length and breadth of the country, although we do cover a large span of the land anyway. No *Clue* show is safe, anywhere from London to Birmingham, Sunderland to Southport, Cambridge to Harrogate, Tunbridge Wells to Leeds and Manchester to Edinburgh is fraught with the danger of a dirty old man getting molested by an excitable young lady!'

Surely these respectable mature statesmen must be horrified at such attention from a gaggle of nubile comedy fans? 'Tim and Graeme appear to think the same way we do – no one can quite believe their luck!' And Barry doesn't feel left out? 'No no no,' he insists, 'It's just a spectator sport, always nice seeing who's turned up this time. Often the same faces! Yes, very . . . heart-warming.'

'How could we not love it?' beams Tim when questioned, 'But sssh, our wives might hear . . .'

Spousal disapproval or no, a Giddy gal or two could usually be found waiting at most of the stage doors as the Teams made their way around at first just England, from a triumphant first night in Bristol, to the last date of the year in Brighton. This was the city from which *Clue* initially began to tour the country, the first recording taking place at the Old Ship Hotel in 1991 in front of only a couple of hundred punters. The second time they popped by they were playing to several times that number at the Theatre Royal – but when it came to that last date of the 2007 tour, nothing but the Brighton Dome would do, filled to capacity with more than two thousand merry, cheering, kazoo-clutching fans.

Up the Rabbit Hole

Before the tour had kicked off, *I'm Sorry I Haven't a Clue*'s fiftieth series had completed recording for the autumn run on Radio 4. It took the show to Croydon, Manchester and finally Peterborough, but ended with no great momentous announcement and only opened with Humph's dismissive intro 'You join us today at the beginning of the fiftieth series of the show. It seems like only yesterday that four comedians got together to prepare a rambling new show based on the flimsiest of formats. One wonders how such a half-hearted amateur creation would fare today? . . . Let's find out.' Another six episodes after thirty-five years only elicited an 'I'd really like to say how much I've enjoyed it, but I'm not allowed to before 9 p.m.' from Humph.

However, the very last recording of 2007 was another break from the norm, with a second Pattinson/Garden-penned panto extravaganza, this time taking its cue from a different literary classic, *Alice's Adventures in Wonderland*. Garden admitted that this wasn't necessarily due to any great affection for the original. 'I'm a kind of fan of Carroll's books, in that I admire his weirdness and twisted logic, but certainly as a kid I found them a bit too scary to love.' Naturally entitled *Humph in Wonderland*, this hour-long special required slightly more tinkering with the original manuscript, to make the part of a pre-pubescent Victorian girl fit the 86-year-old jazz trumpeter. But at the same time, Lewis Carroll's tale somehow seemed to suit the Chairman perfectly, featuring as it does an innocent caught up in a land of frustrating facetious-ness and stupidity, peopled with exhaustingly perverse freaks and clowns. With Stephen Fry busy travelling around every one of the states of America, Tony Hawks happily volunteered to step into his narrator's shoes. Iain and Graeme's reworking of the story continued the trend of mixing Lyttelton's real biog-raphy into the brew too, with Sandi Toksvig showing up to play the role of Humph's childhood nanny, Nanny Viggers, about whom the great man recalled: 'I have quite happy memories of her although I was brought up in the belief that the human backside was specially designed to withstand corporal punish-ment . . . She was small and plump and wore a tight belt across her middle. It gave her the appearance of a cottage loaf.'

> ST: Lord bless you, Master Humphrey, I'm your Nanny Viggers!
> HL: Oh, I didn't recognise you without my glasses on.
> ST: But I have got your glasses on!

HL: Well, give them here, I'm blind as a cat without them.

ST: Oh, you mean blind as a bat!

HL: Looks like a cat to me.

ST: No, it's a white rabbit, Master Humphrey, and you'd best be after it if you want your watch back!

The White Rabbit was Colin, of course, and soon the rest of the gang turned up as the raggle-taggle gang of animals and birds that make up the competitors in the original book's Caucus-race.

They were indeed a queer-looking party that assembled on the bank – the birds with draggled feathers, the animals with their fur clinging close to them, and all dripping wet, cross, and uncomfortable. The first question of course was, how to get dry again . . .

'What I was going to say,' said the Dodo in an offended tone, 'was, that the best thing to get us dry would be a Caucus-race.'

'What *is* a Caucus-race?' said Alice; not that she wanted much to know, but the Dodo had paused as if it thought that *somebody* ought to speak, and no one else seemed inclined to say anything.

'Why,' said the Dodo, 'the best way to explain it is to do it' . . . There was no 'One, two, three, and away,' but they began running when they liked, and left off when they liked, so that it was not easy to know when the race was over. However, when they had been running half an hour or so, and were quite dry again, the Dodo suddenly called out 'The race is over!' and they all crowded round it, panting, and asking, 'But who has won?'

. . . At last the Dodo said, '*Everybody* has won, and all must have prizes.'

'But who is to give the prizes?' quite a chorus of voices asked.

'Why, *she*, of course,' said the Dodo, pointing to Alice with one finger; and the whole party at once crowded round her, calling out in a confused way, 'Prizes! Prizes!'

This is an almost uncannily perfect set-up for the story to provide the same old much-loved games throughout Humph's adventures in Wonderland, as the furry or feathered cast of Tim, Barry, Graeme, Jeremy, Sandi, Tony, Andy, Jack and Rob followed the hero around. Indeed, the combination of silliness, confusion and non-competitiveness of Carroll's 'Caucus-race' – not to mention the sheer pointlessness of the Queen of Hearts' croquet tournament – almost seems like the inspiration for all of *I'm Sorry I Haven't a Clue* in the first place.

When not playing Mornington Crescent down in the underground, coming up with 'Smokers' Book Club' suggestions for Andy Hamilton's Caterpillar or entertaining Barry's Michael Winneresque portmanteau-obsessed Humpty Dumpty with new entries for *The Uxbridge English Dictionary*, the stellar cast slotted uncannily neatly into each of Alice's encounters, with Jack and Jeremy reuniting to play the twins Tweedle Dum and Jack Dee (with Dee doubling up as the grin-festooned Cheshire Cat), Sandi making a scatological appearance as the Queen of Farts, Hamish and Dougal earning their cheers by cropping up as the Walrus and the Carpenter, and time for another positively final appearance from Tim's Lady Constance and Graeme's Moaning Minnie turns – the ideal casting for the pantomime dame double act, the Duchess and the Cook.

It was all perfect Christmas silliness, packed with the same old puns and wordplay as the *ISIRTA* Yuletide specials – 'The sun was unbearable, and the *Daily Mail* wasn't much better' being a line that Announcer Hatch could have delivered with aplomb. But the real thrilling connection to the show's origins didn't become apparent until the courtroom finale, with Tim in the dock as the Knave of Hearts. There may have been no props or costumes, just the cast of *Clue* clique stalwarts spread across the stage, scripts in hand, with Humph taking pride of place on a high stool over on the far right of stage, but the point is that this was the Lyric Theatre – young Tim Brooke-Taylor had been on that exact stage playing the Music Hall comedian Sidney Molar in the courtroom sketch 'Judge Not', night after night, exactly forty-five years earlier. Had the *I'm Sorry* story really come full circle in this, what would turn out to be the very final recording session of *Clue*'s majestic thirty-five-year run?

Well, not really – after all, with Christmas out of the way, there was not only series 51 to start planning, but also the second leg of the tour, this time taking Humph, Colin, Samantha and the Teams further afield, to good old Edinburgh, Cardiff, Brooke-Taylor's Buxton, and then Harrogate, before the big finale in Bournemouth. The real jewel in the itinerary, though, would be the Hammersmith Apollo, more used to playing host to rock bands, and offering *Clue* its biggest ever audience, with over three thousand tickets on sale – tickets which were selling fast.

In the meantime, *Humph in Wonderland* had only to reach the traditional rave-up ending, triggered by the awakening of poor Humph – and of course, it had all been a dream:

HL: You may have noticed I dozed off during that round. That doesn't usually happen – you don't usually notice. Sorry, I just had the most awful nightmarish dream. A bunch of old men were pointlessly listing London place names . . .

TH: Yes, Humph had dozed off in the middle of a round of Mornington Crescent Bridge, and it was all a dream. And so, ladies and gentlemen, as the chill wind . . .

HL: D'you mind? I'm in charge now. And so, ladies and gentlemen, as the chill wind of time carries aloft the solitary snowflake of destiny, and Network SouthEast closes down for the week, I notice it's very nearly the end of the show. But there's just time, however, to fit in a round of 'Swanee Kazoo', in which we meld the soothing lilt of the swanee whistle with the rasping chirrup of the kazoo. Once an unlikely combination, the words 'kazoo' and 'swanee whistle' now go together as naturally as trumpet-playing and magnetic sexual attraction. Cast, I'd like you to provide us with a rendition of 'Winter Wonderland' to feature Tim and Graeme on the swanee whistle, and the rest of you on the kazoo. In the meantime, from all of us, have a very Merry Christmas and a Happy New Year. Goodbye.

Dedication's What You Need . . .

We're on the stage at the Hammersmith Apollo, at about 6 p.m., on Thursday 3 April 2008. There are the three turquoise trestle tables, littered with scraps of script, bottles of water, notepads, and, as Graeme Garden indicates, 'There's the buttons . . .' Out in the stalls Apollo staff are dutifully wandering around with big buckets of kazoos, placing one on each seat, and on the stage Jon Naismith is finalising technical details as the tour's official photographer takes random snaps. Tim Brooke-Taylor runs in with his own camera. 'I just had to take a picture of the outside,' he grins. Ordinarily, wherever *Clue* sets up camp for the evening, the theatres never advertise the fact, with their usual hoardings for the latest Lloyd Webber tour and the like still in place, confusing many a ticket holder. Here in this famed corner of west London, the Apollo has spelled out in foot-high letters 'I'M SORRY I HAVEN'T A CLUE'.

'Have they put our pictures up there?' asks Jeremy. There is a pause. '. . . No.' Tim replies. But there's no time to feel despondent about this, as Humph arrives with Colin in tow and Naismith huddles them all together for a special photo session – this is not the only reason the photographer is in attendance. After a quick run-through of one or two additions to the script, the Teams repair to the tiny green room up a flight of stairs and the giddy fans are allowed into the theatre to take their seats.

'Oh, that's very nice of them!' announces Barry, approaching a fridge conspicuously rammed with cold lagers. 'Yes, one of those would be nice *after* the show,' says Tim, eyeballing his old friend significantly as Baz merrily screws the top off a bottle and takes a glug. Tim and Graeme return to their complimentary prawn sandwiches, and deal with a barrage of questions from green-room guests with a politeness that belies the fact that inquisition is the last thing they need before facing their biggest ever Audience.

'. . . We all agree that it came from Gerry's,' Tim answers between mouthfuls of prawn, while Barry cuts in, 'Yes, it came from Gerry's Club. And I remember Pat Johns was there.' 'Yes, he was the guy that told me,' continues Tim; 'He was pissed . . .' Breaking his silence, Graeme interjects a helpful 'I just know what Tim told me!' before Brooke-Taylor puts the tin hat on the discussion with 'The trouble is, you don't remember any of this because you don't think it's going to be for very long, and then you become a . . . you're lumbered. Heigh-ho.'

At the other end of the green room sits Humph, playing host to his eldest daughter as his manager and companion Sue De Costa fusses around him adoringly. 'Am I looking after you well, dear?' she asks, and he smiles his approval. Having spent the best part of thirty-five years as the most distant member of the gang, arriving alone under his own steam and jealously guarding his privacy to the extent that none of his colleagues had his real phone number and not even Jon Naismith knew his real address (fan mail to be directed to 'c/o The Bull's Head, Surrey'), the Chairman opened up considerably in these later years, and Jeremy Hardy recalls getting to know a completely different Humph as the tour went on. 'The best part of the tour for me was just sitting in hotel bars chatting with Humph after shows. Because he got more and more jovial and convivial as time went on, I think he was making the most of life.' Humph nursed his beloved second wife Jill through a long illness until her death in 2006, and having also been advised in late 2007 to abandon driving himself everywhere, he began to reach out to his old friends more. Hardy continues, 'I found it impossible to go to bed if Humph was still up chatting. He would chat about his family, his ancestry and, of course, music. He stopped chatting only if jazz music was being played in the hotel bar, because he had to listen to jazz; it could never be in the background.'

Coolly slumped in the green room, the smiling jazzman naturally displays not one scintilla of nervousness at going out in front of 3,500 people within the hour. After all, only a few years earlier he and his band had played to over 50,000 young Radiohead fans at Oxford's South Park, having been invited by band member Jonny Greenwood after Humph's band helped out with 'Life in a Glasshouse', a track on the Radiohead album *Amnesiac*. Arriving at the concert, Humph recalled, 'Then a car full of staring, pointing and, I imagined, mocking young people overtook me. When the manic-looking driver wound down his window, I braced myself against whatever ribaldry might come. Then he gave a thumbs-up sign and shouted "Mornington

Crescent!" I had underestimated the power of *I'm Sorry I Haven't a Clue* to smash down the generation barriers.'

Similarly, Humph also betrays little sign of worry over the fact that he's shortly to undergo surgery. He's not letting such a little thing keep him from continuing not only with the *Clue* tour, but his own jazz gigs as well – even if he has recently elegantly signed off from his Radio 2 series *The Best of Jazz* for the last time, after more than forty years of broadcasting. Also, it's been announced that the fifty-first series of *Clue* has been put on hiatus by the BBC just in case plenty of recuperation is needed for the Chairman, and the planned guests including Jo Brand and Victoria Wood, set to make their debuts, have been alerted to the delay. Hardy remembers, 'He was a very emotional man, and it's hard to imagine that he was not frightened about the operation, but every time he spoke of it, he would say that, if he didn't survive it, he wouldn't know anything about it, so he was a winner either way.' Barry also recalls his old friend shrugging off any concerns with 'If all goes well, this year's drama will be next year's anecdote'.

'I heard an old one on BBC7 the other day,' announces Barry, dragging us back into the here and now, 'and it was very straightforward, it hadn't got any sort of ebullience, and we're all talking over each other. A lot of inter-rupting going on, Willie cackling away, Humph pretty straight . . .' 'But it wasn't really until Jon edited it properly . . .' continues Tim, '. . . what Jon does, he manages to leave in rubbish . . .' ('Yep!' agrees Graeme.) '. . . Because he knows there's something really good coming up. Whereas the stupid people would actually cut out everything that went before.'

'That's right,' Barry agrees, and finishes off his lager. 'I'm off out for a breath of fresh air,' he concludes, reaching for his packet of menthol and disappearing down to the fire escape, as Jon introduces the producers of the *Clue* tour DVD, who will be filming the show at the Lowry in Salford the following Sunday. There's only time for a quick 'Have a great show!' from them, though, before it's curtain up, and the guests abscond to join the crowd of merrymakers.

Out in the Apollo auditorium the Audience have manifested themselves in full, tooting their kazoos, reading their programmes, trying on their 'Chairman Humph' T-shirts and, above all, grinning endlessly. Although more than 99 per cent of the population of Great Britain would walk right past him in the street, the sheer volume of cheers which Jon Naismith receives when he strides onto the stage to deliver 'Thora Hird' is astounding. But he's not just doing the howlers tonight; besides showing the crowd *how to play their kazoos*, Jon has a very special announcement to make: 'It may have occurred to all 3,500 of you as you sit there, "Goodness me, what a lot of kazoos, might this be some kind of world record?" D'you know, just the same thought occurred to me! So I emailed the Guinness Book of Records – that's how sad I am – and they emailed me back with the current world record, for the number of kazoos played in one place. They said the World's Largest Kazoo Ensemble involved 2,600 people in New York, USA, on 31 December 2006. So, ladies and gentlemen, may I invite you to kick their arses?' George the photographer joins Jon on the stage – photographic evidence being crucial – as the entire contents of the Hammersmith Apollo raise their plastic *Clue* kazoos to their lips and wildly hum into them.

The noise was of course deafening, but it wasn't a patch on the volume that greeted the Teams and Humph that night. Or indeed the noise of the cheers and whoops that welcomed 'One Song to the Tune of Another', Hamish and Dougal, '84 Chicken Cross Road', Mornington Crescent and, most of all, the emotional 'Swanee Kazoo' finale.

Jon Naismith reflects, 'I'm very glad we did do that tour, because it was a sort of lap of honour for Humph. And what was lovely, at the end of those shows, Humphrey would close the show by playing on his trumpet "We'll Meet Again". And at one of the last dates we did, at the Hammersmith Apollo – this huge venue, three and a half thousand people – there was something magical about that evening. Humphrey played the same piece beautifully, and in the most extraordinary fashion, 3,500 people, as one, stood on their feet and applauded him. And it has been imbued with so much more impact knowing that within a matter of weeks, *days* after that show, he died. It's a wonderful farewell, and I will treasure that memory of three and a half thousand people, standing up as one.'

This Year's Drama
So it was up to Salford, down to Bournemouth, and the tour was done. Between the two dates came Harrogate, the scene of Hardy's debut which allegedly kick-started the rebirth of *Clue* in the first place. Perhaps it was fitting that this was to be the site of Humph's last *Clue* show on 12 April, but it certainly wouldn't be his last performance. For all the fast-selling 'Chairman Humph' T-shirts, and no matter how he was hallooed to the rafters for his inimitable, hugely loved pivotal role on *Clue*, nobody was ever in any doubt that he was, and always would be, a jazzman first and foremost, before he was a panel-game chairman, a comedy performer, a calligrapher, a broad-caster or a cartoonist. The Bull's Head in Humph's beloved Barnes, famed for its jazz evenings, was his second – if not his first – home, playing there regular as clockwork for over forty years – and it was there that he played one of these regular gigs with his loyal band on the last night before entering hospital to undergo surgery to repair an aortic aneurysm. Garden sighs, 'I have to say I was very concerned about him going in for the operation because I knew that a major op with a general anaesthetic at the age of eighty-six is not

something to take lightly, and probably he would come out of it diminished in some way . . . he would have hated convalescence, I know that. It may have meant the end of his trumpeting, which would have been unbearable for him.'

It was bad news for the good people of Bournemouth – Chairman Humph would not be able to make the very last date on the triumphant *Clue* tour. In truth, Naismith had been compelled to come up with contingency plans for Humph's indisposition long before they became necessary, with deputies sounded out for several dates. So close to the full run, though, it became necessary to put out the call for a temporary replacement, and the poor tremulous stand-in, given the task of filling perhaps the single most unfillable shoes in show business, turned out to be Rob Brydon, the baby of the *Clue* clique. Perhaps it was unfair to ask the newbie to be the first person to sit in that crucial central chair since Barry Cryer had waved his white flag thirty-five years earlier, but at the same time, nobody but Brydon would have been able to artfully milk the pity of the crowds for his onerous task with quite such panache. He had after all been playing a neurotic, obnoxious panel-game chairman called Rob Brydon for a couple of years, in BBC3's *Rob Brydon's Annually Retentive*.

This *Larry Sanders*-esque spoof of TV quizzes was a testament to how overblown the comedy panel game had become in the wake of the nineties explosion in the field. Brydon back-pedals somewhat now, admitting 'It'd be wrong to characterise all panel shows as backbiting, Machiavellian things, because they're not. *QI* is a hugely pleasant experience, and even *Would I Lie to You?*, there's not that desperation that we conveyed in *Annually Retentive*. And I can't imagine there's a more creative and constructive environment than *Clue*. On the day when you do it, it's a wonderful process, with no rivalry at all. It always felt like a celebration to me.'

It wasn't an easy job, keeping the spirits up while knowing how Humph was, but Brydon insists 'My reason for filling in for Humph on that particular show was 1) helping out some mates who were in a pickle, and 2) the thought of doing it was wonderful. I said to the Audience, it's like *Jim'll Fix It*! What a treat to deliver those links, you know? But occasionally you'd catch yourself, and feel awfully sad. I would never do it full-time in a million years, I wouldn't want to fill Humph's shoes. But I'm really proud to have got in at the tail-end, and been part of the show's history.' There was an extra surprise for the flustered stand-in when Jon Naismith revealed that Humph had recorded a special announcement for this final date on the tour, from his hospital bed: 'Good evening. This is Humphrey Lyttelton. I can't do the show tonight because I'm in hospital . . . I wish I'd thought of this earlier. Will you give a big welcome to Rob Brydon?'

And so, with that touching kick-off, that Tuesday evening at the Bournemouth Pavilion Theatre unfolded as naturally as possible, the tour reached its conclusion, and the Teams returned to London, to visit Humph in hospital and wait, along with his millions of fans, for the best news possible. Barry recalls, 'I went to see him in hospital, bless him, with tubes in every orifice. They said the hearing's the last thing to go, so keep talking, and we were all saying silly things to him. It was very moving. I was saying, "This is very inconvenient, you know. I'm a very busy man. I've just been for a walk – where were you?" We were doing all this nonsense around the bed.'

But a miserable Friday night brought miserable news. The great man's own website announced: 'Humph died peacefully with his family and friends around him on April 25th at 7.00pm following surgery.' The balloon had burst. The game was up.

Loving Thoughts of Chairman Humph

The outpouring of grief and consternation at the news of Humph's death was in direct proportion to the passionate loudness of his reception every night onstage on the *Clue* tour. No superlative could be superlative enough to describe his achievements, no glowing expression of love and gratitude could glow too brightly. And yet Humph had been one of those rare figures whose status and popularity had allowed his life to be consistently and lovingly celebrated many times while he was still around to be flustered and bemused by the plaudits he received.

Several years earlier, Jon Naismith and the Teams had contributed to a special Radio 4 show, *Humph at 80*, making it abundantly clear how much his every word and indeed pause was appreciated. Tim and Graeme played with differing metaphors in trying to define Humph's mastery, Tim suggesting, 'He's the person that's the conductor in a way, he's lead trumpet, lead fiddle, we take the lead from him, and we will play our bits, we know when it's solo and we know when we're going to be playing ensemble,' while Graeme offered, 'He's more like a tennis umpire, sitting high above the players, looking down and quite remote from them . . . and yet at the same time he's very much part of the performance.' Humph was also featured in *The South Bank Show*, revisiting Eton in the company of Melvyn Bragg, visibly unmoved by the summation of his extraordinary career, and rather keen to move on to the next gig, the next challenge.

But when it came to Jon Naismith's carefully compiled tribute, *Chairman Humph*, broadcast on 15 June, Humph was not there to have his blushes spared. Every member of the *Clue* clique were clearly struggling to express the enormity of the loss, and Hardy put his finger on the problem most succinctly: 'Humph will be remembered with enormous affection; the trouble is all these words have been used up on other dead people. He was a National Treasure, he was our greatest living Englishman, he was enormously charming, very very warm . . .' How can you pay tribute to a man who truly *was* a National Treasure when the term has been used so often? His friends groped for a way to overleap cliché, while making it clear just what a unique man it was that had been taken away from us.

Andy Hamilton offered, 'I think there was also a kind of relaxation in him, he always seemed to have a lot of time. Some of those pauses that he used to exploit after a particularly stupid game ended . . . You know you see some sportsmen who you know are a lot better than everybody else, because they always seem to have more time to play their shots? I always felt that about Humph.' And Jeremy agreed, 'There was such a lack of desperation about Humph, which is great in an entertainer, great in a comedian. A comedian who is not bothered, who does not have to do it, who is not trying to get anywhere, this isn't a rung on his ladder, he's not worried about how many people are listening to the show, he's doing it for fun – absolutely for fun. And that's so liberating for him, and liberating for the show, and made it so much fun for everybody else.'

Sandi also paid tribute, 'Humph is irreplaceable, and the interesting thing, I think, for someone who's passed away, is that I think he'll be remembered alive.' Which was a sentiment that Graeme keenly echoed. 'I think the thing that I admired about him, and which I would like to feel I could take away with me would be his energy, and his hatred of idleness. For such a vigorous and energetic man, working right up to the end is probably as good a way as he would have wished to go. My wife put it rather beautifully, I thought, at the funeral. She said to me, "Well, he died while he was still tall."'

The tribute's narrator Stephen Fry also spoke for many who were listening when he insisted 'I know that I've always thought that when I grow up, I would like nothing more than to be like Humph.' But perhaps the most affecting thought of all came from his friend and admirer of over fifty years, Barry, who concluded, 'I'll never forgive him, he did something totally out of character, he died. And he's left a big gap, and I will never forgive him. God bless him.'

There's no doubt that *Clue* was just one other string to Humph's bow, as he always said about first getting the job: 'I put on the shelf my decision as to whether I'd come and do the show regularly, or whether I'd do it piece-meal – without making any long-term commitment. Which I haven't yet done. But I'll give it another decade or so before I decide whether I'll do it.' And of course he made it clear that he'd really rather be at that infamous gig in Hull, inspiring gales of laughter by complaining: 'Listen, I'll tell you something. If, on 23 May 1921, I'd ever thought that I would live to sit here reading all this codswallop, I'd have turned round and gone right back in!'

Iain Pattinson ruminates on their legendary chemistry, and Humph's celebrated derision for the show: 'The usual cliché about Humph and his delivery is this jazz timing. Where simply on his phrasing, and where he leaves the right length of gap – or what appears to be the wrong length of gap ... He'll bring something to it which, even I, as the writer, hadn't thought was there. I remember once writing a fairly simple line towards the end of the show, saying "Well, we've certainly got through an awful lot of games this evening ..." thinking that he would pause, and let the Audience think about it and get a bit of a giggle on "an awful lot of games". But in fact he read, "We've got through an awful lot of games tonight," and got a laugh. Then he said, "Oh, I think I misread that ..." and got a bigger laugh. Then he paused for about a beat and a half and said, "No, I *didn't*," with the full venom of someone who actually hated being there, and really meant it, and then got a *huge* laugh. So instead of one giggle, he got a big laugh and then a much bigger laugh simply by adding that beat and a half.'

But with time finally called on the game, the truth could at last be told – Humphrey Lyttelton *adored* being the Chairman of *I'm Sorry I Haven't a Clue*, for all fifty series, more than 180 hours of ridiculous gameplay. And he especially appreciated his position once Pattinson was on script duty, eventually being forced to admit, 'Oh, I love it. I love it. In fact, when I get there, to the studio ... as soon as I get the cards with all the links on from Jon Naismith, I have to find a distant dressing room ... and I have to read through these scripts over and over, at least three times, probably more. Otherwise, if I come up on one of his gags, I get the giggles.'

In the wake of the bad news, many people all too quickly began to debate the future of the Antidote to Panel Games, but for most, the priority was, and remains, how best to mourn the man, and celebrate his life. Tim observed with a pang that the very day after Humph's death, mourners began to leave bouquets of flowers at Mornington Crescent, where Willie's blue plaque was certain to be joined by Humph's before long.

Of course, the very best way to pay tribute to Humph is to play his music – that is where you will find his heart. At the same time, though, it's also a tribute to remember Humph by listening to any of the hundreds of episodes of *Clue* – with the BBC CDs having reached more than ten best-selling volumes it's not as if there's a shortage of opportunities to be cheered up all over again by the sound of Humph giving the Teams silly things to do. And if any one person could be said to want those he left behind to be happy – indeed, to be jocular – it was Humph, whose motto was 'It's no good agonising. I don't agonise over many things.' Humph held no truck with self-indulgent good taste at any time – Jeremy admits 'The fact that he would not live forever had been on the minds of everyone involved in *I'm Sorry I Haven't a Clue* for as long as I have been a part of it. But somehow I imagined he would see us all off. I would have liked him to play at my funeral . . . His age was a constant source of humour on the show, but in the last few months we all started to treasure him more dearly, and the jokes had an uncomfortable edge.' But it was precisely because it was Humph, and he was happy to be the source of merriment, that such borderline tasteless gags could go on, right up to the end.

This spirit was underlined by his funeral service on 6 May. Jon Naismith recalled 'It was conducted splendidly by a frizzy-haired humanist and took in all aspects of Humph's life. It was mainly family and friends. Of the *Clue* lot, all the regulars were there including Iain and myself, plus Jeremy, Jack, Rob, Stephen, Sandi and Andy. Barry and Jeremy spoke for the *Clue* team, being funny and very moving, and Elkie Brooks sang brilliantly. As his wicker coffin disappeared with his trumpet placed on top, they played his "We'll Meet Again" solo from the Hammersmith Apollo. That really finished us off.'

On the front of the order of the service was a final Thought from Chairman Humph, which must surely point the way forward for everyone who misses, and will always miss, his presence, be they friend, Audience member, or just one of the millions being cheered up on a rainy and drab Monday evening:

As we journey through life, discarding baggage along the way, we should keep an iron grip, to the very end, on the capacity for silliness. It preserves the soul from desiccation.

Amen.

EPILOGUE

Revels to Come

Despite Humph's philosophy on the subject of agonising, Barry Cryer flatly put his foot down when the press came looking for clues to the future of *Clue*, saying, 'It's too soon to consider the future – there's got to be an agonising reappraisal. He was the very hub of the show: I think it was the Humphrey Lyttelton show, the urbane man in the middle of the idiots. He was the only man I know who could get a laugh with dead air, silence on the radio. Who else would get a laugh with "Mmmm"?' And Tim and Graeme resolutely echoed their old friend's sentiments on the seemingly endless, painful occasions on which the subject arose throughout 2008.

It's understandable that a voluble minority of fans of the show immediately called for an end to the festivities when Humph died. Garden and Hatch had agreed on the perfect presenter back in 1972, and for many, the thought of anyone else stepping into the breach was simply ungraspable. Perhaps these people couldn't remember just how entirely the spirit of *Clue* was personified by Willie Rushton, and how stymied the show seemed with his passing over a decade earlier. Admittedly Humph was far more central to the proceedings – as was astutely noted by journalist Gillian Reynolds: 'All the planets revolve around the Chairman, and he is the centre. And they'll go, "whizz-whizz", "bang-bang", "crash" all around him, and there he is just beaming effulgently . . .' And it was of course at Willie's own bequest that the show should continue for as long as Humph was around – at least. So where the difficulty of finding a successor to Willie felt like a royal accession, the mammoth task of filling Humph's role was more akin to the electing of a new pope. But it was no one else's business how it was to be done – the Cardinals Garden, Brooke-Taylor, Cryer and Naismith would debate the issue in private, and the rest of us would have to patiently await the plume of smoke that denoted a verdict.

Facing Facts

In the meantime, though, there were still laughs to be had, jobs to be done. A very silly scriptbook containing all the doings of Hamish and Dougal was released in the summer with a new print tribute, *Lyttelton's Britain,* not far behind. *You'll Have Had Your Tea* had been produced by Random Entertainment, a new production company founded by Graeme and Jon to keep all their creations under one roof – bar *Clue* itself, which the BBC proudly retained as its own production.

Jon Naismith was as adamant as ever that *Clue* should continue, but knew it was ultimately down to Graeme and co. However, he and Graeme did have some kind of backup with their own new radio panel game *The Unbelievable Truth,* which first debuted on Radio 4 in 2007 and, with Naismith producing and Iain Pattinson scripting, it was a quality show which could easily fit into that prized Monday 6.30 p.m. slot. Naismith had the idea, which was then developed by Graeme, for a show in which a speaker would have to give a lecture on any subject, into which a number of real facts would be surreptitiously slipped amid a torrent of hopefully highly amusing drivel. Competitors would get marks for buzzing in and identifying the truths, and lose them for a wrong interruption – what could be simpler or more inexhaustible than that? Get some quality comics on a panel and let them bicker about nonsense for half an hour, expertly blending absurdity with intelligence in the wake of *QI.*

Unbeknown to either of the creators, the basic précis of *The Unbelievable Truth* also summed up an earlier *Clue* round 'Lies All Lies', which was piloted and scrapped in the same 1985 show which saw Kenny Everett standing in for Graeme. However, when the idea was given a whole half-hour to breathe, it took on a completely different shape, and Jon and Graeme had a hit. The pilot was practically a *Clue* jolly, with Graeme, Neil Mullarkey, Andy Hamilton and Jeremy Hardy delivering the lectures, and holding the subject cards in the centre, David Mitchell. Mitchell's ubiquity on panel games throughout this decade has surely blown Tony Slattery's nineties record out of the water, and you can practically track the status of modern comedy panel games by looking at his CV. But it's hard to blame him or the producers for his omnipresence when it's so clear that booking Mitchell for any quiz improved the quality vastly, being effortlessly funny and quick-witted, and somehow managing the trick of becoming a popular comedian while coming across as the most stereotypical upper-middle-class Footlights graduate that Cambridge has produced in generations. From David Baddiel to Sacha Baron Cohen, Cambridge comics have long tended to shrug off any snobby Oxbridge Mafia prejudices (and the 125th anniversary of the club was characteristically muted), but Mitchell's acerbic plumminess has proven to be his strength, making him ideal Chairman material. His script for *TUT* was not even a hundred miles from what Humph could have been given, introducing the guests as 'The finest comedians in their field . . . let's see what they're like indoors'. But then, Pattinson's scripts have influenced panel games so much that there are very few Chairmen who don't sound like Humph in one way or another.

Incidentally, Graeme won the show's pilot with eleven points, managing to sneak past four facts about bees, among tripe such as 'The offspring of a wasp and a bee is known as a "wee". The wee has no sting but its honey is rubbish, which is why it's never been commercially exploited.' But then he did come up with the game in the first place.

So how has the Antidote to Panel Games influenced modern quiz shows, as we slide into the second decade of the new millennium? Certainly the Antidote has not halted the spread of the disease, with new panel games cropping up continually across all channels. Mitchell has also been the Team Captain on BBC1's *Would I Lie to You?* presented by Angus Deayton, followed by the almost as ubiquitious Rob Brydon, which also takes as its theme the art of comedic deception – albeit in a more celebrity-friendly, mainstream way. Lee Mack's sparring with Mitchell has always made the show at least watchable, and especially when guests of the calibre of Graeme Garden pop up. Their main competition has been the *Big Brother*-obsessed Channel 4 topical quiz *Eight Out of Ten Cats* (always watchable for Sean Lock), and BBC2's *Whose Line*-ish topical game *Mock the Week*, created by Dan Patterson and Mark Leveson. Then there are the two veteran survivors of the nineties quiz explosion, *Never Mind the Buzzcocks* and *Have I Got News For You*, the latter still incapable of replacing Deayton after several years. A strong *Clue* influence has been clear in the way that *HIGNFY* has tried to adapt to the 'Guest Presenter' format by throwing in spoofs of games like *The Price is Right*, but the dramatic variation in quality from show to show, depending on who's presenting, has done the satirical quiz no favours, and speculation that *Clue* could face the same challenges with a rotating Chair fuelled the fears of those who wanted Jon and the Teams to call it a day.

Not long after the *Clue* tour ended, Tim Brooke-Taylor also popped over to the Sky Arts Channel to be the Team Captain opposing Dave Gorman in Sandi Toksvig's cultural quiz *What the Dickens?* This stylish show brought out the best in Tim, and guests of the calibre of Rich Hall and Mariella Frostrup added to the quality – the one real problem was that it was recorded in a tent at the Hay Literary Festival, with terrible sound quality which depleted the atmosphere somewhat when it reached the screen. Toksvig is much more at home as the Chair of *The News Quiz* back on Radio 4, and with regulars Jeremy Hardy, Andy Hamilton and Fred Macaulay at her side, John Lloyd's creation has never been stronger. Jon Naismith laughs, 'She was my choice for Chair when Barry Took was replaced, but they went for Simon Hoggart instead. Jeremy's taken the show up a level in recent years and deserves a regular place on the show, and Andy and Fred are terrific. If only they still had the magnificent Linda Smith.' Besides this warm conclave of *Clue* veterans, Radio 4 still allegedly broadcasts *Quote Unquote*, and of course, after more than forty years, David Hatch's jewel, *Just a Minute*, remains unstoppable, with the 86-year-old Nicholas Parsons clearly inspired by Humph's spirit, determined to remain in harness to the end.

But there has been something missing from the Radio 4 schedules since the loss of Humph. These slick and/or cosy parlour games are all well and good, but who is there to cut through the bullshit and show them up as the Money for Old Rope that they are? Frankly, there has been a dangerous lack of silliness on offer in radio comedy. And there's only one show that can do something about that.

I'm Sorry I Haven't a Clue Again

With apologies to the voluble abolitionists, anyone who pined for the show to be placed in aspic with the loss of its icon was always on a hiding to nothing. The BBC wanted to continue, Jon wanted to continue, the Teams wanted to continue . . . and even Humph made it clear that he would never want to be the cause of an end to all the fun of his old pals being given Silly Things To Do. Barry confirms with a sigh, 'He once said to us a few years ago, "If I go under a bus, I don't want any misplaced displays of loyalty, and the show should go on." Tim, Graeme and I had to talk about this now and then, and it was always painful. We could smugly suggest that we'll continue as a tribute to him. More selfishly, we'd continue because we adore doing it . . . But Humph was the hub. It will never be the same again, I know that much.'

Of course, the papers had a field day with endless suggestions as to who would have the onerous task of trying to fill Humph's size twelves, with the role of *Clue* Chairman becoming like the new James Bond or Doctor Who. Always leading the field was Stephen Fry, despite the fact that he has already devoted a huge chunk of his remaining priceless time on the planet to presenting *QI*, and has endless other arenas in which he must exercise his raging talents. Perhaps the most astute nomination came from Jeremy Hardy, who proposed ex-Pulp frontman Jarvis Cocker as a dry-witted musician who could convincingly remain detached from the proceedings. Otherwise the speculation rumbled on, with the one inescapable proviso – none of the existing players would be prepared to shift sideways into the central chair. They were there as players, until the end.

But what a waste it would be to throw away a pearl like *Clue*, no matter how difficult it may be to find the right chemistry for a relaunch. The show's popularity has increased year after year, the staggering CD sales inspired a new line masterminded by Naismith, releasing uncut recordings in their entirety in the 'Live' range – plus of course another opportunity to get an idea of the atmosphere of the recordings came along with the release of the DVD, another groundbreaking first for any radio show. The internet has increased the size of the *Clue* Audience yet further, thanks to repeats on BBC Radio 7 and the BBC iPlayer and several online *Clue* resources – you can even play Mornington Crescent on Facebook with people all around the world, or join in on Twitter, @isihac72.

There is of course something indisputably British about the show's mixture of wordplay and sauce – in fact, the tribute paid by Jim Broadbent in *I'm Sorry I Haven't A Desert Island* puts it best: 'Though I'm not by nature a patriotic animal, I can listen to the programme and actually feel a tingle of pride at being British. If there is such a thing as the Great British sense of humour, it is here that it must surely be found, with all its absurdity, acerbity, self-mockery and filth. As a measure of my devotion, just as I will get out of a hot bath to turn off *The Archers*, I will stay in a cold bath to wait until *Clue* is finished.' But its appeal is increasingly universal, Graeme says, 'It's a very English kind of silliness, but it does have one or two fans in America, well, quite a few. I'm told that Matt Groening of *The Simpsons* is a fan, but that's only hearsay. He may sue.'

It's no surprise that folk all around the world were having withdrawal symptoms without their twice-yearly fix of *Clue* – its unique atmosphere had become an integral part of Radio 4's schedule. Just as David Hatch insisted that if the BBC were to collapse, the one thing it should cling to is Radio 4, it was now clear that with no *Clue*, Radio 4 could not be truly whole. And so finally the announcement came through – leaving a year for pause and reflection in memory of Humph, *I'm Sorry I Haven't a Clue* would be back in June 2009, beginning a series of guest-presenter try-outs – the old reliable Fry, plus Brydon and Dee – with an eye to finding a permanent new host. A 'revolving chair' had of course been the ideal solution for the loss of Willie, but they wouldn't get caught in the same rut as *HIGNFY* – once the right person was found, that one referee who perfectly bounced off the regulars (or rather, allowed the regulars to bounce around them perfectly), then they would be offered the job permanently.

To a minority, this still may seem like sacrilege, but to most fans of *Clue*, after so long without their fix of top-drawer songs to the tune of others and *UED* entries, the return of this ray of light to Monday evenings – not to mention the announcement of a second UK tour for the autumn – couldn't come quick enough. Without doubt, *Clue* in any incarnation will always be infused with the spirit of Humph – it's as inescapable as his influence on all quizzes. Iain Pattinson wrote, 'Before Chairman Humph, panel games had been chaired by nice chaps (and they invariably were chaps) who hoped we'd all enjoy the show as much as they were going to enjoy delighting each other with their wit and wisdom. After Chairman Humph, we got . . . countless other comedy panel games, where the chairman appears not to want to be there and isn't too fond of either his guests or the subject matter. Humph redefined the role of the comedy panel game chairman.'

And besides, for the three remaining long-term panellists, there could never be a better platform than *Clue*. Tim Brooke-Taylor's lack of full writing credit for *The Goodies* belies a ruthless passion for gaggery, from the most pleasing pun to the harshest satirical barb. Cryer's place as the country's wisest comedy guru and joke craftsman is undisputed, and then there's the man he dubs 'the presiding genius', Graeme Garden, still carrying the real blueprints for the show in his head, still active in all sorts of Radio 4 comedy. And all three are clearly loved. Barry theorises, 'Graeme is the dry one, who'll be silent for a while and then strikes like a snake with the best line you've heard for ages. We always say that Tim is the Audience. They seem to identify with him directly, and he identifies with them directly. Tim is ebullient, and full of beans, and the Audience warm to him. And I'm the joke man! Put another way, Graeme's the witty one, Tim's the funny one, and I'm the other one.' This is not to forget Colin either – when he joined *Clue*, piano-playing accompanists were the norm for so many shows, but now? Sell is the last of a dying breed, and will always have a place in the hearts of the crowd. As indeed will his close friend the Lovely Samantha, whose web of privacy has led to some strange conspiracy theories, but of whom Sell recalls: 'Humph did tell me once that he was playing with his band at a gig, and afterwards a gentleman came up to him looking terribly serious, and Humph thought, "oh dear, this man's going to complain or something, about the music." And this man said, "Mr Lyttelton, may I ask you a question in the strictest confidence?" And Humph said, "Yes, of course you can." And he said, "Do Colin Sell and Samantha really exist?" Humph said, "Oh, Samantha does." And that was that, the man walked away looking perfectly happy with that.'

The stalwart team have a unique chemistry after so long together – two-thirds of *Hello, Cheeky* and two-thirds of *The Goodies* combined. Barry says, 'It's telepathic, when you've known each other a long time, you almost know what each other's going to say, and who's going to butt in next. Now and again we get it wrong, we tread on each other, both talking at once or some-thing, but not often. We give each other little looks, and it's just an instinc-tive thing. Miles Kington said we'd become like a soap – you fall into clearly defined character categories, without realising it. It sort of takes shape through the years, and it takes an outside eye to see something there that we can't see because we're in it.' Cryer is a triumphant survivor from a lost world of British Comedy – Variety, Music Hall, clubland were his nurseries and having worked with every imaginable comic giant over the years while still actively gigging alongside young comics new to the business, he is nothing short of a Yoda figure in the comedy world. He'll be gigging to the end, but there'll never be a better avenue for his gag-slinging than *Clue*, in any form. This is one of the main reasons why *Clue* is so necessary, no matter who's presenting – there's no agenda but to *be funny*, it's just a free arena for the finest jokers in the land to entertain – no need to answer topical questions, no need to worry about repetition or deviation, just dole out the funnies – Cryer country.

Oh, and don't forget the jokes – those poor, grey-headed old jokes that have now been preserved by the *I'm Sorry* team for half a century – they can't be released into the community now. And besides, says Barry, 'I looked after them in their old age, now they can look after me in mine.'

Over nearly fifty years of slow evolution and occasional regeneration, many of the traits of the original Footlights show and *ISIRTA* have been bred out of *Clue*, but the programme is still a direct continuation of the same comedy entity stretching right back to *Cambridge Circus* – and who can name one other show that can claim anything similar? Even the usually erudite John Lloyd finds such an achievement hard to grasp: 'It's a great missing piece of the jigsaw – people go on endlessly about *Python* and Peter Cook, which is all well and good but there's basically this great corpus of work stretching for decades – and consistently good. I mean very very few traditions . . . I can't think of one! I mean, Christ, it's forty-five years! A major piece of work, and universally loved.' And there throughout it all, the one person stretching right back to the start of Chapter One, is Tim Brooke-Taylor. From *Clump of Plinths* originator to warbling star of Radio Prune, right up to today, Tim has jubilantly stayed the course, keeping the fans laughing non-stop since he was an undergraduate. Even when he was at Winchester School, his astute house-master noted, 'No doubt if his A levels fail, Tim could become a film star, or, as he would probably prefer to be, an old-time Music Hall comedian.' Seeing the 67-year-old Tim up onstage at the Lyric, still winking at the Audience as he comes out with yet another prime dollop of sauce, how lucky we are that he was proved right. Tim may play golf, but he's not ready to retire like the rest of his generation just yet, thankfully.

Nor is the 65-year old Graeme Garden – he's still doing what he has always wanted to do since he was tiny: making people laugh. 'It's a curse, really, that I've always loved radio – it was the first thing I wanted to be in, my fantasy career. Of everything I have done, the most fun to do is radio in front of an audience. They're a part of the conspiracy, they can see you but nobody else can. You don't have to learn any lines, and by and large you don't have to fall over very much. You don't have all the technical problems of doing a show for television, or film, where you do it in short bursts. Radio you're just there, just you, the audience, and a script. You can lark about, and make a mistake – sometimes, it has to be said, on purpose, just to get an extra laugh. And the audience are all part of it, and you're creating fantasy worlds with pictures and images, and the audience are there sitting in a theatre, but they're going along with the pretence, and having, I think, a whale of a time. I think a radio audience in full cry is a wonderful thing to work with.' Radio may only have a marginal audience in today's media climate, but those millions who do tune in tend not just to like the show, but *love* it. Perhaps this is why our heroes have stuck to the audio medium throughout.

'When I was a kid,' continues Graeme, 'we had a radio station at home and my dad had brought back, after the war, bits and pieces of equipment, like a microphone, which I discovered I could plug into the back of our radio, and go into another room and broadcast. Trouble was, of course, I couldn't hear it, so when he bought a tape recorder, that was absolute bliss. So radio's always been a terrific love of mine, and sadly not blockbuster movies, otherwise I'd have been better off, if I'd followed that career. It's a medium that listeners and performers absolutely adore, it is such fun to do.' There's an alternate universe in which Steven Spielberg went ahead with his mooted *Goodies* movie project. In this world, Tim and Graeme sun themselves in the LA sunshine, many blockbusters under their belt, and the memories of their radio days – including that silly panel game that lasted only a few years before Hollywood called – are but dim. In this world, their bank managers are very happy men. But as for the rest of us, we millions who have been regularly cheered by their radio output for the best part of half a century ... let's just say that we're grateful for how things have turned out.

Everyone's a Winner
Because, as ever, we are the last part of the puzzle. If anything provides that crucial link between the new relaunch of *Clue* and the good old days, it is us – you and me, the listeners, and the rowdy gang that makes up the Audience, cheering on the time-worn rounds, tooting our kazoos, clapping along to Jeremy's singing, heralding another letter from Mrs Trellis with an approving bellow, and generally lifting the show from a silly tangle of old jokes into a rousing, life-affirming comedy phenomenon. We are what has made *Clue* stand out from the crowd – and we are what will keep the show going. Naismith admits that there was 'almost an ambivalence' about continuing the show without Humph, but the weight of support and encouragement from those who love the show made all the difference in convincing the Teams to

continue. And even if *Clue* does finally reach the end of the line, we'll still carry all these traditions and in-jokes within us. We will always be members of the *Clue* fraternity, whether we're playing Mornington Crescent online or trading new entries for *The Uxbridge English Dictionary* in the pub, and every time members of the *Clue* clique meet, Humph, Samantha and the Teams will be remembered. Whenever two or three are gathered together in *Clue*'s name, then they will recall Samantha's charitable activities, or pass the time constructing a letter to 84 Chicken Cross Road, or recall some of the more audacious Late Arrivals. Audience, take a bow.

Hopefully, our continued support will see *Clue* once again rise from the ashes, still organically moving with the times and getting away with joyous old jokes. '*Just a Minute* has a rigid format, and stands and falls by its performers, and there's nothing wrong with that,' says Cryer, 'We've never had a rigid format. We've never had a complete blueprint of, "there it is, that's what we do."' And even Garden admits 'In theory it could go on forever, but I guess the dinosaurs thought that before the meteor strike.'

Nevertheless, on Sunday 26 April, 2009, a year and a day after the loss of Humph, the first episodes of series 51 were recorded, with Fry taking the reins at Her Majesty's Theatre, Haymarket in tribute to Humph – with Victoria Wood finally taking her place on the panel, to boot. So who's to say whether there ever will be an end to this game? Humph was the show's icon, the real centre of its phenomenal success, and with his loss, the show will have to find new forms, new traditions – even new jokes. But for all that, the marriage of Iain Pattinson's words and Humph's delivery will always be seen as one of the finest partnerships in comedy history, the meat of every show has always been the Silly Things that the best minds in the comedy world are given to do, so why not let play continue under the *I'm Sorry* banner, rather than with some makeshift replacement? There's no real reason why Mornington Crescent should not be played by comedians currently unborn, in *Clue*'s hundredth series ('A lovely thought' – Cryer). The transient nature of other Antidotes to Panel Games that have come and gone, shows that we only really need one, with its own traditions stretching back to the Cambridge Footlights of half a century ago – a fine, immortal blend of saucy puns, random silliness, irreverent references and, of course, a complete ambivalence to point-scoring. After all – what do points mean?

I'M SORRY BIBLIOGRAPHY AND OFFICIAL RELEASES

Prune Products

Cambridge Circus, Parlophone, 1963
I'm Sorry I'll Read That Again, Parlophone, 1967
I'm Sorry I'll Read That Again, BBC Records, 1978
I'm Sorry I'll Read That Again: The Classic Scripts, Javelin, 1985
I'm Sorry I'll Read That Again, Vols 1–5, BBC Audiobooks, 1989–2005

Commercial Clue

Unexpurgated Highlights from I'm Sorry I Haven't a Clue, Robson Books, 1980
I'm Sorry I Haven't a Clue: The Official Limerick Collection, Orion, 1998
The Almost Totally Complete I'm Sorry I Haven't a Clue, Orion, 1999
The Little Book of Mornington Crescent, Orion, 2000
Stovold's Mornington Crescent Almanac, Orion, 2001
The Uxbridge English Dictionary, HarperCollins, 2005
The New Uxbridge English Dictionary, HarperCollins, 2007
The Doings of Hamish and Dougal, Preface, 2008
Lyttelton's Britain, Preface, 2008
I'm Sorry I Haven't a Clue, Vols 1–11, BBC Audiobooks, 1993–2009
I'm Sorry I Haven't a Clue Anniversary Special, BBC Audiobooks, 2003
I'm Sorry I Haven't a Christmas Clue, BBC Audiobooks, 2004
I'm Sorry I Haven't a Clue Live, Vols 1–2, BBC Audiobooks, 2006–2008
I'm Sorry I Haven't a Clue: In Search of Mornington Crescent, BBC Audiobooks, 2007
Humph in Wonderland, BBC Audiobooks, 2008
Chairman Humph: A Tribute, BBC Audiobooks, 2008
I'm Sorry I Haven't a Clue: Live On Stage, BBC DVD, 2008
('Chairman Humph' and 'Mornington Crescent' T-shirts – check eBay!)

Books by the Teams

Brooke-Taylor, Tim:
Rule Britannia, BCA, 1983; *Tim Brooke-Taylor's Cricket Box*, Stanley Paul, 1986; *Tim Brooke-Taylor's Golf Bag*, Stanley Paul, 1988

Cryer, Barry:
You Won't Believe This, But . . ., Virgin, 1996; *Pigs Can Fly*, Orion, 2003

Garden, Graeme:
The Seventh Man, Eyre Methuen, 1981; *The Best Medicine: Graeme Garden's Book of Medical Humour*, Robson Books, 1984; *A Sense of the Past*, Ward Lock, 1985; *Graeme Garden's Compendium of Very Silly Games*, Methuen, 1987; *The Skylighters*, Methuen, 1988

Lyttelton, Humphrey (Selected):
I Play As I Please, McGibbon and Kee, 1954; *Second Chorus*, Jazz Book Club, 1958; *Take it From the Top*, Robson Books, 1975; *Why No Beethoven?: Diary of a Vagrant Musician*, Robson Books, 1984; *Notes from a Jazz Life*, (with Digby Fairweather and Peter Manders), Northway, 2002; *It Just Occurred to Me . . .*, Robson Books, 2007; *The Best of Jazz*, Robson Books, 2008; *Last Chorus: An Autobiographical Medley*, JR Books, 2008

Rushton, Willie (Selected):
Willie Rushton's Dirty Book, Private Eye, 1964; *How to Play Football*, Margaret and Jack Hobbs, 1968; *The Day of the Grocer*, Andre Deutsch, 1971; *The Geranium of Flut*, Andre Deutsch, 1975; *Superpig*, Macdonald and Jane's, 1976; *Pigsticking*, Macdonald and Jane's, 1977; *Unarmed Gardening*, (with Frank Ward) Macdonald and Jane's, 1979; *The Filth Amendment*, Queen Anne Press, 1980; *The Reluctant Euro*, Queen Anne Press, 1980; *The Incredible Cottage Annual*, Grandreams, 1982; *W. G. Grace's Last Case*, Methuen, 1984; *Great Moments of History*, Charles Herridge, 1985; *Adam and Eve*, Bell and Hyman, 1985; *The Alternative Gardener*, Grafton, 1986; *Marylebone Versus the World*, Pavilion, 1987; *Spy Thatcher*, Pavilion, 1987; *Every Cat in the Book*, Pavilion, 1993; *Humphrey: The Nine Lives of the Number Ten Cat*, Pavilion, 1995

Books by others

Carpenter, Humphrey, *That Was Satire that Was*, Victor Gollancz, 2000; Foster, Andy and Steve Furst, *Radio Comedy 1938–1968*, Virgin, 1996; Fry, Stephen, *Paperweight*, Mandarin, 1993; Hewison, Robert, *Footlights!*, Methuen, 1984; Lakin, Warren, *Driving Miss Smith*, Hodder and Stoughton, 2007; Lakin, Warren and Ian Parsons (eds), *The Very Best of Linda Smith*, Hodder and Stoughton, 2006; Margolis, Jonathan, *Cleese Encounters*, Orion 1998; McCabe, Bob, *Life of Graham*, Orion 2005; McCabe, Bob, *Pythons on the Pythons*, Orion, 2003; Muir, Frank and Simon Brett (eds), *The Penguin Book of Comedy Sketches*, Penguin, 1992; Oddie, Bill, *One Flew into the Cuckoo's Egg*, Hodder and Stoughton, 2008; Oddie, Bill and Laura Beaumont, *From the Top*, Magnet,

1985; Palin, Michael, *Diaries 1969–1979: The Python Years*, Weidenfeld and Nicolson, 2006; Parsons, Nicholas, *The Straight Man*, Orion, 1994; Perry, George, *Life of Python*, Pavilion, 1994; Ross, Robert, *The Complete Goodies*, B. T. Batsford Ltd, 2000; Ross, Robert, *The Goodies Rule OK*, Carlton Books, 2006; Wilmut, Roger, *From Fringe to Flying Circus*, Eyre Methuen, 1980

Other Sources

Archive Hour: Humph at 80, BBC Radio 4, 2001; *At Last the 1948 Show*, Pye Records, 1967; *At Last the 1948 Show*, Pinnacle DVD, 2007; *Bill Oddie Talks to Mark Lawson*, BBC4, 2007; *Comedy Controller* (Oddie), BBC Radio 7, 2006; *Current Puns*, BBC Radio 4, 2007; *Dawn French's More Boys Who Do Comedy* (Cleese), Saunders and French for BBC4, 2007; *Distinctly Oddie*, Polydor Records, 1967; *The Goodies – The Complete LWT Series*, Network DVD, 2005; *In Conversation with . . .* (Brooke-Taylor and Garden), Paul Jackson for BBC Radio 4; *The Last Word* (Hatch), BBC Radio 4, 2007; *Legends: Humphrey Lyttelton*, BBC4, 2008; *Play it Again*, Diverse Productions for BBC1, 2007; *Radio Heads* (Hatch), BBC Radio 7, 2006; *The South Bank Show* (Humphrey Lyttelton), ITV Productions, 2007; *Shooting Stars*, BBC2, 1996; *Swing When You're Laughing*, BBC Radio 4, 2004; *Two Old Farts in the Night*, 4 Front Video, 1996

Links

Archive resources: missingepisodes.com; Cambridge Footlights: footlights.org; John Cleese's official site: thejohncleese.com; John Cleese podcasts: johncleesepodcast.co.uk; Official BBC ISIHAC Site: bbc.co.uk/comedy/clue/; Official Goodies Fan Club: goodiesruleok.com; Official Humph: humphreylyttelton.com; Officially unofficial ISIHAC Site: isihac.co.uk; Random Entertainment: randomentertainment.co.uk; Saucy Gibbon: the-goodies.co.uk; Supporters Club: cam.net.uk/~aaa236/isirta01.htm; UK Gameshows: ukgameshows.com; Unofficial ISIRTA: britishcomedy.org.uk/comedy/isirta.htm; Wilmut's Pages: rfwilmut.clara.net

"I'M SORRY, I'LL READ THAT AGAIN" (1)

Thursday's read through : 39.40
+ laughs : 44.40

WITH

JO KENDALL

Cut: Kummerwal (2.40)
6.00   Beach Erosion (3.20)

TIM BROOKE-TAYLOR

GRAEME GARDEN

Choose between:

DAVID HATCH

Swinging (2.30)
Tomato (1.40)
Footman (4.03).

BILL ODDIE

Insert: RAF (5.00)
6.00   Beethoven gags (1.00 in all)

JEAN HART

Intro to She's Gone

34.25
29.55
4.30
1.25
3.05

(weather to start
tomato after she's gone.

THE MUSIC OF DAVE LEE

PRODUCER — HUMPHREY BARCLAY, 122 AEOLIAN.

SCRIPTS — BRIAN COOKE AND JOHN E. MORTIMER
  ELIZABETH EVANS
  GRAEME GARDEN
  BRIAN JONES
  PETER VINCENT AND DAVID McKELLAR
  HUGH WOODHOUSE

SONGS — BILL ODDIE

RECORDING FRIDAY 28th MAY 1965: 7.30 - 8.15 p.m.

STUDIO THE PLAYHOUSE   STUDIO MANAGER: David Turner.

REHEARSAL 3.15 p.m.   ASSISTANT
      STUDIO MANAGERS: John Bussell.
R.P. REF. TLO. 521/831.   Tony Wilson.

* 3.15 - 4.00 Read through cuts + details
3.30 - 4.15 Band rehearse
4.15 - 5.00 Songs.   5.15 Run through (1) 6.00 - 6.30 Run through (2)
5.00 - 6.00 Band break
6.00 - 6.45

EPISODE GUIDE

'I'M SORRY I'LL READ THAT AGAIN'

CAMBRIDGE CIRCUS. Rec. Nov Brd. Dec, 1963. The Light Programme. Prod. Ted Taylor, Humphrey Barclay.
With Jo Kendall, Humphrey Barclay, Tim Brooke-Taylor, Graham Chapman, John Cleese, David Hatch and Bill Oddie.

SERIES 1 (ISIRTA PILOT 1, 2, 3) Brd. April 1964.
With Tim Brooke-Taylor, Anthony Buffery, John Cleese, David Hatch, Jo Kendall and Bill Oddie. (Note: BBC Worldwide releases recognise the three try-out pilots as series one, just to add a frisson of exciting confusion to the proceedings.)

SERIES 2 Brd. Oct–Dec 1965. Prod. Humphrey Barclay.
With Tim Brooke-Taylor, Graeme Garden, David Hatch, Jo Kendall and Bill Oddie.
1) Critics Credits. 2) Swan Lake Commentary. 3) The Singular Case of the Workington Shillelagh. 4) The Battle of Whispering Mouse. 5) The Adventures of Little Martin Copperwick. 6) Mike Spanner – Private Eye. 7) England, Our England. 8) Dr Why and The Thing. 9) The BBC.

SERIES 3 Brd. March–June 1966.
With Tim Brooke-Taylor, John 'Otto' Cleese, Graeme Garden, David Hatch, Jo Kendall and Bill Oddie. (The default cast from now on, although Graeme was absent for series 4 and nearly all of series 5.)
1) Ireland. 2) Moll Flounders. 3) Ali Baba. 4) Nelson and The Battle of Piccadilly Circus. 5) Dr Heckle and Mr Jibe. 6) The Angus Prune Story. 7) Ten Little Emergent Nationals. 8) World Of Sport. 9) Julius Caesar.10) The Occult and The Unexplained. 11) Robin Hood. 12) Tim Brown's Schooldays. 13) Liverpool Special.

SERIES 4 Brd. Oct–Jan 1966–67.
1–13) The Curse Of The Flying Wombat.

JACK and THE BEANSTALK. Brd. Jan 1967.

SERIES 5 Brd. April–July 1967.
1) The Knights of the Round Table. 2) Champion The Wondermouse. 3) William Tell. 4) Dr Clubfoot In The Antarctic. 5) The British Army. 6) Cleopatra and Caesar, or Jeremiah Pig and the Transvestite Hippo. 7) Princess Goldilocks and The Perverted Goblins. 8) All Hands On Venus. 9) The Lone Stranger, or The Wild and The Woolly. 10) The Ghost Of Objectionable Manor. 11) Othello. 12) The Inimitable Grimbling. 13) Odysseus. 14) The Dessert Song.

SERIES 6 Brd. April–July 1968. BBC Radio 2. Prod. David Hatch, Peter Titheradge.
1) Bunny and Claude. 2) Dentisti. 3) The Vikings. 4) Incompetence: The Story Of The Arkwright Family. 5) 10,000 B.C. 6) The Tale Of McMuckle Manse. 7) Operation Chocolate. 8) Beau Legs. 9) Macbeth. 10) Robinson Prunestone. 11) The Roaring Twenties. 12) The Legend of Lady Godiva. 13) The History of Cinema.

DICK WHITTINGTON and HIS WONDERFUL HAT. Brd. Dec 1968.

SERIES 7 Brd. Jan–April 1969.
1–13) Professor Prune and The Electric Time Trousers.

A CHRISTMAS CARROT. Brd. Dec 1969.

SERIES 8 Brd. Feb–May 1970.
1) The Taming Of The Shrew. 2) Canterbury Tales. 3) The GPO. 4) Tales Of The Circus. 5) Billy Bunters of Greyfriars School. 6) The 3:17 To Cleethorpes. 7) Henry VIII and His Six Wives (All At Once). 8) Jorrocks! 9) The Return Of The Son Of Bride Of Dracula's Cousin Frankenstein's Wife's Lover's Hair-Dresser's Gibbon's Mummy. 10) The Harder They Fall, The More They Hurt Themselves. 11) 20,000 Leaks Under The Sea. 12) Oedipus Rex and His Red Hot Momma. 13) The Raymond Nostril Story.

DR ZHIVAGO and HIS WONDERFUL LAMP. Brd. Dec 1970.

SERIES 9 Brd. Nov–Dec 1973.
1) Lawrence of Arabia On Ice. 2) Jack The Ripper. 3) Star Trek. 4) The Search For The Nile – or Swedish Chartered Accountant On The Job. 5) Song Of The South. 6) Oklahoma! 7) Alice In Wonderland. 8) Ice Cubes Down My Cleavage, or The Coldtitz Story.

BLACK CINDERELLA TWO GOES EAST. BBC Radio 4. Brd. Dec 1978. Prod. Douglas Adams and John Lloyd.
With Jo Kendall, Graeme Garden, Tim Brooke-Taylor, Bill Oddie, David Hatch and the voice of John Cleese. Plus Peter Cook, Rob Buckman, Richard Murdoch, Richard Baker and John Pardoe.

ISIRTA REUNION SPECIAL. Brd. Dec 1988. Prod. Richard Wilcox.

'I'M SORRY I HAVEN'T A CLUE'

SERIES 1 Brd. Apr–July 1972. BBC Radio 4. Prod. John Cassels. (Pilot recorded November 1971, Prod. David Hatch.)

1) *Graeme Garden, Tim Brooke-Taylor, Bill Oddie and Jo Kendall were given silly things to do by Humphrey Lyttelton, with Dave Lee setting some of them to music.* **No Ball.**

2) *Barry Cryer chairs Tim and Bill versus Graeme and Jo.* **Plumbers' Ball.** 'Mr and Mrs J Soir and their son P Soir . . .'

3) **Clothing Manufacturers' Ball.** 'Mr Nick R Elastic, and Eve Ning-Dress . . .'

4) *Humphrey Lyttelton chairs Tim and Bill versus Graeme and John.* **Zookeepers' Ball.** 'Mr and Mrs Teeter and their daughter Ann Teater . . .'

5) **Greengrocers' Ball.** 'Gary Baldy-Biscuits and Mr and Mrs Choke and their son . . . Norman Choke . . .'

6) **Farmers' Ball.** 'Our friends from Scotland the McSpreaders . . .'

7) **Doctors' Ball.** 'Mr and Mrs Cillin, and their daughter Penelope . . . no need to be familiar . . .'

8) *Barry Cryer chairs Tim and Bill versus Graeme and Jo.* **Furniture Salesman's Ball.** 'Chester Drawers, Dai Ning-Table and Stan Dard-Lamp . . .'

9) **Fishmongers' Ball.** 'Mr and Mrs Sleepinthesubwaydarling, and their dog, Fish.'

10) *Barry Cryer chairs Tim and Bill versus Graeme and John.* **Musicians' Ball.** 'Hans' niece Anne Boompsidaisy . . .'

11) **Mechanics' Ball.** 'Mr and Mrs Drover and their son Alan Drover.'

12) *Humphrey Lyttelton chairs Tim and John versus Graeme and Jo.* **Stage, Screen and Radio Ball.** 'Mr and Mrs Orrowsworld, and their son Tom . . .'

13) **Geographical Society Ball.** 'The Australian Ambassador and his wife and their pet Koala, Lumpar . . .'

SERIES 2 Brd. Apr–June 1973.

1) *Humphrey Lyttelton chairs Tim and Bill versus Graeme and Barry.* **Funny Foreigners' Ball.** 'From Germany, Herr und Frau Zat-Dodishes, and their son Hans . . .'

2) **Sportsmen's Ball.** 'Mr and Mrs Ontal-Bars and their son Horace . . .'

3) **Television Ball.** 'Mr and Mrs Python's-Flying-Circus and their son Arthur.'

4) **North American Ball.** 'Mr and Mrs Cude-Steak, and their daughter Barbie . . .'

5) **Archaeologists' Ball.** 'Priest Orick Remains, Terry Dactyl and Mo Zaic-Floor . . . Sutton who?'

6) **Military Ball.** 'Corporal Punishment and Major Jump . . .'

7) **Historians' Ball.** 'Mr and Mrs Robinson and their fireplace, Alfred The Grate. And their butler, Hastings . . .'

8) **Clothiers' Ball.** 'Spotty Bow-Tie and his brother Dickie . . .'

9) **Astronauts' Ball.** 'Mr and Mrs Control-Houston and their effeminate French son Miss Jean Control-Houston . . .'

10) **MISSING.**

SERIES 3 Brd. Aug–Oct 1974.

1) *Humphrey Lyttelton chairs Tim and Willie versus Graeme and Barry.* **Booksellers' Ball**. 'Mr and Mrs Jonathan Cape, and their son The Great S. Cape . . .'
2) **Publicans' Ball.** 'The Port Family, Tony Port and his wonderful elderly sister, Fine Old Ruby . . .'
3) **MISSING. The Teachers' Ball.**
4) **Clerics' Ball.** 'Mrs and Mrs Perior, and their Mother, Sue Perior . . .'
5) **The Politicians' Ball.** 'Wave something tasteful for Mr and Mrs Secretary and their hairy song Furry Ian Secretary . . .'
6) **Pharmacists' Ball.** 'Mr and Mrs Tick and their daughter Emma Tick (Groan) . . . oh, it makes you sick.'

SERIES 4 Brd. July–Sept 1975. Prod. Simon Brett.

Graeme Garden, Tim Brooke-Taylor, Barry Cryer and Willie Rushton were given silly things to do by Humphrey Lyttelton, with Colin Sell setting some of them to music.

1) **BBC Ball.** 'Mr and Mrs Ory and their hermaphrodite child Jack-Anne Ory . . .'
2) **Schoolteachers' Ball.** 'Mr and Mrs Tation and their son Dick . . .'
3) **JOHN JUNKIN, in for Tim. Fairyland Ball.** 'Mr and Mrs Arthur Elf tender their apologies and send their only son, Bymis . . .'
4) **JUNKIN. The Housewives' Ball.** 'Mr and Mrs Swasher and their daughter Dee Swasher . . .'
5) **Common Market Ball.** 'Suspend if you will your critical faculties, for Mr and Mrs Reaches-Newlow and their son Stirling Reaches-Newlow.'
6) **Estate Agents' Ball.** 'Sammy Detached and Gary J-Joining . . .'
7) **Economists' Ball.** 'Mr and Mrs Cums-Policy and their unemployable son, the Unworkable Ian Cums-Policy . . .'
8) **Anatomists' Ball.** 'Dame Bones and Rupert Churd-Spleen . . .'

SERIES 5 Brd. March–April 1976.

1) **Footballers' Ball.** 'Ernest, Muriel and Nicholas had just arrived, but now we've got to say: "Bye, Ern, Mu, Nick!"'
2) **Politicians' Ball.** 'Homosexual Bill with his Queen's Speech . . .'
3) **Astronomers' Ball.** 'From Ireland, Mr and Mrs Centauri and their son Alfie Centauri – and don't forget the Irish stew, it's meaty-o'rite . . .'
4) **Geographers' Ball.** 'Mr and Mrs Sippy, and Madge and Min Orca . . .'
5) **Electrical Goods and Allied Industries Ball.** 'Con Trast and Jack Plug, who has good connections . . .'
6) **Tailors' Ball.** 'Glad Rags and Leo Tard . . .'

SERIES 6 Brd. Aug–Oct 1978. Prod. Geoffrey Perkins.

1) **Mornington Crescent debut. Mad Scientists' Ball.** 'Those sinister sisters Bella Lugosi and Doris Karloff . . .'
2) **MISSING. The Criminals' Ball.** 'Mr and Mrs Eny and their son Lars Eny . . .'

3) **Artists' Ball**. 'All the way from The States, Mr and Mrs Trait, and their father, Pa Trait.'
4) **Aristocrats' Ball.** 'Ma Quiss and Ma Chioness . . . And the Right Hon. Baby . . .'
5) **MISSING.**
6) **MISSING. Shakespearean Ball.** 'Is it Sir Toby Belch? Toby or not Toby . . .'
7) JONATHAN LYNN, in for Willie. **Vets' Ball.** 'Mr and Mrs Wobbles and the dog, the Collie Wobbles . . .'
8) **Travellers' Ball.** 'Oh, there's Alf Ganistan . . .'
9) **Drunkards' Ball**. 'Mr and Mrs Tasanewt, and their son Piers . . . and his parrot, Litic . . .'
10) **The Old Testament Ball**. 'Gladys and her respectable whale . . . and Joan, her randy whale . . .'

SERIES 7 Brd. July–Sept 1979.
1) **Confectioners' Ball**. 'PC Cake and his dog, Biscuit . . .'
2) **Politicians' Ball**. 'Mr and Mrs Norder and their little girl Laura Norder . . .'
3) **Broadcasting Ball**. 'Carla Television and a drunken Viking, Lars Of-The-Summer-Wine . . .'
4) **Science Fiction Ball**. 'Mr and Mrs Vasionofthebodysnatchers, and their son, Ian . . . Vasionofthebodysnatchers . . .'
5) DENISE COFFEY, in for Willie. **Gourmets' Ball**. 'Mr and Mrs Toast and their good food guide son Egon . . .'
6) **Estate Agents' Ball**. 'Our visitor from Australia, Lou Outback . . .'
7) **Advertisers' Ball**. 'Welcome Ma Goodness and Ma Guinness . . .'
8) **Gardeners' Ball**. 'There's the lovely Cynthia. Everybody say, 'Hiya Cynth!' . . . It grows on you.'
9) COFFEY. **Transport Ball**. 'Captain and Mrs Dingcraft, and their son Len Dingcraft . . .'
10) **Common Market Ball**. 'Freda Muvmovement and Belle Jum . . .'

XMAS SPECIAL. Brd. Dec 1979.
JOHN JUNKIN, in for Barry. **Christmas Ball.** 'Here come some traditional visitors, the Family Row . . .'

XMAS SPECIAL. Brd. Dec 1980.
Christmas Ball. 'From Italy, Donna Youdrinkand-Drive . . .'

SERIES 8 Brd. Aug–Oct 1981.
1) **Royal Ball**. 'Mr and Mrs Slist, and their discredited daughter Honor Slist . . .'
2) **Criminal's Ball**. 'The Chinese Detective Ah-Salt, and Ali-Buy . . .'
3) **Hollywood Ball**. 'From Torquay, Mr and Mrs Ruinous, and their son Will, known as "Torquay's Will Ruinous" . . .'
4) DENISE COFFEY, in for Tim. **Explorers' Ball**. 'Dr Presume, full name Livingstone I Presume . . .'

5) **Big Game Hunters' Ball**. 'Amos Kito-Net, and Zebra Carr . . .'
6) **Keep Fit Fanatics' Ball.** 'Mr and Mrs Ontal bars, and their son Horace Ontal-Bars . . .'
7) **Household Furnishers' Ball.** 'Ray Diator, and from Wales, Dai Van . . .'
8) COFFEY. **TV Awards Ball**. 'Wendy Boatcomesin, Bo Nanza and Heidi Hi . . .'
9) **Cricketers' Ball**. 'From Scotland, Jock Strap and Wee Kitt Keeper . . .'
10) **Music Lovers' Ball.** 'Mr Moonlight, and the Moonlights' Son, Arthur.'

SERIES 9 Brd. March–May 1982. Prod. Paul Mayhew-Archer.
1) **Oriental Ball**. 'Sweet Ann Sourpork . . .'
2) **Financiers' Ball.** 'Mr and Mrs Needle-Street and their son Fred Needle-Street. And his Old Lady . . .'
3) **Linguists' Ball.** 'Mrs and Mrs Viderci amd their cockney son 'Arry Viderci, and Lyn Guaphone.'
4) **Students' Ball.** 'Polly Technic, Alma Mater, and Algie Bra.'
5) **Sailors' Ball.** 'Mr and Mrs Dupsherises, and their rather posh daughter Hooray Dupsherises . . .'
6) **Ecclesiastical Ball.** 'EQ Maniacal-Movements and Si Nod, tipping the wink . . .'
7) **Journalists' Ball.** 'Dolly Telegraph and Evelyn Standard . . .'
8) **Theatrical Ball.** 'Mr and Mrs Doctor-Inthehouse and their daughter Sarah Doctor-Inthehouse, and Hugh L. Nevergetadrinkattheinterval . . .'
9) **Holidaymakers' Ball.** 'Stuart S. Canihaveapaperbag, Dick Chair and Sam Tropez.'
10) **Builders' Ball.** 'All da way from Ireland, Mr and Mrs O'Dawes and their daughter Patti O'Dawes . . .'

SERIES 10 Brd. February–April 1983.
1) Guildhall School of Music and Drama DENISE COFFEY, in for Barry. **YELLOW PAGES. Jewellers, and Painters and Decorators.** 'Nick Lace and Stringer-Pearls and Walter Colours.'
2) COFFEY. **YELLOW PAGES. Massage Parlours and Sculptors.** 'Giselle-Anne Ameur and Christopher Rub-In and Winnie the Pool.'
3) **YELLOW PAGES. Property Developers.** 'The Imposing Eddie Fiss, Gus Hump and Terry Stouse.'
4) **YELLOW PAGES. Grocers and Gunsmiths.** 'Miss Tit and Molly Gatauney.'
5) **YELLOW PAGES. Family-Planning Clinic.** 'Vast Hector Mee and Ivor Headache-Darling.'
6) **YELLOW PAGES. Plumbers and Sewage Contractors.** 'Michaelangelo will paint your cistern for you . . .'
7) Middlesex Hospital. DENISE COFFEY, in for Graeme. **YELLOW PAGES. Horticultural Wholesalers.** 'Patrick Mower and his sister, Lorna Mower'.
8) COFFEY. **YELLOW PAGES. Garage Services.** 'Emma O'Tee, Phil Erup and Jack Erup'.

9) Imperial College. **YELLOW PAGES. Farmers.** 'Si Ledge, Clive Dunge and Pearl Barley . . .'

10) **YELLOW PAGES. Marriage Guidance.** 'Di Vorce, with Al Imony.'

SERIES 11 Brd. April–June 1984.

1) **Gamblers' Ball.** 'From Las Vegas, the family Shootcrap, and their son Les Shootcrap.'

2) **Car Salesmen's Ball.** 'Who's that lovely lady over there? Cor! Tina!'

3) **Vets' Ball.** 'There's D. Stemper and Ray Bees over there . . .'

4) **Removal Men's Ball.** 'Mr and Mrs Drawers and their son Chester . . . He's a tall boy . . .'

5) Imperial College. **Insurance Salesmen's Ball.** 'Ian Surer and his friend, Justin Case . . .'

6) **Electricians' Ball.** 'Meg O'Watts and her murderous husand Killer O'Watts . . .'

7) **Security Services Annual Ball.** 'Mr and Mrs Out-for-the-Burglars, and their daughter Alison Out-for-the-Burglars . . .'

8) **Catering Equipment Purveyors' Ball.** 'Sue Pladle. She's come with Stewart Prune, oh she's leaving . . .'

9) MIKE HARDING, in for Tim. **Charities' Ball.** 'There's Charity Biggins . . . I thought she was at home!'

10) HARDING. **Sports Equipment Ball.** 'Mr and Mrs Nginto-Touch, and their rugby-playing Maori friend Kiki Nginto-Touch . . .'

EVERYMAN'S GUIDE TO MORNINGTON CRESCENT. Brd. Dec 1984.

SERIES 12 Brd. May–July 1985.

1) **Dancers' Ball.** 'All the way from Norway . . .' 'This is going to be Lars Waltz, isn't it?'

2) **Fishermens' Ball.** 'Mr and Mrs Dozen-Oysters and their son Oliver Dozen-Oysters . . . and his brother, Arfur.'

3) Samantha's debut. KENNY EVERETT, in for Graeme. **Beauticians' Ball.** 'Mr and Mrs Schlair and their daughter Faye . . .'

4) EVERETT. **Gamblers' Ball.** 'Ladies and gentlemen, here he comes – Mr Bernard Cribbage and Miss Roulette Lenska!'

5) **Embassy's Ball.** 'There's Aunt Eager and Bob Ados . . .'

6) **Morticians' Ball.** 'Will you welcome please, spluttering fellow from Wales, Dai the Death . . . who seems to be having a coffin fit.'

7) BILL TIDY, in for Graeme. **Expectant Mothers' Ball.** 'Mr and Mrs Tisntis, and their daughter Betty Tisntis . . .'

8) TIDY. **Photographers' Ball.** 'Mama Razzi, and her husband Papa Razzi . . .'

9) **Farmers' Ball.** 'Fertilizer Minnelli singing some songs by Noel Cowherd . . .'

10) **Newsagents' Ball.** 'Here comes Joan Collins. She's got a male on Sunday, two mirrors and an observer . . .'

SERIES 13 Brd. July–Sept 1986. [With original *Radio Times* billing]

1) JOHN JUNKIN, in for Barry. **Communications Ball.** 'Mr and Mrs Confidential, and their daughter, in the army, Private Ann Confidential.'

2) [*I'm Sorry I Haven't a Clue II*] JUNKIN. **Wild West Ball.** 'Mr and Mrs Derek Nimmo, and their son GERRY NIMMOOOO!'

3) [*I'm Sorry I H . . . t a . . . e – Edited highlights of I'm Sorry I Haven't a Clue*] MIKE HARDING, in for Graeme. **Travellers' Ball.** 'The Peruvian Usatac Family, and their son Billy Usatac . . .'

4) [*I'm No Longer Sorry I Haven't a Clue and Why Should I Be?*] **The Vicars' Ball.** 'Mr and Mrs Ment and their newt, Esther Ment . . .'

5) [*I'm Sorry I Haven't a Clue How to Set Out a Cast List*] STEPHEN FRY, in for Graeme. **Caterers' Ball.** 'Sue Flay's just collapsed . . . It's OK someone's given her the quiche of life.'

6) [*Clint Eastwood is the Man with No Part in I'm Sorry I Haven't a Clue*] FRY. **Nannies' Ball.** 'The Siamese Twins Mew Ling and Pu King . . .'

7) [*Having Fun with Goats. With the gang from I'm Sorry I Haven't a Clue*] HARDING. **Teachers' Ball.** 'Wendy Bellgoes and Hans Upwhoknows.'

8) HARDING. **Health and Efficiency Ball.** 'Herr und Frau Pimples and their son Goose.'

9) FRY. **Musicians' Ball.** 'Andrew Lloyd Webber with his fan, Tom of the Opera. And his Cosy fan, Tootie.'

10) FRY. **Secret Service Ball.** 'Mrs and Mrs Can-Dagger, and their daughter Cleo Can-Dagger . . .'

XMAS SPECIAL. Brd. Dec 1986.
[*I'm Shorry I Haven't a Cluezy Woozy*] **Christmas Ball.** 'Shall we get all the ones called Chris out of the way early on? Mr and Mrs Mas-Comes-Earlier-Every-Year . . .'

SERIES 14 Brd. Aug–Oct 1987. Prod. Paul Spencer.

1) **World War II Ball.** 'Interesting family, the We-Shall-Fight-Them-On-The-Beaches, and their daughter Michelle . . .'

2) STEPHEN FRY, in for Tim. **Shakespearian Ball.** 'All the way from Wales, there's Nye Theraborrower, and his girlfriend Nora Lenderby.'

3) **Wine and Cheese Ball.** 'Cabaret Time: Welcome Dip Dunk and The Twiglets.'

4) [*Bob Says: I'm Sorry I Haven't a Clue*] FRY. **Weatherman's Ball.** 'Please welcome Lord and Lady Frost, and their son Sir Vere.'

5) **Criminals' Ball.** 'Kneel with obeisance to a little known Nordic God, Offa Thebackofalorry.'

6) **Motorists' Ball.** 'Will you welcome from Sweden, please, Lars Yearsmodel . . .'

7) **Sailors' Ball.** 'Mandy Pumps and Wendy Boot-Comes-In . . . And Captain Slog.'

8) **Americans' Ball.** 'Sitting Bull and his wife Lying Cow . . .'

9) **Rag Trade Ball.** 'Mr and Mrs Parker, and their friend Annie Rack.'

10) **Doctors' Ball.** 'There Sue Positry . . . she's coming up in the world . . .'

SERIES 15 Brd. Jan–March 1989.

1) **Gardeners' Ball.** 'The Dendrums and their daughter Thora . . . Rhoda couldn't come . . . And Graeme Garden!'

2) **Schooldays Ball.** 'Mr and Mrs Mathics, and their daughter Martha Matics, and her friend Algy Bra.'

3) BILL TIDY, in for Barry. **Delicatessen Ball.** 'There's Olive Oil and her son, Flower. And their friend Polly Unsaturates.'

4) **Licensed Victuallers' Ball.** 'From Spain, Mr and Mrs Over-The-Eight and their son Juan Over-The-Eight . . .'

5) STEPHEN FRY, in for Barry. **Fleet Street Ball.** 'There's our old friend Hugh Whatascorcher!'

6) **Keep Fit Ball.** 'The Bolic-Steroids and their daughter Anna . . .'

7) TIDY. **Car Dealers' Ball.** 'Emma T. Test making a welcome return . . .'

8) **DIY Ball.** 'All the way from Ireland, Mr and Mrs O'Dawes, and their daughter Patti O'Dawes . . .'

9) FRY. **Dickensian Ball.** 'Mr and Mrs Gin and their daughter Faye . . . doing the Twist.'

10) **Roman Ball.** 'Will you welcome please Mr and Mrs Swall and their son Adrian . . .'

SERIES 16 Brd. Feb–March 1990. Producer: Jon Magnusson.

1) **Ecological Ball.** 'Welcome the Sellafield cows, and a bull. Oh he's lit up, that's the glow bull . . . warming.'

2) **Detectives' Ball.** 'From France, Jacques Hughes, with Jean D'Armori.'

3) **Chefs' Ball.** 'Welcome from Italy, that well known Italian-Scot Mac Aroni and his Auntie Pasta and French whore, D'ourve.'

4) **Vicars' Ball.** 'The Right Hon. Ismay Shepherd, with the Lord Ismay-Shepherd . . .'

5) **Travel Agents' Ball.** 'Mr and Mrs Sand, and their son Charles Norman – C.N. Sand . . .'

6) **Fashion Ball. MISSING.**

SERIES 17 Brd. Nov–Dec 1990.

1) **Euro Ball.** 'Mr and Mrs Amin, and their underwater sun, Subs Idi . . . ?'

2) **Painters' Ball.** 'Cabaret Time! Easel Knieasel jumping over 20 Caravaggios . . .'

3) **Conservative Party Ball.** 'Mr and Mrs Unscrupulous Bastard, and their son A. Unscrupulous Bastard . . .'

4) **Circus Performers' Ball.** 'Mr and Mrs E. Doodle-Dandy, and their Yak E. Doodle-Dandy . . .'

5) **Cowboys and Indians Ball.** 'On the bill is Frankie Howerd and Andrew Ridgeley . . . That's Wig-Wham.'

6) Mrs Trellis' debut. **The Scouts and Guides Jamboree Camping Ball.** 'Rub yourselves together please, for John Knot, and his Granny Knot, and the sheep, Shank.'

SERIES 18 Brd. June-July 1991.
NO BALLS! ('We've dropped the Balls – the programme's finally reached puberty.')
1) The Old Shop Hotel, Brighton. BILL TIDY in for Tim. **Limerick.** 'While listening to Radio 1 . . .'
2) TIDY. **Limericks.** 'I once spent a weekend in Hove . . .'
3) TIDY. **Limericks.** 'I was courting a girl from the North . . .'
4) TIDY. **Limericks.** 'One evening, while playing at whist . . .'
5) TIDY. **Limericks.** 'While having a drink with Ken Bruce . . .'
6) TIDY. **Limericks.** 'On thumbing my way through *The Sun* . . .'

SERIES 19 Brd. Oct–Dec 1991. Prod. Jon Naismith.
NO BALLS!
1) PAUL MERTON in for Graeme. **Limericks.** 'One lunchtime, while quaffing some ale . . .'
2) MERTON in for Graeme. **Limericks.** 'I've an enormous collection of Strauss . . .'
3) BILL TIDY in for Graeme, DENISE COFFEY in for Tim. **Limericks.** 'A man with a gift for the fiddle . . .'
4) TIDY/COFFEY. **Limericks.** 'At the Commons, with newsman John Cole . . .'
5) PAUL MERTON in for Graeme. **Limericks.** 'If you meet the Archbishop of York . . .'
6) MERTON. **Limericks.** 'A sandwich prepared by Crewe Leith . . .'
7) **Limericks.** 'If you're hoping to travel by train . . .'
8) **Limericks.** 'When drinking a cup of Early Grey . . .'

SERIES 20 Brd. May–June 1992.
1) PAUL MERTON in for Graeme. **Celebrity Sponsors.** 'My Fair Ladyshave' and 'Oklahomebase'.
2) **Fishermen's Film Club.** 'And Cod Created Woman' and 'Kramer Vs. Fishcake'.
3) Brighton. **Vegetable Film Club.** 'The Adventures of Tom Soya'. and 'The Texas Coleslaw Massacre'.
4) Oxford. **Confectioners' Ball.** 'Mr and Mrs Gums and their son Wayne Gums . . .'
5) **Ornithologists' Film Club.** 'The Forbidden Gannet' and 'All Quiet On The Crested Grebe'.
6) Oxford. **Bakers' Film Club.** 'The Last Temptation of Crust' and 'BRING ME THE BREAD OF ALFREDO GARCIA'.

SERIES 21 Brd. Nov–Dec 1992.
1) Buxton. **Official Sponsor.** 'Alfred Hitchcock's "Tesco"' and 'North by Nat West'.
2) **Her Majesty's Film Club.** 'The Last Days of Sodom and Balmoral'.
3) Paris Theatre, London. **Farmers' Film Club.** 'My Left Foot and Mouth' and 'Beef Encounter'.
4) **Limericks.** 'A romantic named Percy Bysshe Shelley . . .'

5) Chichester. PAUL MERTON in for Tim. **Undertakers' Film Club.** 'Robocorpse' and 'Bring Me the Rest of Alfredo Garcia!'

6) MERTON. **Limericks.** 'While playing a tough game of patience . . .'

XMAS SPECIAL. Brd. Dec 1992.
Santa's Film Club. 'Three Wise Men and A Baby' and 'King Kong Merrily on High'.

SERIES 22 Brd. Nov–Dec 1993.
1) Edinburgh Festival. **Medical Film Club.** 'Up Stethoscope' and 'Coldfinger'.

2) **Vicars' Film Club.** 'What's Up, Flock?'

3) Bury St Edmunds. **Motor Mechanics' Film Club.** 'Die Lada' and 'Robin Reliant, Prince of Thieves'.

4) **Zookeepers' Film Club.** 'Camel. Ot' and 'The Gnus of Navarone'.

5) **Gardeners' Ball.** 'Mr and Mrs Radicator and their son Slugger!'

6) **Chefs' Film Club.** 'The Last Mango In Paris' and 'Prawn Free'.

XMAS SPECIAL. Brd. Dec 1993.
Santa's Xmas Ball. 'Mr and Mrs O'Manger, and their son Wayne . . .'

SERIES 23 Brd. May–July 1994.
1) Windsor. **Butchers' Film Club.** 'Let's get 'Jurassic Pork' out of the way . . .'

2) **Farmers' Song Book.** 'I Wonder Who's Kissing Her Plough'.

3) Oxford. **Barmen's Film Club.** 'The Booze Brothers' and 'Tequila Mockingbird'.

4) **MISSING.**

5) **Doctors' Book Club.** 'Paddy Doyle Hahaha You Can Put Your Trousers Back On Now'.

6) **Fruiterers' Film Club.** 'Brewster's Melons' and 'Kumquat's Up, Doc?'

SERIES 24 Brd. Nov–Dec 1994.
1) Bath. PAUL MERTON in for Tim. **Lumberjacks' Film Club.** 'Joan Collins is . . . The Beech!'

2) MERTON. **Entomologists' Film Club.** 'Charley's Ant' and 'A Moth In The Country'.

3) Paris Theatre. **Painters' Film Club.** 'The Lady Varnishes' and 'Renoir Dogs'.

4) **Highland Film Club.** 'Hebrides For Seven Brothers' and 'Look Back At Angus'.

5) Chester. **Motor Mechanics' Ball.** 'Here come the Absorbers and their son Jacques!'

6) **Roman Film Club.** 'Rome Alone' and 'Hadrian's Wall Street'.

SERIES 25 Brd. May–July 1995.
1) Brighton. **Doctors' Song Book.** 'Knees Up, Mother Brown'.

2) **Butchers' Film Club.** 'Beef Encounter, directed by David Lean' and 'O, Liver'.

3) Watford. **Undertakers' Song Book.** 'Some Embalming Evening, you may stuff a stranger . . .'

4) **Train Drivers' Film Club.** 'The Sidings of the Lambs' and 'The Odd Coupling'.

5) Radio Theatre, Broadcasting House. **Ornithologists' Ball.** 'Mr and Mrs Shag, and their children, who are far too numerous to mention.'

6) **Fishermans' Song Book.** 'Shark The Herald Angels Sing' and 'Stickleback Writer'.

SERIES 26 Brd. Nov–Dec 1995.

1) Hackney Empire. TONY HAWKS in for Tim. **Antique Collectors' Film Club.** 'Porcelain Bess' and 'The Last Auction Hero'.

2) HAWKS. **Car Mechanics' Song Book.** 'Begin the Big-End' and 'Nissan Dorma'.

3) Harrogate. JEREMY HARDY in for Tim. **Newsagents' Song Book.** 'Hello Dolly Telegraph' and 'Penthouse of the Rising Sun'.

4) HARDY. **Weather Forecasters' Film Club.** 'A Fish Called Michael' and 'Play Mistral For Me'.

5) Stratford. **Painters' Song Book.** 'Happy Degas Here Again' and 'How Much Is That Doggie In Formaldehyde?'

6) **Elizabethan Film Club.** 'Sword Fight at The OK Corral' and 'Goldenhind, with Doublet-Hose 7'.

XMAS SPECIAL. Brd. Dec 1995.

Swanee Kazoo. 'Winter Wonderland', with Humph's band.

SERIES 27 Brd. June–July 1996.

1) Brighton. **Launderette Attendants' Film Club.** 'Bring Me The Vest of Alfredo Garcia' and 'Sink The Skidmark'.

2) **Furniture Makers' Song Book.** 'Nellie The Elephant's Foot Umbrella Stand' and 'Don't Laugh At Me Cause I'm A Stool'.

3) Richmond. **Fashion Designers' Film Club.** 'Ben Kingsley as GUCCI' and 'For Whom The Bellbottoms'.

4) **Biblical Song Book.** 'I Need A Hebrew' and 'I'm In The Mood For Leviticus'.

5) Cheltenham. **Financiers' Film Club.** 'Withdrawal and I' and 'Nightsafe on Elm Street'.

6) **Cheesemakers' Ball.** 'Pray silence and grovel a bit for the Family Ooh! And their daughter Poor Sal . . .'

SERIES 28 Brd. Nov–Dec 1996.

1) Liverpool Playhouse. **TV Seasons – Gardening.** 'The Great Train Shrubbery' and 'Growbag In Anger'.

2) **Butchers' Song Book.** 'Some Day My Mince Will Come' and 'Never Mind The Bullocks'.

3) Northampton. **Builders' Film Club.** 'All About Eaves' and 'Schindler's Loft Conversion.'

4) **Dog Fanciers' Song Book.** 'Good Collie, Miss Molly!' and 'Hey Chewed' and 'Labrador Rigby', by The Beagles.

5) Cambridge Arts Theatre. **Undertakers' Ball.** 'Here come Mr and Mrs Reaper, and their son Graeme Reaper . . .'

6) Brd. 14 December 1996. **Biscuit Makers' Film Club.** 'The Singing Digestive' and 'La Dolce Ryvita'.

SERIES 29 Brd. June–July 1997.

1) Bath. PAUL MERTON. **Smokers' Film Club.** 'Tar Wars' and 'Look Who's Toking'.

2) **Computer Programmers' Song Book.** 'QWERTY QWERTY Chip-Chip' and 'When I'm Cleaning Windows 95'.

3) Brighton. DENISE COFFEY. **Cobblers' Song Book.** 'David Sole sings 'Peggy Shoe' . . . ? Good god, that's the best one . . .'

4) **Australian Ball.** 'And will you welcome Mr and Mrs O'Reef, and their wonderful son Great Barry O'Reef!'

5) Canterbury. STEPHEN FRY. **Weight Watchers' Song Book.** 'I'll Never Get Over You' and 'My Sweet Lard'.

6) **Builders' Ball.** 'All the way from Ireland, Brendan Beam and James Joist.'

SERIES 30 Brd. Nov–Dec 1997.

1) Wimbledon. PAUL MERTON. NEIL INNES in for Colin. **Hairdressers' Song Book.** 'Dandruff Keeps Falling Off My Head' and 'Shave Your Missus For Me'.

2) MERTON/INNES. **Zookeepers' Ball.** 'Will you please welcome Mr and Mrs De Beast, and their son, Harry.'

3) Newcastle. TONY HAWKS. **Criminals' Song Book.** 'Wouldn't It Be Robbery?' and Cat Burglar Stevens' 'Morning Has Been Broken Into'.

4) HAWKS. **Stockbrokers' Ball.** 'Mr and Mrs It-Crash, and their son Mark It-Crash . . .'

5) Almeida Theatre, Islington. SANDI TOKSVIG. **Pensioners' Film Club.** 'Senior Citizen Kane' and 'Honey I've Shrunk'. Bring Me The Truss . . .

6) TOKSVIG. **Old Testament Ball.** 'Ron and I are running the bar. If anything goes wrong, it's due to Ron and Me. Ah, there's Tara Babel . . .'

Willie Rushton Tribute. Brd. April 6th 1998.

SERIES 31 Brd. April–June 1998.

1) Windsor. JEREMY HARDY. **Hairdressers' Film Club.** 'Perms of Endearment' and 'Top Bun'.

2) HARDY. **Hoteliers' Ball.** 'Will you welcome please Mr and Mrs Rouserpress and their son Corbett Rouserpress.'

3) City of Varieties. Leeds. PAUL MERTON. **Welsh Film Festival.** 'Dai Hard', 'Dai Hard 2' and 'An American in Powys'.

4) MERTON. **Overweight Ball.** 'It's cabaret time! Tummy Steele, George Belly and Fats Domino singing "Blubbery Hill".'

5) Southsea. SANDI TOKSVIG. **Airline Pilots' Song Book.** 'Cheapy Cheapy Seat-Seats' and 'Stanstead By Your Man'.

6) TOKSVIG. **FootBall Managers' Ball.** 'Will you welcome Mr and Mrs Sthebastard-In-The-Black, and their son Hugh . . .'

SERIES 32 Brd. Nov 1998 – Jan 1999.

1) Glasgow. FRED MACAULAY. **Hospital Book Club.** 'Bridget Jones' Diarrhoea' and 'The Chronicles of Hernia'.
2) MACAULAY. **The Scottish Ball.** 'Delightful to see the House-Muirs, and their son Stan . . .'
3) Cardiff. MAX BOYCE. **Welsh Song Book.** 'Knocking On Evans' Door' and 'Don't Look You, Bach, In Anger'.
4) BOYCE. **Driving Instructors' Ball.** 'From Spain, Mr and Mrs Gears, and their song Manuel Gears.'
5) Birmingham. JEREMY HARDY. **Pensioners' Song Book.** 'We're all going on a SAGA holiday . . .' and 'Staying Alive'.
6) HARDY. **Computer Operators' Film Club.** 'Thoroughly Modem Millie' and 'The Charge of Delete Brigade'.

I'M SORRY I HAVEN'T A DESERT ISLAND. Brd. 11 Jan 1999.

SERIES 33 Brd. May–July 1999.

1) Guildford. FRED MACAULAY. **Royal Song Book.** 'We Are The Champion', by Queen, and 'The Funky Coronation Chicken'.
2) MACAULAY. **Countrymen's Ball.** 'From Germany, welcome Herr und Frau Gidiot, and their song Villie Gidiot . . .'
3) Plymouth. TONY HAWKS. **Fishermen's Book Club.** 'The Little Book of Clam' and 'Great Exaggerations'.
4) HAWKS. **Radio Ball.** 'Mr and Mrs Bennett When-Will-They-Stop-Mucking-About-With-The-Schedules . . . and their son, GORDON–!'
5) Nottingham. JEREMY HARDY. **Vegetable Song Book.** 'Bohemian Raspberry' and 'Sitting With Some Dock and Some Bay'.
6) HARDY. **Cobblers' Film Club.** 'All Michael Winner films, they're all a load of cobblers.'

SERIES 34 Brd. Nov–Dec 1999.

1) York. SANDI TOKSVIG and JEREMY HARDY in for Barry. **Builders' Song Book.** 'I've Got You Under My Skip' and 'The First Quote Is The Cheapest'.
2) TOKSVIG/HARDY. **Shakespearean Ball.** 'Will you welcome please, Mr and Mrs The-Fourth-Part-One, and their son Derek.'
3) Milton Keynes. PHILL JUPITUS. **Music Lovers' Ball.** 'I'm delighted to announce that the Rackers Family have arrived. I can see Pa Rackers there, and Baby Rackers. And here she is, Mrs Rackers.'
4) JUPITUS. **Parliamentary Song Book.** 'Mandelson's Wedding March' and 'Ramsay McDonald Had A Form'.

5) Greenwich. ANDY HAMILTON. **Frenchman's Ball.** 'Mr and Mrs Fembargo, their daughter British Bea Fembargo!'

6) HAMILTON. **Greek Film Club.** 'Grease', obviously, and 'Homer Lone'.

XMAS SPECIAL. Brd. Dec 1999.
Golder's Green Hippodrome. STEPHEN FRY. **Swanee Kazoo.** 'Santa Claus Is Coming To Town', with Humph's band.

SERIES 35 Brd. May–June 2000.

1) Woking. NEIL MULLARKEY. **Insects' Ball.** 'Mr and Mrs T, and their daughter Ann T.'

2) MULLARKEY. **Dog Breeders' Radio Times.** 'It's Top of the Pups! With Good Boy, Slim!'

3) Stoke-on-Trent. SANDI TOKSVIG and JEREMY HARDY in for Graeme. **Smokers' Song Book.** 'Amazing Grass' and 'I can't Get No Full-Strength Capstan'.

4) TOKSVIG/HARDY. **Farmers' Radio Times.** 'G.M.T.V.' and 'Changing Rams'.

5) Lyttelton Theatre, South Bank. STEPHEN FRY. **Cheesemakers' Film Club.** 'The Guns Of Mascarpone' and 'Fromage To Eternity'.

6) FRY. **Pensioners' Book Club.** 'The Almost Totally Complete I'm Sorry I Haven't A Clue Who I Am' and 'Senseless Senility'.

SERIES 36 Brd. Nov–Dec 2000.

1) Bournemouth Pavilion. SANDI TOKSVIG. **Swanee Kazoo.**

2) TOKSVIG. **Singing Relay.**

3) Coventry. TONY HAWKS. **Fishermans' Radio Times.** 'A Hook At Bedtime' and 'The Brill'.

4) HAWKS. **Equestrian Ball.** 'There's Peggy Mount with her friend Lucy Lastic – oh, they're off!'

5) High Wycombe. JEREMY HARDY. **Military Ball.** 'Please welcome Mr and Mrs Voidable-Civilian-Casualties and their daughters Anna Voidable-Civilian-Casualties . . .'

6) HARDY. **Dogs' Chat Up Lines.** 'Fancy doing it human-style?'

SERIES 37 Brd. May–July 2001.

1) Reading. JEREMY HARDY. **Beekeepers' Film Club.** 'The Cook, The Thief, His Wife And Her Bee' and 'Her Bee Rides Again'.

2) HARDY. **Complete Jokes.** 'What goes "tick tick, woof"? A dog marking homework.'

3) Sheffield. LINDA SMITH. **Spanish Radio Times.** 'Julio Wants To Be A Millionaire?' and 'Drop The Dead Don Quixote'.

4) SMITH. **Pharmacists' Ball.** 'All the way from Saudi Arabia, please welcome, Sheik Thebottle!'

5) Norwich. SANDI TOKSVIG. **Ladies' Film Club.** 'For A Few Doilies More' and 'Bring Me The Headache of Alfreda Garcia'.

6) TOKSVIG. **Musician's Opening Lines.** 'I suppose a pluck's out of the question?'

SERIES 38 Brd. Nov–Dec 2001.

1) Wolverhampton. TONY HAWKS. **Golders' Film Club.** 'Fiddler In The Rough' and 'Bring Me The Wedge . . .'

2) HAWKS. **I.T. Ball.** 'Our resident I.T. expert Samantha tells me she has to nip out to meet a young man who's having problems configuring his new PC. She says he's just called to say his zip is down, his floppy keeps popping out and he feels . . . he feels he needs more bytes on it.' 'Oh, Boot-Up Boot-Up Ghali . . . so good they named him twice!'

3) Brighton. PHILL JUPITUS. **Italian Radio Times.** 'The Weakest Linguini, starring Parmesan Robinson.'

4) JUPITUS. **Pessimists' Song Book.** 'There'll Be Bluebirds Over My Just-washed Rover.' and 'I Remember *You*.'

5) Bristol. ANDY HAMILTON. **Menswear Department Ball.** 'Mr and Mrs Poke-Tayloring, and their daughter Bess.'

6) HAMILTON. **Policemans' Song Book.** 'Super Intendent Fragilisticexpialidocious!' and 'Fit Me Up Before You Go-Go'.

XMAS SPECIAL. Brd. Dec 2001.

London. HARDY. **Swanee Kazoo.** 'Rudolph The Red-Nosed Reindeer.'

30th ANNIVERSARY SPECIAL. Brd. 13 April 2002.

The Playhouse, London. STEPHEN FRY. **Pensioners' Ball.** 'All the way from Russia, Mr and Mrs Ickle-Stockings, and their son Serge . . . great friend of the Ickle-Trusses.'

SERIES 39 Brd. May–June 2002.

1) Bradford. SANDI TOKSVIG. **Parliamentary Ball.** 'Mr and Mrs Envelopes and their son Bryan Envelopes . . .'

2) TOKSVIG. **Plumbers' Song Book.** 'Sitting on the Blocked-Up Bidet' and 'Fifty Ways To Bleed Your Boiler'.

3) Leicester. JEREMY HARDY. **Pharmacists' Song Book.** 'Ibuleve, for every drop of rain that falls . . .' and 'Anusol Man'.

4) HARDY. **French Radio Times.** 'Un, Deu, Milkwood' and 'Merde She Wrote'.

5) Hastings. BILL BAILEY. **Estate Agents' Song Book.** 'House Of The Rising Damp' and 'Gazumping Jack Flash'.

6) BAILEY. **Musical Conversations.** 'Won't You Come Home, Bill Bailey?' and 'Just Walking In The Rain'.

SERIES 40 Brd. Nov–Dec 2002.

1) Malvern. ANDY HAMILTON. **Conservative Party Song Book.** 'The Blue Rinse Matrons of Virginia Water' and 'Douglas Hurd It Through The Grapevine'.

2) Blackpool. TONY HAWKS. **Devils' Song Book.** 'Route 666' and 'I'm Horny'.

3) HAMILTON. **Equestrian Ball.** 'All the way from Ascot, here's Mr Singh. That's Ray Singh, from Ascot . . .'

4) HAWKS. **Weight-watchers' Book Club.** 'Two-Kilo Mocking Bird' and 'Fatty Potter and The Loss Of A Stone'.

5) Sadler's Wells. SANDI TOKSVIG. **Ornithologists' Song Book.** 'You've Got To Pick A Poxy Cockatoo' and 'Kum Ba Ya, Mallard'.

6) TOKSVIG. **Dancers' Ball.** 'Mr and Mrs Plum-Fairy and their horse Shergar . . .'

SERIES 41 Brd. May–June 2003.

1) Darlington. TONY HAWKS. **Women-Only Film Club.** 'Twelve Perfectly Reasonable Women' and 'Spend It Like Beckham'.

2) HAWKS. **Gardeners' Theatre Club.** 'Henry Ivy' and 'Prune Back In Anger'.

3) Buxton! HARRY HILL. **Entomologists' Song Book.** 'My Old Man's A Dust-Mite' and 'I'm A Pink Toothbrush, You're A Wasp'.

4) HILL. **What's The Link?**

5) Torquay. JEREMY HARDY. **Babies' Film Club.** 'Prambo' and 'Lock Stock and Two Smoking Pampers'.

6) HARDY. **Pensioners' Song Book.** 'Walk-In Bath To Happiness' and 'Don't Go breaking My Hip'.

SERIES 42 Brd. Nov–Dec 2003.

1) Winchester. SANDI TOKSVIG. **Russian Song Book.** 'Chek-chek-chek-Chekhov.' and 'Putin On The Style'.

2) TOKSVIG. **Swanee Kazoo.**

3) Eastbourne. JEREMY HARDY. **Fishermens' Theatre Club.** 'Calamari Jane' and 'An Inspector Trawls'.

4) Leeds. ROSS NOBLE. **Builders' Book Club.** 'Grout Expectations' and 'The Joy Of Flex'.

5) HARDY. **Menswear Department Film Club.** 'Lord Of The Flies' and 'All Quiet On The Vest and Pants'.

6) NOBLE. **Censored Songs.**

I'M SORRY I HAVEN'T A CHRISTMAS CAROL. Brd. Dec 2003.

Logan Hall, University of London. With FRY, TOKSVIG, HARDY, SMITH, HAWKS, HAMILTON.

SERIES 43 Brd. May–July 2004.

1) Dartford. TONY HAWKS. **Aristocrats Song Book.** 'Pass The Duchess' and 'The Heir That You'll Breed'.

2) HAWKS. **Car Mechanics Book Club.** 'The Silencer of the Lamborghinis' and 'The Day Of The Jack'.

3) Belfast. JACK DEE. **Butchers' Book Club.** 'King Solomon's Mince' and 'The Old Curiosity Chop'.

4) DEE. **Drinkers' Book Club.** 'The Grolsch That Stole Christmas' and 'Schindler's Pissed'.

5) Salford. JEREMY HARDY. **Bakers' Song Book.** 'Puff The Magic Pastry' and 'Give Pies A Chance'.

6) HARDY. **Naturists' Film Club.** 'A Man Called Horse' and 'Twelve Dangly Men'.

SERIES 44 Brd. Dec 2004 – Jan 2005.

1) Basingstoke. LINDA SMITH. **Daily Mail Song Book.** 'Who Let The Frogs In?' and 'String 'Em Up Before You Go Go'.

2) SMITH. **Hirsute Person's Film Club.** 'To Kill A Mockingbeard' and 'Thoroughly Modern Mullet'.

3) Kingston-upon-Hull. ANDY HAMILTON. **Lawyers' Song Book.** 'M'lud, Glorious M'lud' and 'Do You Know The Way To Sue Jose?'

4) HAMILTON. **Gluttons' Film Club.** 'Dial B For Burger' and 'Pies Like Us'.

5) Tunbridge Wells. JACK DEE. **Grumpy Song Book.** 'Long and Whining Mode' and 'Strop In The Name Of Love'.

6) DEE. **Accident and Emergency Film Club.** 'A & E Which Way But Loose' and 'Around The Ward In 80 Days'.

SERIES 45 Brd. May–July 2005.

1) Ipswich. JEREMY HARDY. **Menswear Song Book.** 'I Like Driving In My Cardigan' and 'Silly Glove Songs'.

2) HARDY. **Smokers' Book Club.** 'A Tale of Two Ciggies' and 'Harry Pothead and The Philosopher's Bong', by JK Roll-ups.

3) Rhyl. ANDY HAMILTON and TONY HAWKS in for GRAEME. **Highway Code Songbook.** 'Braking Uphill Is Hard To Do' and 'Gearstick On Your Collar'.

4) HAMILTON/HAWKS. **Welsh Film Club.** 'Bend It Like Brecon' and 'Taffy The Vampire Slayer'.

5) Oxford. HARRY HILL. **Babies' and Toddlers' Song Book.** 'I Just Crawled To Say I Love You' and 'Teats For Two'.

6) HILL. **Electrical Retailers' Film Club.** 'Cassette Blanca' and 'Lady Chatterley's Hoover'.

EDINBURGH FRINGE SPECIAL. Brd. Sept 2005.

Edinburgh. ROSS NOBLE. **Scottish Film Club.** 'Sporrans of Arabia' and 'Dundee Bloody Dundee'.

SERIES 46 Brd. Nov–Dec 2005.

1) London Palladium. JEREMY HARDY. **Funeral Directors' Song Book.** 'Laid Out In Red' and 'My Old Man's Dust'.

2) HARDY. **Monkeyhouse Film Club.** 'Baboon On The Forth Of July' and 'She Wore A Yellow Gibbon'.

3) Brighton. JACK DEE. **Cheesemonger's Song Book.** 'Que Cheddar Cheddar, Whatever will brie, will brie, the feta's not ours to see . . .'

4) DEE. **Unhealthy Eaters' Film Club.** 'A Chocolate Orange' and 'The Good, The Kebab and The Ugly'.

5) Harrogate. SANDI TOKSVIG. **Naturists' Song Book.** 'Eine Kleine Naked Musik' and 'Blue Moon'.

6) TOKSVIG. **Vatican Film Club.** 'Pope Eye The Saviour Man' and 'Rome Alone'.

IN SEARCH OF MORNINGTON CRESCENT. Brd. 24 December 2005.

SERIES 47 Brd. May–June 2006.

1) Bristol. JEREMY HARDY. **Indian Restaurant Song Book.** 'Girlfriend In A Korma' and 'Ring Of Fire'.

2) HARDY. **Snobbish Film Club.** 'Ferris The Butler's Day Off' and 'Sun-Dried Tomatoes at the Whistle-Stop Café'.

3) Birmingham. ANDY HAMILTON. **Cold and Flu Song Book.** 'Greensleeves' and 'Eternal Phlegm'.

4) HAMILTON. **Gardening Film Club.** 'The Germinator' and 'Back To The Fuchsia'.

5) Halifax. ROB BRYDON. **Bathroom Songbook.** 'I've Got You Under My Sink' and 'Shave Your Missus For Me'.

6) BRYDON. **Builders' Film Club.** 'Crouching Builder, Hidden Charges' and 'The Subsidence Adventure'.

SERIES 48 Brd. Nov–Dec 2006.

1) Southport. JEREMY HARDY. **R.S.P.B. Ball.** 'Here's a rather angry Mr Oddie, yes, he's a Cross Bill . . .'

2) HARDY. **Misers' Film Club.** 'Copperfinger' and 'Tight-Arse Andronicus'.

3) Victoria Palace Theatre, London. ROB BRYDON. **Fishermen's Ball.** 'A very big welcome please for Mr and Mrs Bigguns-Lately and their daughter Courtney Bigguns-Lately . . .'

4) BRYDON. **Hospital Patients' Song Book.** 'Knees Up, Mother Brown' and 'Lady In Bed'.

5) Sunderland. TONY HAWKS. **Gardeners' Ball.** 'From China, Mr and Mrs Willow and their tiny son Wee Ping Willow.'

6) HAWKS. **Dog Lovers' Song Book.** 'All You Need Is Woof' and 'Pearl's A Springer'.

SERIES 49 Brd. June–July 2007.

1) London Coliseum. STEPHEN FRY. **The Old Testament Ball.** 'Welcome please Sam Lila, and Sam's Son, Andy Lila.'

2) FRY. **Learner Drivers' Film Club.** 'The Brake Fast Club' and 'Start Key and Clutch'.

3) Cardiff. ROB BRYDON. **Ornithologists' Corner Shop.** 'If you're thirsty, some PG Tits, and Lapwing Souchong.'

4) BRYDON. **Farmers' Songbook.** 'On A Clear Day You Can See Four Heffers' and 'Can't Get You Out Of My Herd'.

5) Wimbledon. JEREMY HARDY. **The Butchers' Ball.** 'Big welcome for Mr and Mrs Pie, and their son the well-known villain Han Pie.'

6) HARDY. **IT Film Club.** 'I.T.'s A Wonderful Life' and 'Fatal Attachment'.

SERIES 50 Brd. Nov–Dec 2007.

1) Croydon. ROB BRYDON. **Hairdressers' Ball.** 'Oh, Dan Druff and his daughter Pecia. Allo, Pecia!'

2) BRYDON. **Bartenders' Film Club.** 'Bringing Up Babycham' and 'Days of Chunder'.

3) Manchester. JEREMY HARDY. **Farmers' Radio Times.** 'Pig Of The Week' and 'Veal Or No Veal'.

4) HARDY. **Furniture Makers' Song Book.** 'Side By Sideboard, sing by The Artist Formerly Known As Plinth'.

5) Peterborough. JACK DEE and ANDY HAMILTON in for Tim. **Butchers' Song Book.** 'Force-feed The Birds' and 'Sausage In A Bottle'.

6) DEE/HAMILTON. **Overweight Radio Times.** 'Absolutely Flabbiest' and 'Life On Deep-Fried Mars'.

HUMPH IN WONDERLAND. Brd. Dec 2007.
Lyric Theatre, London. With HAWKS, TOKSVIG, HARDY, DEE, BRYDON, HAMILTON.

'YOU'LL HAVE HAD YOUR TEA'

SERIES 1 Brd. Dec 2002. BBC Radio 4. Prod. Jon Naismith.
With Barry Cryer, Graeme Garden, Alison Steadman and Jeremy Hardy.
1) The Musical Evening. 2) The Murder Mystery. 3) Romance in the Glen. 4) The Shooting Party.

SERIES 2 Brd. Feb–March 2004.
1) The Vampire of the Glen. 2) Fame Idol. 3) The Fitness Club. 4) The Poison Pen Letters. 5) The Monster in the Loch. 6) Trapped.

HOGMANAY SPECIAL. Brd. Dec 2004.
With Humphrey Lyttelton, Tim Brooke-Taylor, Colin Sell, Sandi Toksvig and James Naughtie.

SERIES 3 Brd. Aug–Sept 2006.
1) Gambling Fever. 2) Something About Mrs Naughtie. 3) The Subsidence Adventure. 4) Inverurie Jones and The Thimble of Doom. 5) Look Who's Stalking. 6) Porridge Votes.

BURNS NIGHT SPECIAL. Brd. Jan 2007.

LIST OF ILLUSTRATIONS

Pages 6–7: The Clue tour, courtesy of Graeme Garden

Page 8: Backstage at the Apollo, courtesy of Graeme Garden; The Hammersmith Apollo, courtesy of Tim Brooke-Taylor

Text Pictures:

Pages 3 and 163: sketches © Graeme Garden

Page 352: Script © Humphrey Barclay

INDEX